A Celebration of Young Poets

Canada – Fall 2007

Creative Communication, Inc.

A Celebration of Young Poets
Canada – Fall 2007

An anthology compiled by Creative Communication, Inc.

Published by:

CREATIVE COMMUNICATION, INC.
1488 NORTH 200 WEST
LOGAN, UT 84341

Copyright © 2008 by Creative Communication, Inc.
Printed in the United States of America

ISBN: 978-1-60050-145-6

Foreword

The poets between these pages are not famous...yet. They are still learning how language creates images and how to reflect their thoughts through words. However, through their acceptance into this publication, these young poets have taken a giant leap that reflects their desire to write.

We are proud of this anthology and what it represents. Most poets who entered the contest were not accepted to be published. The poets who are included in this book represent the best poems from our youth. These young poets took a chance and were rewarded by being featured in this anthology. Without this book, these poems would have been lost in a locker or a backpack.

We will have a feeling of success if upon reading this anthology of poetry each reader finds a poem that evokes emotion. It may be a giggle or a smile. It may be a thoughtful reflection. You might find a poem that takes you back to an earlier day when a snowfall contains magic or when a pile of leaves was an irresistible temptation. If these poems can make you feel alive and have hope in our youth, then it will be time well spent.

As we thank the poets for sharing their work, we also thank you, the reader, for allowing us to be part of your life.

Thomas Worthen, Ph.D.
Editor
Creative Communication

WRITING CONTESTS!

Enter our next POETRY contest!
Enter our next ESSAY contest!

Why should I enter?

Win prizes and get published! Each year thousands of dollars in prizes are awarded in each region and tens of thousands of dollars in prizes are awarded throughout North America. The top writers in each division receive a monetary award and a free book that includes their published poem or essay. Entries of merit are also selected to be published in our anthology.

Who may enter?

There are four divisions in the poetry contest. The poetry divisions are grades K-3, 4-6, 7-9, and 10-12. There are three divisions in the essay contest. The essay division are grades 4-6, 7-9, and 10-12.

What is needed to enter the contest?

To enter the poetry contest send in one original poem, 21 lines or less. To enter the essay contest send in one original essay, 250 words or less, on any topic. Each entry must include the student's name, grade, address, city, state, and zip code, and the student's school name and school address. Students who include their teacher's name may help the teacher qualify for a free copy of the anthology.

How do I enter?

Enter a poem online at:
www.poeticpower.com

or

Mail your poem to:
Poetry Contest
1488 North 200 West
Logan, UT 84341

Enter an essay online at:
www.studentessaycontest.com

or

Mail your essay to:
Essay Contest
1488 North 200 West
Logan, UT 84341

When is the deadline?

Poetry contest deadlines are August 14th, December 4th, and April 8th. Essay contest deadlines are July 15th, October 15th, and February 17th. You can enter each contest, however, send only one poem or essay for each contest deadline.

Are there benefits for my school?

Yes. We award $15,000 each year in grants to help with Language Arts programs. Schools qualify to apply for a grant by having a large number of entries of which over fifty percent are accepted for publication. This typically tends to be about 15 accepted entries.

Are there benefits for my teacher?

Yes. Teachers with five or more students accepted to be published receive a free anthology that includes their students' writing.

For more information please go to our website at **www.poeticpower.com**, email us at editor@poeticpower.com or call 435-713-4411.

Table of Contents

Fall 2007
Poetic Achievement
Honor Schools

* Teachers who had fifteen or more poets accepted to be published

The following schools are recognized as receiving a "Poetic Achievement Award." This award is given to schools who have a large number of entries of which over fifty percent are accepted for publication. With hundreds of schools entering our contest, only a small percent of these schools are honored with this award. The purpose of this award is to recognize schools with excellent Language Arts programs. This award qualifies these schools to receive a complimentary copy of this anthology. In addition, these schools are eligible to apply for a Creative Communication Language Arts Grant. Grants of two hundred and fifty dollars each are awarded to further develop writing in our schools.

Ascension of Our Lord Secondary School
Mississauga, ON
Maureen Ahmad*

Avondale School
Grande Prairie, AB
Sandy Bakos
Leanne Glenn*

Bayview Elementary School
Nanaimo, BC
Kathy Domina*

Brentwood College School
Mill Bay, BC
Beth Melhuish*

Burnaby North Secondary School
Burnaby, BC
Ms. D. Bettles
Jennifer Cowley
Pat MacKenzie*
Mr. Pare
L. Seehagen

Collège Jésus-Marie de Sillery
Sillery, QC
Roberte Bolduc*
Julie Bussiére

Dr F D Sinclair Elementary School
Surrey, BC
Cheryl Andres*
Mrs. Aylett
Mrs. Davies
Mrs. Gill

Ecole Akiva
Westmount, QC
Jessica Sinyor*
Helaine Tecks*

Ecole Secondaire Jean Grou
Montreal, QC
Maria Polychronis*

Forest Hill Public School
Midhurst, ON
Anita Lazor*

John Cabot Catholic Secondary School
Mississauga, ON
Chris Chin*

Linsford Park School
Leduc, AB
Tracy Ratzlaff*

Macdonald High School
Sainte Anne De Bellevue, QC
Karen Jones*
Ms. McGovern

Mennonite Educational Institute
Abbotsford, BC
Ruth Froese*

Milverton Public School
Milverton, ON
Steve Rueffer
Kim Whittaker*

Muskoka Falls Public School
Bracebridge, ON
Reta Houston*

Nationview Public School
South Mountain, ON
Rhonda Deighton*

St Anne School
Saskatoon, SK
Mrs. Johnson*

St Noel Chabanel Catholic Elementary School
Wasaga Beach, ON
Mrs. Taylor*

St Peter Catholic High School
Orleans, ON
Mrs. Mailhot
Melodee Mulligan*

The Study School
Westmount, QC
Isabelle Fahmy*

Uniacke District School
Mt Uniacke, NS
Emily Levy-Purdy*

Villa Maria High School
Montreal, QC
Meghan DeJean*
Ms. Di Scala
Nadia Fabrizi
Jade Winsor

William G Davis Public School
Windsor, ON
Ms. T. Butcher
Heidi Sales

William Mason School
Choiceland, SK
Andrew Blackburn*

Language Arts Grant Recipients 2007-2008

After receiving a "Poetic Achievement Award" schools are encouraged to apply for a Creative Communication Language Arts Grant. The following is a list of schools who received a two hundred and fifty dollar grant for the 2007-2008 school year.

Acadamie DaVinci, Dunedin, FL
Altamont Elementary School, Altamont, KS
Belle Valley South School, Belleville, IL
Bose Elementary School, Kenosha, WI
Brittany Hill Middle School, Blue Springs, MO
Carver Jr High School, Spartanburg, SC
Cave City Elementary School, Cave City, AR
Central Elementary School, Iron Mountain, MI
Challenger K8 School of Science and Mathematics, Spring Hill, FL
Columbus Middle School, Columbus, MT
Cypress Christian School, Houston, TX
Deer River High School, Deer River, MN
Deweyville Middle School, Deweyville, TX
Four Peaks Elementary School, Fountain Hills, AZ
Fox Chase School, Philadelphia, PA
Fox Creek High School, North Augusta, SC
Grandview Alternative School, Grandview, MO
Hillcrest Elementary School, Lawrence, KS
Holbrook School, Holden, ME
Houston Middle School, Germantown, TN
Independence High School, Elko, NV
International College Preparatory Academy, Cincinnati, OH
John Bowne High School, Flushing, NY
Lorain County Joint Vocational School, Oberlin, OH
Merritt Secondary School, Merritt, BC
Midway Covenant Christian School, Powder Springs, GA
Muir Middle School, Milford, MI
Northlake Christian School, Covington, LA
Northwood Elementary School, Hilton, NY
Place Middle School, Denver, CO
Public School 124, South Ozone Park, NY

Language Arts Grant Winners cont.

Public School 219 Kennedy King, Brooklyn, NY
Rolling Hills Elementary School, San Diego, CA
St Anthony's School, Streator, IL
St Joan Of Arc School, Library, PA
St Joseph Catholic School, York, NE
St Joseph School-Fullerton, Baltimore, MD
St Monica Elementary School, Mishawaka, IN
St Peter Celestine Catholic School, Cherry Hill, NJ
Strasburg High School, Strasburg, VA
Stratton Elementary School, Stratton, ME
Tom Thomson Public School, Burlington, ON
Tremont Elementary School, Tremont, IL
Warren Elementary School, Warren, OR
Webster Elementary School, Hazel Park, MI
West Woods Elementary School, Arvada, CO
West Woods Upper Elementary School, Farmington, CT
White Pine Middle School, Richmond, UT
Winona Elementary School, Winona, TX
Wissahickon Charter School, Philadelphia, PA
Wood County Christian School, Williamstown, WV
Wray High School, Wray, CO

Young Poets
Grades 10-11-12

Note: The Top Ten poems were finalized through an online voting system. Creative Communication's judges first picked out the top poems. These poems were then posted online. The final step involved thousands of students and teachers who registered as online judges and voted for the Top Ten poems. We hope you enjoy these selections.

Top Poem Grades 10-11-12

Only a Man

It seems as though before youth's blossom had unfurled it was already withering,
The creeping vines of mortality obscuring the sun and choking out the air,
Life was like a near-ripe fruit, delicious to look upon but rotten in its core,
Insects tear at it with a fury born of despair at their own shameful existences,
The droning and buzzing of souls that were long lost before they were found.
The stone that hangs around my neck grows ever heavier with the passing of seconds,
Each brief moment an eternity and a myth at once,
As death's cold hands grip my shoulders I feel that I've not long to be.
Innocence withers with experience to be replaced by an all consuming self-loathing,
The search for purpose is like finding a leaf upon the vast ocean,
Fate and destiny remain clouded playing their childhood games, mocking from afar,
Always whispering the faintest secret that I fail to hear.
I peer into the vast abyss of death that so many fear,
I know then that it is not so different from this life and I may breathe again.
One may exist but a second and change the world,
If death were to lead you away today,
Then we have served our purpose.
Just as a pawn may change the game of chess,
A drop of water may tip the scales,
So too may one man change the course of his fate and the fate of the world.
Though he may have withered and died his memory lives on in all that is.

Chris Brown, Grade 12
Christ The King Secondary School, ON

Top Poem Grades 10-11-12

Lady Tongue, Lady Love

Sharpened tongues of two doth clash;
Betwixt each crass, euphoric lash,
Lies slicing wit as rapier's tip,
Slays crude defenders of my ship.

Within harsh humor's hollow wakes,
A gentler guard whose spirit takes,
A most disturbing course at sea,
On winds of foul epiphany.

A shipwreck's final flag shall wave,
Belike thy love shall dig my grave —
And such a ship shall drown this day,
Than turn to mutiny, I pray.

Planks crash down, cross deck to deck,
As ship sinks to become shipwreck.
To raid my riches, but seek not gold,
With stolen keys to my heart's hold.

To passion's plight, I grant thee spite,
Lest I sway to fancy's flight,
Of handsome, craven, selfish sin:
'Tis love I loathe, yet love I'm in.

Sabrina Cook, Grade 12
South Kamloops Secondary School, BC

Top Poem Grades 10-11-12

Pen

The pen that I write with, it's keeping me clean…
It keeps me from being a mindless machine…
My thoughts and ideas, some good and some bad…
But my pen doesn't care, when it's all that I have…
My pen does not fight, my pen does not judge…
My pen does not cry, or hold onto a grudge…
My pen can be used, my pen can be shared…
My pen will not lie or pretend that it cares…
My pen is like me, more so than I know…
It won't last forever, it will soon have to go…
It's cheap and it's simple, it works time and again…
It's the only constant in my life, my constant common pen…

Melissa DeCiantis, Grade 12
St Francis Xavier Secondary School, ON

Top Poem Grades 10-11-12

Ending

Autumn air —
crisp, exhilarating.
I stand alone.
Darkness descends around me,
inescapable.
My fiery branches quiver.
Leaves once vibrant, hang low.
Sadness reverberates
to my in'most core.
Longing for what has passed
fades with every blown breeze.
Devoid of moisture,
fragments of me drift away.
I'm stripped of cover.
Footsteps flatten
what once belonged.
Brisk, frosty morning air
nips at my bare flesh.
A glimpse of sunlight
uncovers the raw truth —
Winter has arrived.

Jennifer Janzen, Grade 12
Killarney Collegiate Institute, MB

Top Poem Grades 10-11-12

Fallen

Daring each other to stare right back,
Too scared to move or to attack,
Raise the finger, someone to blame,
It's a bloody war, not a game,

Men and women, living in fear,
Afraid to lose all they hold dear,
Hiding under mountains and under rocks,
Always checking the Armageddon clocks,

Fallen countries need no more sin,
Peace is war, the same as it has been,
History is changing right on the page,
Now entering the new dark age,

Finding new and better ways to split,
Fat Men, Little Boys, can't believe they did it,
Flattened buildings triumph cry,
Underneath the blood-soaked sky,

Washing hands of it all,
Mustn't be late for roll call,
Orders and lies are fed to us,
We love the fight, for war we lust.

Matthew Richards, Grade 10
Henry Wise Wood High School, AB

Top Poem Grades 10-11-12

A Time to Let Go

When the boat of friendship begins to sink,
It's as though you're drifting away;
Away from the closeness you once shared
Into silence that's dark and gray.

Something unexplainable comes between,
Putting cracks in what once was steady and strong.
The hurt and the sorrow may fade with each day,
Though the cherished memories remain lifelong.

Laughter and tears; the talks and the fun,
Sharing our thoughts and fears and emotion,
Spending each possible moment together
With loyalty, honesty, trust, and devotion.

Friendship compares to a piece of soap;
Hold it loosely, it will greatly repay;
But tighten your grip
And it shoots away.

New friends will come as old ones go,
People you never thought could be.
Accept the change, allowing friends to change:
Only then will you be truly free.

Jennifer Roseboom, Grade 12
Timothy Christian School, BC

Top Poem Grades 10-11-12

The Labyrinth

You walk a maze with no exit
Winding in and out without success.
Venturing deeper, becoming surreal
Fear and anxiety is all you feel.

Another wrong turn and then one more
All you wonder is what you're walking for.
Never an answer, only desperation
Anxiety builds and you start to run.

But a quick pace is not the fix
It's not your fitness, smarts, or wits.
Solid beats your heart inside your heavy chest
Vibrating your entirety in a sign of protest.

There is no slowing down, oh no not now
Feet pound hard and the tears begin to drown.
A splash of a puddle and the squish of mud
Running in circles that do no good.

Suddenly a glimpse at the light of day
But then it's gone as the colours bleed away.
Alone again and as it will remain
There is no quitting once you start this game.

Kendra Scanlon, Grade 12
Notre Dame High School, AB

Top Poem Grades 10-11-12

Any Thoughts?

Are your ideas your own?
Did you dream them yourself?
Did you buy them on loan?
Were they sold off a shelf?

Are the thoughts in your head
Something from you alone?
Made of dribbled-in words,
Or been cultured and grown?

Who gave them to you?
Was it mommy or peers?
Was it thrown from the media,
Stuffed into your ears?

We are so affected
By views not our own.
We let them control us.
Will true selves be shown?

And the question remains,
Will you think for yourself?
Or stay locked up in think-chains
Like everyone else?

Leah Siczkar, Grade 12
Hillcrest High School, ON

Top Poem Grades 10-11-12

Birthday Bash

Walking to the mall one day with a pocketful of cash
Thinking of all the things to buy for my birthday bash
A new dress, some shoes, and decorations too
New movies, some lights, and a bag of balloons
The music will rock, the food will delight
The cake will impress and I'll be a sight
A thousand new presents I will possess
I am excited, I must confess
Hundreds of dollars I will spend — but wait!!!
As I was walking to the mall that day
I saw a little girl all dressed in gray
An ugly outfit it was indeed
But the poor thing was for sure in need
She looked at me quite dearly so
And then my heart quickly filled with woe
Her hungry face was such a sight
That my self-absorbedness had taken flight
I saw before me now a new road
With two arrows pointing where to go
I made a decision in a flash
And swallowed all hopes of a birthday bash.

Arshila Varind, Grade 11
Applewood Heights Secondary School, ON

Top Poem Grades 10-11-12

Masked Identity

You cannot say you know me,
Because even I don't know,
Who I am on the inside,
The side I do not show.

I wear an invisible mask,
Every day of every year.
I cannot face rejection,
It is what I most fear.

But with this mask comes also,
A small dent in my pride,
For the real me you will never know,
The real me I must hide.

But you cannot judge me,
When I wear my mask,
And for me to take it off,
Would be too great a task.

One day I may be able,
To put my mask upon the shelf,
And then I will reveal to you,
My true inner self.

Candice Whitehead, Grade 12
Bradford District High School, ON

Shattered Heart...

My heart's in several pieces that never seem to fit
Why can't I just forget?
I say I moved on until I see your face
Remembering all the sweet embrace
Sometimes it's so hard to explain
What I feel deep down and when you are near
Suddenly it's all so clear
I love you I really do
But everything you do just hurt me so
Every day I see you with someone else and my world just falls into pieces.
Pieces that never seem to mend but all they do is get broken into a thousand bits over and over again
Why do you keep doing this to me in the end you'll never find someone who'll love you half as much as me
I won't wait forever I don't want to wait forever yet somehow I know you'll never love me again
My love never seems to be enough I want to move on and never remember the side of you so tender
Yet when I look into your eyes that side is all I see
Hoping someday you'll come back to me

Maria Bassil, Grade 11
L'École Arménienne Sourp Hagop, QC

A Biblical Knot

Can He, God, the unknown — all omniscient, all powerful — produce in one word:
Truth, what the Book strains to convey in its pages
Redemption, love, mercy — by the Sword
A sword of Truth? The Word of God? Is that what that is?
"The wages of Sin are death," and yet Samson, David, my heroes, were not smitten dead,
But forgiven and blessed; they were kissed with a fire akin to the judgment fire
Save they remain unscalded: held in good favor so that they may follow in Christ's stead
An aversion to rules is unacceptable! No superiority, no mortal exceptions to punishment of sinful desire
Even the lusting of Bathsheba as she scrawled wet kisses of fate upon a king's damp forehead
Night after night, propitious as Job's restitution, fatal as Cain's jealous intent
Even in this all things proved trivial; wrists were slapped; few tears shed
Death of a husband, death of a son, the wrong victims were taken; no need to repent
Do the rules still apply?
God must have his laws twisted; the Book smudged; but still on him do we rely.

Caitlin Meyer, Grade 10
Brentwood College School, BC

The Road to Battle

On the eleventh day of the eleventh month at the hour of eleven,
Canadians take the moment to remember the soldiers who are at peace in heaven:
The brave men who fought for our country's liberty and peace,
and those who even gave up their lives to make the future inhabitants of Canada live life with ease.
The newly wed groom who left his wife to go fight,
and the grandfather who said farewell to his grandson and took flight.
The father who tried to explain to his daughter that he will be back,
the son who smiled one last time at his mother and slung over his shoulder his sack.
They all marched, one by one, down the road to battle.
They fought at war together little by little.
War that meant death, injury, nightmare, catastrophe,
but represented freedom, liberty, peace; a trophy.
These soldiers have marked a special place deep inside our souls.
They still remain in our hearts in the form of ghouls.
And today, this is why at the eleventh hour of the eleventh day of the eleventh month,
we take the moment to remember the warriors who fought during the days of this month.

Dhabisha Kohilanathan, Grade 10
Villa Maria High School, QC

Screaming Silence

Tears drip down either side of my face
The day is gone it won the race
It must be proud, everyone knows its name
Killing was its claim to fame
It knows its power, we entice its glory
Hesitation compels me from telling my story
Like an evil that will attack if you begin to expose
Its powerful secrets that everyone already knows
Something sensitive to talk about, but necessary at times,
Needs to be screamed, more vivid than rhymes
My mother's life was stolen by the infamous cancer
It drifts through families like an innocent dancer
Wrapping its legs gently around its prey
Then leaving it lifeless, on every given day
Everyone knows, everyone's affected by the fear
That at every second, there's one more tear.

Chloe Freeman, Grade 12
Rockridge Secondary School, BC

Dress Rehearsal

You put on your make-up, you put on your smile,
Your cue will be next but in a little while;
Not caring…It's only dress rehearsal.

Rags on the street, they lead to a kid
The coins, they clatter but you're the better bid;
Not caring…It's only dress rehearsal.

The lights shine, the cameras go,
The action is signaled, you messed up your show;
Not caring…It's only dress rehearsal.

Every day the same, with smiles all fake,
Not saying the apology, the one you had to make;
Not caring…It's only dress rehearsal.

No more yesterday, you only have today
Not even tomorrow, for tomorrow will be today;
Not caring?…Life's no dress rehearsal.

Gina Bak, Grade 12
Mennonite Educational Institute, BC

forks and knives

little betrayers,
the crooked stripe of eyeliner
ten boxes of q-tips neatly lined up at the stairs
the little tremor, at the base of your throat
gives you away.

i sit on my bed, matching my socks,
fingertips that
used to radiate are now pressed together,
my bones now fragile little birds.

i hear the swish of cymbal in my ear,
your fingers (remembering them)
plucking at air,
when you were nervous.

Nikki Rozario, Grade 12
RH King Academy, ON

I Am an Eraser

I help fellow students erase their mistakes
All the groaning and laughing as I work
Screeching bits and parts of the paper
Trying to erase
Bit by bit
Word by word

I come to school clean without a spec
And usually I arrive home filthy And sometimes even wrecked
Day after day going to school
Along with some friends; Pens, pencils, crayons, Sharpies too!
Meeting a "new" is what school is a part
Sometimes my eraser bits get in the way, I get blown away
My adrenaline running across the paper And onto the table
Suddenly, I fall Off the edge

I weep with lead stains
And I quickly pick myself up
I'm calm, soft, and easy to use
I stay with my friends in a sack
And I wait for more mistakes to come my way
Through obstacles I go To try to renew another's heart desire
But sometimes I know, I also have to help myself as well.

Sarah Tam, Grade 10
Burnaby North Secondary School, BC

Writing in Summary

It's hard to write,
When guide lines are all I see.
Regulations here, rules there,
Restrictions everywhere I look!
The words are putting up a fight,
On the paper they do not want to be.
I might as well be struggling with a bear,
The words do not want to be a part of this book.

There's no end in sight,
To start it is the key.
It really isn't fair,
My thoughts and creativeness were what the rules took.
I try with all my might,
To make the words come to me,
But they're still hiding; wake me from this nightmare.
Don't go cower in some little nook.

When I try to write,
Calming long poems are what I see,
It's hard to pen something short from here to there,
Oh look!
I've run out of room.

Jordan Fiegehen, Grade 12
Innisdale Secondary School, ON

The Mountain

Mountain, so beautiful
Your stunning, snowy peak
Some will seek.

You soak in the sunlight,
Towering above the terrain,
As if it's your own domain.

You are a beautiful landscape,
Where many creatures roam,
And there they find a home.

Your vast structure,
Is surveyed by plenty
And loved by many.
Lois Neels, Grade 11
Timothy Christian School, BC

I Know That You Miss Me

I know that you miss me
But please do not cry
I will always be watching you
From my home in the sky

A cool breeze on your face
A sight of a beautiful butterfly
I will always send as a reminder
That we will be together again

Life on earth is but one
Small moment in time
I am finally home eternity is mine
Love always your butterfly
Tasha Howard, Grade 10
Ecole Secondaire Du Sacre-Coeur, ON

Jesus Lives

Jesus lives I am so glad,
I know He loves me day by day.
When I do things, good or bad,
He's still beside me all the way.
The world to me its riches offers,
But I despise its fullest coffers.
The world forsakes me in the end,
But Jesus is my dearest friend.

Jesus lives, my joy is full,
My Saviour fills me with His peace.
Why He loves I'll ever mull,
His gifts to me, they never cease.
When Jesus died on Calvary,
Some were as grieved as grieved can be.
But then He rose up from the grave,
His plan was done the world to save.
Alissa Waldner, Grade 10
Milltown Academy, MB

I Am a Radio

I am a radio
As your alarm I will always keep you on time, on task and alert
Ready for a new day with the latest tunes and latest news
Sometimes I may be a little fuzzy but only when something's in my way
If there's anything bothering me I may sound distant and unclear
Once you get to know me I can be loud and exciting
Or soothing and relaxing depending on your mood
I will always take into consideration how you feel
I can be very different and appeal to different personalties
With my different stations I can get along with different types of people
At times I do repeat myself not knowing what's already been said
It does tend to get annoying but then onto the next song I go
I am very informative I do tons of research
And I have the dish on the latest weather, celebrities, fashion and news
At the end of the day you can always count on me
To reflect your day and to leave you with a comfortable night
I am a dependable radio.
Joyce Dy, Grade 10
Burnaby North Secondary School, BC

A Cry for Help

The children cry oh night be day the tears dissolve my skin.
Death comes rolling down the road to kill the sin that has always been.
These children's tears turn day to night, the clouds roll forever past,
my life's like a thousand daggers deep sunken into beings that could never last.
The children scream and I scream back, they ask for help that will let them live,
oh children why do you ask me this for it's the one thing that I cannot give.
So let it be known your screams were heard, and I responded as best I could,
for you are the children beyond the night like a face beyond its hood.
Tye Justin Shoaf, Grade 10
Pembroke Street School, BC

Rodin's Martyr

Martyr, I wish you would sicken me
with your selflessness, your piousness.
I wish I could envy you with great vicious strides.
You have your immortality now; you are one of the gods.
You died and you are remembered.
I want to be remembered, too, want to be known
and recognized and thought of, lusted after like Helen,
stretched out in time like you.
I want your naked grace, your sprawl,
your fearlessness, your calm, unflawed in death.
I am lovelorn; I want you in my arms,
I want to hold your body next to mine, kiss swollen cold lips,
a hesitant scribe of history, admiring your fallen body,
wondering over your clutched hands and your swell of dark hair.
Martyr, I wish you would love me.
I wish I wasn't so juvenile in comparison,
juxtaposed with you, a faint mockingbird.
I wish I wasn't so small, so ugly. I cannot join you where you have gone.
You will never come alive under my hands,
you will never open your eyes, see me, kiss,
because I am human, and you are dead.
Adryon Kozel, Grade 10
Brentwood College School, BC

Reminiscing

I'm blaming you for what I went through,
I never expected any of this from you.

I loved you with all of my heart,
You promised we'd never be apart.

I loved you with all of my life,
You cut me down just like a knife.

Somehow it always felt wrong,
My feelings for you were so strong.

You held a special place in my heart,
I loved you right from the start.

You were the sparkle in my eye,
The truth behind every lie.

You were my happiness when I was down,
The huge smile behind my frown.

Whatever happened to our love?
It's lost in our memories, shoved.

Sarah Khan, Grade 12
John Cabot Catholic Secondary School, ON

Bottled Up

Building the bomb little by little
Shut behind glass walls so fragile, so brittle.
More ammunition arrives on a flow
Building the pressure secretly, on the low.

Inside the glass walls it's filled to the top
Shut, locked up just waiting to pop.
It does in an instant, a second of that
The walls explode, shatter to a flat.

Years of building fallen so fast
Broken in pieces, triggered to a blast.

A crater of damage redundantly spawned
through anger, sadness, guilt, and lost bonds
A prevention of pain if the bomb was never made
or defused and stopped by asking for aid.

Bombs can't be built inside glass walls
because once ignited, everything falls.
If we hold in our emotions since the time of birth
just like the bomb we will cause and feel hurt.

Rochelle Francis, Grade 11
Ascension of Our Lord Secondary School, ON

The Butterfly

After endless nights of coiled darkness
It is time to break free
Pushing through a tomb of silky cotton
Its muscles exert themselves
Layer by layer
Until the tiniest of holes
Is punctured
And light rays illuminate the sheltered cocoon
With newfound determination
To reach this impossible destination
This nirvana
It rips its hand-spun prison
Into pieces
And with wings of sun kissed stained glass
And dew drops
Flies into the misty heavens
An independent creature of the Earth

Hilary Ilkay, Grade 11
Earl Haig Secondary School, ON

Falling in Love

There was something still missing
He was never sure what it was
But when he looked in her eyes
As beautiful as a butterfly in the morning
He realized he was in love.

He would never forget her again
For as long as he lived
He remembered her lips of cherries
And her creamy chocolate coloured hair
He took the first step towards love.

He knew it would never happen
But he gave it one chance
And once achieved successful he felt
Like a new spring morning with dew on the grass
He finally found what was missing. Love.

Jonathan Dingwell, Grade 11
Morell Regional High School, PE

Life Is What You Make It

You cannot pick and choose what comes your way,
You can choose to continue on with your day.

Some times are tough, and some are not so bad,
You can choose to forget what makes you sad.

Changes will be good and bad,
You can choose to embrace all,
Or you will never know what you could have had.

Chance is inadvertently decided by choice,
You can choose to take advantage, shout out and rejoice!

Life can only be what you make it,
Do not sit back and let time take it.

Meghan Oxley, Grade 12
Charlottenburgh-Lancaster District High School, ON

I Am from My Past

I am from nomads, moving here and there
New houses, new schools, new friends every year
I am from both love and hate
A mother depressed and confused, a father lost to his weakness, a family that never knew
I am from foreigners
Comfortable customs, only to us
I am from a family as big as the sea
Grandmother so beautiful, aunts as heroines, cousins as my best friends
I am from disfunction
Abuse, neglect, and fear
I am from my best friend
A me-sized teddy bear
I am from shyness
Following me through life, keeping me quiet and alone
I am from art
Words and drawings to say what I want you to know
I am from courage
The courage to change my life, to start anew
I am from a jumbled past
One that has made me, me
A me that is different from you

Desirae Mindel, Grade 12
Captain Meares Elementary Secondary School, BC

Infatuation

I love her far more than any man loves wealth

Her picturesque emerald eyes will render any man's heart asunder
Her majestic hair assures all life that our creator indeed made no blunder
Her soothing voice I know must be the unwritten angelic requiem of hope
Her eloquent personality will even teach dictators how to cope

I love her even more than you, my dearest of dear friends
I must continue on and on…No my friend, I stop must you from ranting on
You are bewildered my friend, you say you must but I say you lust

I beg to differ, her supercilious personality is indeed quite sad
I must now ask, is it possible for an infant to enumerate the conversations that you have had?
I do not think this girl wears her hair any different to the modern maiden.
I do not even know why her eye color concerns you, being as you're never the subject in which they are laid on

You do, no doubt admire her far more than any dictator desires desolation

You are supposed to be my friend, how dare you utter such slights
I love this woman with everything that essentially composes my heart
Yes a friend indeed, that is the only fact in which you are right
Ultimately what you are in love with is an illusion of a work of art

Try as you may
Try as you might
But I am truly sorry my friend
You are a victim of love at first sight

Negus Taylor, Grade 11
Ascension of Our Lord Secondary School, ON

The Boy

Every day he sits by himself
with a frown on his face.
Nobody ever talks to him.
They say he's a disgrace.

He eats alone in the corner.
He does not look around.
Some people laugh and some make jokes,
but he doesn't make a sound.

Nobody thinks twice about it.
It doesn't leave his mind.
He wants to have friends and fit in;
they say he's not their kind.

The next day, our teacher tells us,
a sad look in his eyes,
that boy couldn't live through the pain.
He committed suicide.

Sharayah Clark, Grade 12
John Paul II Collegiate School, SK

Self-Release

I sometimes escape to the recesses of my mind,
the rough contour of my thought.
I'm not alone, with myself
for company and all the voices
replaying over and over.
Walls protect me so no one sees.
So reclusive. My only reference
for judgment is myself.
No one referees my conclusions.
And it all fades away.
I can breath fresh air again.
I can escape back to the present.

Sarah Arbeider, Grade 12
St Thomas More Collegiate School, BC

Crushed

As I walk across these once deserted lands,
I wipe the dirt clean off of my hands
That built up on sun-dried fingers
The tears didn't wash it away; it lingered.
My mind runs wild, along with the wind
since the day I was born to the day I have sinned.
Every bits of sanity slip away from me
and slowly become parts of history.

Love and hope were just an illusion
That built up in me along with pain and confusion.
I cross my weak hands and pray to the skies,
Confessing all of my secretive lies.
I once saw a land filled with peace and compassion
But the passion bleeds and leads to drastic action.
What I used to believe I can no longer see
and if seeing is believing what does that make of me?

Chantel Pereira, Grade 12
St Thomas Aquinas High School High School, ON

Do Not Assume You Know Him Well

Do not assume you know him well
His words, although a pretty sound
It is far too hard to tell.

Our love, wasn't it too strong to sell?
Or did it sell for a petty pound?
Do not assume you know him well.

Should I waste my breath and yell?
Or is it too late, have you already gone around?
It is far too hard to tell.

I thought that I knew well, you would never rebel
For we were close and tightly bound —
Do not assume you know him well.

But if I fell,
Would you have picked me up, my Emanuel?
It is far too hard to tell.

His place is not on this earth, but hell.
Not of the skies above, but below the ground,
Do not assume you know him well,
It is far too hard to tell.

Olivia Teixeira, Grade 12
Father Leo J Austin Catholic Secondary School, ON

Lest We Forget

Soldiers are standing in a row,
bowing their heads solemnly low.
They're getting ready for battle to take place,
having only some idea of what they'll face.

They look their brothers in the eye,
knowing that on this day, some may die.
A soldier falls to the ground,
gunshots are heard all around.

Their bodies shake and quiver with fear,
hoping the end soon will be near.
One by one the soldiers fall,
though once they stood so brave and tall.

On the fallen they find a letter,
loved ones sent hoping for the better.
We'll always remember those young men who died,
while not forgetting all that they sacrificed.

Lest We Forget

Shelan Faith, Grade 11
William Mason School, SK

When It Happened…

The first time it happened…
I loved him.
The second time it happened…
I forgave him.
The third time it happened…
I hated him.

And I swore to myself
He would never hurt me again

Meghan Broddy, Grade 12
Sir John Franklin School, NT

The Closing

It's dark outside
It's quiet and black
Running so far away
Never to turn back
Can you look at me
And see anything but perfect
If I try to reach out
It proves not to be worth it
Tired all the time
I'm losing my grip
Holding on for dear life
On the inside, wanting to slip
To be there for you
when you're not there for me
To lend you a hand
And still you don't see
Maybe it's the arguing
I can't take it anymore
All I know is
You just closed the last open door

Stephanie McLeod, Grade 12
Elmwood High School, MB

Irony

Everyone has ups and downs,
They may be doctors or clowns.
Fat, short
Poor, shabby
Pregnant, young
Unless you walk in their shoes,
Judging them is like abuse.
Good, die
Strong, lose
Evil, gain
Things happen ironically,
People lie chronically.
Unlucky, timing
Rude, behavior
Accidents, happen
Irony is like a knife,
Getting "stabbed" is part of life.

Tamar Silverbrook, Grade 11
Northern Secondary School, ON

Love Is Life

Love is such a mysterious thing,
It causes hate and suffering,
But it also causes happiness and joy,
It's something that you can't give up on,
You must always believe in it,
It may hurt at times but you must keep trying to find it,
If you're heart gets broken try again,
Maybe next time you'll find your soul mate,
When starting again don't think of all the bad things that happened last time,
But think of the good things that made it all worth while,
You'll get your heart broken many times,
But it's worth it in the end,
When you get older you'll know what I mean,
When you look back on your life,
You'll see how all of those relationships shaped and made you who you are,
You'll see all the lessons you've learned from each and every one of those people,
Good or bad they made you,
Who you are and who you will be,
So never give up,
If you get knocked down get right back up and try again,
Love is life and life is love.

Andrea Craddock, Grade 10
Frances Kelsey Secondary School, BC

A Thousand Words

If a picture is worth a thousand words,
Then why do we write?
We could save so much time filling our heads with images,
But would we understand those pictures?

Why is that girl crying?
She's surrounded by beauty.
A royal life, but the tear is still there,
Forever frozen in time.

Words are truly a gift.
They create personal pictures for everyone who reads them.
They provide insight, bridging the gap,
Allowing us to see so much deeper.

Words can create a mood,
A dark, dank, haunted castle,
Or a green, fresh, fragrant meadow.
We can see, hear, smell, touch and taste every word we read.

A picture truly is a king's treasury,
But so is a word.
Each concept opens a door into our imagination,
Letting us create the meaning of the image, or the image from the meaning!

Kara Wheat, Grade 10
Northern BC Distance Education, BC

An Ode to a Phone

Oh, how I love my merciful phone,
But sometimes I wish it were made of stone,
Because the only thing I do is drop it,
But there is nothing I can do to stop it.
And even when I find ways to lose it,
My phone comes back to me like I knew it,
Oh, merciful phone, you always forgave me,
No matter how bad my infractions seem to be,
And I take your qualities to heart,
As I aspire, with those qualities, to take part.

Not only do I admire you for your qualities,
I also love you for your numerous abilities,
The way you dial your numbers so fast,
I sometimes wonder how you could last,
Those countless hours I am able to talk,
You bear the weight without one single squawk,
Still when you notice me you give me a warning,
But even when you do you still last until morning,
Oh, merciful phone, no matter what I do to you,
In the end you still operate like you're brand new.

Dorota Smolarz, Grade 12
John Cabot Catholic Secondary School, ON

The Way of My Life

You are the one gardener of my life,
who sowed the seed of goal in my dead life,
and germinated it with a great whole soul.
You are the one mentor of my life.

You are the one potter of my life,
Who heated me in a kiln of hope,
and made me strong so that I don't get weak.
You are the one mentor of my life.

You are the one goldsmith of my life,
Who cast the mold and gave form to my life,
and shaped my life to shine.
You are the one mentor of my life.

You are the one hero of my life,
Who took darkness from my life,
and brought brightness to my life.
you are the one mentor of my life.

I am the cover and you are the book,
Which tells the story of my struggle,
And speaks the words of dreams and triumph,
You are the one mentor of my life.

Steffi Christachari, Grade 12
George Harvey Collegiate Institute, ON

The Horse

The horse wouldn't stop neighing
So we shot it with a tranquilizer dart
You know truth
How she is all too content to flick the first domino
We must force their quiet
And retard blabbering lips
A little girlie asked a question
So we threw her Dolly in the mud
And we powers had to calm our bulging veins
Eventually the common brain will rust shut
And we will take a mortar and pestle to their curiosity
You know thought
How she gets so angry when provoked
Why, just think of the consequences
If brains are granted the power to improvise
You know the horse wouldn't stop neighing
So we shot it with a tranquilizer dart

Paloma Lev, Grade 11
Thornhill Secondary School, ON

Father

A tiring day has claimed a young girl.
Awaiting her arrival is a peaceful escape.
Strong arms gently fan like wings.
Rested upon his solid shoulders
Is a head of long brown waves,
Juxtaposing his short, thin grey hair.
His fresh, familiar scent is comforting to her senses.
Tears of love grow in her eyes,
Trickling one by one onto his bone-white shirt.
Work-worn hands grip a pair of sharp, bony shoulders.
Wise, blue eyes peer into a mind full of frustration.

She is now happy.
She is in the warm arms of her father.
Her thoughts are reassured
She listens to his soothing whispers.
Her distress vanishes
He sympathetically pats her fragile back.
Gone is the deprivation she once felt,
Replaced with love.

Tahira Penman, Grade 10
Brentwood College School, BC

Mother

There is no one else like her.
She is the most wonderful woman in my life.
She is there to support me.
She is there to care for me.
She is there to love me.
When I call out "Mom" she immediately answers me.
She gives me all the attention and respect.
She shows me right from wrong,
Good from bad.
She always supports me and gives me advice.
I love her and could not live without her.

Chantel Bianco, Grade 11
Ascension of Our Lord Secondary School, ON

Soar*

By my side
   Helped me up
      Let me soar
         Raised me.
Without you I wouldn't be who I am.
Time passes and I know there isn't much time left for us to share.
So I will cherish the moments I have and grasp them with all I know to keep them deep in my heart, soul, memory, forever.
I hear that you are leaving, and my mind goes blank, my eyes fill with tears and my tummy is filled with upsetting knots. I can't believe life without you. All the things you have been through, and you are still strong and beautiful and I admire that. You raised me to be a beautiful, strong, intelligent, loving, forgiving woman. I know eventually in time I will heal and be filled with happy thoughts, tears of joy, and a tummy at ease, but for now all I want is you here now to fill my mind with happy thoughts, to wipe my tears away, and make my tummy feel better one last time,
        one last moment,
    before I let you go,
and let you soar.

Elissabeth Michailidis, Grade 12
John Cabot Catholic Secondary School, ON
*Dedicated to my Yaiyai

His Kiss

The first kiss, Always meaningful,
Always powerful, Most of all memorable.

As your lips brush, His against yours.
Almost touching, Just enough space in-between.

His hands on your waist, Just the simple touch gives you those butterflies.
Those butterflies that fly up and down your spine. His human touch is knee-weakening.

As you breathe in his scent, You look into his eyes,
As he grins and looks at you, Your heart melts.

He whispers the three words, Those three words everyone wants to hear,
Your heart pounds against your ribs, As if it was trying to escape into his.

As he lets his fingers run through your hair, You can see the desire in his eyes,
As he cups your face, And settles in for the longest kiss.

C St-Amant, Grade 10
Ecole secondaire Le Caron, ON

Timeless Existence

I am here.
I am the gentle wind blowing a crispy golden leaf from its home on a tired tree, and guiding it safely to the ground.
I am the snowflake, falling gracefully from the sky like a tiny gift from God,
which lands on your nose as you stand in a frozen frame.
I am the tulip sprouting new life through the earth, outside of a hospital where a baby girl is being born.
I am hiding in the wind, in the trees, in the sky, in the earth.
I am living in your heart, in your thoughts, every feeling, every word.
I am every hue of colour reflecting back at you in the mirror
while the rest of your world is fading into a melancholy blend of black and white.
I am every smile protruding through your lips as the fibers of your being are being woven into something magnificent.
I am every tear drop being released from the brilliant sparkle in your eye and rolling down your face into a beautiful oblivion.
I am love.
I am here.

Sonya Sydoryshyn, Grade 12
John Cabot Catholic Secondary School, ON

Alone

A teardrop clear and vacant of a wish that isn't said
A thought that isn't spoken of a hope that's mostly dead
A past of silent memories of times we'll never know
A dream that is forgotten of a future long ago.
A star that once was shining now relinquishes its light
And all that is above us is the darkness of the night
The tear that drops form rain clouds frozen slowly as it fell
To shatter on the pavement as a cold and empty shell
A bitter spark of chaos fills the silence with a scream
Of long forgotten wishes and a never spoken dream.

Jenny Smart, Grade 11
London Central Secondary School, ON

The Clock Is Ticking

The clock is ticking
It's time to straighten yourself out
Time to realize what you're doing
Understand what it's all about
Your words have become worthless
No longer worth hearing
It's time to understand this
Because your words are no longer worth fearing
The numbers are starting to increase
Your time has almost run out
You're affecting me like a contagious disease
My patience has run out
Just remember that this was your chance
To stop this, and everything else from sinking
To fix what was broken, and look at things from a new glance
The clock is ticking

Sophia Affleck, Grade 10
Killarney Secondary School, BC

Powerful Minds

I believed you when you told me the secret
That our hearts will always be true
But, when you left a note on my pillow
I didn't want to believe
You made me believe that I was yours forever
Time has come for me to let go
It saddens my heart but I'll manage to smile
Remember, the things you told me
We have powerful minds
Just for today I'll do my best
I know way down deep inside I'll find myself
Saying a prayer now and then
Believing in myself
School teaches us how to think
Through experiences, we learn to survive
Yeah! Our minds are powerful!
Yet, I still have a difficult time
Concentrating is so difficult
Our minds can run away
Think positive and believe
Our minds are powerful!

Sha-Lynn J. Bird, Grade 12
Waweyekisik Education Centre, SK

Light, Then Darkness

For years beyond count
The Faeries have been sought
By both love and hate
None have ever been caught

Faeries can be found
At far ends of the Earth
In forests and cliffs
They've lived there since their birth

Should one venture there
The Light Faerie they'll meet
She has praise for good
But contempt for deceit

Gorgeous to behold
She is loved by many
But betray her once
She won't love you any

Should you displease her
There is no hope for you
For the Dark Faerie
Only evil is true

Mel Duncan, Grade 10
Chateauguay Valley Regional High School, QC

River

I am swift and polished;
An endless torrent of liquid desire,
Dangerous for all that challenge my wrath,
Yet irresistible to those who have felt my splendour.
Steadfast, I climb over smooth rocks and jagged boulders
Watching the lofty firs as they dance in the wind.
They wave in a cordial fashion as I pass,
But I've no time for greetings.
I can feel the sun rising, kissing me
Softly on the cheek as it transcends the all-seeing mountains.
I laugh at those mountains, for they are unmoving.

I am wild and untamable,
Slowing only to indulge in the majesty of my playground.
I know every round curve of the bed in which I lie.
I caress each bend as I flow on,
As if it were a lavish blanket.
But I never sleep.
I will not rest until I have reached
Into the depths of the infinite ocean that waits for me
At my end.

Adelaide Backer, Grade 10
Brentwood College School, BC

The Misfitted

A song of love,
a song of death.
A bright white dove,
and my last breath.
Coming close to you,
and parting fast.
A love so true,
that could never last.

Domenico Commisso, Grade 12
St Mary's High School, ON

The Guitar Solo

Tension builds up,
As the song is being played.
The crowd cheers wildly,
And the guitarist is dazed.

Now it's time for the solo,
Will it be great?
His first live performance,
Will determine his fate.

Fingers moving so gracefully,
On his guitar.
Eyes stare with awe,
At his talents he has so far.

The solo is over,
No more to be played.
The audience is stunned,
At the creation he made.

Tanner McEwen, Grade 10
William Mason School, SK

Fictional Safety

A safe world,
Free of corruption;
Otherwise known as fiction.

In truth,
Our safe world
Is nothing short of frightful.

Leaders lie;
Men die;
All cry.

Evening news
Plays the horror,
Censored to comfort.

Life continues uninterrupted
For the delusional
Without a regard for the truth.

Jonathan Dick, Grade 12
Dr Charles Best Secondary School, BC

Paintball

The sounds of war surge all around me, and the battle cries are long and clear.
I dive into hiding, fearfully waiting, for the sounds of the guns to ring near.

I can see my enemy circling, as slowly, backwards I edge.
But I know that I cannot stop him, as he drops beneath the ledge.

Slowly I shift my gun, changing my point of vantage;
Cautiously I take my aim, hoping to have the advantage.

Carefully I prepare to shoot, afraid to be the first to fire;
Crouching low I consider my choice; the wrong one could prove to be dire.

Suddenly, his shot rings out, and quickly I'm forced to react.
I fire fast, hoping for accuracy, as faster he continues the attack.

Without warning I'm hit, and quickly I fall.
The battle's now over, the war of Paintball.

Brittany Reddicopp, Grade 10
Mennonite Educational Institute, BC

Two Magicians

All eyes turned as the first note sounds.
The room grew silent and still.
The only sound was made by the piano keys, and a soft rustling in the background.
His fingers flew over black and white as all stood in awe.
All at once a burst of sound joined the piano's song.
Her song gained strength as the piano's went on.
The violinist matched the pianist's skill.
Her fingers were flying as fast as his.
They played with one mind, one heart, and with one true passion.
The love of the music spurred them on, until all hearts were filled.
All at once the music stopped, but no one moved for fear of breaking the spell.
The pianist turned, surprised to see the crowd that had gathered 'round.
The violinist smiled a knowing smile at him as she placed her spell binder away.
As if from a signal, the spell was broken and great applause burst
forth for the two magicians as they melted away into the crowd.

Hawna Murray, Grade 11
Magrath Jr/Sr High School, AB

City of Heaven

The church bell rings
To mark the passage of 15 minutes
Reminding me
That I have been walking on an endless cobbled road.
I am filled with images of the surrounding I had once seen.
The Roman house in ruins,
The Medieval castle upon the hill,
The golden fields,
The lush tress,
The gazing sun.
I am overwhelmed with the steady stream of images running through my mind.
But it is at this moment
That I realize I am in the city of heaven,
I am finally home.

Sarah Inglis, Grade 12
Surrey Connect School, BC

Fall and Winter

Leaves scattered about in the air,
Red, yellow, orange, brown
Dancing to sounds of nature
The fall is coming, let's change colors
the sky is grey and damp,
the stars are hidden in the clouds
The geese fly south, warmer coats are worn,
the chipmunks collect the rest of the nuts
the rabbits once grey
begin to turn a snowy white
The bear yawns loudly
preparing for a long winter's night
The snow begins to dance
The wind blowing lightly, brings the snow up like fairies
the days are shorter and the nights are longer
Lights go on, filling the dark sky with pretty colors
Children's' laughter heard, snowmen here, snowballs there
the evergreen tree's branches, that of a fairy snow queen
The ice dragon roars as the nights grows warmer
The south wind is coming
and so is more sun

Jessica MacPhail, Grade 12
Christ The King Secondary School, ON

Wanting

You know you want it.
It's right there.
It's within your grasp.
Go on, get it!

Reach a little further.
Try a little harder.
The effort can't hurt you,
It'll just make you stronger.

You're sneaking your way in,
Closer to the prize.
The ultimate quest
To your ultimate desire.

Why can't you do it?
Aren't you strong enough?
The ever draining goal,
The ever reaching hand.

But, what happens when you get it?
Does it start all over again?
Why would you want it,
When it's reaching for your hand?

Chloe Hurtubise, Grade 12
Charlottenburgh-Lancaster District High School, ON

Large, Perennial, Woody Plants

The sky outside is white and blue
the clouds, the sun, a gentle hue
The trees they call, "Come out and play!
Come laugh and sing and climb all day!"
"But, I can't come out to laugh and sing,
or climb your limbs or anything!
There's work to do, there's school today
They've locked me in, I cannot play!"
So there I sat with sunken heart,
the trees they watched, their boughs apart
I slowly turned without a peep
And heard the trees begin to weep
But then there was a sudden crack
The trees had launched their first attack!
"The trees!" I cried, "The trees are here!
I now have nothing left to fear!"
"We've come to take you far away,
we want you to come out and play!"
And so I rode off with the trees
Today's the day that I was free.

Damien Doepping-Schumacher, Grade 12
Ridgeway and Crystal Beach High School, ON

Typical Morning

Awakened by the traveling lamp,
she moves easily out the door.
The earth is damp,
it rained again the night before.

Through the trees and out the other side,
just past the gnarled tree trunk,
she sees the new and wet, speckled hide
standing for the first with a little spunk.

He arrived in the early mist of morn,
starting a new journey on this day.
Waiting for so long to be born,
to reach this Earth for a longer stay.

As she waits patiently aside,
she remains quiet while a tear is drawn to her eye.

Brittany Thibault, Grade 11
William Mason School, SK

Summer

The style of summer dramatically changes,
Expression travels like the wind on my shoulder

People change and so does fashion,
But people change to a certain passion

Hair colour, eye colour, personality and clothes
It all changes as the sea water flows,

Rainbows, sunsets are all beautiful things
As we sit, lie and share our feelings.

Monika Tezak, Grade 12
John Cabot Catholic Secondary School, ON

The Player

The harsh beat pounds in the ears, of the figure on the bench
Blurs the world, creates the fears, along with that foul stench

Outside the room is a different story, where among the crowd I am waiting
The people around me are shouting glory, to the opposing team we are hating

The cue is revealed for the players to stand, and be shown in the crisp cooling air
Last minutes to remember what is planned, and endure the moments so rare

The players skate out and the adrenaline rushes, the warm up has begun
Stick handling great saves and body crushes, I shout "we are number one"

First period, second period and finally the third, while hot sweat drips down the face
As time has paused, not a voice can be heard, with a slap shot they've won the race

The buzzer sounds and the team assembles, around the player who shot
The helmets come off and with a tremble, a girl was in that spot

Tara Joubert, Grade 11
Holy Cross Regional High School, BC

The Lion of March

He floated in like down, on the warm gentle breeze, coming from the mouth of the storm. For when he arrived from his long and cold journey, he began tearing at the skin of Mother Earth. With a stern blow of his hand, he began ripping trees, and rocks, and land away from the Mother who has carried us all. For he blew and blew, causing waves higher than the Wall of China, flooding everything.
For his eyes were as sharp as a shaft of lightning, and when he clapped at the terrible disaster he had made, it caused a loud bang, like the thunder in the evening sky. For his voice was pale like heavy rain on a tin roof, and when he uses his arms and hands to mix and play with the weather, he causes a terrible vortex sucking everything up. And when he has finished tearing everything away, he hurls it into the air, causing even more wreckage, and more is shed from the Earth. Yet when he has done all the terrible things, with no pity at all, he leaves everything lying dead on the ground, causing a terrible mess. Yet he has crept in like a lion waiting for its prey, then he strikes, and leaves, leaving everything in a wreck.
But in the end, the very symbol of a lamb lay still in the grass, with only pure beauty, lay the lamb. And as the old saying goes, "if it is in with a Lion, then it shall be out with a Lamb."

The Lion of March

Aaron Wells, Grade 10
Captain Meares Elementary Secondary School, BC

Lonely

I lay here under the sun, watching the clouds go by. As if life were a piece of cotton and I could just dive in it. I am what I am and I can't be what I never will. I am alone. They say I am the new kid and I will never fit in. They try to harass me and take away my dignity. O how I pray to Thee in heaven to let my soul go free. Let my family and I live in peace and harmony. I wish I could talk to someone, and let them know what I feel, too bad I have no friends and all of the class hates me. Getting good grades and having an accent meant nothing to me, all I ever wanted to do was to go to the movies with a couple of buddies. I watched the sunset at the harbor today. Gave me confidence, and a new technique to get them easily. I tried to help them out, and get them good grades. They started to appreciate what I did and invited me to hang along. I started to hang with them, soon I realized, I joined the wrong crowd. I was a lie, a cheat to them. They used me to get what they needed. Under the peer pressure, I couldn't hold back, so I took it without asking and was held back. Interrogated and searched, this was not my way, I was a good kid until that day. Later I took a walk in the park, there was a nice breeze. I wished I could share this moment with someone I believed to be with me. I am lost. I am alone. But I have heart and soul. I pray every day and I help around the house. Hope one day they shall recognize, maybe it will be thanks to this poem I write tonight. All I want is to have respect and gain some dignity, for I am a human being and I need some air to breathe.

Fardan Ali, Grade 10
The Woodlands Secondary School, ON

Hibernation

It's said you move like a river, Time,
but rivers are much too fast.
Rather, you trudge sluggishly along
as though you have nowhere to go.

Gah! Hurry up, O lazy Time!
I have things to do!
I have my dreams, my aspirations…
Why must I wait for you?!

If I were a little bear,
I would find some sleep
and escape into blissful slumber
as I await my spring.

What can be done?
Nothing…nothing at all…
Alas, I'll have to wait it out.
No hibernating for me.

Brian Proctor, Grade 12
Simonds High School, NB

Soldier

A tear trickles down her face
She bows her head to say a prayer,
He is gone, no longer part of her embrace
And remembering the last time she caught his stare.

Before he left and said goodbye
She kissed his cheek and whispered, "I love you"
In her head she always wondered why,
He left her to save a stranger, someone who he never knew.

Kneeling down she touches his grave,
A flower she places across
She knows he was so exceptionally brave,
He saved someone's life,
In turn his was a loss.

Katlin Dewar, Grade 10
William Mason School, SK

Powerless Nature

When rivers flow through majestic mountains
And chickadees warble soft sanguine songs,
The world's too busy purchasing new kitchens,
Or wondering if their pant legs are long.
If colourful rainbows began to burst
Throughout the blue hazy azure, like grand
Dazzling fireworks above, cracking
Into a dark starry heartland,
Instead, a most beautiful sight, we ignore
For the pleasant polyester in shirts.
Pretty pictures of purses from brochures,
Intoxicate us to buy skimpy skirts.
We are benighted to Nature's allure,
Fretting instead over acquisitive amours.

Simon Lam, Grade 12
Burnaby North Secondary School, BC

My Heart

The anger in my self-broken heart,
Is swallowing my precious soul.
I want to hide my sin,
Into the deepest corner of my mind.
I feel as if I may die soon.
All the Suffering and pain I've been given,
I return to those closest to me.
Lies catch up after all this time,
Running away but never actually taking a step.
Did you find the girl you were looking for?
Did you conclude that she wasn't me?
I have tried to be someone I was never before,
And in turn I changed myself.
I can't remember the innocent me.
I miss her deeply, like the bottomless ocean.
Her time on this world is ended and cut short.
Can I keep pretending to be the happy one?
The world around me is trying to take my life.
I don't care, and I never have, although maybe I should.
I just wish that you would see me,
As that one girl, with the beautiful heart.

Christina Bremner, Grade 12
Garden Valley Collegiate, MB

Too Far Away

Her ear against his chest
She listens to his heart
Nothing mattered more
Than this pounding in the dark

Never growing tired of the sound
She would lay there for hours
Without it she was nothing
Like a field without flowers

The two were inseparable
Some might say, unimaginably so
Wherever he went, she would follow
It was like they formed one solid bow

When it was his time to go
She found herself longing for this sound
The sound that so many times put her to sleep
Was now escaping her and falling to the ground

Though she knew one day he would return
His arms open, and ready to meet
For now he was too far away
And she couldn't feel his heartbeat

Kate Gosselin, Grade 10
Villa Maria High School, QC

Masquerade

The hush of the meadows
Draws us in,
I can't breathe.
I could get lost in your eyes,
So beautiful and unnatural,
But it wouldn't even matter.
You stand there,
Unnoticing,
Unreal, and
All I do is wish
For the impossible.
Whispers are all I hear,
Sending shivers up my spine.
Hold onto me, beautiful.
Save me from the depths
That you don't realize I'm sinking into.

Grace Loeschmann, Grade 10
Mennonite Educational Institute, BC

A Private Sunshine

I'm sorry that I hurt you so deeply
And that my wound cut me so
If we were not what I expected
If I may have ruined this all too slow
Most of all I hate this outcome
And how happy we have become
For this sadness is my soul's best friend
And an addiction that you mustn't mend
For if you wish to please me
If you wish we may still speak
But leave me to my dark despair
For then, is my passion at it's peak

Martika Crumly, Grade 10
Westsyde Secondary School, BC

Moving On

What has happened, has happened.
I need not dwell on it anymore.
The future lies ahead,
Calling me to move on.
I move on with a desire
For something better.
Knowing that I cannot change the past,
But I can change the future.

I need not know what lies ahead
Because of the faith that I have.
The faith in myself
The faith in my heart.
Times can be hard, but they can change.
I will keep standing strong
And never look back again.
I'm moving on.

Emily Seitz, Grade 10
Holy Cross Regional High School, BC

Vicissitudes

There's not much to talk about when there's still 85 years to live.
I'm young and full of energy.
I decided to take the path to a happy, long lasting life.
I plan to enjoy and cherish every single moment of my teenage life,
Since there's no such thing as the butterfly effect.
I don't take advantage of those who are inferior to me;
Even though I criticize very often, I try hard to keep them all to myself.

I was reluctant in relationships, but eventually,
I learned the concept of giving and taking.
Trust was the only word in the world I cannot write or say…
Until these trustworthy individuals finally put an end into my demise.
I felt guilty for not telling them about my past,
But that was the finest option I had…
'Til now.

An unraveling mystery,
An infallible remedy,
A lifelong vendetta,
A painful memento.
Vicissitudes.

Beatrice Balano, Grade 10
Philip Pocock Catholic Secondary School, ON

The Beginning

She took a small, nervous step towards the ever growing front doors,
terrified at what could happen past those gates.
She thought back to all the other schools she'd been to,
and hoped that this one would be different.

She dreaded waking up, because she knew she would face;
another day of tormenting, another day of pure evil.
She yearned for the day when she could actually be excited to go to school.

But these new doors gave her hope,
hope that maybe this place would be different.
She took another, bigger, step.
Her heart raced faster and faster.
She saw her newfound peers slowly file in,
optimistically filling in every detail of their eventful summer.

She took another, more confident, stride towards the door,
placed her hand cautiously on the door knob,
shut her eyes tightly, and took a final deep breath.
She pushed aside the doors of wonder, and gradually opened her eyes.
She saw the lobby that would greet her every morning,
and bid her good-bye every afternoon.
She paced silently to her homeroom class, scanned the room vigilantly,
sat down, and began a new chapter of her life.

Marize Bakhet, Grade 10
Mennonite Educational Institute, BC

Saving the Best Part of Me

I went down with a fight
My heat broke beautifully
Into a million little pieces
To stretch over vast distances
And swallowed the world whole.
My soul crashed gracefully
Into every river and stream
It moved quickly to come together again
And swam freely in the deepest parts of the ocean.
My mind climbed quickly
To the top of trees and city scape
It drifted slowly across the sky
Soaking in every detail.
My body dug deep into the ground
Warming at its core
Casually moving from place to place
To find where it belongs.
One day my mind body heart and soul
Will be together again
The world will make sense
And be a much more beautiful place.

Sarah Bunda, Grade 12
Huron Heights Secondary School, ON

Depths of War

A battle forever fought,
an unmistakable loss for some.
While others take it for granted,
to fight is unmerciful, yet sacrificial.

Somewhat unwanted at times,
yet is the mistake that most answer to.
Why disturb the calm waters of life?
To merely take on and cause a wave?

As we know, it will build up,
causing a tide, that will soon bring down,
the life that they gave theirs for.
But as it floods,

it drowns out all forgiveness,
merely building up the hate.
This, the cause for the beginning of conflict,
now as an ocean, will the waves ever be calm?

A wanted reflection, in which brings up the reason,
for this everlasting memory of valor.
Will not be forgotten,
nor remembered to be merciful.

Alycia Kolish, Grade 11
William Mason School, SK

War Land

You can wish for your life
You can dream of your wife
They can be mean
They also have been seen
Your family can wait and dream and cry
Your family can pray up high
But the only thing you remember
Is the sound of your friend's fear
But the only thing you remember
Is the sound of the flying bullets
They can wait and dream and cry
They could still wish before they learned you died

Valerie Boyer, Grade 11
Ste Agathe Academy, QC

Out of the Dark

This burns inside;
To be understood is all desired;
But failure is to come.
A wall surrounds;
A barrier exists.
There is a choice,
But confidence cannot be mustered.
This secret, this burden is pain;
What shows is a lie;
What shows is what is expected.
Alone is when truth surfaces;
But it means to be in the dark.
The heart and mind is the truth,
When nothing is expected,
When nothing is to be proven.
Their existence — to be respected;
Strength is returned.

Joanna Ngo, Grade 12
Burnaby Mountain Secondary School, BC

My Butterfly

You were a butterfly;
A real beauty.
Fluttering around flowers,
humble and innocent.

A naive smile,
that brings people up;
Now has transformed,
into a wicked leer.

You became greedy.
Taking over one blossom;
Sucking all the honey,
from the wilted flower.

What happened to my butterfly?
Where is her beauty?
I miss you,
oh beautiful butterfly.

Karmila Harder, Grade 10
Mennonite Educational Institute, BC

Power of Feeling

"Feeling is first." He began to soothe, "That's not what God said." She replied less smooth.
"You're right," He smirked "he only hinted this truth." "Explain," she whispered, "where is your proof?"
He acted surprised. "You are all the evidence we need. Adam was lonely so God made you to set his feelings free.
All you share with Adam is a foolish little feeling. God made you with a desire, your only purpose; your meaning."
He held in his snicker as her face fell downcast. "Why else would God have created you so different and last?"
"Why should I be concerned?" she suddenly smiled. He then laughed very loud, "Oh, my simple child,
You will never understand the mind of a man for all that he is missing is the touch of your hand.
Yet you are missing all of Adam's rare wisdom, there is only one way you can be just like him."
"I am happy the way I am." and with that she turned away. "Happy being used and eventually forgotten one day?"
He knew the woman's greatest fear — to be alone and unloved. And it was that fear that caused her to pick the fruit from above.
Her weakness is still a part of us; it's a curse we still must slay.
Don't try to be "more" than what you are, or the fear of Eve you'll pay.

Kilah Sawatsky, Grade 11
King's Christian Collegiate, ON

Recollections of Another

Abusive dad. Alcoholic dad. She tried so hard to defeat,
The evil burdens forced upon her with scarce amounts of food to eat.
One day she lost a loved one. That was the day she lost her best friend.
Together, they had planned their futures, and made a pact to stay together until the end.

To this day, no one is able to realize, the misery that continues to run through her veins.
No psychiatrist could comprehend her depression, leaving her with unanswered questions…and memories that remain.
She felt her grandpa understood her pain, for she knew in World War II he fought.
She felt a connection between her loss and that of he and his fellow comrades, being shot.

Soldiers fought dusk to dawn every day, many never even had it planned.
Regardless, they were sent on a mission and gained peace and freedom across our land.
In return, it's not that much to ask of us to give a moment of thanks each November,
To prove our appreciation of the troops, those men and women who never surrendered.

Megan Riege, Grade 11
Stoughton Central School, SK

In the Hourglass

Life.
Life is love.
Life is tough.
City lights come to life and illuminate the sky at the midnight hour,
as creatures slither and crawl, roaming the planet's depths.
The moon shines brightly in a pitch-black sky, a ball of enchantment playing with the stars.
Life goes on. The world goes around.
But where do we go when time stands still?
Still like turquoise waters in the midst of a forest.
Do our bewildered spirits leave our bodies and fly?
Fly with the swirls of light shimmering in the north?
Fly above the sun, to a place where warmth becomes our friend?
Or do we fall?
Fall into an ocean of memories, into the pond of the past?
Some say guardian angels take us on their wings to a paradise beyond words.
Some say our hearts stop beating and that is it.
So do we even go anywhere at all?
Or do we simply stay snuggled beneath the earth's dirty feet,
silently sleeping an eternal slumber?
If only the sands in the hourglass could speak sweet whispers.

Kyle Ventura, Grade 12
John Cabot Catholic Secondary School, ON

Teardrops and Fairy Tales

Mommy tell me a story,
Not like the ones in books,
A fairy tale just for me.
Mommy don't start the story,
With castles, kings, and queens.
Put daddy in the story,
Then add you and me.
Mommy, can we have a dog too?
And we'll live in a really big house,
With lots and lots of toys.
Tell me a story just like that,
Only make it better,
Just like all mommies do.
When you tell the story, you have to tuck me in,
And say you love me, and don't forget a goodnight kiss.
I know you can't tell me stories now, that's okay I'll wait.
Mommy, promise you'll tell me a fairy tale,
Daddy says you will,
When I get to heaven too.

Whitney Hunter, Grade 10
Little Flower Academy, BC

September Hunt

My eyes open to the scenery, awakening,
Toes numb, smell of ashes from the fire.
Dew soaked through the blanket, my body shivering,
For me, it is an autumn morning desire.

To get this feeling is such a thrill,
To be like a predator on a hunt,
I wait and wait for my first kill,
A moose is near, I hear its grunt.

Colours, a burning fire as I look abroad,
Even the smallest leaf has its beauty.
The autumn smell as the dew thawed,
Reminded me I was still on duty.

Lost in nature's splendor, I will always remember
The cold morning hunt that September.

Alexandre Harvey, Grade 12
École secondaire Catholique Sainte-Marie, ON

Early Mornings

Getting up early is way too hard
7:00 is way too early, I'd rather sleep
Early mornings are like an unmatching outfit
You feel awful and tired
Plus the dreaded sound of your alarm clock
Shocks you out of a deep, restful sleep
If we never had to get up early,
I wouldn't be up before noon
Getting up just makes you grumpy,
And if you're grumpy you don't want to be,
At school or anywhere,
but sleeping.

Elizabeth Argue, Grade 10
Burnaby North Secondary School, BC

Time Tells

My words were breaking as I was standing there.
So sad to break promises you swear you were going to keep.
You miss the times when you were inseparable
Now all you want to do is separate.
So sad how everything used to be great
So sad now I find things in you to hate.
Maybe you were a little too fast for me
Too bad we gave up on each other so easily.
It was you I grew up with, it was you who taught me how to live
But you hurt me so bad. I took you back
But you hurt me so bad…
Tears flow like rivers. How could I go back?
Things were going crazy, and I'm not sure who to blame
Things were going crazy, and I didn't feel the same.
I wish things could have gotten better
But sometimes silly little wounds grow bigger…
Bigger, bigger, until they become painful scars
It's time to try and heal, it has gotten too far.
I hated to part, but now we're both better
I still think of you sometimes
But I'm glad I knew better.

Samantha Meadows, Grade 12
John Cabot Catholic Secondary School, ON

Forever Will I Stay

I shiver with every breath I take,
This world has become scary.
There's no one behind me but I,
Lost in my reverie of success,
Shadowed by one's failures,
Longing to know the purpose of life.

I overlook the endless ocean,
Such beauty in the wonders of the Earth.
Who so brilliant pursued such a charming sight?
Each night I lay my head to rest,
And speak fathomless words from my heart,
Curious of who is listening,
Your presence in acknowledgment.

The intensity of your love Father,
I could not pull away.
Was it fate that I found you?
After years of searching.
Or was it You that courageously followed this lost soul?

Evidently, someway,
Into your arms You took me,
And forever will I stay.

Celine Mohammed, Grade 11
Ascension of Our Lord Secondary School, ON

Invisible

Perhaps she is dead,
Merely a ghost of a memory,
Empty, hollow, forgotten

Confused, she wonders
Why the world is in a frantic race,
When hers is dead

In silence she waits
To somehow escape
The past that consumes her

She is fading.
Who will see her? Who will find her?
Before she becomes invisible.

Jenelle Franz, Grade 10
Mennonite Educational Institute, BC

Lost in This World

I stand here.
I feel alone.
I know you are there,
But do you really care?
I don't know what to feel,
Is it lust or love I have for you?
You make me smile.
You make me laugh.
You make me care.
But I feel alone,
Lying here without you.
Not able to kiss.
Not able to feel.
Just lost in this word.

Kyle Perry, Grade 11
IE Weldon Secondary School, ON

Driving in the Dark

When you're driving in the dark
Your vehicle is a speck of light
Surrounded by blackness

Out there could be anything,
Or everything

Whatever you want it to be
When you're driving in the dark
Anything is possible

You can do whatever,
Go wherever

Driving in the dark is freedom
As long as you keep driving
And as long as it stays dark.

Amy Kenwell, Grade 12
Marymount Academy, ON

An Athlete's Race

Sometimes your will is tested, to see how strong you are,
I will go far.
Stomach knotted, but muscles warm, I'll fly instead of jog,
I am the underdog.
There's no room to breathe or space to move, spectators admire,
I hear starting gunfire.
Feet find rhythm and pound in sync, focused on catching,
I feel paces matching.
My body's a marvel, this is overwhelmingly tough,
I have trained enough.
I won't slow down; it's not an option despite the fact I'm sore,
I have done this before.
Then unfamiliar voices cheer me on, because for them I will not quit,
I have grit.
It hurts, but pain is temporary and glory's what I need,
I pay no heed.
The schools we run for blur together and gone are teams or sides,
I see exhaustion override.
The finish line is straight ahead, but still I know I can,
This is who I am.

Megan Sunners, Grade 12
Ridgeway and Crystal Beach High School, ON

Mom

I love the way you're always there,
It shows that you care,
You make me happy through times of sorrow
You tell me that everything will be all right just wait and see tomorrow.
When father was dying you told me to stop the crying.
When I felt like giving up you told me to continue trying

Millicent Mensah, Grade 11
Ascension of Our Lord Secondary School, ON

Starlight

A
star
in the
sky, does
not mean
much on its
own. It's small,
and dim when compared to the sun. However, when many small
lights come together, a beautiful tapestry is formed. The
dark night sky is brought to life through the efforts
of the small stars that keep shining, even
when they are hidden from us by the
sun's overpowering rays.
Stars are elegant on their own,
but to make a difference on a
dark night, they   need each other.
If only people   would listen
to the   wisdom of
the   stars
one   day.

Brianna Conway, Grade 11
Mother Teresa Catholic High School, ON

A Clock

I am a clock
I have numbers on my face
My hands go around and around
I keep you on time and on track

DING

I may be as light as a bracelet
Or as heavy as a tower
I may be loud but it's only for a good cause

DONG

I may be called your boss
For I tell you when to do things
But I may work for you too
Make me remind you

I am always there for you
You carry me around
I am easy to find,
Almost everywhere

Michael Ho, Grade 10
Burnaby North Secondary School, BC

The Karma of Karma

Karma gives as Karma gets

Lie and be lied to
Hurt and in return, be hurt.
Injure someone, and receive a bruise.
Cheat and pass, but ultimately fail.
Ignore and lose your voice.
Steal, and be stolen from.

Karma is cause
And Karma is effect.

Give and get.
Be kind and in return, receive compassion.
Respect and be respected.
Befriend and gain friends.
Love and be loved.
Smile and be smiled at.

Karma is a gift.
Love it,
And it will shower you,
With the gifts of love.

Stephanie-Lynn Papineau, Grade 12
Earl of March Secondary School, ON

Sanctuary

My eyes shut tight
Leaving me in the darkness of a starless night
Whispers around me fade
I can hardly stay awake

Ice runs down my back
Frozen, like an ice pack
Heavy and still
My body, lifeless

I never really understood
When drifting off to another world
Lost in my thoughts and memories
I take my last sweet breath into my sanctuary

Rana Bahsous, Grade 12
John Cabot Catholic Secondary School, ON

The Flame of Dance

The heat of the dance, the cool of the stage,
The hush of the audience, the flip of a page,
The soar of the music as it brings to life
The dancer's magic of this winter's night.

Flits of pink, swirls of rich blue,
Jots of black, dresses of golden hue.
Leaps and spins, glides and falls,
Hold the audience enchanted, enthralled.

The lights dim, the music fades,
So ends the delightful masquerade.
But the dance still lives, an enigmatic flame,
That lights a passion in the dancer's frame.

Arpita Bajpeyi, Grade 12
Sir Robert Borden High School, ON

I Am Free

Gliding along through the garden,
soaring from stone to stone.
Rays of light reflect from tears,
not from the golden sky alone.
I am a bird, I am free.
Free from country, free from nation.
Free from wanting, free from obligation.
I am far above the ground.

Whirling past glistening gems,
sailing through worlds of radiance.
The end is never met with fear,
all days are spent in a glowing dance.
I am a fish, I am free.
Free from hate, free from lies.
Free from identity, free from disguise.
I am far below the ground.

We make the world, and we must be free.
We make the world, we must be free.

Nicolas Veltmeyer, Grade 11
Citadel High School, NS

For Dad

Thought you'd never go
Time really doesn't pass by slow
Precious were the days as they went by
And I don't think that one passes that I don't think of you and cry
I took it for granted, that whatever I'd be handed
Would be resolved by just one call
My life will never be the same, without looking at your face.
I think of your laugh when I feel sad
It helps to heal what seems so unreal
We had a special bond and I know it's never gone
But every day will be so long
Without hearing you sing another song.
Got to keep telling myself that it isn't goodbye
And I know you're always by my side
You always loved me and fought with all you had
But there is not a soul that truly understands
We can't see you now and look into your eyes
But the day will come when I see you on the other side.

Angelina Dukart, Grade 12
Allan Composite School, SK

Stand Up

I am the words for those who can't speak,
Or I can be your strength when you begin to feel weak.
I am the ears for those who can't hear,
Or I can be your confidence when you face your fears.
I can be your friend when you feel all alone,
Or I can be the one to shelter you because you don't live in a home.
I can be your tissue when you feel you need to cry,
Or I can be the one to push you forward when you no longer want to try.
I am the person who can stand up and make a change,
It's just up to the rest of the world to follow me if they want to do the same.
I am a person to speak up and make violence stop,
I am the final seconds when there is not another minute left on the clock.

Jessica Gordon, Grade 10
Dartmouth High School, NS

The War Inside a War

Innocent people killed, being shot for no reason.
Bombs are always going off, blood splattering everywhere.
Our soldiers will fight, fight for what's right,
Other people will battle because they just want to fight.
Little kids, some not even born, are getting killed every day,
The cute little children are being taken away.
Families are broken, hearts are torn out,
Parents get killed, children are alone,
Children get killed, parents are alone.

However, no one cares; they just go on with their day.
What really matters, is if we all get paid.
The war can go on, and no one will stop it,
The war will kill people, little kids just to top it.
War will always go on; we can try and ignore it,
And it won't affect you until it knocks on your door and you're dead.

Zane Jiwa, Grade 12
Dr Charles Best Secondary School, BC

Rose, Life

When all was gone, there came the twilight
Sitting at a corner, I looked on with delight
Not a bird was singing, not even a sparrow
Nor a critter was running, hidden in their burrow

Yet a rose was standing, in a sea of grass
Its red seemed exotic, even through the glass
The falling moon cast, a gracious shadow along
The slender body of the rose, it knew where it belong

Atop the meadow, swinging in a breeze
Beyond the horizon, where moments freeze
As the sun rose up, the rose quivered in dawn
Upon once a place where the moonlight shone.

I ran down the lawn and jumped over a hose
Sprang down the pebbled path and picked the rose
Soon as I touched it, I was atop a mountain
With auras ubiquitous, life in a fountain

Tony Xiao, Grade 12
Burnaby North Secondary School, BC

Dark Blue Nights

On dark blue nights,
We climb the mountains,
Where the stars connect us all.
With eyes closed,
The eagle soars through the sky,
And the blind man now sees the world for what it is.
The eclipse of gentle eyes, filled with fire,
In the dream I live each day,
Are cast wings of shelter,
As love is reflected in miracles and truth.
Still as daggers pierce the flesh,
A new man is born.
Changed into perfection,
He sees his world around him.
For the outcome is just beginning,
And our future has no end.

Matt Panetta, Grade 11
Br Andre Catholic High School, ON

One Snowy Night

These walls are breathing.
The night is heavy.
There is some lonely solace in their voices,
And vibrations of their breaths.
This opaque music we share
Paints the world with acrylic lyrics:
Emotional lines,
Oblivious to reason.
Within his madness
He found beauty
We lost, contained by sanity.
The music stops.
The silence is exhausted.
They were just strangers after all.

Belinda Gu, Grade 11
Sir Winston Churchill Secondary School, BC

Requiem for Drunk Drivers and Their Passengers

The blur of the city lights
Fly by the car window.
Unconscious of the cool wind
Whipping his hot face.

One block past the bowling alley,
One hour past midnight.
He leans out the window,
And shouts his name out to the world.

He chases the sun
So that the night could last forever.
He chased the sun too heedlessly,
And the night did not last much longer.

Never mind his wreck of metal,
Leave it all behind.
He's got his lover's hand,
And they are to the air.

Floating across the sky,
They are sure to see the blur of the lights
Beneath their feet;
As they chase the sun forever.

Dennis Tour, Grade 12
Brookfield High School, ON

Facing Reality

I am a caterpillar stuck in a cocoon
A cocoon of war
Unable to flee, or seek help
Unable to spread my wings
And save the world
Around me, children are dying
People are crying
Refugees flee
Leaving loved ones behind
Hoping that one day,
They will be together again
Children are taken away from their families
To become soldiers
The only battle truly worth fighting, is the battle for life
One day, I will break free
Free from war, poverty, and neglect
I'll grow wings and fly
Away from horror
Away from death
Away from bloodshed
I am a butterfly, and I will change the world.

Gonee Saini, Grade 12
Abbotsford Collegiate School, BC

A Winter's Wish

The snow dances towards me in rejoice,
Off to it's place of destiny,
Predetermined only by nature's choice,
To feel complete in white sanctity.
As I reach for one,
To make a winter wish,
It decides to have some fun,
With the breeze's tempting kiss.
Though one wish may have fled,
There will forever be another,
To acquire its place instead,
Until the rebirth of summer.
As the white hope flows,
I reach again now,
For a cold crystal to enclose,
Another warm vow.

Maria Tippler, Grade 10
Villa Maria High School, QC

How Can I Ever Forget About You?

How can I ever forget about you?
Your sweet smile makes me melt;
Your kind, loving eyes makes me proud;
To be your girl;
To have you forever

How can I ever forget about you?
I may be busy;
Or out of reach
But to let you know;
You are always on my mind;
Even though we don't talk for a while

How can I ever forget about you?
I still love you;
My feelings about you haven't changed
This is to let you know;
That you are always in my heart;
Even though I'm not there, with you
How can I ever forget about you?

Cansas Flett, Grade 11
John Taylor Collegiate School, MB

The Cry of Nature

Forests disappearing,
Animals dying,
Glaciers melting,
Skies turning gray;
Is there no hope left?
It is never too late
To start taking action
Because humanity as a whole
Can secure a better future.

Thanh Nguyen, Grade 12
The Woodlands Secondary School, ON

Evacuated

Desperate, angry, and frightened, how must it feel to be an evacuee?
To be moved from your home, to leave your friends behind?
What if they don't make it? But you do, what guilt would you feel?
And if your house becomes splinters, where will you go?
All your belongings into a pile of trash.
Would you feel that you had nothing left to live for? Or would you feel at all?
Maybe the numbness of pain would consume, and take you down to its icy depths,
Leaving you stranded there. How do you recover from such a tragedy?
What if your parents stayed? Your sons, daughters, cousins?
To have such a lack of blood left, to carry on a noble family name?
This could be the end of a lineage.
Natural disaster or not, you want to stay.
Keep the things most important, safe with you. Next to you.
But they won't let you. You're dragged away from house and home
From love, and what seems like life. To keep you safe, and only you.
You must be important. But you don't want to think that way.
There's so much more importance being left behind.
Go back, go back! You fight them off, but they lead you away.
To something called safety. But your home is safety. Just to stay is all you ask.
But will they listen?
No.

McKenzie Spies, Grade 11
Lloydminster Comprehensive High School, AB

Hockey Only Has One Champion

I sit down on the cold, hard, bench,
Smelling that unique, winning stench,
That no one understands, as I quench,
The thought of bonding without mention,

The single black discus that is the objective,
But my thought interrupts with what he said is,
Play hard, play fast and play seductive,
That is the only way to be productive,

And we listen to what the man in the hat has to say,
Without say, quietly, silent, in order to slay,
As he gives our battle commands and the prices we pay,
And we reminisce on these thoughts as we ready to play,

Standing on that black rubber waiting to take action,
To step out on that ice as the black and white gliding faction,
On this frictionless battlefield without traction,
Doing things people couldn't possibly imagine,

Moving from one end to the other taking no prisoners,
All working together, as a unit, until we're declared winners,
CHAMPIONS, victorious, trembling at the thought of becoming sinners,
To the one religion we worship that forbids sorrowful quitters.

David Ferro, Grade 12
John Cabot Catholic Secondary School, ON

Soaring to the Sky

Celestially dancing in the moonlight;
The vision of gracefulness is puzzling
Comprehension is disregarded;
Yet instincts lay their concentrated mark
The occurrence does not go unnoticed
That's when they all inquire
Why do you dance?
Little are they aware
That this is the question that should never be asked
No more confinement to a box of air
I wish I could even soar to space,
While envying the stars and the planets
Expressive and breathless motions
Allow my spirit to float away
From the haunting to which it pertains
I yearn for moments like these;
No longer desiring of living in wasted space
Yet I stay here and overwhelm myself
With images created by my far-fetched imagination
I crave for another lifetime
In which dancing is art for art's sake

Cristina Olteanu, Grade 12
Bayview Secondary School, ON

√Me = Sin (You)

And what this has led to.
Days spent trying to plot you.
Perhaps it is cruel of me to call myself
a byproduct of your cruèlty,
but in no *d/v* at all, I am
        transformed, and horizontally compressed
by a factor of *x* —
— by the factor of your *sin*.
You meld me, melt me down,
bring me shuddering to my knees…

I would like to be factored out again, please.

Before I *knew* you,
I traced figure-eights on my paper, instead of hearts
because I liked to imagine
they were Möbius strips
or the loops of infinity,
ready to carry me to you on the wingèd heels
of topological mathematics.

Today I find, upon closer inspection,
that these loops are covered with black ants,
forever crawling on the same side, without escape.

Alena Wang, Grade 12
Burnaby South Secondary School, BC

Daddy's Little Girl

When I was two you played with me
Even when you said you were too old to play silly games
When I was five you came to school with me
Because I was scared
When I was ten you bugged me about boys and cooties
I got mad but I still loved you
When I was fifteen you always tried to be in my life
I didn't say I love you anymore, I didn't want to
When I was twenty you lent me money for college
I took it without saying thank you; I forgot to say I love you
When I was twenty-eight you led me down the isle
I was so happy
I didn't need to be daddy's girl anymore
I was too old to play silly little games with you
Now you're sick, at the end of the game
I wish I said I loved you more
I wish I could still be daddy's little girl

Virginia Aspinall, Grade 10
Merritt Secondary School, BC

Not

These cruel petals dropping slowly down
Are caged by death, beauty gone quietly.
Hushed whispers: Love or Not? is asked again.
Her questions spin out, weaving a romance —

A fairy tale, with an ending unsaid.
The final chapters are written on these,
The thin membranes of flower, lovely yet
Dead, used answers of the desp'rate query.

Speaking with fragile strength, delicate words
Stop. Wet eyes blink. Lips purse. Silent waiting.
"NOT." Choking, gasping — quiet while her throat
Swallows the dream and the story it wrote.

Makaela Peters, Grade 10
Mennonite Educational Institute, BC

A Deadly Demon

I pounce out from the darkness like a mouse
Climb inside of you and, victim, you are mine
The doctors may see me
You can only feel me
My existence will cause you to go quietly
Like the others six feet down
I am like the top of a mountain in the Arctic
The silent surrounding numbs you
Crash, slam, slap, moan, cry
Like an elephant being slaughtered in the jungle
You are powerless to stop me
I am the strongest thing you know
You will not want to hear what I say
But you must, for you have no choice
I kill people, hopes, and dreams
I have an unused heart
I will be your downfall
I am Cancer

Lindsay Reynoldson, Grade 11
Merritt Secondary School, BC

Broken

I couldn't breath, I couldn't think.
We heard their shouts.
Foul. Piercing. Offensive.
Doors banged, glass crashed.
She screamed "Get out!"
Crying. Hiding.
Wishing it would end…
I felt her hurt, I heard his anger.
My heart broke in two.
My family. My life.
Me. Gone.
I held my sister, comforted her, protected her.
Held her ears from the pain.
Their words…
Heartless. Spiteful. Torture.
It went quiet, the door slammed.
She cried.
"It's over" I said.
I crawled out, opened the door.
He was gone.
We were broken.

Tayla Wiebe, Grade 12
Georges P Vanier Secondary School, BC

Dumb, Senseless

He loves you.
That is plain to see.
Even green-tinged eyes see the light in his
when he thinks of you.

Twin passions drip from our hearts' tongues.
Your ears are deaf to mine
while his spoon into your soul.

A dumb fool,
smiles when you smile,
Holds the words that threaten your mind's ease
deep in howling darkness.

Take his love of equal value.
Let it simmer in your affections,
Bask in his favours, his innocent passion.
My ardour comes world-weary.

Willingly, secret yearning hides,
festering under despondent joy.
My net of ignorance drapes in quiet words,
so that your smiles may turn
weightless to mine.

Cindy Mei, Grade 12
Hugh McRoberts Secondary School, BC

Weep

This dark deserted church parking lot,
stale coffee, and a weary heart.
Are things that tear my life apart.
A fear so deep one can't see it,
surrounded by all of the lies that feed it.

My unguided soul lay down
as if another building came crashing to the ground.
onto what we call our future,
I weep and whimper as the days come nearer
another year will come and pass — just as the last.

Luke Perrin, Grade 12
Kennebecasis Valley High School, NB

Risking Rejection

Isn't it worth
Risking rejection
To have something you want?
If you don't risk rejection,
You will never have it any ways,
You didn't want it bad enough to try.
What is the purpose of wishing,
If you are not going to go for it?
Knowing you might not get it,
But going for it any ways,
Because you love it too much
Not to take the chance of
Not having it,
You'd rather risk rejection,
Than face the fact
That you might lose what you love,
And you didn't even try.
Risk rejection,
Receive respect.

Jackelyn Gignac, Grade 11
General Panet Sr Secondary School, ON

Those Eyes

I see those eyes,
usually so gentle and true.
They are the first thing I notice
every time I look at you.

Why am I the hunter
And you the deer?
Caught by surprise,
frozen in fear.

But I'm not a hunter
I mean you no harm.
I'm sorry if I hurt you before,
there's no need for alarm.

I'm not a hunter
I wish you knew that it's true.
Please soften those eyes
and let me see inside you.

Caroline Czekajlo, Grade 10
St Thomas More Collegiate School, BC

The Dream Horse

Out on the hilltop at sunset he stands —
A jet black shadow against the sky
Surveying his kingdom of hills of sands,
He listens to the wind's high cry.

Mane and tail a-blowing in the wind,
Nostrils flared and head held high —
He'll follow the lure of the singing wind
On pounding hooves which learned to fly.

Fearless, though the coyote howls,
Fearless, out on the hill he stands,
Wild and free as the swift-winged fowl,
Freely he roams those hills of sands.

Naomi Unrau, Grade 10
Austin Mennonite School, MB

Emotions

Love is nonexistent
Faith dwells among a few
Bliss is being belittled
Trust — I never knew
Hope is not an option
Harmony — hard to find
Lies are nowadays common
Joy was never mine
Tears now come easily
After I befriended misery
I'm now submerged in sorrow
Yearning for a better tomorrow
Now I think of my mind as greater
As my heart was the proven traitor
It's unconditional love and devotion
Resulted in this outbreak of never-ending emotions

Abigail Pereira, Grade 12
John Cabot Catholic Secondary School, ON

I Had a Vision

I had a vision.
I had a vision of beauty
Of harmony,
Of beat,
Of rhythm.
I had a vision of a land
Of rivers,
Of mountains,
Of rolling gold fields.
I had a vision of power
Of unity,
Of strength,
Of glory.
I had a vision of angels
Of spirits,
Of souls,
Of ghosts of the wind
I had a vision.

Colleen Bunyan, Grade 10
New Norway School, AB

Autumn Leaves

A frost, the first frost of the year,
now rests upon the earth.
Crystallized on window panes
And wilted flower petals,
upon the naked tree branches
and their discarded leaves.
Nature's cast-off decorations
are beautiful, even in death.

Quickly fading colours
are briefly admired by all.

The fallen leaves cover the ground
in a blanket of earthy tones.
A warmer, richer, foreshadowing
of the snow that is soon to come.
They add to the crisp autumn air
a soft but poignant smell,
The sweet aroma of decay,
as leaves rejoin with earth.
Nature's cast-off decorations
are beautiful, even in death.

Nina Schroeder, Grade 12
Mennonite Brethren Collegiate Institute, MB

Soft Spoken Emotions

My heart whispers softly, words that are unfamiliar to me.
But my heart only ever seems to speak
When I'm in the comforting presence of you.
Softly, the words flow, like a silent river throughout the night,
Guiding me steadily, in the direction of you.

The blossoming of the sweet smelling roses in spring
Reminds me of your beautiful, heartwarming smiles.
The twinkle in your blue eyes is devastatingly captivating,
And as I look deep into your soul as they shine,
My thumping heart is left, yearning for so much more.

I listen to your voice, with great concentration,
Dazzled by each and every word that you seem to say.
I imagine us walking on the beach, hand in hand,
As the cool water brushes up upon our skin,
And our warm feet sink into the dampened sand.

I pray each and every night — as I lay in my warm bed,
Drifting away slowly in my thoughts of you —
That our magnificent connection never ends.
Hoping that my now incredible life
Forever remains the same, with you held tightly in my arms.

Jordan Smith, Grade 12
Hon W C Kennedy Collegiate Institute, ON

The Love I Feel for Wakeboarding

Water is like glass, no one's around, morning's the time to go.
Rough water makes wakeboarding intense and having the feeling of power knowing I'm in control.
The rope tightens; I feel the knot in my stomach.
Cutting back and forth, outside and inside the wake, the water spraying behind me.
Lifting off the wake, the intense height.
Wakeboard off the water my body soaring through the air.
Feeling the wind in my hair, the water in my face.
Bending at the knees, grabbing the board with my hands knowing I can handle the tricks I like to put out.
In the air soaring then landing on the flat water.
Falling.
Then knowing you can get up and try, try again.
The powerslide looks like you're under a waterfall.
The feeling of the final seconds of your run knowing you accomplished the trick you have been trying to do.
When my turn is up again, I can try something new.
Watching my friends try tricks and learning from their mistakes.
At the end of the day knowing I had fun, I laughed I learned.
Knowing tomorrow will be another boarding day.

Ashton Edwards, Grade 10
Merritt Secondary School, BC

If I Was a Mermaid
If I was a mermaid

I would sit by the water's edge and comb my silky golden hair.
I would soak in the sun's rays and breathe in the salty air.

With the ocean as my deep, dark world and every fish as my companion
I would disappear beneath the waves, as high as the Grand Canyon.

I would float along the current and hum a lovely tune.
Be desired by all the fishermen, but as untouchable as the moon.

With the dolphins as my chariot and the coral as my throne
I could venture into a majestic world, far beyond what is known.

If I was a mermaid

I would never long for a life on Earth and cherish my enchanting world far beneath the shore.
I would never take for granted the wonders that I had and seldom long for anything more.

Danielle Bruno, Grade 12
John Cabot Catholic Secondary School, ON

The Anonymous

She is hard to describe, but how can I not try, to put in words the beauty she has inside,
In her mind she holds the hands of time, in her eyes; the key to one's tangled mind,
In her kiss; passion beyond it, that leaves you breathless and floating in bliss,
Her voice is like a la-la-bye, if you listen; it will make you cry,
Her worth are soothing, like a glass of wine, that makes you leave all your troubles behind,
In her arms; you will be safe from harm, but its really a crime to be so blessed,
cuz in that very moment you forget about the rest, and then and there you will be put to test,
a test of trust and loyalty; that'll make you weak and look about 40,
Her heart; its a mystery, oh! how I long to hear of its history,
who has been there, who is there, and who will always be there.
These are all stories of the anonymous, who's story appears to be way beyond us.

Darren Bennett, Grade 12
Ascension of Our Lord Secondary School, ON

Not You

The world knows you for what you have become.
But I remember you for who you used to be.
You always said you'd be a star,
You were right, you've put your name up in big lights.
But now would you pick up the phone if I called?
The crowds they cheer loud,
But do they cover my voice inside your head?
So many friends surround you,
But do they know your favorite colour's blue?
Does your big house feel like home?
With echoes and ghosts protruding from every wall?
You caught your dreams I know,
But what did you lose on the way?
Would you recognize me,
After all these years gone by?
You sing upon a different stage every night,
But I don't hear you, I can't hear a sound.
Because your soul's not singing.
Because it's not you, that's not you up there,
And we both know that it is true.
That's not you.

Rebecca Rempel, Grade 10
Mennonite Educational Institute, BC

My Beautiful Country

Canada is such a beautiful country
It has so many great things to offer.
A place to call home and piece of mind
There isn't a place any better.

Children grow up in stability
And become wonderful loving adults
Everyone is so helping and nice
O Canada, you have no faults!

With the perfect blend of cities and fields
And the combination of so many races,
Canada is such a unique place
Because every day you see so many different faces.

From the Atlantic to the Arctic to the Pacific
Canadian land connects it all together.
Really hot and really cold
Best describes the Canadian weather.

Canada is such a beautiful country
It is a safe place where so many people differ.
The land is vast and the weather is crazy
But there isn't a place any better.

Cassandra Cole, Grade 12
Ecole secondaire Catholique Sainte-Marie, ON

Light Bulb

I am a bright shining light bulb
I tend to light up a room
Although, some days I can
Be brighter than others
At the end of a long, tiring
Day I just get burnt out
Flick, flick, flick, on, off, on, off
Always trying my best to provide for others
People, like bugs, enjoy being around me
I give my best shot to help the community
Feeling safe and sound
I am a bright shining light bulb

Larissa Chin, Grade 10
Burnaby North Secondary School, BC

Love Hurts

Soundly, sleep, my little sheep
Now you may fall deeply asleep
you are now resting in peace
While the rest of us feast you are my ray of sunshine
Like the day you vowed to be mine
We were two peas in a pod
And you are in the presence of God

You were adored
By beautiful Lenore
You gaze upon me from the starts
Which makes me feel that you are not far
I will see you
When it is my cue
I love you from the bottom of my heart
But I hate that we are apart

Gilles Frappier, Grade 10
École secondaire catholique L'Horizon, ON

A Moment of Silence (Ode to the Voice)

We'll use it
But abuse it
Losing it will drive us hysterical
Crazy, like a scalene triangle

Silent like a mime
Working for a dime
Silence is an art
But be smart

Things are better left unsaid
But don't let this disease spread
Learn to appreciate
And don't hate

There's no more time
The bottom line
A world with no voice
Is only noise
So make your choice.

Kristine Mar, Grade 12
John Cabot Catholic Secondary School, ON

Why?

A weary heart, a teary eye
Trying to find a reason why
He left this world so early
Without a single goodbye.

From fighting a war for our nation
Or a disease within the person,
She had no last chance to touch,
Her one and only son.

A father indeed he was,
A man whom she still loves
Tried so hard to defeat,
A battle he could not overcome.

And while she sits there wondering
About the war we are currently fighting,
She starts to ask herself,
Why,
Are all our soldiers dying?
Kelsey Picard, Grade 11
Stoughton Central School, SK

Never Gone

Remember us, and all we've done
The blood we shed under setting sun
The times we feared and cried aloud
Remember us, and make us proud.

Remember us, our name and face
The crosses that now mark our place
The cause that we were fighting for
Remember us, heroes of war.

Remember us, the brave deceased
Our sacrifice and strive for peace
Our bodies lying under dawn
Remember us, we're never gone.
Caroline Frappier, Grade 10
Villa Maria High School, QC

The Big Picture

It's not how you see it,
It's how they view it.
It's not what you do,
It's what they put on the news.
The world won't listen,
If you're not the main person,
And all the tangles you get in,
Mean nothing to them.
Think you're alone,
But we're all blind to each other,
We have one another,
So why are we fighting the Big Picture.
Bronwynn Panek, Grade 12
Seaquam Secondary School, BC

My Sisters

What a dynamic duo you two used to be,
Until Mom came home and told you there would soon be three.
When I was a baby you thought I was fun,
Until the midnight crying had begun.
As I grew into a child, you thought it would end,
Yet time with you I always wanted to spend.
And now that I look back on my annoyingness,
I have to say that I'm sorry, sis.
So I wish to thank you,
I am so grateful, oh if you only knew!
Thank you for letting me borrow your clothes,
Even though I did anyways if you said no.
Thank you for teaching me how to drive,
Even though you thought that you wouldn't survive.
Thank you for always helping me with my homework,
Even though my perfectionism drove you berserk.
Thank you for coming to save me from the bug,
Even though it had long since disappeared underneath the rug.
Thank you for taking me out late at night,
When I had a craving for french fries that I just couldn't fight.
But most of all I want to thank you, for being my big sister, through and through.
Kaley Fitzsimmons, Grade 12
John Cabot Catholic Secondary School, ON

Snowman

Looking out my window on a cold starry night
There was a snowman who's face was full of fright
For in the morning I rose and his body was still froze
And as I looked at him in the warm, warm sun I wondered has his end just begun
For many things were changing it was rearranging the snow into the mud
Soon the water would be flowing, flowing down the rivers
And this is why I saw the snowman quiver
And this is why I think back to that night at the window
Knowing that the days would be longer, the sun would be stronger,
and I would always hope to be younger
So as you can see our lives are a mirror of the snowmen
Because no man's life goes on without change

Delane Wilburn, Grade 10
William Mason School, SK

Thoughts…

As I sit here and ponder what to say,
My restless fingers paused over a landscape of endless possibilities,
I wonder what you would want to hear today,
What sort of kingly sized words I could use to describe what I see.
How do I convey to you the enormity of the mammoth in my sight?
The looming figure towering above all my judgment,
All the things I am supposed to know, speak, understand, are blotted out.
But I find myself here, in a cool shade, the sun still glowing around the abundance,
I am safe, though completely out of my own control; I have no fears, no doubts.
There is an overwhelming peace and sanctuary in the long, soft grass of our meadow,
And slowly, what was once a mammoth, is a tall, spiring tree,
Offering shelter and rest to the unsure below,
This is where I'm meant to be, with you, and you with me.
Hannah Webb, Grade 12
Grand Forks Secondary School, BC

A Mystery

I am filled with regret
The pain of distress, is butchering my soul
I am trapped knowing you are gone.
I am only left with recollections,
In which those might not be great.
The things you say, one shall not forget,
I know I am your one and only
I know we are meant to be,
Whether we are as one, or apart
You are my better half and I am yours
Trying to remember my decision,
Will be one of the most difficult things I have ever done
I was your life and you were once mine
And in some ways, still are
We are connected like no other
But times have changed and things are different now
Maybe it's best,
For us both to move on
We'll figure things out eventually
But for now, let's just leave it,
A mystery.

Brittney Lebel, Grade 12
Trafalgar Castle School, ON

Brackets (Change Everything)

Like a finger on frozen glass (Makes a smear that lasts)
So love has marked my soul (Your love alone)
And if Jack Frost is an artist (You are my da Vinci)
His touch (Your Smile)
Is an impression (On my world)
I wish color could speak (For me)
Turn grey into violet (Your heart)
Oh, how you've sculpted! (My heart)
But like the wind, (Nature's Monet)
My courage blows away (To build in strength)
And goes away(But I'd let you know)
If I were Anne Frank (And you were a diary)
Every page
Would be full.

Jessica Noujeim, Grade 10
St Patrick's Regional Secondary School, BC

Writer's Block

Stuck in my mind,
On the flypaper of thoughts
An idea sits waiting,
Waiting to fall from my ever-ready fingertips
And land,
Glued forever to the blank pages before me.
My hand stops, hesitates;
A pause, the calm before the storm.
In a flurry the idea flies away,
Away from that which had trapped it before.
My paper lies blank,
Still waiting for its emptiness to be filled,
But there is nothing.

Caitlin Lamb, Grade 11
Burnaby Mountain Secondary School, BC

To Be Young

Lollipops and gumdrops
Candy canes so sweet
Just some of the many things I really love to eat
Teddy bears and other fluff
And all the rest of that cozy stuff
Innocence and pure of heart
The world is free of shame
So big a place for so small a face
Things will never seem the same
All is simple and all is fun
What else but everyone's number one
Every place is another playground
Every experience is something new
Desserts and toys and all the joys
Not a day without something to do
Imagination
Fascination
More love than who or what else
To be free to be happy
To play, laugh and learn
Oh what it's like to be young

Cassandra Nardi, Grade 11
Villa Maria High School, QC

Thinking of You

Every night I look at the sky,
Just to say good night to you.
I admire the beauty of the shining stars,
because they shine like your eyes.

When I stare at the bright night,
I can see your beautiful smile.
The bright moon and the shining stars told me,
our friendship is a gift from God.

We have been together in good and bad times,
And you understood my fears and sorrow.
You taught me to have courage and faith,
And I'm thankful to you.

You are the brightest star in my life
We shared our pain and tears together,
You gave me comfort and advice
You were always there for me.

Many circumstances pulled us apart,
But you are my best friend.
Though we are miles apart,
We still share the same stars.

Karthika Harikumar, Grade 11
Ascension of Our Lord Secondary School, ON

It Rains on Tuesdays

An orchestra of colors conducts the light into the world,
As an ensemble of rain and melancholy counteract.
The light rain is the beginning of a downpour,
That will never ever end.

The vivid colors of sunflowers and daffodils,
Decorate the dreary and calamitous of poverty.
While the sharp red of roses capriole over the blues and greens,
It floods as gunshots interrupt the tranquillity in our lives.

The silence — is it gone?

Whereas the mass-circulation of newspapers and magazines
Ignite the mediums of news and entertainment,
The rain on Tuesdays extinguishes.

Lips stop, eyes widen, eyebrows raise, and lips drop.

The precipitation evaporates before impact with the anhydrous soil,
Illustrating the beauty and wonders of nature before,
And the sunset, like a wax candle — is it blown out forever?

Konrad Listwan, Grade 10
Turner Fenton Secondary School, ON

Forgive Me

I see a light, beyond my sight, break through the blood stained glass.
It strikes my skin, a warmth within, a fleeting memory passed.
I smell the air that lingers there, inside this soul of mine.
A cry rings out, a violent shout, I'm running out of time.
I feel my spirit drift away, on wind kicked from a storm.
Promises made, now debts unpaid, for I have been reborn.
So many lies, have compromised, the walls that I've built up.
I'd tear them down, right to the ground, if I had strength enough.
I taste a tear, fueling my fear, the lights are growing dim.
My Savior has forsaken me, for I've forsaken Him.
My foul deeds, grow up like weeds, those who could count would see,
Why I wish I could come back, in hope you'd forgive me.

Josh Ruegg, Grade 12
Ridgeway and Crystal Beach High School, ON

Imagine a Place

Imagine a place where there is no famine,
this place is a quieter and happier place to be than anywhere else,
no war, no suicide, and no sin.
Everyone tries to be perfect as can be,
a place where there is eternal life,
a great view of all the earth for all of this place to see.
All people at this place would listen to this one person,
everybody will get along and listen to his commands,
nothing to interrupt you in this place.
Peaceful and graceful forever more,
beautiful clouds all around,
maybe one day this world would be this place,
this place called Heaven.

Alysha Aussant, Grade 10
Vanier Collegiate, SK

Earth Removers

Scraping down into the earth
Removing trees throughout the day
Running machinery until it hurts
Going to be a good day for pay
Furiously battling your push
Working the gears with force
Removing waste from the bush
Tracking the ground like a horse
Time to take a break for awhile
Looking for your lunch kit
Your chainsaw later needs a file
Pushing a boulder with a big hit
Sun is setting, another day has gone past
Looking over the job one more time
Let's get these work trucks and fill them with gas
Another day has gone with no breakdowns, what a good sign

Zachary Chevrier, Grade 11
William Mason School, SK

Love

Love, a feeling society strives for,
    but can only be found in one's heart.
Unlike many other things it can't be bought from the start.
Love is a priceless gift from God,
    that one should cherish greatly.
Love is a commitment shared by two,
    once you find it, you know it's true.
Love is surreal,
    the way it can make one feel.
A powerful force where the stakes are high,
sometimes it's forever and sometimes it's good-bye.

Nicole Fernandes, Grade 12
John Cabot Catholic Secondary School, ON

Black Waltz

Vivid colours,
Feelings alike.
Held in the city of lust.
We are lovers.
Grant the florist,
Shiny coins,
For the Andean sage on my lips.
Your symbol for love
    My black flower.
A silver lining,
Around its black heart.
And symphonies.
My black flower
    Falls to the ground,
As you sweep me
Into your broken waltz.
Clumsy romanticism,
Toe on toe.
We stumble along
Our cobblestone streets.
Alone.

Allana Ziorjen, Grade 12
Haliburton Highland Secondary School, ON

Perfect Mother

God made me a mother,
    She never grows old.
Her face as beautiful as the sun,
    Her heart as pure as gold.

My love for her is weird,
    Hard to explain.
Sometimes I make her laugh,
    Sometimes I cause her pain.

The love for my mother,
    Is like my first goal.
I cherish with all my heart,
    And every part of my soul

God made me the best mother,
    Now you can all see.
That God made me a mother
That will always be there for me.

Nash Boateng, Grade 11
Ascension of Our Lord Secondary School, ON

Dire Black Rose

My heart and soul are bleeding red.
Your thorns have pierced through and
Yet you expect me to forgive and forget.

My heart and soul are bleeding red.
Your black petals have uncurled showing all the deceit,
Yet you expect me to forgive and forget.

My heart and soul are bleeding red.
Your tainted center has scarred my heart and
Yet you expect me to forgive and forget.

My heart and soul are bleeding red.
Yet you expect me to forgive and forget,
You are a corrupt and dire black rose.

Felicia Sieppert, Grade 11
Drumheller Outreach, AB

A Battle Cry to Dunsinane

A selfish player on the stage of life;
With deceit, demise, Macbeth played his part.
With flags of Malcolm and the Thane of Fife,
We rise to fight the king of blackened heart.
Leafy shrouds have hidden our noble deeds;
Birnam Wood is the mask of death and blood.
Our army, the soldiers of moss and reeds,
Hearts set in stone, have amassed a dark flood.
We are the deadly act on Judgment Day,
That shall roar, and purge that hell-bound Macbeth.
No soldier, nor guard, shall keep us at bay.
My hands, they shall grasp, until his last breath.
The ghosts of my son and wife haunt my days,
My sword seeks your blood, Tyrant, show your face!

Steven Slowka, Grade 10
Christ The King Secondary School, ON

King My Queen

I start with a kiss,
And begin with a ring,
Will you be my miss,
As I become a king;

I love you with all hearts,
And care with all my love,
My heart has two parts,
You and I bound is enough;

True love of ours combined,
Can never be put in a word,
Our two hearts in bind,
I love you is what we heard.

Andrew Rodman, Grade 11
Markham District High School, ON

Drown

Rivers flow endless
ocean laps on one another
continuous yet melodic
I quietly pray, chant
peaceful tunes
sink into my skin
my bone
I drown within
deeply
carefree
back in basic
away from civilization
into single cells
the call of mother nature awaits
patiently
endlessly
for its children to awaken

Elva Li, Grade 11
Burnaby North Secondary School, BC

Awakening

As I run down the rail,
on a crisp fall morning,
a crunchy orange blanket
crumbles beneath my feet.
My breath exhales
in puffs of steaming air.
My feet strike the ground,
in a rhythmic cadence,
that drives me faster, faster.
The touch of frost on the trees,
glitters in the gold morning sun.
The path and the scene
call to me.
My legs, my heart,
pump in unison.
My spirit soars.

Kelsey Foote, Grade 12
Killarney Collegiate Institute, MB

We're the Real Changes

Can you feel the blazing cold?
Such a misconception of the weather outside.
Blown away by the chilled leaf diseased winds,
Soon to change and differentiate into snow engulfed surroundings.
The weather is ceasing its present state,
To move on to another sense of time,
A different moment of our year,
The formation of another beautiful coming era,
The sense of all around beginning to die for winter's entrance,
But us, we're always growing from sprout to grace.
We're changing along with these seasons,
A sense of joy becomes of all this change around us,
But along with this easily comprehensible joyful exchange,
Hides just one other thing.
The bright shift the humanity faces, children of these seasons to partake in.
Flourishing, dying and soon regrowing into many magnificent beings.
Flourished beings, ever so grown to perfection.
We're the real creation of the changing season,
In fact a comparison, thought gorgeous, surely.
We follow in the footsteps of its evolution,
And create it to be our own, reform.

Brandon Faucher, Grade 11
Heritage Regional High School, QC

The Night's Spectacle

When the sun finishes its descent upon the sky,
The nighttime players begin their commence.
The stage is set with a background of the rainbow,
And the crickets begin their song.

The darkness slowly entwines your senses,
While whispering rumors and plots in your ear.
Capturing the mind, so you can't help but wonder,
Of this spectacle, oh so magnificent.

The stars slowly appear in their rehearsed places,
To perform for you the show created by time.
They tell you of great deeds long past,
While they wink at you from behind a cloud.

The wind twirls your thoughts, ensnared as you are,
Keeping you waiting in suspense for the next twist.
Showing you every part of the character's mind,
Allowing you false hopes for your favorite's destiny.

The moon's final scene begins with her shining glory,
As the clouds draw ever nearer until they are too close.
She cannot escape her fate as the gray veil covers her last breath.
Stillness draws nigh and darkness until the sun chooses to rise again.

Katrina Campbell, Grade 10
J L Ilsley High School, NS

Outlines

It is dark where I am.
Eyes widen, thirsting for light,
outlines emerge.
Silhouettes in the faded darkness
moving, never-ending ebbing flow of the
steady beating of the rhythmic pulsing of the:
no, imitations.
In daylight, objects;
now, only tints and shades of shadow.
Darkness, so often overshadowed by the light,
grows brighter, brighter:
excruciating brightness of the night.

I turn, slowly, searching,
where is? Where is my.
My? No, no matter, let it go.
Only an outline, sketch of
emptiness in the nothingness,
effaced by the brightening night.

Adrian Budhram, Grade 12
Bayview Secondary School, ON

The Perfect Leaf

I step into the crisp clear air,
Welcoming with every breath,
The path of intertwining leaves,
Invite me on a quest.

Each leaf holds it's own beauty,
Portrayed in different ways,
To find a leaf of flawlessness,
Would take some countless days.

The path of these shriveled lifeless leaves,
Begin my never-ending story,
That each leaf leads to just another,
So bask in each one's glory.

Jordana Polito, Grade 11
Aurora High School, ON

In Honor

Though Papa is the one who left,
Mama is the one, who's gone,
She got a phone call late last week,
After that —
She died…inside.

Two doors down the hall,
Is her bed from mine,
And after the call,
I woke suddenly because mama,
She cried.

I walked into another realm,
When I walked into her room,
And when I asked her what was wrong…
"Sergeant Peters…He says Daddy is gone."

Jessica Reed, Grade 10
Merritt Secondary School, BC

My Feline Friend

He greets me at the door.
Rubs against my weary legs,
Follows me around and begs.
So loud; impossible to ignore.

He leads me to his empty bowl,
Let's out a strident cry,
Looks deep into my eyes,
As though he's studying my soul.

I pour some tiny pebbles
Into his empty little bowl.
He races to eat as much as he can,
He's lost all self-control.

Alas, the bowl is empty,
Sound of satisfaction.
He sits down right beside me.
I pet him; no reaction.

Like a pile of dirty laundry,
Curled up in a ball of fur.
He's in his deepest sleep,
Let's out a faint but constant purr.

Monica Stanuch, Grade 12
John Cabot Catholic Secondary School, ON

Bucking Horse

Some days I feel as though I am
On a horse that bucks too hard,
And won't stop 'till he does the damage
Of breaking every bone
In the body that I call home.
And no one dares step in his path
While he displays his coltish ways,
For when you do
Fear is the least of your worries.
Yet most of the time he's a harmless foal
Playing at the edge of the fire
Hoping that he won't get burned by the sizzling, smoking coals.
Someday he might realize the harm that he's done
Finally learning to be a respectable mount
His episodes no longer fun,
And even though he's young enough
Some things can't be undone.
So that's why I'm starting now
To tame this colt within me
Before he gets too hard to catch
And sails off right before me.

Abbey Parsonage, Grade 10
Consul School, SK

The Open Door

You've always dreamed of a bright, sunny day, with the door always open, to show you what the world has become, but you've never felt that. The sky is always dark, filled with pain and terror, and the door is always closed. You are forced to never see the beauty of what remains on the other side of life. Cuts and bruises scar you, but in a place where you can never find them — your heart, a fragile place of no tomorrow. You pray so hard for a day when life where you come from becomes a better place; a place where the day is always glowing and the sun is always shining. Well, one day, that day came. Out of the darkness came a face — you, a face of tomorrow. You came to show me that life is better if someone is there to share it with you. So you held out your hand, and I couldn't resist. Feeling your hand in mine made me feel so alive and different. I always knew that now we could always experience a bright sunny day. We could always experience the beauty of what lies on the other side of life. Those cuts and bruises are now healed and my heart is no longer fragile, but stronger. And at last, the door is open, but you're coming out with me.

Rachel Mason, Grade 11
St Thomas More Catholic Secondary School, ON

The Unforgiving Wave

The dancing waves charmed the sun kissed beach, as the cool wind moved with grace.
It was like any other day, in this tropical paradise.
Then suddenly the ocean is pulled to the core with the strength of a magnetic force.
An eerie silence surrounds the scene with dreadful calm that's unlike the sea.
Then it happens, a raging hundred-foot wave, within seconds it reaches the beach.
Crashing onto the rocks, crushing trees as if they were twigs.
Immersing the earth, absorbing and extracting away the beauty.
The screams and the confusion, the mad rush and the scramble.
Useless against that aggressive powerful force.
Nothing could stop them from being dragged off like rag dolls.
Poor fishing villages are crushed to the ground.
Empty classrooms are flooded and destroyed.
Homes are crumpled like autumn leaves, along with their hopes and dreams
Within minutes all is destroyed.
Happy honeymooning couple is no more, the young wife is now a widow.
The family that saved up for their special holiday, those children are now orphaned
Left behind are the echoes, the echoes of the souls that are lost in the depths of the sea.
And the tears and the anguish of those they left behind.
The ocean is serene once more. The calm waves continue to hit the beach,
But the lives of those people, it will never be the same.

Neluni Dassanayake, Grade 12
John Cabot Catholic Secondary School, ON

My Dreams of You

My dreams of you are like newborn pups
Growing their first coats of golden fur
Like the rhythm of drums in a tropical, Latin fiesta
Like a baby's first steps in a cotton meadow of sparkling snow
Like the scent of Cousin Nikki's perfume, fervent, fruity
Like a thrilling chill of a fierce, arctic current
Like the warmth of a reunited embrace
Like the hushed hum of silence in the deepest rainforest
Like the crunch of an apple from the Tree of Life in the Garden of Eden
Like stormy rain clouds over Kenya
Like the salt of a healing tear of happiness after infinite despair
Like the roar of Croatian fans at a World Cup soccer game
Like a supernova in an immaculate, velvet sky
Like swinging off an old, billowing willow tree screaming, and diving into a crystal lake
Like the shimmering zest of Niagara's tranquil mist
Like sitting in a gothic church with a spectrum of vibrant reds, yellows, and blues creeping in through a jigsaw of stain glass windows

Yasmina Havlicek, Grade 12
Burnaby North Secondary School, BC

Prayer

An unfamiliar voice lingers in my mind
Is it you?
I yearn to find myself in the darkness
Do my pleas not reach your ears?
I'm always wishing,
That one day my prayer will reach you
The silent figure that stood in the doorway
Holds my life in his hands
My vision is slurred with illusions
Could it be I'm terrified of my own reflection?
I'll grasp my fear close to my heart
And never let you see my weakened smile
Isolated in this nightmare
I'm blinded by fake bliss I can't escape
Am I walking through life meaninglessly?
Your unseen embrace gives me courage
The ray of light that flows steadily,
It calls out to me, scattering precious miracles
Hope and faith
I'll keep listening to the voice that tells me I'm not alone
And walk toward the planned future.

Ana-Maria Castillo, Grade 12
Gleneagle Secondary School, BC

Am I Canadian? Eh!

Am I Canadian? Eh!
I don't live in an igloo or eat blubber.
I have to have my Timmies every day.

Linked to the Trans-Canada Highway,
I go from St. John's to Vancouver.
Am I Canadian? Eh!

On a hot summer day,
I barbecued beef for supper.
I have to have my Timmies every day.

Fishing on Hudson Bay
With my dog sled and ice auger,
Am I Canadian? Eh!

Farmers bailing some hay
For our harsh cold winter.
I have to have my Timmies every day.

His commitment goes without say;
Steven Harper is our prime minister.
Am I Canadian? Eh!
I have to have my Timmies every day.

Joshua Dufresne, Grade 12
Ecole secondaire Catholique Sainte-Marie, ON

Not Enough

Over the rainbow there is no sun
Just a broken projection
Of what used to be
All we have left is memories
That's not enough

I still cry
For the shattered hope
You'd create
Every time we'd almost touch

It burns so much that
Dark sunglasses
Cannot conceal these tears

Knowing you don't feel the same
Hides my rainbow of memories
Behind clouds of disappointment

My broken heart bleeds

Paige Clare, Grade 12
Dr Charles Best Secondary School, BC

Hockey

The ice is all smooth
As all the players
Get ready for the game

The fans all cheer
The home team is winning tonight
As the period ends

The players hustle toward the puck
Playing their very best game
Checking, bumping, passing, shooting, and SCORING

Jonathan Gritter, Grade 11
Immanuel Christian School, MB

Dead on My Feet

So beautiful, he waits, for me, it's so sad to see,
He leans, oh so casually, against, the wrought iron gates.

Chalk like, his complexion, irritated, his expression,
As I, his obsession, makes, my confession.

I whisper, biting my lip, of him, and another,
Of how, I must pick, only one, or the other.

Jealous, eyes narrowed, he's calm, glaring angrily,
Almost, cupid's arrow, seems, it has missed me.

'That's fine,' he smiles, shocked, I wait,
Silent, all awhile, casually, against the gate.

Leaning in, he kisses my cheek, gently, he slides past me,
Vanishing, where I can't see, crying, I feel dead on my feet.

Tiffany Lemoine, Grade 12
Simonds High School, NB

Interior Battles

She cries out for him,
In the dark of the night.
This emotion isn't a whim.
It's an inner fight,
For the one whom she desires,
Who lifts her soul higher.

But fear is holding her back,
And at her soul it eats away.
He could give what she doth lack.
Still, she keeps her love at bay.
No matter what she could gain,
She is still scared of all the pain.

But when the healing has been done,
Ready to love, to him she shall run.

Jessica Thomas, Grade 12
Holy Cross Regional High School, BC

I Don't Wanna Go Swimming

I don't wanna go swimming
I hate the smell of chlorine
People pee in these waters
Are pigs getting slaughtered?
Screams can be heard as I enter
I think it's hell in there
It even ruins my hair
I don't see a point going there
It just ain't fair
Bacteria is crawling on my arm
Feels like an awful ant farm
I don't wanna go swimming

Carrie Ho, Grade 10
Burnaby North Secondary School, BC

Ted

When I see him
I see some self centered guy.
He's big, tall and strong
With brown hair and deep blue eyes.
When he's mad,
His face is red,
Overflowing with anger.
Tears roll down his face,
His insane, crazy face.
At his house,
He broke a lot of things.
He broke chairs and doors
And made holes in the walls
Bing, bang, boom!
There goes another door.
But behind all this,
He has a heart of chocolate.
He's sweet in various ways.

Dominique Doutre, Grade 10
Ecole Secondaire La Citadelle, ON

Timid Hearts

Constant cries of pain and hunger.
No one to care or keep them safe.
Not even the words of others can comfort their tiny timid hearts.
Every day the pain reminds them of the days that lay behind.
Reaching out for something that's not there.
The constant reminder of the people that have come and gone.
Black eyes watch the sun rise and set, enjoying everyone as if it was the last.
They stand holding hands singing the words that I can't understand.
Their voices ring through the air,
Knowing someone's watching their little black dirt covered faces from above.

Danae Siemens, Grade 12
Mennonite Educational Institute, BC

Hidden Clover

The speech prepared in my heart,
is one I've tried to speak out in the past.
And now that I feel it breaking apart,
I have no choice but to blurt it out fast.
The bar was set up far too high
Always trying to skip and fast forward.
I hoped somehow life would just pass me by.
But now I feel the bar must be lowered.
Life to me was sitting out while the others played
Rehearsing lines in my head before I spoke.
Watching them spread their wings while I just stayed.
Sleeping in when everyone else awoke.
How could I fail if I never tried?
How could they hurt me if I was never there?
Above everything else I held my pride.
If they knew how I felt, they would not care.
If I could relive my life I'd slow it down and feel every emotion I pushed aside.
I'd cherish every feeling and refuse them a place to hide.
I'd treasure the smaller things because the bigger things were so few and far between.
And now I know that past the stones lay the clovers just waiting to be seen.

Kayla Sousa, Grade 12
John Cabot Catholic Secondary School, ON

Foolish Heart

My eyes filled with tears as I saw him with the girl
His arms were relaxed and wrapped around her neck
The boy joked and the girl laughed — how simple it was
Who do I have — no one.

I'm scared of telling you,
not wanting to let go,
not wanting to turn away
The nicer you are, the harder it is for me
Loving you is foolish,
you already have someone
Trapped in this state for more than a year,
I should look for someone new
But I only end up hurting them, and me because I keep thinking of you
Is this all there is to love?

Karen Lam, Grade 10
St Thomas More Collegiate School, BC

If Only It Were Easy

If only it were easy
To live life to the fullest
Instead of dreaming of what could be
And living through what seems to be a never ending conquest

If only it were effortless
To be gay
And to not obsess
Over the little things
That always leave you in dismay

If only it were simple
To find what we're looking for;
Whether it be in yourself or in other people.
But whatever you find always leaves you wanting more

If everything was as you wanted it
Wouldn't it be that much easier to quit?

Catherine Sollazzo, Grade 10
Villa Maria High School, QC

Snow Day

Monday is here and my dreary eyes awake;
The sound of my alarm is too much to take.
I squint as white light reflects my mirror,
In doubt that school could not seem nearer.

When the blinds open, the sight triggers an emotion.
Those that are overjoyed never complete their work,
The frustrated students are known for their devotion,
And anxious ones seek adventure while hiding a smirk.

This white painting should not be described too greatly.
The day is often dangerous and something adults dread
Snow day is a miracle where journeys broaden endlessly.
It rarely occurs, but when it does, delight is always spread.

Angela Guadagno, Grade 10
Villa Maria High School, QC

Duration

Forever we are waiting.
Time wearily passes
Over hordes of prosaic tasks
And never-ending classes;
Pause.

And still, we wait
For the promising toll of the bell,
The auditory indication of finality,
For heaven to claim its pow'r over hell;
Anticipate.

And on it goes.
The blissful robins sing,
With the propitious sunny glow.
We dread the sepulchral pendulum swing;
Go.

Mairi McGowan, Grade 10
Brentwood College School, BC

Seconds Please!

We see the signs in restaurants,
We see the signs in bars,
Then why do we feel the need,
To push the limit so far?

He lights a match,
I gaze in concern,
How could he kill himself,
And his family in return?

The smoke enters our lungs,
With no exit,
I think to myself,
I sure do hope he regrets it.

Second hand smoke kills us slowly,
Inside and out,
I can do nothing,
Except sit down and pout.

I have a fact,
That will put your mind at ease.
If smoking continues,
We will always be able to ask for "seconds please!"

Sanaya El Sayad, Grade 10
Villa Maria High School, QC

Skit's a Friend Yeah

Caw a fabled line,
a contemplation of glee,
you frail parrot of their fancy.
"What's for dinner, Skit?"
Parakeet stew my dearest songbird.
I'll play with you
(Hide and seek)
if you play with me.
Let's count together:
(It's too dangerous alone)
"One, twelve, six — eighteen."
(How quickly we've grown)
Search the basement.
(So you're up in the attic?)
Crack-up the steps.
(Don't titter, I'll hear!)
"But the fear, Skit, the fear, Skit! It's too late now dear."
"Come out, come out or go-go go ba-ba-ba-bananananas!"
Pecked by a feather, the cracked parrot did split.
"Giggle-de, giggle-de, har-de-har-har!"
(I'll never be far)

Lucas Greig, Grade 12
Ecole secondaire catholique Saint-Charles-Garnier, ON

Human

What's with this world we are living in?
The only difference between right and wrong is a line,
A line that fades over time and eventually disappears.
The only truth in our lives is that of our friends, family, and loved ones.
The right appears at the wrong times and is only there when we no longer care.
What's with these lives that we're living?
Greed taking over generosity.
We beg for things to go right in our lives,
But ruin others in the process of making it so.
We grieve from the deceiving, the hate, and the pain.
We pursue hurt to gain pride and make ourselves a name.
This name is but merely a word,
A word that expresses the idea of change but not the action of it.
This word is "human."
We all think we act in special ways,
The truth is we don't, we are all the same.
Human is not angry, is not kind, and is not shy.
It is a word that masks the hundreds of thousands of emotions bottled up inside.

Jacey Sharpe, Grade 10
Minnedosa Collegiate, MB

falling out of love

i'm high above when she tells me, now peering down overwhelms me,
a hopeless certainty, her eyes are searching me,
for answers but her questions are cancers, i have no cure,
so here we hang unassured,
death is undeterred and i'm so scared it hurts,
i exert, i search but all i find is sweat, which makes her slip worse,
cursed, we fall like a summers end or like emotion dripping from a dying man's pen
we once were but never again, does god wait for me at love's end?

Vinay Dhir, Grade 12
William Lucas Centre, BC

Someone Just for Me

I see them every day
There are always two
Never one, never three; why isn't there someone just for me?
They are always smiling; holding hands
Their lips touch together in a kiss; I want to do that too.
They play their games meant for two
Everyone ignores me, I am not like them, I have no one just for me.
Not like them
Just a shadow; an annoyance
But I always wonder is there someone just for me?
Someone to smile with
To hold hands; laugh with
To kiss and to play games with? Someone just for me?
I like someone; I wonder if they are that someone
Meant just for me, only me.
We could laugh; we could kiss
We could smile, someone just for me.
I wonder if there is
Someone just
For me.

Danielle Nauss, Grade 11
Forest Heights Community School, NS

Bleak

I could not imagine
I could not live
I could not think
Without it
You ask me
"Who do you love more?
Music or me?"
And I cannot answer
Because it is not fair
I love music
And I love you, too
It cannot be compared
It makes taste to the world
Lets life be wonderful
Color to my eyes
Neither food nor water
Happiness or joy
Can be greater than music
It is my heart
My beat
My savior.

Eric Chow, Grade 11
Burnaby Mountain Secondary School, BC

Walking the Right Path

When you are on a journey
Walk the right path
Just look up at everything around you
Look at all the birds flying and the clouds drifting
They are following you

The Creator loves you
He loves the way you follow the right path
He knows what you are feeling
And what your emotions are
He knows what path you are walking

The right path is for you
Just walk it and take comfort
It will bring you to a wonderful world
Inside you to your secret soul
Just look up and say
I thank You for walking with me on this path

The right path will bring out your best
Just walk it and never give up
It will give you a positive experience in life
It will take you somewhere in this world
Always walk the right path

Holly F. Badger, Grade 10
Kehewin Community Education Centre, AB

The Tangible Fades the Intangible Remains

Smiles take form with mild satisfaction.
pleasing the outside with expected reaction.
memories of old loves hidden under the rocks.
hearts outbeat the tick tocking of clocks.
lowered lashes of willows weeping out loud
lying above ground picking out the clouds.
abuse of a substance…said the worst of any kind.
but we are fallen jewels said the rarest of any find.
held high by most but not seen for what we are.
wishers. pretenders. descendants of stars.

Christine Simons, Grade 12
John Cabot Catholic Secondary School, ON

Getting Over You

Loving you felt like I was being drugged;
I woke up each day and my mind was so fogged.
Your kisses were one of my major addictions;
I always took more than the normal prescription.
We stopped speaking over the phone at nights,
Yet I struggled to stop my emotional fight.
Though I wasn't sure I guessed it was over;
I had no regrets, though I wished it were sooner.
You played one of the biggest roles in my life;
I was blinded to all of your stupid lies.
They say experience is the greatest teacher;
I'm glad it took you to make me much wiser.
As for gettin' over you I'm doing quite all right;
You were just one of the men on my way to Mr. Right.
Being friends is not really much of an option;
And nothing you can say will alter my decision.
I have a life of my own which I intend to live;
I have set my goals which I'm now ready to achieve.
Don't try to stop me now you best believe it's true;
It only took one man to make me know I'm over you!

Endy Williams, Grade 12
George Harvey Collegiate Institute, ON

You Cannot Find Me

I am all around you as we speak,
Unbelievable, immortal, unreachable and bleak,
You cannot find me, no matter how hard you try,
I am within you, on earth, in water and sky,
I torture your fantasies, and live your realities,
I am the ruler, the supreme, of all humanities,
I have brought down the civilizations of eons passed,
Sent the futures of gods into the fires of hell, cast,
Your mission, your pathway, your only wish,
It sets its will against you, and leads into the abyss,
The love you lust, when all dreams are dying,
That comfort you seek, when your soul is crying,
That ounce of strength you summon, when all hope is lost,
The moment you seize, no matter the cost,
To your very knees I will force you to hail,
Your time is running out, you have yet to fail,
For you cannot find me,
I am your holy grail.

Laura Gudowski, Grade 12
Wellington Secondary School, BC

Autumn

The wind dances with branches on trees
Air stirs as the leaves mingle
The sky cries tears from above
Leaves are turning so brightly
So brightly they seem to be burning
The sounds in my ear tell me all is well
Days are short
The night air is cool, soothing my heart

Kaitlyn Nicholson, Grade 10
Merritt Secondary School, BC

Sunday Feelings

I'm blank for words,
But I have a hurt to express.
The more the days,
The more I feel less.
I'm sad, I'm sick,
What more can I say.
I'm a teenager with problems,
And they just won't go away.
I hate being alone,
I can't do what I can.
I don't know who I'll be,
Or even who I am.
I'm not ready for new,
I can barely handle things old.
I want my heart warm,
I don't like when it's cold.
This poem is so over,
In fact it did not start.
This poem has no soul,
This poem is my empty heart.

Jillian Wilson, Grade 10
Hazelton Secondary School, BC

Writing Is...

Like a bee flying
Back
And
Forth
From the hive
There is a job to be done
A boring stressful job.
It has to be completed
Before winter
A bee has no idea on what freedom is.
Because he is always working
But when winter comes,
His job is finished.
He can feel relaxed.
There's always something missing,
A job that has to be worked.
Only when your time is up
Are you complete.

Jordan Yntema, Grade 11
King's Christian School, BC

Dance of Death

Under sound of heavy footsteps, her voice trampled.
She cannot cry out, nor plead for others sympathy,
But entwined with antipathy they disregard a somber human soul.
Her lips are sealed with curse of addiction.
She begs, muttered noise echoes throughout her intentions
And she begins to move, and dances the dance of death,
Her body moves as in a trance, yet she is unable to escape her shackles
Imposed by that of a insignificant snow-white crystal
Burned and melted in the fires of abhorrence and iniquity
Burned with the fires of Hades, abode of the dead
Thus she must dance the Dance of Death
Beelzebub bickers and kindly watches her fate, His prize won
But in her head, in her head she fights, fighting to hold on to the very ledge of life
The footsteps continue not one stops, they are locked in a predetermined beat
Glaring eyes watch her stumble, and succumbing to the dreaded silence of anguish
She falls
Quietly against rain stricken streets
Filled with fear and despair, she beckons for compassion
Yet Silence bestows, and a heartbroken woman gives up her soul
Ignored and Forgotten
To death's realm she trudges on

Sean Formby, Grade 12
Holy Cross Regional High School, BC

Man

And they say he was made in the image of God
Well then pray tell why he is flawed?
His eye can only spot the skin, eyes, hair, nose
Conceive he cannot the complexity of a rose

He can notice the splendour of the red petal
And the attractive odour that will settle
But in the mind's eye flawlessness is still the goal
And in the heart can lie the perfection that was stole

He walks with a falter, for he sees himself and
Places his existence at the alter; a trivial grain of sand
For they only see him if he bears a mask
An Adonis build, trim, thus in his brilliance, bask

Michelangelo's David is distracting, and the image screens the mind
Where previous morals were acting. Hence, towards life he walks blind
And were he too poor to provide
Woman will abhor, no wife will twin his stride

And in this state he will remain
It is too late, it is too great a stain
And so they say he was made in the image of God
There can be no day when precision will trod

Pamela Miller, Grade 12
Bashaw School, AB

A Cat's Perspective

The smell of old books wafts through the air,
Light from the window makes the television screen glisten.
I've licked all the dirt and grime off my hair,
And lie comfortably on the couch, and listen.
It's serene down here, quiet, listless and calm,
When suddenly the silence is broken.
Down from the stairs he lumbers with his palm
Outstretched so that he may start strokin'.
His weight, as he sits, sinks him into his place,
And I begin to meander away.
But as his fingers rub my scalp, and around my face
I decide I might like to stay.
There I lie on the couch with my glorious masseuse,
I examine my surrounding as present.
I listen, sniff, sense for any abuse,
But it is only quiet, cool, and pleasant.

Brandon Green, Grade 10
Brentwood College School, BC

In the Middle

Do you remember back in elementary school?
Two people fighting, both wanting to sit next to you
Stuck in the middle, not wanting to cause more fights
you sat there in silence starring up at the lights
Six years later your sixteen years old
Stuck in the middle of a friendship gone cold
Not wanting to choose sides or fuel the fight
You stood on the sidelines and held on tight
Six more years go by, now your twenty-two
Starring at the doctor who just told you the news
Now your stuck in the middle of a whole new fight
Holding on to life with all your might
Seven long years and your twenty-nine
Looking around the home it took so long to find
Now your in the middle of your husbands life
Who's been there forever, through all your strife
in the middle is a hard place to be
Between what's expected and the need to be free
Just try to remember that its all right
Just keep going and don't give up the fight

Evelyn Dillman, Grade 11
Musquodoboit Rural High School, NS

Christina Luchetta

Christina Luchetta
Wide eyed, brown haired, artistic
Sister to Micheal
Who loves art, fun, excitement
who feels safe around friends
Who needs love, safety and complexity
Who gives laughter, friendship and kindness
who fears spiders, clowns and being hurt
who'd like to see Paris
Who dreams of happiness
A student of Ascension
Christina

Christina Luchetta, Grade 11
Ascension of Our Lord Secondary School, ON

What Is a Canadian?

When I think French, I think of
large Catholic families.
When I think French, I think of
their many pastries.

When I think English, I think of
their royal family.
When I think English, I think of
aristocrats, and conservatives.

When I think Asians, I think of
their intelligence in technology.
When I think Asians, I think of
their delicious foods.

When I think of Africans, I think of
their long, hard history.
When I think of Africans, I think of
their many forms of art.

When I think Canadians, I think of
French, English, Asians, Africans.
When I think of Canadians, I think of
a mix of the best.

Julie Sullivan, Grade 12
École secondaire Catholique Sainte-Marie, ON

Age

Talk to me
As though we had never met
Like my face was new
In the glass of your eye
As though my skin did not stretch
With the weight of your children
And my skeleton hung straight
In its canvas
Like we have not sat, half our lives
In this room
The TV our telegram
As though the night fell on us
With expectation and delight
How wide our bed has grown
And we were not hoarded
Like chattel, forever moving onward
With our eyes to the ground
Hands bound behind us
Please,
Talk to me as though
You love me still

Amanda Merritt, Grade 11
Timberline Secondary School, BC

Winter

As Winter's grasp grows steadily still,
Replacing summer with piercing chill
Green colours linger, caught by time
Seemingly cut from their flourishing prime
Autumn's tease, fallen leaves, assisted greedily by cooling breeze
December's blanket, in cold air's wake,
Covering grass, and freezing lake
Stretching throughout, seen all from afar
Smothering leaves, reflecting the star.
Nights grow cold, so dark, so bold, love's soft touch, too rough to hold.
And as trees grow stiff and frost fills sky,
Reminding me the end is nigh,
Distant the memories, of tracks in the snow
Like a leaf to a branch, I simply let go
To love lost, love found, no path but to drown, in ecstasy, in bliss, in changes profound.
Hands and heart grow weary and blue,
The days seem colder, Winter's cue
And beauty is frozen, sleeping sublime
Only to be awakened again sometime.

Matt Davis, Grade 12
Notre Dame High School, AB

Do You Remember?

Do you remember when the world was at your fingertips? When everything was just a game? I remember, do you? Do you remember how differently the world looked? I do and it was beautiful. Every tree rich with unpicked promises.
Back then every new discovery was a hidden treasure. The rainbow after the rain, was never just coincidental phenomenon but to me, oh so much more.
A staircase to climb, and climb I did. My mind became a porthole, through which I could reach another world. Do you remember what fun we had? I do. Every day was something new.
Oh such fun we had. Eating ice cream on hot summer days, playing hopscotch and hiding among the trees. Then there were all of the secrets we told and all of the laughs we shared. It seemed that we could continue in our childlike innocence forever but it was not meant to be. Soon those days of bliss became a distant memory. You changed. You began to find your fun in other places. And soon like all of the games and times we shared, you put all of your memories of the back shelf and I too became something of the past. These days you don't even acknowledge my existence, but my friend have you honestly forgotten. Maybe one day you'll go back to that shelf and you'll uncover a box that has been hidden away and discover the treasure within. Maybe one day we'll both walk hand in hand down memory lane and revisit the place of our youth.

Camellia Morris, Grade 11
Pierrefonds Comprehensive High School, QC

Memories

I remember a time when everything was good,
the world was a peaceful place or so I understood.
My childhood contained events that molded me in every way.
The good times help to overcome the hardships we face today.

My grandpa told me stories pertaining to the past.
He taught me valuable lessons about how the memories last.
You see, he fought in a war similar to the present one in many ways.
He was lucky to make it back alive, but his brother remains there to this day.

Gunshots, bombs, and tanks all around constantly fearing for their lives.
Soldiers unaware if they would make it, back home to see their wives.
They fought for our country to give us freedom and security. We can't begin to imagine the obstacles they overcame.
Those who made it back were forever changed they will NEVER be the same.

Chelsey Knibbs, Grade 11
Stoughton Central School, SK

Ascension

Bathed in black, the night engulfs all,
Seemingly infinite, only to enthrall
Everything good, as they cannot coexist;
Darkness cannot have light in its' midst
And any felon of this law, darkness shall erase.

The unlighted world creates conflicts amass,
That neither Satan nor Lucifer could easily surpass,
And humans unlock their deepest desires.
While the universe aligns its infernal fires,
The effulgence rises slowly, eminent with grace.

Now completely discernible and recognized by all,
The contentions' tenor began to readily fall.
Burning through vapor, and calamity all the same;
An emotional window; elation lacking a frame.
Light beginning to reveal its indubitable face.

Breathtaking euphoria, zestful beauty,
The fluorescence radiates with loyal duty,
Lifting upwards, the world in totality,
Towards the paradise of flourishing vitality,
Luminance ascends all into their blissful place,
Defeating the dark and conceiving the embrace.

Nathan Tippe, Grade 12
Archbishop Carney Secondary School, BC

Ta-Da!

Enter stage left,
Character number four,
Spotlight! Spotlight!
The director calls from his special chair,
Actors mill around,
Decked out in gorgeous costumes,
I stand among the chaos, of their new production,
And I stare at my newly found script,
(Exeunt All)
It says,
And I realize the line doesn't work,
Because there is no one else on the stage,
But me,
Standing in the sun's spotlight,
Alone,
Taking orders from no director,
Striking a pose,
With a confidence that appears,
And dissolves,
In a flash,
Of the camera.

Alexandra Carrière, Grade 11
Centennial Regional High School, QC

The Waiting

Mist catching in my hair,
Eyelashes surrender too.
I see each drop under the light;
That of a passing stranger
Or one standing still —
A tall black post in the station —
And feel its grace against my skin.
Cold sharp needles,
That is what the raindrops are,
A sweet serenade of the limitless sky
They pierce my line of sight,
Hold my breath caught in my throat,
Engrave into my heart and mind
That what I now await
Is not at all worth waiting for.

Elizaveta Salnikova, Grade 12
Burnaby Mountain Secondary School, BC

God How Could You Do This to Me?

God how could you do this to me?
How could you take him from me?
God how could you do this to me?
I feel like I am dying without him.
God how could you do this to me?
God please give me the words to say to him
I don't know how to express my feelings to him.
Please just give me a sign, give me the words to say to him.
God how could you do this to me?
When I see him I want to tell him that
I really like him and that I wanted to be with him.
God how could you do this to me?
He is killing me inside I see him with other girls
and it feels like someone is stabbing me in the heart.
I was serious about us
but I guess he is just like the others.

Kimberly Harrison, Grade 11
Ascension of Our Lord Secondary School, ON

Conquest

I dangle my hands behind my hip, allow them to
Swim and sift through my chalk bag as the
Powdery substance glazes my skin which will
Embark on a hellish campaign to conquer.

I attach myself to the jagged stone,
Let its chilling moisture cool my hands
Grasp and cling, muscles tense, adrenaline flows
Through veins bulging out of chapped, coarse skin.

Crimp and pull; I ascend as if my body is floating
Satisfaction drives me to make another move up
Flag a leg out, balance, reach and grasp a wall
Higher than your house, more serrated then a knife.

The crux of the climb is below me, the pinnacle imminent
A synergy of athleticism, strength, and confidence empower
I top out and have achieved first conquest of the climb.

Michael De Paoli, Grade 10
Brentwood College School, BC

When Child Becomes Adult

As I stand here and watch the time
I think about where it might have gone
It seems like only yesterday I was
learning how to walk
But know,
as I walk,
to my biggest accomplishment
Where child becomes adult
Where adult becomes the future
As I grab my diploma
I recap my past
and take my knowledge
and begin my first step
The step in a new journey,
New adventure,
New Chapter

Jennifer Leblanc, Grade 12
McCoy High School, AB

I Am a Puck

I am in every play,
I glide on the ice,
I soar through the air.
I ring off the pipes,
And caught by the net.
I slam into the thick pads.
I whip around the boards.
I bruise you when I hit you.
I go from stick to stick.
I am a puck.

Jean-Luc Tatto, Grade 10
Burnaby North Secondary School, BC

Generation Cable Bleed

Tonight I'll watch with caution
As screens consume my landscape,
And let life lose its stronghold
As apathy seduces.
And once, again, revert
To that too-familiar numbness,
'Til death arrives on horseback,
Young and fast and painful.
For now, content, I'll languish
In this culture of the instant,
For all our substance lacking
Reveals our stalled transition.
How apt — they call it static,
This digital abyss.

The world may burn, tonight —
Outside my window, even —
And yet, I would not see it —
Unless, of course, they filmed it
And it bled onto the screen.

Lauri-Beth Lewis, Grade 12
Stratford Central Secondary School, ON

Autumn Leaves

The autumn leaves fall — red and yellow
And shape the warmth of the ground
The fruits of spring seem to slowly mellow
And shape the earth so round.

The dancing leaves hold a dance
In midair, where the beautiful fragrance carries them
Prancing through the sweetness of romance
Singing softly to the crystalline gem.

The maidens shyly bow,
The gentlemen take the maidens by the hand
Musicians! — play the music slow, maybe we can delay the snow
Let us all make a last stand.

Euphony quiets into a subsidized chatter
The wind has brought with him some terrible news
What's the matter? — A bird ponders as the leaves scatter
It is here! It is here! The cold-hearted winter's here!

Another year, another year
Our show has ended for now — it's true
It is here! It is here! The cold-hearted winter is here!
It is here in chase of the autumn leaves — my friends, adieu!

Hannah Sung, Grade 11
Bayview Secondary School, ON

I Will Never Surrender

Ignorance
A plague that sweeps across the nation like wildfire
Projecting its cruelty unto those whom refuse to surrender to its wrathful grip
Besieging the minds of the seemingly innocent and pure
I will never surrender

Prejudice
It exists everywhere
Sprouting randomly and spreading like viral infection
Surrender or fall victim to its abominable mission
I will never surrender

Envy
Unveiling the evil that exists in us all
Provoking hateful and pernicious thoughts
Until it seeps its way into all life
I will never surrender

Hope
It saves us from all other evils in this world
It does not infect or consume
It merely reigns over all that try to fight it
I will never let it go

Kyle Wilson, Grade 10
Brentwood College School, BC

Apathy

I feel so sad and dead inside,
Like a gold leaf falling on the ground,
I feel so weak and faithless,
Like a disease newly found.

The power in my body has completely vanished,
I have no will to go on,
The power inside has long ago faded,
I have no will since it's all gone.

My heart is slowly bleeding away,
And my tears are turning black,
My heart longs for happiness,
And my tears may never go back.

Just a dream fading in my memory,
Just something caged and never free,
Just a dream of you and me,
Just something never meant to be.

Alicia Bleaney, Grade 11
Johnston Heights Secondary School, BC

Raging Fury

The eye of the storm is its most calm, but
The fury that ensues brings destruction.
As it tears into you like a deep cut
All you can do is run for protection.

As the rage and the wrath overwhelm me
Thoughts of revenge and reprisal ensue.
Spontaneous actions are done blindly
And dangerous thoughts soon come into view.

But soon my heart strongly beats against it
And to anger I'll no longer submit.

Isabelle Khoo, Grade 12
Father Leo J Austin Catholic Secondary School, ON

11 Questions

If you truly love me will you prove it through your touch?
If you truly care will you act upon that feeling?
Will you show me all that I am worth?
Or will you let me take the fall?
Will you take my hand and lead the way,
Through this dreary and vile life?
Or will you watch me slip into the darkness?
The road is blocked with walls of hate,
Will you break them down with your love?
Will you save me from my tower way above the clouds?
Or will you flea in fear and weep in my defeat?
So tell me darling all I want to hear,
Tell me lovely all I want to know,
When comes the end,
When comes the last,
Will you love me?
Or will you let go?

Ashley Brown, Grade 10
Brookfield High School, ON

Eternal Love

My love for you is growing
Each day without you knowing
Though you may be gone
I'll wait for the dawn
To carry me high
So that when I die
My soul will be with you once again.

I can feel my heart swelling
Even without me telling
How much, with heart and soul, I love you
And I know, without you being here, you love me too
Without you my heart and soul
Will never be whole
Until I am with you once again.

And now, at last, I can see your smiling face
I can see you moving with silent grace
I can feel your sweet breath
Can this really be death?
My heart is filling with uncontrolled love
You're still smiling and cooing like a dove
And, my soul lifting, I am with you once again.

Julie Vance, Grade 12
Mother Teresa Catholic High School, ON

A Student's Struggle

This right here is about a student's struggle.
His worries about failing and getting into trouble.
But you see it's not that he fails intentionally,
The problems that he faces are not always evidently.

He goes through issues just like everyone else,
But always feels like it's just himself.
The path that he takes is always cold and dark,
There can be times when it's good…but then it goes dark.

In that time he hopes for a light,
A light to make that path shine bright.
To keep focused and not lose sight,
To never ever give up on a fight.

People walk by,
Don't really ask why.
What some people see,
Other people just deny.

In the end…comes much experience,
Because the student's struggle is a testament to perseverance.

Raffaele Romano, Grade 11
Ascension of Our Lord Secondary School, ON

Contradictory

I tell her she is beautiful,
But she does not believe me,
Because louder than my voice,
Is the voice of a TV.
I tell her she is beautiful
Right before I put her to bed.
But then comes a magazine
Contradicting all that I said.
Your flaws are not ugly they're what make you unique.
But they tell her with just a little make-up you will look "oh so chic!"
Your lustrous red hair is beautiful,
Just like the sun.
But now she wants to dye it because they say
Blondes have more fun!
For false beauty we pay thousands of dollars to go under a knife,
But while just reading this poem 4 kids in Africa just lost their life!

Sherina Forte-Jones, Grade 10
Villa Maria High School, QC

Sunset

Pastel pinks, brilliant oranges and dusky purples
illuminate the fading sky
As the sun slowly evaporates behind the infinite horizon
All is still
The glistening ocean reflects the smiling, dancing stars
that nudge themselves through the lively colors of the sunset to be noticed
Slowly but surely
the sunset will give away
to the pale shining dollar in the sky
called the moon.

Tassha A. Johnson, Grade 10
Porter Creek Secondary School, YT

Your Time

This is your time to dream, your time to love, your time to share,
Your time to hope, your time to think, your time to care.
This is your time to laugh, your time to succeed, your time to make amends,
Your time to help, your time to achieve, your time to make a new friend.
This is your time to be loyal, your time to be honest, your time to forgive,
Your time to speak, your time to shine, your time to live.
This is your time to smile, your time to learn, your time to make a choice,
Your time to accept, your time to believe, your time to have a voice.
This is your time to experience, your time to express, your time to roam,
Your time to explain, your time to travel, your time to seek the unknown.
This is your time to be selfless, your time to trust, your time to grow,
Your time to ask questions, your time to get answers, your time to know.
This is your time to lead, your time to wonder, your time to fly,
Your time to understand, your time to take risks, your time to ask why.
This is your time to have fun, your time to build, your time to discover you,
Your time to make memories, your time for peace, your time to do something new.
This is your time to win, your time to beat the odds, your time to stand,
Your time to listen, your time to be brave, your time to join another's hand.
This is your time to be curious, your time to be unique, your time to bear it all,
Your time to be determined, your time to be wise, your time to knock down that wall.

Jaclyn Stief, Grade 12
St Thomas Aquinas Catholic Secondary School, ON

To the Seasons

Canadian scenery is so gleaming
it's beautiful through and through.
Sometimes you could swear it is glowing.

Spring time brings fishing
with a sky oh so blue.
Canadian scenery is so gleaming.

Summer brings swimming
with a wonderful view.
Sometimes you could swear it is glowing.

Fall brings leaves falling
with the wind that blew.
Canadian scenery is so gleaming.

Winter brings snowing, skiing and snowmobiling
with a little bit of snowboarding and ice fishing too.
Sometimes you could swear it is glowing.

What is truly a treat about all the seasons is the traveling
with everything new.
Canadian scenery is so gleaming.
Sometimes you could swear it is glowing.
Tiffany Willard, Grade 12
Ecole secondaire Catholique Sainte-Marie, ON

Straight Edge Black Sheep

In the state of my being
I try to bring essence to the meaning
Of the right to stand for worth
That we all belong to the earth
As for your own person, for justice and right
With the trials of our own great fight
Against all that is bad
And for those who live sad
Unknowing lives for all time
And breathe air that screams crime.
We are, or should be, our own master
Though some are puppets made of cheap plaster
Because they are the sheep
Under conformity they eat, breathe, and sleep.
I am a black sheep, of whom many shun
I carve my own path and follow none
You all look at me as an enemy of society
Because the way I look and the way I dress with no propriety
But I am no different from the best no matter
How I look to you, don't judge me, I am me!
I am my own person, unique, a black sheep…
Tori Larson, Grade 10
William Mason School, SK

Respect for Women

Women grew out of a mixed up past
their strength and confidence always would crash
no say or opinion in the past
Women were always mistreated and put last
but this is a beginning, one where we can start fresh
and treat women with honour and respect
the men should all listen and try to accept
that we're the same both equal and true in everything we do
Women around the world should all have rights
but in some places they still put up a fight
I think it's time for a change
a change for a chance
a chance to make a difference
a difference in our society
We should all give it our all to make them the best
to honour and reward them for their great success
because we are all equal, created in the same way
so they should live respected each and every day.
Timothy Homem, Grade 11
Ascension of Our Lord Secondary School, ON

Nothing More Than…

Nothing stronger than everlasting love,
Nothing as free as the wings of a dove,
Nothing more creative than the work of the Holy Molder,
True beauty lies in the eyes of the beholder.

Genuine serenity is found in the rustling leaves of trees,
In the wind, in stormy seas.
Bonding is found in friends, in the success of a nation;
Sincere men treasure nothing more than God's creation.

Undoubted strength rests in true words.
Those that allow readers' minds to fly freely as birds
For style and quality are seen at their best,
In wholehearted poetry distinguished from the rest.
Arnav Agarwal, Grade 10
Father Michael Goetz Secondary School, ON

Remembrance

God take me home.
This is not what I signed up for.
I feel no honor, no pride.
I feel guilt beyond imagination.
I kill men
Who have lives of their own.
Who, like me, want to see their children grow.

I kill them for what?
Peace?
I see no peace happening,
No shaking of hands.
All I see are pools of blood.
Mangled figures surrounding me.
Men, giving up their lives thinking they will be remembered,
Yet have already been forgotten.
Christie Arlotti Wood, Grade 10
Little Flower Academy, BC

A True Friend

She'll always be there.
Forever she'll care.
When life goes all wrong,
She helps you be strong.

If you share your doubt,
She will reach out.
She'll hold you tight,
Chase away your fright.

She'll hold your hand
And take a stand.
Whatever it takes
To ease your shakes.

When all seems vain,
She will remain
Beside you forever
Through every endeavor.

We all will change.
Our friendships will range.
Some leave our side,
But true friends abide.

Sharlene Van Dyk, Grade 11
Timothy Christian School, BC

Time Is Evil to the Innocent

Time is so rude to me
No matter what I do,
thousands I saved
the hundreds I arrested,
I will be forgotten.

For the moment I'm a hero
A object of love and bravely,
An icon for children to grow for
a symbol of greatest,
For now that is.

The names of evil will live forever
Their crimes written in blood,
My name nowhere to be seen
Forgotten in rough draft of life,
Time is so very cruel.

My own family shall lost my honour
As time erases at greatest and just,
Leaving the blankness in my life
Stealing my respect from the public,
The harsh reality, it is true.

Stephen Miller, Grade 11
Charlottetown Rural High School, PE

Terrible Beauty

Crush Despair,
As one has crushed oneself in the realization,
Of the terrible beauty of self-observation.

Raymund Jacildo, Grade 11
WL MacKenzie Collegiate Institute, ON

Remember Them

Covered in mud, as if it were a blanket,
Trying to get warm, trying to sleep
But there is no place to sleep, there's no place to get warm
Because they are at war
Fighting for what is right.
For the women and children back home
For the innocent people, who are pressured into such horrible situations.
The men and women of our armed forces fight for those who are unable
To defend themselves.
They fight for me, they fight for you
Not only do they fight in the present day
But in the past
And we remember them for this.
We remember how brave they were and how they were just like us,
Normal human beings
Who decided to stand up for what was right
When the world was enclosed with evil.
Some returned, while others stayed against their will.
Fighting for the day when peace blankets the world.
All we can do now is pray and hope for that day to come soon.

Emily Bromley, Grade 11
Renfrew Collegiate Institute, ON

A Look at You

A look at you is like a look at a picture because it's worth a thousand words
You're like a gun, because you can steal a breath for quite long
A falling star that will never fall, and for your request, I will answer the call
You're a masterpiece from another dimension
Because we haven't ever seen something to this extension
A posture that will give all musicians a bad name
Simply a view that anyone would love to frame
A look at you can bring happiness and much perfection
But to others it's regret, disappointment and imperfection
Your reaction can decide a fate
Your reaction can lay a body to rest
Your reaction can open a gate
Your reaction in us brings out the best
A look at you cannot last long enough
Because your shine is blindness to the best of us
A beauty that Shakespeare couldn't tragically end
And Tchaikovsky couldn't musically express
A look at you shows a delicate flower with some distress
Then let me be your water, heat, comfort and health
And that's my rebuttal Mr. Speaker
For why this diamond shall not be sold, even for a million.

Lior Grimberg, Grade 12
Bayview Secondary School, ON

Broken Love

I look beyond the mist of stars,
But there was no trace of him.
His last kiss lingers on my lips,
Like a drop of honey slowly melting,
They killed him; I know they did.
He was darker than I and better than they,
But it never mattered because I loved him,
Which is the reason why they chased him around.
So, I walk some more and fall to the ground,
When I see his bloody body covered with dirt.
His soul had fled an hour ago,
I can see it on his beautiful face.
But it hurts to know that the eyes I loved
Fail to recognize me anymore,
As the moon fades into the dark blue sky,
I have the urge to lie down and die.
But I take him in my arms and my heart shatters,
Is colour the only thing that matters?

Suganya Kandasamy, Grade 10
Lindsay Place High School, QC

Driving Backwards

She met another bad driver along the way
Constantly driving towards dead ends.
They both knew in time they would crash
(Together or apart they were unsure)
The chase had them both intoxicated
Were they spellbound?
Held by the mirage (false hope, fake names)
Never heeding caution, bleeding
As stop signs fly by, she walks backwards
So as to better see his face.

Priyanka Dhaliwal, Grade 11
Mulgrave School, BC

All I Have

All I have is my pen and paper
My pen and paper is all I have
My thoughts and secrets is what it holds
And my life is what unfolds
It allows me to let down my guard
Within this paper you'll find my heart
All I have is my pen and paper
My pen and paper is all I have
You'll find out things, even I've never known
On paper I put myself first, that's clearly shown
I sit by myself, releasing my pain and fears
And also wiping away, my tired tears
All I have is my pen and paper
My pen and paper is all I have
On this paper I have yet to find a new face
Hoping the old one will leave without a trace
My pen and paper understand me
In return I confide in laying down my dreams
All I have is my pen and paper
My pen and paper is all I have

Tracy Watt, Grade 12
Peel Alternative School South, ON

The Days of Power

In ancient times, in long lost lands
When Pharaohs ruled o'er fields and sands.
Great things were done on their commands
Those were the days of power!

Osiris ruled the world of dead,
Anubis — final judge, it's said.
Some gods had creatures as their head.
Those were the days of power!

Now, Other gods had rule divine,
But after them came, next in line,
The Pharaohs with their gold and wine.
Those were the days of power!

Great monuments were then raised up
And in their light the kings did sup
With scarab, sphinx and golden cup.
Those were the days of power!

But nothing great can last for long
Two thousand years Egypt stood strong
And now is mourned in soulful song.
Those were the days of power!

Aron Zahradka, Grade 10
Brentwood College School, BC

Up in the Sky

If it feels sometimes
That your wings are broken,
And it seems
Like you can't fly,
Just close your eyes
And say:
"I'm strong, I'll make it.
I do believe. Amen."
And trust me,
You'll feel the growing wings again.
You'll fly up high,
Without falling.
With joy,
With smile on your face.
You'll feel relief.
No stress, no tension.
You'll rein your world,
You'll make it be
So light and easy,
Like in your dreams,
Which did come true.

Violetta Nadtochyy, Grade 12
Newmarket High School, ON

Strike a Fire

Let's pretend the world's on fire,
place ourselves in our own desire.
Cry for help and scream for heart,
let's pray to God we never part.
I'm here for you, you don't want me,
I hold the matches, and say it's to be.
Strike a fire, a sudden mistake
I wasn't here for you to break.
Still you're wearing your famous crown,
and I just want to be happy now.
For once, I'd like to see your eyes,
filled with everything but despise.
A great flame of hope you've created,
but I know for sure we won't make it.
Too bitter, too kind, I'm sure you're fine.
Please place your hands here, they fit great with mine.
I know you will just leave this way,
with nothing more you'd like to say.
A fire we once shared apart,
never together and never to start.
I think I love you, but you forgot.

Joanne Dzierza, Grade 10
Holy Cross Regional High School, BC

Autumn's Fire

Crackling leaves smolder at my feet
Encompass the ground,
extend toward the sky.
Gold, orange, crimson —
they drift down from above
to glance off my head.

I fall into the blaze.
Sparks shoot up to envelop me.
Gazing upward
I see the gnarled remains of a tree
maintaining a protective watch.

The sun beams its approval.
A ladybug crawls across my upheld finger.
One, two, three, four, spots
mar its red wings.
Sudden movement startles it into flight.
Unbidden giggles spring forth.

Looking up I see my mirror image
laughing back at me.
Autumn's colours take us in their embrace
spreading warmth to our very core.

Tari Goertzen, Grade 12
Killarney Collegiate Institute, MB

The Girl Who Haunts My Dreams

I peer into the darkness,
As I drown inside my thoughts.
I feel as if I'm heartless,
That I'm left without a shot.
She took something I never owned,
Just a broken memory.
I'm leaking underneath this cloak,
Of my drunken misery.
It's so hard to hold back now,
When I feel so much inside.
The faint sound of your voice and coffee
linger in my mind.
But now you tell me truths,
About your sincere emotions.
The "just-a-friend" excuse,
Hits me in one steady motion.
Reality has checked me in its frightening mental ward.
Why am I stuck inside my mind, in this demented storm?
I leave things untouched, put them high up on my shelf
Because in the end, I'm the only one who can save myself,

Emilie Lacaille, Grade 11
Aurora High School, ON

Frostbite

Dark night on the lake
wind blows swiftly and loudly
harbinger of frost

Nathan Roane, Grade 11
Ascension of Our Lord Secondary School, ON

A Child Again

Walking on the winding country road
Feeling the warm, clean breeze
Gazing at the cloudless sky
A stunning backdrop for the swaying fields

I long to walk into those fields
To lie down and hide myself from the world
To play and laugh like when I was a child.
But what would they think?

They'd laugh and say, "How childish!
She doesn't act grown up!"
But why should I care what they say?
Being a child again sounds like a dream.

Suddenly the fields pull me into them
The sun and skies are laughing with glee
I start to giggle as the joy bursts from me
And I run, skip, trip and fall

I'm in the middle of a great golden field
I'm hiding myself from the hurtful world
I'm playing and laughing with the sun and skies
I'm a child again!

Sylvia Wollman, Grade 10
Twilight Colony School, MB

Be There

Be there dear guardian.
The time has now arrived;
I am proud to be Canadian.

Walking through a garden
And wishing I'm still alive,
Be there dear guardian.

The joy has now darkened,
The troop in down to five.
I am proud to be Canadian.

Bang! Bang!
It's time to dive.
Be there dear guardian.

I got hit in the abdomen;
Please let me still be alive.
I am proud to be Canadian.

I think I'm in heaven;
My heart has just died.
Be there dear guardian.
I am proud to be Canadian.

Tracy Gravline, Grade 12
École secondaire Catholique Sainte-Marie, ON

Foul Shot

Went up for the shot at the basket
Stands at the line to shoot
Ref tosses the ball
Dribbles — One…Two…Three…
Head up…
Elbow in…
Tight…
Flick…
Extend…
Arch…
Swish?
Yes!
Cheers all around, again?
The ball is in hand
dribbles — one…two…three…
head up…
elbow in
flick, extend, arch
swish?
No.
Why.

Haley Glendinning, Grade 11
Merritt Secondary School, BC

Remembering

When we are in our later years,
When we have gone our separate ways,
I want to remember those days.

The days when we made snow angels;
The days when we sat in the sun;
When our spirits were one.

I want to remember what brought us together.
All the pain and the tears we cried,
And when we couldn't forget our pride.

These memories we've made
Have left our lives blessed,
But remembering is the ultimate test.

Devon Jolie, Grade 10
Lester B Pearson Sr High School, AB

Hey Pal

hey pal, let's be friends
you make me write my best poems:
wander, stop, start, wonder
maybe someday I'll give them to you,
maybe today, maybe your birthday
tied in a silver paper package
or scrawled here on loose-leaf
hey pal, let's be friends
I like your silly faces, I like your poser-flip hair
and the V on your forehead
making you an avid fanatic of Battlestar Galactica
but you are more, you are cooler
you are the commander of the school of rock,
coaxing from us the ferocity/beauty that lives
untrumpeted in our music —
hey pal, let's make music all right pal, let's be friends
let's hug 'til our air is squeezed out completely;
a kiss or two never hurt anyone did it?
hey pal, let's be friends — let's witch-dance in the moon;
I'll salsa, meringue, or even rumba in your honour.

Naomi Hyba, Grade 12
Canterbury High School, ON

For Those of Us Who Cannot Truly Live

The crackling fires of unnatural lives
Lived underground in blatant misery
Unheard by the ears of the naive,
Ignorant to every plea
cry
wail
tear
in silent frustration.
Not hearing, not seeing, not wanting more
…inconveniences.
We are the underachievers, the underpaid
The overworked, the overlooked
The awaiters of justice and dreams.

Carey Viejou, Grade 12
Rutland Secondary School, BC

The Fear of Non-Existence

Some say they have an undying fear of death.
To say that one's fear of death is undying is quite fascinating.
This fear always lives, within them. Immortal. It remains. It perpetuates.
Like the lingering scent of a fire that has been extinguished.
But what truly is fascinating are the remnants of dust and smoke always left behind, when one thinks they have ceased a fire's existence completely.
What ceases to exist is the medium. The vehicle through which its flame is carried in. The physical body of gold and red and sometimes blue.
Flames do not fool, it is not their intention.
They are not to be blamed for something they have no control over.
And they are not to be blamed for their destiny.
For a burning flame shares our same human fate: our fate is to exist, always.
To never truly die. To live forever. To linger like dust and smoke after our fires have been extinguished. After our physical bodies of gold, red and sometimes blue, have passed on, our eternal flames remain, our undying spirits perpetuate, and our immortal souls continue on without ceasing.
Some say they have an undying fear of death, when in reality they fear their soul's non-existence.

Jessica Carlo, Grade 12
Notre Dame Catholic High School, ON

Freedom's Facade

Staring deep into the relaxing, ripples of the River Thames
The swishing and soothing waves took me to another world
A world in which I submerged into profound thought
The waves called to me but Vauxhall Bridge stood guard
Firm and strong, it wouldn't let me go
The mob of water molecules started a wave and with every synchronized swirl,
Beckoned me to join them in their salty sanctuary
The cleanest river, in its black cloak stood inert as the cool London air brushed over its surface
The weird scent found its way to me and took me by the hand, leading me home
Down I plummeted
I felt as free as a bird
I experienced the breeze rush through my hair
I froze for a second in midair
In that moment, I became one with the wind
I was the wind
I anticipated a warm welcome but, then
I plunged into the cold, murky and deceitful waters
Swimming to the shore, I vowed I would never; neither would I let anyone else,
Find themselves staring deep into the rebellious ripples of the River Thames

Victoria Awa, Grade 12
St Thomas More Catholic Secondary School, ON

Imprisonment

C onflicts that are of the mental and physical state which binds us to their reality
O pen minds, open emotions, open reactions all caged like a beautiful bird in ones canopy
N eeding space within life's space but restricted like the government confidential information
S truggle, the movement of our freedom, historic in achievement, monumental in size but only to we who believe it
P resence, unknown to the people, us the people seem to never be free from this evil
I nspired to seek comfort and faith, a place for one to escape, the falsehood of society
R aces race to the goal, the beauty of our bodies now wasted like coal, stop. Our generation has a poisonous soul
A cceptance is sad, those creeping eyes that watch us are mad, drifting us and our sanity
C ontemplation is cheap, a characteristic of the souls that are weak, never accepted to us who only allow fact in our speech
Y earning for freedom from this incarceration, look to the heaven, move forward and stop the waiting and free yourself from this
   Imprisonment

Jordon Samuels, Grade 12
Woburn Collegiate Institute, ON

A Knight

Holy man is his name
Virtue and fealty is his game
Whether shielding a comrade
Or slaying a foe
A Knight is God's general
Attired in Chain mail from head to toe
When charging through the bloodstained field
This sentinel has only but his lord's faith to wield
His mind is not clouded, nor veiled with doubt
He roars at his enemies, in the midst of a bout
Falling for his faith, is this Knight's Iron Will
In his kingdom's town square, lies a statue of him still
Although it is now worn down and rot
His chivalry and braveness will not be forgot.

Brandon Langlois, Grade 12
General Amherst High School, ON

Together

The scars are burning.
The feeling of this is hurting.
Your eyes are burning with a passion.
I see you and I feel sick.
My stomach boils.

It kills to see you leave
When we're together,
But it hurts even more
When we're not together at all.

Your gaze is powerful.
Your eyes are beautiful.
I look at them and die.
I can see you in the reflection of my eyes.
You look hurt, confused, and dead.

I couldn't have asked for someone better.
You give me everything I need.
Your eyes are the jewels of my life.
I wish we were together now.

Mike Keus, Grade 12
Morell Regional High School, PE

Innocent Murder

Holding a pulsing heart in my shaking hand,
I look upon it in confusion;
it's vulnerability frightens me,
gentles my hold.
But time is running out.
I can't feed this heart's needs,
cannot respond to its love,
simply cannot give up my own heart.
But as I watch this miracle shatter,
into a thousand glorious shards of emotion,
I desperately wish to defy nature,
to sacrifice my own heart,
to replenish this broken one,
that died for me.

Milena Scekic, Grade 11
Burnaby South Secondary School, BC

The Mountain

The mountainside, still looming high,
Doth freeze the travelers trusting so.
Now half have died; unearthly quiet
Unfolds around them as they go.

The eagle's cry cracks dawn-streaked sky
But cold still burns the struggling hike.
Still the men sigh, We shall not die;
Salvation, hope is now in sight.

The snow attacks and frozen backs
Push hard to climb the deadly slope.
They pant and heave, and lastly leaves
The fading glimmer of their hope.

The last one falls as unkind squalls
Sing long the tale of life lost here.
Yes, victory is lost as all
Fall prey to snow, the foe austere.

The mountainside, aflame with pride
Unconquered by the travelers yet.
Now all have died; but glory high
Will yet be sought: and death be met.

Luke Sawczak, Grade 11
Toronto District Christian High School, ON

Myriad

rage
scream the love away; scream for another day
scream 'cause you can't go on
nausea
spinning from end to end; spinning from friend to friend
spinning and sickening
tears
cry, you're not strong; cry, it's too long
cry 'cause nothing helps
distance
walk for a while; walk for a mile
walk 'cause you don't know where you'll end up
bliss
smile, everyone believes you; smile, it must be true
smile 'cause the edge is only a little farther ahead
deep
bury it down; bury, don't make a sound
bury and forget it
fall
collapse and pass out; collapse into the crowd
collapse…and that's the *finale*

Theresa Do, Grade 11
Holy Cross Catholic Academy High School, ON

When You're Gone*

I didn't know I'd lose you
I didn't care
I told you to shut up
But you always just stood there

Looking at me with those
Kind eyes of yours
Smiling as I walked in mock annoyance
Out the door

I watched you leave
I heard your goodbye, full of laughter
I watched your steps never falter
I saw the grass your skirts rustled

I loved to hug you
I loved to breathe you in
I loved your smile and your beauty
The crescent moon on your chin

I watched you cook endless meals
I watched your suffer countless pains
I miss your warmth
I want your love
But never again

Sarah Shahid, Grade 11
Glenforest Secondary School, ON
*Dedicated to my grandfather,
Ehsan-Ul-Haq

Silence*

Silence. In a school, it's a terrifying thing.
The world has stopped spinning,
and for one moment, you can hear a scream.

Then nothing. The silence returns.

You can see the sorrow,
etched onto the faces of the people who knew him.
Their eyes screaming in pain.

Then nothing. The silence returns.

Those standing by are helpless,
as those they love disappear in a shroud of despair.
Leaving only the outline of who they once were.

Then nothing. The silence returns.

Little by little, our loved ones will leave the dark,
but they do not come out the same.
They are haunted by the past, thinking they could have done more.

Then nothing. The silence returns.
Then nothing. The silence returns.

Amanda Bilevicius, Grade 11
Shaftesbury High School, MB
*Dedicated to those who have suffered the loss of people they love.

Castle of My Mind

Castle of my mind,
Goes deep,
Like a vast chasm.

Dungeon of suspicion,
Spreads far and wide,
Causing fear, intense spasm.

Vestibule of knowledge,
Beautified marvellously,
Broadens my sight.

Amphitheatre of love,
Causes tears,
Euphoria to an infinite height.

Castle of my mind,
Is adorned,
Day by day.

Kingdom of my life,
Like an adroit architect,
Shapes it out of pure clay.

Arash Lotfi, Grade 10
Catholic Central High School, ON

Flow

The soft pink cherry blossoms
That cover the overhanging limbs
Hide a formidable sight

The shimmering liquid that slips over the cool stones
Spits up an icy mist while following its winding path
Whose job it is to guide the stream to the crystal blue sea
The view, so incredibly fanciful, instills a sense of order and peace
The comfort that washes over one
Like the clouds that envelope the mountains in the distance
Seems to stop time and the thrill of the moment wipes away all anguish and anxiety

One feels utterly isolated, alone and totally abandoned by the world itself
These feelings are mirrored in a deep green strand of sea grass
Waving lazily back and forth with no will in life
But to be guided by the current

So lovely is this setting, a sanctuary where beauty is bred
And whilst I gaze into the depths of the shimmering stream
I vow to return to this sacred dwelling
And lay my eyes upon the silver stream once more.

Alexander Carr, Grade 10
Brentwood College School, BC

Blistering Instant

The ground beneath her turns to ice,
and she falls.
Searing words slip from her lips.
The blazing edges of each letter
burn into him.
His now flaming heart
transfers to his eyes
and pleads her to stop,
but like a five year-old in a playground
the words sliding off her tongue.
His ears begin to burn and boil
and run down his sides, dying,
and taking his other senses with them,
leaving him numb.
His heart now joins the mass at his feet
he begins to freeze internally,
and his wounds from her fatal speech
begin to burn deeper into him.
Balance is lost and he falls,
onto the ice
in the shadow of her.

Alicia Smith, Grade 12
Haliburton Highland Secondary School, ON

Where I Belong

It's the place where I feel so safe and strong,
where there's nothing I can deny,
Canada is where I belong.

When we gather together to sing our song,
on the one and only first of July,
It's the place where I feel so safe and strong.

From the fields that are wide and long,
to the mountains up so high,
Canada is where I belong.

Nothing better than its hockey on pond,
and also its fine golden rye,
It's the place where I feel so safe and strong.

From all places to travel along,
to the parks and sites,
Canada is where I belong.

I know, in this country, there's nothing wrong,
Which is why I'll hate to say good-bye.
It's the place where I feel so safe and strong,
Canada is where I belong.

Jeremie Ducharme, Grade 12
École secondaire Catholique Sainte-Marie, ON

Jubilant Symphony

Deep inside me, lies a symphony,
a rhythm reaching out to seek
the lyrics of a laughter.
I wear a smile which
tingles everyone with elation.
It spreads a pizzazz of joy and
rings a belief of liberation,
to break free and enjoy.
Blooming within me is a power to inspire,
lead and guide those
who need the taste of euphoria,
to create a chortle of a trillion sounds
and perplex the world to full throttle.
My symphony leaves my soul,
and fills the others with hope.
I know that altitudes are
fun to reach with jubilant beliefs,
but what is youth without altitudes to overcome?
So I carry my symphony over the highest peaks
and then down to slopes of ease
and flashing memorable snaps!!

Tanvi Ahuja, Grade 12
Kwantlen Park Secondary School, BC

You Can Count on Me

Whatever you're going through,
You can tell me and I'll listen.
I'll be here whenever you need me.
I'll cry with you and laugh with you.
Hold onto good memories,
And forget bad ones.
Certain wounds won't heal,
But I'll help mend them.
You can't change the past,
Rewind or fast forward time.
I just want you to know,
In good times and bad,
I'll be there for you.

Dawn Smith, Grade 10
St Marys District Collegiate and Vocational Institute, ON

Winter

A leaf is falling to the ground,
The air is feeling cold,
The changing sights make no sound,
The summer has now become old.
The birds in the north start to fly away,
And brown bunnies start to turn white,
The horses look up from eating their hay,
To see the geese beginning their flight.
During the night clouds form in the sky,
So thick that they cover the starlight,
Children wake in the morning and start to cry,
Snowflakes have fallen and everything's white.
The coldness of winter has so quickly come,
And it has brought so much joy to some.

Kim Dewar, Grade 11
William Mason School, SK

Life from Two Perspectives
Compressed clusters of carbon mate maturely as molded monocoques are formed.
Joined by light lacquered lugs,
fibers of carbon are weaved perpendicularly on purple pipings.
Meanwhile,
a batch of random parts rolls freely on CNC conveyors,
as a team of ingenious inspectors inspect the internals individually.
At birth,
The soft saddle acts as the head of a body,
pushing itself out of an expandable opening.
Throughout adolescence,
Our tires, acting as a foot,
absorb asymmetrical bumps on asphalt.
Like all forms of life; we age.
Days followed by months,
Years after decades,
Our coatings begin to shrink and shrivel like the skin of our older siblings.
The luxurious lacquering finish is no longer sleek and luxurious;
but there is always someone special who still sincerely loves us.
Dangling deadly down from distressed beams,
along with ageing antique displays,
we wait for a new niche of hell or heaven.

Hank Jien, Grade 12
Elgin Park Secondary School, BC

Liquid to Solid
My veins filled of this powerful liquid, these memories in and out of the past
I welcome home this inner fear, I have the feeling my end will be fast
It scares me to know that this is near, I pray every day to make this my last

I am the one who made me high, I screamed out loud in my mind
Giving up and saying goodbye, in the dark a lost road I can't find
So into myself up in the sky, always bringing you down I was so blind
Running away just to go and fly, scarred now, but these eyes once shined

Down and confused walking in the night
How it was just won't be the same, a possibility help put up a fight
The pulling desires brought me the shame, seeing it and being it is an ugly sight
My life should never be like a game, I help myself to make this right
Tears and prayers put out this dark flame, gaining strength comes out bright
Sorry I hurt you, I am to blame, I was in the dark but now found the light

Phylaine Razor, Grade 12
Waweyekisik Education Centre, SK

The Sound of Love
A bride is getting married in two days.
She has picked out a beautiful gown.
But there is something missing.
The bride brought the dress back to her tailor.
She took a silver bell out of her pocket,
And asked the tailor to sew it on for her.
The tailor doesn't understand.
"My fiancé is blind," the bride said,
"I want him to hear the bell, and know that I am coming."
In life, if you listen closely, you can always hear a subtle sound of love.

Mary Jie Yang, Grade 11
Woburn Collegiate Institute, ON

So Strong

So strong, for what purpose?
The ring of a siren.
The ring of the phone.
The ring of his finger
Removed before the swelling takes over.
His hand cold to touch and hold and kiss.
And some of us hate the fact that this may be the closest
We ever got.
Not his father anymore
And now it is too late for them to understand the other.
But regret is slightly lessened by the hope
That somewhere in his inability to live
He can hear.
Gone is not a term defined lightly.
The room is left purging tear ducts.
And we know how frustrated
He would be
If he knew.
And just the thought and just the touch and just the —
Not so strong, anymore.

Kristina Carley, Grade 12
St Thomas More Collegiate School, BC

Winter in Montreal

Winter was like this:
Cold, windy, snowy
But because of Global Warming,
Winter is like this:
One day cold, one day warm
One day snow, one day rain.
Global Warming not only affects us,
It also harms animals, plants, and marine life.
It is up to us, to protect our world
If we don't do anything about Global Warming,
Then the winters that I once knew will be no more.

Robin Brodrick, Grade 10
Villa Maria High School, QC

The Judge

Love at first sight, does not exist
A stranger's delight, is what persists

Unwelcome it is to stop and stare
I cannot say that this is fair

Indeed, learn to love; let not your eyes wonder
For he next to you also stares over yonder

True beauty is within; thus not an expression
Your heart you shall listen, feed not this obsession

Learn not to judge; yet judge your learning
For all make mistakes, when heads are turning

This sin is upon us and in our descent
Ever-present it is, so forgive and repent

Stéphane Perrault, Grade 11
École Notre-Dame-des-Vertus, SK

Bullet

It fell from the sky through all the ash and rain
And as the day came to pass it was never the same

Fear and sorrow caused men of arms to dream
Of mothers a long way 'cross stormy seas

Whilst burning flames crept from the midst of darkness
Eating the dreams of hope for a reason long forgotten

Where warriors knelt, spirits flew high
Forced was a young boy to cry

As, for a short time, the bells of heaven sound
Gentle hands lift soul from the ground

To a peace long since deserved
For an age of suffering down upon Earth

And down in the mud, the boy wept on
For the friend who was now long gone

While others turn their heads to ignore
There was no time for tears in war.

Alicia Scott, Grade 11
Chateauguay Valley Regional High School, QC

Tranquil Retreat

Fluttering leaves
cast dancing shadows
across the typed page,
as their tangy sun-drenched aroma
tickles my nostrils.
The lofty canopy shelters me
like a giant umbrella —
a tranquil haven
from a world
that rankles sorely.
Occasionally,
a distant voice echoes
in my consciousness,
reminding me of familial security
only a short distance away.

I long for summers such as these,
sanctuaries from tedious halls of learning,
where literary fantasies can transport me
to faraway realms,
as the tree encloses me
in its comforting embrace.

Lindsey Bylo, Grade 12
Killarney Collegiate Institute, MB

The Old Oak Tree

Oh, the old oak tree —

Its leaves shining emerald green
in the sun's vibrant rays.
Limbs emerge from the trunk's embrace,
reaching for the heavens.
An unending adventure
waiting for children,
filled with fun and excitement.
Their laughter
fills the long summer days,
and echoes in the twilight breeze.

Autumn descends —

Relentlessly.
The leaves shrivel and float
gently to blanket the ground.
Cold fall winds
whistle ominously.
The bare branches
of the old oak tree
hang vacant and barren.

Travis Falk, Grade 12
Killarney Collegiate Institute, MB

Maybe if I Dream

Maybe if I dream,
I'll find my shooting star.
I'll reach deep inside,
And wish really hard.

Maybe if I dream,
I'll find what I need.
I'll try my very best,
And maybe I'll succeed.

Maybe if I dream,
You'll finally notice me.
I'm praying real hard
Cause you can set me free.

Maybe if I dream,
I'll stand up really tall.
I will count on you,
So don't let me fall.

Maybe if I dream,
I'll find my shooting star.
I'll pull it from my heart,
And love you real hard.

Krista Barre, Grade 10
Bishop Carroll High School, AB

The Truth Is Undercover

Cloaked behind the finest silks,
The truth is undercover.
Peeping from pashmina curtains,
The truth is undercover.
Scaling ancient stone walls,
The truth is undercover.
Wealth is the perfect disguise;
The truth is hidden, the truth is forbidden.

Cristina Forlini, Grade 10
Villa Maria High School, QC

Gull's Noon

In great swoops and joyful soars, I brave
The waves on a dancing breeze,
Slicing through wisps of frail cloud.
Below is the blue; a shallow sea.

Now I look upon a beach.
I yearn to land in the silk-white sand, and
Play with the rush of the breaking tide,
Seek a snack from tender-pink conch that roams within my reach.

Or maybe, I should snap up a fish from the dark, sharp coral,
Feel the flashes of colour slip, and fade from its body.
I hunger to relish the flavour as it runs and rips down my beak, and
Stains my white feathers a terrible red.

But again, I take to the warm moist air,
Escaping the waves as they trample each other in hasty hurry.
I scream in joy at my flitting shadow below me,
My voice is a screeching echo.

Stephanie Ridenour, Grade 10
Brentwood College School, BC

Crazy

Outside first, it's what they see.
It's a pity that it is not much better than the real me.
Check, scrutinize, judge your shell.
Don't worry, the sickness isn't so bad, only a living hell.
Outer pains become real, swell in your mind.
Soon to take over, disguised, sweet and kind.
Melting like chocolate, smooth as cream.
You don't need them anymore, "I don't need them!" you scream.
The illness transformed, becoming like nourishment.
Numb with tingles, you smile in wonderment.
Frail and delicate, compliments you gladly accept.
Looking in the mirror still painful, distorted reflect.
Regret, memory; "Why?" You cry.
Inside your heart tangles, strangling, your defenses die.
Liquid from wells overflow to escape,
You struggle and you punch, blocking out the distorted shape.
Your eyes turn black, letting in more than is there.
How could you go so far, and why does no one care?
Your ideas block out, your mind hazy.
You have now met your monster, welcome to crazy.

Marlena Legault Monton, Grade 10
Villa Maria High School, QC

Flying Overhead

A carcass, abandoned in the woods.
Killed by a disease
ravaging one animal and the next.
The gorilla died young.
Only five months she lived.
Her mother left her just hours ago.
Her heart broken.
Two halves.
She was her first born.
Now just a carcass
in the barren woods.
But she is not alone now
Her scent, caught,
by the feeders of the dead.
Closing in on their latest meal.
Deepening her mother's pain.
Thus, the perpetual cycle of life continues.
She knew they would come, feeders of the dead.
For that is why she left.
Couldn't stand to see it;
The vultures, flying overhead.

Carmen Yung, Grade 11
Earl Haig Secondary School, ON

The Deer Hunt

Today I hope to shoot a deer
My sights are set I listen with my ear
We drive in the truck looking for tracks
I am really jittery, I tell myself to relax

We see something out in the field
I hit the breaks and slow to a yield
I grab my binoculars and take a look
It was just does, I checked my book

I can't shoot does so I continue on
I look for deer I have my mind set on
I see some more so I stop the truck
I see them run and I almost got stuck

We see them again, I check with my scope
It's a big buck but it was down a slope
I crept towards them in hope to get a shot
I am wearing a big jacket, I start to get hot

I put my sights on the biggest deer
I pull the trigger and then I peered
It fell and we drove over to it
A 170 size buck that oughta do it

Eric Doerksen, Grade 11
William Mason School, SK

Butterfly Musings

I wish you were a butterfly.
With two strong wings you'd cruise the sky.
I wish worries grew little feet,
And ran away — wouldn't that be sweet?

I wish that you would not cry tears,
That you'd understand that someone hears.
I wish I could buy you a diamond ring.
Each little sparkle would lessen pain's sting.

I wish that I could coax a smile,
From battle worn eyes where depth is miles.
I wish that your place could be mine,
And, holding your hand, we'd pass the time.

I wish that we were butterflies,
With our strong wings we'd cruise the sky.
And claim our place amongst the stars.
The butterfly victory would be ours.

Hannah Marazzi, Grade 10
Mennonite Educational Institute, BC

The King's Cry

The lion stands strong
With a flicker of humour in the eye.
The all-mighty roar,
The kind of the jungles' cry.

He, the other,
Thought he could purge.
Soon to discover
What intelligence it surged.

A fight to the death
Seemed only fitting.
One must murder:
One must be victim.

Sinking jaws in deep,
Victory overshadowing all.
The crown: his to keep.
Standing strong, standing tall.

Jaide Davis, Grade 10
Mount Boucherie Secondary School, BC

Winter Coldness

You see your breath,
the foggy smoke.
Your teeth chatters,
uncontrollably.
Your hands are frozen,
they're dug into your pockets.
Few steps away from school,
anticipated to get in
away from this cold
that the winter brings.

Kimberly Calayag, Grade 12
Burnaby Mountain Secondary School, BC

Life as Me

I don't live the lifestyle of the rich and the famous.
I live the lifestyle of struggle, filled with trouble
I keep my head level, although the ground beneath me is unlevel
I don't stumble or crumble,
I just grind it out knowing in the end it'll all prove worthwhile.
Wake up feeling like the hulk
Rising at 5 o'clock, knowing you could never handle my bulk.
Yes, I'm black and because of that,
I'm the first they're trying to crack
Trying to figure me out like I'm a code to crack,
But to understand me it's not as easy as that.
Judging me like they're the jury, pushing me to unleash the fury.
It's got me so low, I feel like the brothers picking cotton years ago,
Grilling them under the sun of Ohio.
This stereotype that the black man is put up to, I'd never want to be the one to prove it true,
White, Yellow, Red, Black are nothing but skin tones, I learned that on my own
Now it's up to the world to understand it and move on,
Because this racial profiling's been going on for too long.
Now I pass the torch on to you,
The story of your life is up to you, what will you do?

Maketo Binzangi, Grade 12
École secondaire catholique Renaissance, ON

Remembrance Day

Remember those soldiers and Veterans that fought and supported our country. The ones that never gave up when it got rough. They fought so we could keep our freedom. We should remember the soldiers that were lost in battles and the ones that are alive today. Soldiers are strong and brave, but the true hero lies deeper inside.

Katie Oliver, Grade 11
Lincoln M Alexander Secondary School, ON

From Rags to Riches

Gone but not forgotten, Soul alive, Spirit on fire,
However my body may be rotten.
I can remember those days; Hollis Queens was the heat,
Snatching chains, robbing others the life was on the street.
Then it all turned around after being locked up for something I never did
Changed my hearts beat, beat, beat

Life was passing me by, quicker than I grew,
Beating others, smoking marijuana was killing me quicker than I knew.
So I turned to the art of Dj-ing, at the time just a hobby nothing ever less
It became my safe haven like a bulletproof vest.
On the tables I was like a genius writing a test,
And I would never ever fail just like a ship that never sailed.
So I put myself together with two Emcees and a legacy was born named Run-Dmc.

First a hobby then career, easier than sitting back and drinking beer,
I would never ever think or wonder that during the prime of my life I would be left, six feet under.
So it can be said that God wanted me quick at the age of thirty-seven
Where there are clouds underneath us and no one gets sick.
Now I'm an angel,
Gone but not forgotten, Soul alive, Spirit on fire
However my body may be rotten.

Jasraj Sadyora, Grade 11
Middlefield Collegiate Institute, ON

Celestial Bliss

a crisp breeze — Embraces nature's shadows;
The smell of lavender and ripe roses
And lingering dew on fresh morning grass

waves in promenade — Defining the quintessence of rhythm;
A sea star's wish
Flying on golden dust
Past the silhouettes of horizon

of starry autumn nights — Amidst red-hued leaves;
The moon's gentle glow
Illuminating secrets from the sky

a drift of snow — Blanketing wooden planks;
Standing in a fur-lined coat
Encircled by falling flakes

The imagination
A mere ethereal illusion
Yet so welcoming and infinite in capacity

Unknowing of limitations
Allowing the intangible tangible

Living in a paradise of my own creation
I lose myself in its radiant perfection
And succumb to the most beautiful of minds

Priscilla Chu, Grade 12
Burnaby North Secondary School, BC

Nighttime Sunroof

A brief skyward glance,
A daring second peek.

Revealing,
  Amazingly,
    A secret place so filled with
      Bright lights.
Orbs of circular wisdom,
  Knowing
    All yet telling so very
    Little.
A sea of constellations,
  As it has been said.
Floating endlessly in a plane of
  Nothing.
  Empty nothing.
    The epitome of null.
Night time sky, like a warm safety blanket;
  Always there yet never
    here.
StarryNightSkyThroughANightTimeSunroof.

Garrett Arnold, Grade 12
Oakridge Secondary School, ON

The Fairies

As I crouched behind the forest's trees,
My ears met their hushed tunes.
Earth and rock left on my knees;
Their wings as white as the moon.

As I crouched behind the forest's trees,
My eyes met their bright eyes.
Their sweet scent left upon the breeze,
As they danced beneath the night skies.

As I crouched behind the forest's trees,
My eyes met their soft glows.
Enchantment left the forest's trees
As their voices slowed.

As I crouched behind the forest's trees,
My ears met soft sweet breaths.
They settled into broken leaves,
And quietly they slept.

Jamila Punjani, Grade 11
Burnaby Mountain Secondary School, BC

Eat Up, Eat Up!

hang your clothes in the daytime
darling girl,
you know not what lurks in
the nighttime.

slicing potatoes and killing dinner
he gathers with his love
and across the treetops the
petty yelps of fear sound,
as the dark approaches.

such a world of wanderers,
this is!
we know not what comes in the
midnight!

eat up! eat up!
I hate it when I drink from your cup;
I am only guilty and never thirsty.

there is no hope for the village.

Stefana Fratila, Grade 11
Lord Byng Secondary School, BC

A Son

The women who gave me birth.
The one that is always there for me.
Caring and loving for me.
Is what she does the best.
Always at home or at work where she's always at.
Even in the kitchen cooking for the rest.
Today and the days before, she always there.
Hoping for many days to live.
You had done so much for me ever since.
And this is why I love you.

Kenny Alvarado, Grade 10
Ascension of Our Lord Secondary School, ON

The Waterfront

The smell sweet as rain
Reminds me of fresh cut grass.
The cool breeze
Sends shivers down my spine.
The colors so bright and vibrant
Just like a dragonfly in a field of flowers.

The nights are warm
Like a long summer's day.
I long for the day
That I can return
To my heaven on Earth.

Lounging on the beach
With the toasty sand between my toes
I can only imagine
The smile of the ocean
On the next summer's day
When I launch into the cold crisp water
Of my favorite place on Earth.

Sarah Hardy, Grade 10
Merritt Secondary School, BC

Ocean Wanderlust

Its dark depths are among the undying,
Wanderlust it feeds.
The brightest light dares not disturb it,
Wanderlust it needs.
Few gaze beyond the forbidding surface,
Wanderlust it leads.
It guides me to my ocean slumber,
Wanderlust in me.

Sylvia Braun, Grade 10
Mennonite Educational Institute, BC

Walk Through the Garden

Walk through the garden
Crush the petals below
Shoes off, toes first
Jumping into cool mud

Walk toward the pond
Squelching mud between open toes
Eyes closed, palm open
Hand grazing the water's surface

A graceful step forward
Silhouette dancing along the edge
Shoes off, toes first
Sinking into the ticklish chill

Break the surface in ripples
Cannonball into the deep
Eyes closed, palm open
Exposed stretches of skin tingling

Yasmin Cokay, Grade 10
Villa Maria High School, QC

My Run Home

I'm up to bat in the top of the first
3 strikes blow right by me
It's not tee ball it's baseball
The pitcher stared me down like I was nothing
I didn't swing not even once
But my time was done, back to the bench

Next time up I finally swing but still no contact, not even a foul
Next pitch I hit the ball but right to the pitcher's glove
It was an out, but also a great failure
One more time up the pitcher's getting tired
Then suddenly I felt a vibration in my bat
The ball's in the air and going further and further
I start to run; the faster I run the faster my heart beats
I feel a rush as I race rapidly through first base
Then finally the ball hits the ground

I am as happy as a kid on Christmas
I spread a smile from cheek to cheek but the play's not over
As I round second base I think to myself I'm the next Babe Ruth
I get past third base, just ninety feet away from glory, fame, eternal happiness
I slide under the tag
I made it I'm home

Julio Castillo, Grade 11
Philip Pocock Catholic Secondary School, ON

A Day in the South

The sun scorches the last stubborn droplets of water hidden beneath layers of dirt.
The road is a tornado of suffocating dust,
Whirling endlessly down the county's main street.

Sticky children sit on the steps of the abandoned ice cream parlor,
Drinking warm bottles of syrupy orange soda pop.
The structured world of school seems ridiculous and distant.

A boy is seen chasing a hoop with a worn wooden stick.
His mother can be heard yelling her disapproval,
Her arms elbow deep in moisture extracting lye suds.

The hazy August sun grows bored.
Unhurriedly it departs leaving behind
A bronzed and dry southern paradise.

Lost in a dream, the bayou creaks in slumber.
Crickets scream their high-pitched contentment,
As twilight yawns and swallows the day.

Fire bugs flicker in giddy elation.
Crocodiles grin as they eerily lurk in velvet pools of sinister depths.
Another day in the South sways along, drunk with tangy confection.

Janyne Laing, Grade 12
Cut Knife High School, SK

Teardrops from Heaven

Little drops come raining down.
One lands in my hand,
    falls off,
       and shatters as it hits the ground.

I lift my eyes to the clouds.
Another one hits my nose,
    my lip,
    my cheek.
Leaving their marks in tiny mirrors,
    reflecting the vision,
      that is the rain.

I look at the scene laid before me.
Puddles gather,
  flowers sparkle,
and I know
that all this is created,
because God is crying
Teardrops from Heaven.

Jacqueline (Jacqui) Omichinski, Grade 10
Mennonite Educational Institute, BC

Ecstatic Dogmatism

Who knows the name of jealousy, anger, or deceit?
Who knows the names of every child dying or in need?
Who knows the name of gluttony?
Who knows the name of pride?
Who knows the name of ignorance,
where mankind subsides.
Who knows the name of poverty?
Who knows the name of AIDS?
Who knows the name of slavery
or how humanity came to fade?
Every day is just like the last
the rich get richer,
the poor get poorer,
the sick get worse and die.
Who has the courage to take these things
and look them in the eye?
Ignorance is the word of the day.
For all eternity
it's ignorance; we're ignorant.
It rules society.

Angeline Abinoja, Grade 11
Johnston Heights Secondary School, BC

Unwanted

You are the flower and I am the tree.
You bloom and I break
You are picked up and I am pushed over
People stop and stare at you
I only receive a glance
Your sweet nectar is gathered up
My leaves are brushed away
You are the flower and I am the tree,
People see you and ignore me.

Nicole Ainsworth, Grade 10
William E Hay Composite High School, AB

A Treasure Gone Forever

I wish to hold you in my arms again
But you're not coming back
And I have to support the pain
Every time I mention your name
Day by day I await you
I know that I can't see you
But deep down inside
I feel you by my side
You are my treasure
And I'll love you forever

You are my baby little sister
Yet you don't know that I am your brother
I don't know for how long it will be hidden
But all I know is that without you I'm broken
You were taken from me
At a very young age
You could barely say my name
I don't even know your real name
You're gone and nowhere to be found
But I know that I will always have you in my heart

Gabriel Wagner, Grade 11
Polyvalente Marcel Landry, QC

Bare Feet Sand

I hate the way
It fills between my toes.
My sensitive toes are sinking
With every step I take,
Drilling further and further
Into an agonizing scream.
I can see where the water floods the sand.
I embrace the cool breeze
From the lake's surface,
It comforts me.
Back to reality, the sand is like a bear
Climbing a tree.
It forces itself further into my skin.
"Leave me be."
The dryness of the sand is unbearable
At this point.
I take one last leap
SPLASH! I'm in
For a moment I'm relieved,
Until I find myself
In an even bigger situation.

Kimberly Spehar, Grade 10
Burnaby North Secondary School, BC

Love Conquers

Love conquers all hate,
comforts and reassures all.
Always hopes and trusts.

Tricia Samaroo, Grade 11
Ascension of Our Lord Secondary School, ON

Relationships

I don't want to deal with you, your issues
With what people are saying about you.
You don't see it but it affects me too,
The lies, the rumors, the labels.
I try talking to you, make you see your mistakes.
And I'm there for you. I help you with your problems,
If one day I try talking to you about mine,
You tell me I'm selfish and that the world doesn't revolve around me.
When really, it doesn't revolve around YOU.
You're not like a goddess, celebrity or anyone famous.
You make people feel small compared to you.
It's like you became an empty box, no feeling, no nothing.
You're like a doll, pretty but fake.
I'm done dealing with your mistakes
I guess you need to learn yourself,
But it's disappointing to see you change.
To see you walk down the wrong path.

Carla Luna, Grade 10
Burnaby North Secondary School, BC

A Jigsaw Puzzle

I am a jigsaw puzzle.
At first, when you don't know me
I can be very confusing and hard to understand
But once all my pieces come together, I'll be clear.
Sometimes, I'm a million pieces to solve, other times it will be easier.
I'm unpredictable from time to time and I'm like glass.
With one hit, I can break apart.
I'm enjoyed by some who like to take their time with things,
But get frustrated by others that don't have patience.
If you don't put my pieces into the right place,
I can turn out pretty ugly.
I am quiet and patient.
No matter how long people are gone for, I'll be sitting there
Waiting for them to come back to me.
I am a jigsaw puzzle

Cecilia Pow, Grade 10
Burnaby North Secondary School, BC

Descending from Up High

As the wind brushes against my face;
as the seasons drag winter close behind it,
nothing can make my life longer.
The crack of my stem begins the cushioned fall
to where I become a blanket.
The breeze slowly sweeps me softly away from my landing
as the pavement scribbles wrinkles across my surface.
I pass leaves that lurk in the corners like thieves behind the shadows.
The weather becomes a burden upon my shoulders
and the morning dew becomes puddles on my back.
The crisp cold turns the water into diamonds of ice,
making me sink into the ground due to the weight of the world;
leaving me no choice but to lay still
until the next gust of wind brings me to a new destination.

Jalissa Weymouth, Grade 11
Merritt Secondary School, BC

There Was a Young Man

There was a young man from Japan,
Who sifted for gold with a pan.
He sat by the river,
Said a lady, "Come hither,"
Feeling richer he said, "Yes I can!"

Kirsten Snoek, Grade 10
St Marys District Collegiate and Vocational Institute, ON

My Song…

My Song…

The song I sing for you,
telling you the things you knew but never learned,
telling you the meaning of your love
and showing you the meaning of mine

My love…

tomorrow you will awake to the smile
that uncovers the veil of complexities
of sharing a life with you,
the game of love is harder than before
but more worth the while

My friend…

through the ages we pass, shifting and slipping through time.
By your side I (choose to) stay,
never fully comprehending why your intoxicating presence
holds me magnetically by your side
where I see beauty

Sahara Sloan, Grade 12
Esquimalt Community School, BC

September 24, 2007

Who knew that a phone call
could be so powerful.
After the phone was hung up,
the tremors and the tears came,
racking my whole body.
There was no stopping them.

What if he hadn't made it?
What if he hadn't ducked?
What if the truck had been heavier?
They say if any of these factors
had been different
my friend would not be here today.

His story is a true miracle.
One that he will now be able to tell
for the rest of his life.
He will have a few scars
and the memories
but all he had really wanted
was a carton of milk.

Megan Williamson, Grade 12
Burnaby Mountain Secondary School, BC

Spreading My Wings

I try not to say hurtful words
    The words don't seem to stumble,
but just like seasons
have their time
                this is mine,
I know it seems
    like I'm not your little girl anymore
    but you have to see
I'm growing up
"I'm at the startin' line of the rest of my life
    As ready as I've ever been"*
Have the patience to learn, that
                I love you
just let it go,
 I'll grow up, yet
  I will always be your baby girl,
and you'll always be my hero, my dad.

*From "Ready Set, Don't Go" by Billy Ray Cyrus
Laura Grajales, Grade 12
Burnaby Mountain Secondary School, BC

Why Must It Hurt to Say Goodbye?

We all know this pain
A little all too well
The sorrow that comes
When we must say goodbye
We all know it will come
So then tell me
Why must it hurt to say goodbye?
Young children don't always understand
Why daddy
Won't come home
And why mommy
Won't stop crying
Why must it hurt to say goodbye?
Death affects us all
So why is it so hard?
To help someone
Who has lost a loved one
Who had to say goodbye
So please tell me!
Why must it hurt to say goodbye?

Adrienne Wager, Grade 11
William Mason School, SK

Passion

Hold on to the passion
For which we seek
Life is like a broken heart
That cannot weep.

Hold on to the passion
For when passion cries
Life is a burning flame
That never dies.

Jorie Kramer, Grade 11
Lloydminster Comprehensive High School, AB

War: A Poet's View

The country takes a breath,
It knows what's coming.
War has been declared
And already they're numbing,

Preparing for dead
Preparing for evil dealings,
Hardening their hearts
To the deepest of feelings

The guns cracked loud,
And some saw their friends fall
And the look in their eyes
Was the worst part of all

Their bittersweet songs
That their hearts did sing
As they said good-bye
To everything,

Ring out today
As a lonely stand
From those who gave all
To save our land.

Holly Anderson, Grade 11
Eagle Butte High School, AB

The Reason Why I Love You

King of all kings
Your joy shines within
Your love is paradise
You are life everlasting

Worthy, kind, helpful and caring
You are
Holy of Holies
Your forgiving love
Draws me to you

Your miracles of life
Your listening heart
The happiness of life
You share with us
Is the reason I love you

You gave me
The right to choose
And Lord that's the reason
I love you

Natalie Quesnel, Grade 11
École Notre-Dame-des-Vertus, SK

The Tempest

The bone shattering cold bestows on me a bite
The cold hearted demon has left no sign of a fight
The maniac of wind slashes upon my innocent face
The sad truth is that he knows not of a resting place
The snow dances spiraling and twisting violently
The only thing I see later on that day are people who are lonely
Their hearts have been incarcerated by that misery around them
They do violent crimes in confusion
And all that is left is to
Pray for them

Oscar Ramirez, Grade 12
George Harvey Collegiate Institute, ON

Shelby

When I was fifteen I found out about you.
Found out enough to hate you, think of how to break you, get rid of you.
I never wanted you.
It took nine months to create you, but oh how that time flew by.
I grew to like you, to want to know more about you, which then grew to love.
It was time, time for you to come.
I was scared.
Nervous.
Happy but sad.
The doctor came, and said get ready, today's the day.
I was right by my mother's side, just as scared as she was.
They pulled you out, it took some time but there you were.
I never saw anything more beautiful.
How could I ever hate you?
You cried.
I cried.
I'm seventeen now, and live every day to see you at the end of it.
Thank you.

Geri Rising, Grade 12
John Cabot Catholic Secondary School, ON

Lies

Another day has come and passed,
Just like the one before it,
And the one that has yet to come.

As we age,
We live to die another day.
Just as the past does, we truly lie to tell the truth,
Just as the lie before it and the lie yet to come.

As we lie about the truth, the truth becomes a lie,
The present becomes a past of lies filled with anger and rage.

Imagine living a life you thought was yours,
Unravel a dark secret woven in tears ready to fall into a puddle of blood,
Not knowing the prophecy of your future, scared and weary about life.

Finally, waking up to realize it was only a dream,
You learn to trust your mind,
Your mind will not lie to you.

Wade Atkinson, Grade 10
Sisler High School, MB

The Good Old Days

Remember the good old days?
We were always in our secret hiding place.
When the fun would never end.
Everything seemed to blend.

Now everything's a blunder.
Who should be given all of the blame,
I will constantly wonder.
I always thought that we were going to stay the same.

Never realizing that one day,
We're going to grow up.
Never realizing that one day,
We're going to change.
Never realizing that one day,
Our childhood is going away.

Remember the good old days?
I'm not sure about you,
But I sure do.

Dave Cordoviz, Grade 10
Holy Cross Regional High School, BC

Love

Love
Is her only life
Her formation.
Her true way to see
Love
Is her dream
Love shatters her soul
Love
Warms her.
Love
Is her peaceful time.
Her constant need.
Love is the only thing
She lives without.

Love
Makes her smile
Out of the heart that is broken
Love is her path.

Rachel Acey, Grade 11
Lloydminster Comprehensive High School, AB

She's an Angel

She's an angel,
With iridescent wings,
And a crown of golden flowers atop her head.
She's an angel,
With her lilting voice,
That floats between the trees.
With eyes and hair so bright,
She can light up the night.
She radiates with inner warmth,
That fills my heart with peace.

Kristen Stephenson, Grade 12
Oakridge Secondary School, ON

A Waterfall

One dull dark morning
A waterfall of color
Glowing out my door

Sean Lefebvre, Grade 11
Mother Teresa Catholic High School, ON

Freedom and Imprisonment

My ears are blocked,
I can only hear the pulsing of my heart within.
I feel like I'm swimming in a stream of thought and memory.
And I'm happy. I'm in my own little world.
My eyes are closed allowing me to see the differences
Between freedom and imprisonment.
My lungs are yelling out,
"Breath, you have yet more years to live."
My mind is telling me,
"You have suffered enough. Stay where you can be happy."
But my heart is louder than both combined.
It tells me in its wise words,
"If you stay here, you'll only be imprisoned in your mind.
Unable to move, and asking the following question:
'What have I done all my life?'
Continuously.
If you let your soul breath, you'll have the choice
To change your life for the better, and that's freedom.
Follow the light of the sun
As disguise of God showing you the way to happiness.
Love awaits you on the shore."

Mélanie Houle, Grade 10
École secondaire catholique L'Horizon, ON

…Bless The Eternal…

Thousands Of Silent Jews
Surrounded by electrified wire
WE WAIT
Gathered with faces stricken
And falling light
WE WAIT
Lord Of The Universe
Our sick minds are troubled
WE WAIT
TO PRAY
Blessed be the name of the Eternal
Why, why bless him
WE WAIT
Because he let thousands burn
Because in his might he created Auschwitz
WE WAIT
We wait for our God
To witness the greatness of our God
WE WAIT
Rising Up
With our God

Haakin Fried, Grade 12
Peace Wapiti Academy, AB

Temiskaming Shores

Oh Temiskaming Shores, you are the boat and we the oars.
We steer you where we want to go;
You take us places that we do not know.
We stick with you during the sun, and the downpours.

Oh Temiskaming Shores, I remember a time not long ago
When you were not a one, but a three:
Cobalt, New Liskeard and Haileybury.
Although Cobalt did not amalgamate, Dymond stood up and took your place.

Oh Temiskaming Shores, your hockey team is now the puckhounds.
What happened to old rivalry?
Now on the ice, yellow, black, and white is all we see!
It is hard to know what room you're in, because all the board says is puckhounds vs puckhounds.

Oh Temiskaming Shores, we are going through so many changes:
City police turned into OPP
And the town hall moved to Haileybury
AHHH! With all these changes the town just buzzes.

Oh Temiskaming Shores, you are the boat we are the oars.
Even if we do not like some of it
We stick with you because we love it.
And in votes, oh Temiskaming Shores, you are the one who always outscores.

Natasha MacDonald, Grade 12
École secondaire Catholique Sainte-Marie, ON

The Accident

She caught the rain in her gathered skirts.
Stopping in the middle of the street to tie the ropes of wind together with her fingertips.
Ducking, as a car flew over her, and screaming, crashed into a nearby wall.

Arms flailing in the distance for help. Smoke exhaling into the air, choking on cotton clouds.
Essence, streaming like liquid despair, over stones, through cracks in the cement.
Writing the memory of itself. Quietly.

Humming motorcycles approach. Insects on wheels. Shiny black eyes staring into distance.
She watched him forget how to move. Saw as he stepped into the sky on graceful feet.

That's when the wind fought back —
suddenly wiping the air out of her lungs,
choking her with the ropes she'd made,
handlebars — locking her into place — sealing her on the ground.
Hard cold cement. Oil running through her outstretched fingers.

She's forgotten how she got here. She's forgotten it all.

Sounds crinkle in long-dead ears.
Have they noticed yet?
Or does he still capture the red and white lights with his motionless form?

The motor-insects stare on.

Jillian Hunt, Grade 12
Kelowna Secondary School, BC

Poetry Anthology

I see people walking down the street
And I just wonder
What's with all this violence?
I think to myself and wonder
Why can't we have some silence?
Don't you know?
He knew someone who died
Can't you see all the tears he's cried?
Wondering where he is
She's making his favorite sauce
Two rings from the telephone and all she hears is
Sorry for your loss
With tears rolling down her cheeks
There is nothing but silence
She turns and drops the phone
As she hears the sirens
With the doorbell ringing
And the banging on the door
They take off their hats and bow their heads
She knows her son is no more.

Kristin Smith, Grade 11
Glenforest Secondary School, ON

I Dreamed

I dreamed of a love so true
And then one day
God sent you
When our eyes met
I had to turn away
Only to regret
That one grateful day

Antonia Debattista, Grade 11
Ascension of Our Lord Secondary School, ON

The Escape

Let us escape
To the farthest reaches of the world
Where we can pretend to exist
My angel
But we are already making believe

Is this real then, my love?
These bittersweet moments touch my heart
So I can smile again
My friend
My dearest you are not my friend

You are
My breath in the cold of winter
My heartbeat in the night
My reason
For life? Or for reasons themselves…

Do call me in the quiet of morning
Dead night
And you answer

Jayne Nestor, Grade 12
Michael A Riffel High School, SK

Will I Always Think of You?

Sitting by the water's edge,
I stare out into the open.
I think of you.

At home making dinner,
I try to remember ingredients.
But I can only think of you.

I live my life,
My normal routine.
I always think of you.

The one small thought,
It grows and grows.
I call it you.

Will I live on,
Then die in peace?
Or will I always think of you?

Victoria Back, Grade 12
Sir Robert Borden High School, ON

Placebo

You did it quietly; more like silently.
A silence so thick that I couldn't move,
couldn't scream, couldn't make a sound.
But I still heard my heart break.
And then everything was distant.
I could heal, if only your memories would fade away.
But this infection drives deeper,
perverting me further,
and crying isn't the curing medicine.
You infect me so far; I just want to forget.
You said you could make it better;
But you're still here.
And the memories, a flood;
I was sitting beside you screaming,
but it was silent. So silent.
I could heal, if only your memory would fade away.
You refuse to fade,
and I know you can't make it better.
You infect me so far; I just want to forget.
But you're still here. Just placebo.

Alyssa Cooper, Grade 12
Quinte Secondary School, ON

This Epic Crash

An instant of incredulity,
for a wave of terror punishes the
innocence of our day leaving nothing
to clutch in sorrow, no last words to ease
endless nights of tears and disbelief.
As accusations sprout beneath the drools of our
solidarity fanatics who seek blame
and refuse the offer of fault,
the world is left to wonder.

Ted Carr, Grade 12
Dr Charles Best Secondary School, BC

A Kid's Dream

Ginormous trees
protecting me from the world.
Offering walls with peek holes
that capture my eye.
They cannot still
the tormenting winds
that seek me out.

My safety lies
in this self-crafted haven.
Miniature treasures
adorn my watch tower.
This sanctuary,
upheld
by a gnarled branch.
Extending from the forest.

Grasping the rope,
I ascend to my faithful
watch tower.

Michelle Williamson, Grade 12
Killarney Collegiate Institute, MB

Little Angel

So beautiful she looks today,
Wearing a new white gown.
Four strong men escort her to me;
She smiles, but makes no sound.
A single white rose I hold for her,
To remind us of our love.
Delicate and special it is,
With the innocence of a dove.
Her eyes are closed, her skin so pale;
She took a mighty blow.
Now she lies in a wooden bed,
And I must let her go.
Gently I lean down to her,
And carefully kiss her cheek.
"Farewell for now, my little angel;
Again someday we'll meet."

Lisa McQuarrie, Grade 11
Sydenham High School, ON

A Song

On the five-lined staffs,
Rains notes of rhapsody.
A sonata of art and timelessness,
A refrain of Renaissance,
Repeats with a rondo of inspiration.

An ensemble of imagination
Waltzes beyond treble and bass.
On the five-lined staffs,
Perches a nightingale, awaiting flight,
A conductor of his own song.

Sunny Wong, Grade 12
Burnaby North Secondary School, BC

Too Late

A moment lost in the dictionary.
Time heats up, while trapped in the surging firm.
Typing numbers, writing notes, the clicks of a stapler;
My troubled mind knows all but the twitching clock.

A ring pierces through the ranting,
I pick up to heed the caller, as he rants about every single problem.
I begin to assure the man, as my thoughts began to collapse in my head.
I hung up the wretched phone,
I rise to clear my mind,
I needed a light, as my mind went into nightfall.

The clock ticked faster, people begin scolding me for leaving my workplace.
My mind continues to exhaust.
The clock ticks faster, my boss roars about someone getting fired.
I feel terrified.
The clock ticks faster.
My breath is gone.

I stared at the clock, as the tick grew slower and slower.
Why now? Not even after I achieved one single dream?
The clock said nothing, it just ticked slower.
Slower.

Derrick Matthias, Grade 10
Merritt Secondary School, BC

Reassurance

Short, time ran, devouring faster than the sun's fuel,
Numbered was Earth's life span; O was this poison cruel.

Dim, did the light of day, the darkness filled the space,
The only question, Nature heard say; "What's happening to this place?"

As did the rain diminish, mustard with greed the trees did turn,
Earth's time was now finished; the pain began to burn.

She watched in grief, as her home caught fire,
"Who is this thief?" The answer was swift, the flames grew higher.

The sun turned black, the Earth turned white,
Turning brightness into night; impairing such beauties sight.

The silence blundered like an angry tune, in harmony with dead stars,
No planet was immune; to the dark icy scars.

People are so hideously seduced by paradise of soil
So easily are they reduced with conflict of oil.

Their minds corrupted by lofty, ideal humors
Which slowly become deadly, power-hungry tumors.

Aly-Shah Jamal, Grade 10
Burnaby Central Secondary School, BC

Life

It runs straight forward to my ear
Like nothing was right at all
The message I shall not hear
Came to me with such a fall

It was by far the most painful thing
Because I broke her heart
It rang the bell that shall ring
And now I fall apart

The torment I will not let seek
For if I do my word is dead
Agony from me will leak
But there is a road ahead

I suffer from a lifeless pain
For many do not know
An honest anguish that will remain
Because she is so low

Anita Martell, Grade 11
Waweyekisik Education Centre, SK

Our Own World

Friendships start, friendships end,
Who will be tomorrow's friend?
Jumping in, we go too fast,
High school relationships rarely last.
Stories spread fast like wildfire,
Everyone clouded by a selfish desire.
But the older we get, the more to do,
So homework grades are slipping too.
One mistake and we get grounded,
A place to escape, but we're surrounded.
So let me dwell in my chaos of misery,
Let me escape from the world of reality.
If only for a second, that breath of air,
And then back to the world that's so unfair.
In my room, every thought that spins,
Guilted by life's bittersweet sins.
Now building up that collection of anger,
Holding my head 'cause it only spins faster.
A knock on my door, the courage I gather,
"Welcome to the world of teenage disaster."

Louisa Dal Cengio, Grade 10
Holy Cross Regional High School, BC

Winter Is Here

Winter is near,
And it is the best time of the year.
When the snow starts to fall, you can hear all the kids cheer.
The first snow storm arrives in November,
All the shoveling we will all remember.
During the night the snow is so white,
That even with the darkness,
Outside looks so bright.
Winter is no longer near,
With all the snow winter is clearly here.

Alexandra Cadillo, Grade 10
Villa Maria High School, QC

Monster

a monster in my bed

Bar the windows!
Bar the doors!

here we go again.

close your starry eyes
don't let it see the light
fading

close your starry eyes
and maybe tonight
it will go

Quickly

wriggle away
under the covers
avoid the chasing fingers
cold and wet — they slip
after you
press into
your tainted skin

don't open your starry eyes
because you know
it's him

Sunet Slabbert, Grade 12
Sir James Dunn Collegiate and Vocational School, ON

Stop — Listen

The earth greets with the fresh smile of the morning
Possibilities are like endless blooming flowers,
Waiting to be chosen.
The season sings a ballad for all to hear,
So stop — listen.

With every step, a new note sings,
And a new instrument introduced,
In the orchestra of life.
Stop — listen.

The concert of creation is free,
but seldom truly hear it.
So stop — listen.

As the wind hums along,
And the new day beckons,
The puzzle of life continues
But the river will still run, and the birds will still sing
keeping to the beat of the symphony.
So stop — listen.

Megan Patterson, Grade 10
Mennonite Educational Institute, BC

The Great Hunt

The morning of a cool late fall day.
Getting out of bed the sun was in the east.
It is a perfect day for Whitetail deer hunting.
Having a nice soothing cup of coffee, for the morning.
The guys show up just on time.
We all hop into the truck and hope for a great hunt.
We start our adventure to the south.
We get to our favorite spot called the honey hole.
What a surprise there it is the godfather of all Whitetail.
It just stands there feeding with 9 other does.
It stands at 200 yards from the road.
We all silently creep out of the vehicle.
We all take aim and finally someone shoots.
The shot made a puck noise and we knew it was a hit.
So we all waited patiently and suddenly the deer fell to the ground.
Everyone was excited since it was the biggest deer ever shot.
The legend still goes on today.

Adam Mardell, Grade 11
William Mason School, SK

The Volleyball Game

The teams come out to a cheering crowd.
The warm up begins.
You can feel the tension in the air.
Music is blaring out of the stereo getting the teams excited.
The ref blows the whistle and calls the captains,
He lays out the rules and tosses the coin,
Home team calls tails and takes first serve.
The captains walk over to the team huddle,
All the players are shaking with excitement,
Adrenaline is pumping through their warm bodies.
The coach tries to calm them down,
But it's hard when he is also vibrating with joy.
Both teams are pumped and ready to go.
In the huddle the team starts bouncing around,
"What time is it?" chants the loud boy,
As the rest of the team follows up with "Game Time!!"
They finish the Chant with the team name.
They shake hands with their opponents.
The Whistle blows, the crowd cheers and the first serve floats over the net,
Everybody in the gym is wondering the same thing,
Who will come out on top?

Daniel Bond, Grade 10
William Mason School, SK

The Tree That Grew from Concrete

Long live the tree that grew from concrete that couldn't grow anywhere,
Without the proper conditions, it fought through its despair
A diamond in the rough all right
That tree could not even take a bite
Of rich soil like the rest
No one came to make its nest
Long live the tree that grew without fresh air
It learned to grow, with no one's care

Jon Skarsten, Grade 11
Earl Haig Secondary School, ON

Waiting on Love

I have never felt like this before,
My face is happy yet my heart is sore.
I am not sick, really, I feel just fine,
I feel this way because I want you to be mine.

I love when I am hanging out with you,
An hour flies by in a minute, or two.
My time is up and I am forced to leave,
I'll see you soon, which is what I believe.

I sit at home and wait for your call,
When you finally do I get weak, and nearly fall.
The time quickly passes, and we both say good-bye,
My ears cannot wait for your mouth to say hi.

I may not be with you, but my heart always is.
My life is perfect because he is mine, and I am his.
No matter what, I am thinking about you,
You are my comfort when I feel blue.

You're the reason I feel so full of joy,
I couldn't have met a more perfect boy.
Every minute is like a wonderful dream.
Skyler, I don't know how, but we're a perfect team.

Tiffany McKenzie, Grade 11
Holy Rosary High School, AB

In Loving Memory — Budd

Taking it one day at a time,
One heart wrenching day after another.
The house is silent,
The silence bores holes in you
Sending you quietly insane.
You long to hear his laugh,
His laugh at nothing,
Once more.

God's tears, they just keep falling,
In a steady rhythm,
Like the beat of my favorite song.
He too feels our pain.
Knowing the world will never be the same.

We will mourn for a while,
Some longer than others,
But just remember all the good times.
The fun, the laughter, the Christmases, the birthdays.
We will never stop loving him,
We will never stop missing him.
We are his family, and he will never stop missing us too.

Jessica O'Connell, Grade 11
Mennonite Collegiate Institute, MB

Time

Time passes by,
And I absolutely can't stop thinking of you
When I see you smile,
My world is lightened up.

Time passes by,
And still I can't seem to forget you.
You're certainly the one I want,
But you seem to be slowly walking away.

Time passes by,
And I'm still waiting for our happy ending.
Since the day you looked me in the eye,
I knew right there that this was truly meant to be.

Time passes by,
And you're still in my head.
Now I'm wishing that,
Tomorrow will be a different story.

Jena Lapierre, Grade 10
Charlottenburgh-Lancaster District High School, ON

Hoping for Love

My love for you I cannot explain
My unexpressed feelings leave me in pain

You wield such faith, compassion and beauty
Your looks so inspiring just trying to be "yours truly"

Your always good attitude, you don't care what they say
Always living in freedom or looking another way

When I first saw you, first stared in your eyes
Such wondrous delight like the stars in the skies

I swore I saw Heaven and a future so bright
The thoughts filled my mind, it was love at first sight

Do you see what I see? When I look towards you
Always sharing, caring and filled with love too

I know how I feel, hoping we'll be together
If this were to come true I'll pray it forever.

Jeremy Burkinshaw, Grade 10
Macdonald High School, QC

When Things Gone Bad

When things gone bad,
Don't ever be sad,
Cause I will always be by your side.
When days aren't bright,
Also timing isn't right,
Just hold me tight,
Sunshine will come to your sight.
When you are tired and give up try,
All the good things seem to be far in the sky,
I'll make a balloon so you can fly,
So you can fly really really high!

Ivy Wang, Grade 11
Burnaby North Secondary School, BC

Free Falling

I gaze upward,
imagining victory,
as I reach for the crown.
I am a bear,
as I take the trunk in my grasp,
leaves rattle, twist, and fall to the ground.
Eyes focus on the prize — a golden leaf.
As I lunge from branch to branch,
safety is out of the question.
Passing nests and hollows,
the wind begins to weigh heavily.
The end is near.
One last branch —
CRACK!
Free falling to the ground,
twigs assault my body left and right,
I slam upon the hard, bare ground.
My body, my ego sore, but not broken.
I gaze upward,
take a deep breath and stand,
ready for round two.

Spencer Beazley, Grade 12
Killarney Collegiate Institute, MB

Footprints?

Have you ever felt the urge to scream
only to see if anyone looks up?

An aimless amble
through the exclusive laughter
that doesn't fit

17 strangers I've known for 12 years
where choice is not a choice
and I'm left with no match
An unequivocal oddity
not worth the effort to understand

The thing about circles
is that once they're formed
additions become ambiguous
It's human nature to resist change

How do you become a memory
if you don't feel like part of the present?
An inadvertent absence

Have you ever walked through the sand
only to see if you even exist?

Brittany Serafini, Grade 12
Cut Knife High School, SK

Love

If you find the right person love is like a clock
It will keep going and going and it will never stop
When you look into that person's eyes
You will know you have the ultimate prize
Treat that person like royalty
Do what you can to make sure they're carefree
Give that person the utmost respect
And do what you can to love serve and protect
Remember that conflict is inevitable
But at the end of the day you are still my angel

Stacey Acheampong, Grade 12
John Cabot Catholic Secondary School, ON

Inside a Silent Dream

I look over the wonderful city, standing on top of a building.
How beautiful the twilight of spring is,
Like a silk garment worn by the sky.
    I want it to be night forever.
The streets empty of all the crowds and cars,
The smooth shade between every building,
The glow of streetlights in every direction,
    Everything is silent.
I want to soar above the city, gazing upon a silent scenery,
To fly higher, watching over as everything shrinks beneath my feet,
Diving headfirst into the gentle atmosphere,
    And then rise again.
The sun is descending behind the buildings.
Let me flow along the direction of the sunset
Over the resting city.

Lynaya Penniston, Grade 10
Kildonan-East Collegiate, MB

Jaded

I remember a time when you and I were once us,
Makes me wonder if I lost or gained in that long-term investment I made.
To this day that has been on my mind,
Seems like so much time has passed since the last embrace we shared,
Back when we cared,
But did that ever stop?

Now I stand alone.
Stony gazed and hard hearted,
Since the moment we parted,
Guarded the rock hard fortress my heart had started to become.
Others are repelled by the electric fence of cutting words I use in my heart's defense,
I tell them and myself that I want to be on my own.

Hence the loneliness I feel inside.
But my pride makes me hide behind a mask of strength and satisfaction,
This is my reaction,
How I act when I don't want to feel.
I seal all the emotion to the back of my mind,
Become numb to the real.
I find temporary peace inside.

Khadija Derie, Grade 12
John Cabot Catholic Secondary School, ON

Kitsch

Dancing under the leaves of fall,
Weaving my way under as I call,
Where are you my darling?
I miss you, I'm longing,

Your gentle embrace, feelings I can't replace,
An ephemeral pleasure, love I can't measure,
Your soft kiss, an eternal bliss,
Memories I can't forget, dreams I can't regret,

My eyes are crying, my heart is broken,
Running and looking, all that I've given,
Wasn't even enough to keep your love,
You just flew away so high above,

You left me all alone in the darkness,
With nothing to fill my emptiness,
Will I live forever with this sadness?
I don't care, I only wish for your happiness,

Leonard Au, Grade 11
College Jean De La Mennais, QC

The Severed Garden

The sky changed color in system ripples of light,
The garden is true,
Chariots traverse the heaven of doom,
The day is bright,
The night is young,
Filled with compensatory possibilities of fun,
As the sun goes down and the people run,
The song of peace is never sung,
Mysterious strays and forgotten ways,
Scare not true beings of day,
'Til the night is over and morning comes,
The jumpled fields off dazed,
Will forever be one,
Flying wonders of freedom,
The chariots gone undone,
The night together for once,
'Til the next day is done,
And the severed garden is one.

Jake Simpkins, Grade 12
General Amherst High School, ON

Real Eyes, Realize, Real Lies

Waking up next to the person you love most is a great feeling
Waking up with black all around, results in you not seeing
People take their eyesight for granted
When it's all gone you're walking a little slanted
Walking around school with your eyes shut tight
Was weird getting around with absolutely no sight
It was hard getting around I was surely not used to it
Having someone guide me just made me want to quit
When it was all over and I could open up my eyes
I was happy that I could see, I breathed a big heavy sigh
Now I know not everyone has it as great as some do
From now on in I'll treat it as special as not having the flu

Jessica Correia, Grade 12
John Cabot Catholic Secondary School, ON

Jim's Shoes

God,
I think You laid a cross too heavy,
A burden too strong
For a small person like him.
I want him to be an angel,
So give him my wings.
I want him to fly,
So give me his load.
I secretly pray for him
And the burdens he hauls.
I yearn for him to grow,
For Your shoes are too big.
And when I cry myself to sleep,
I cry for both him and me.
Because he's dying inside;
His pain I can't even compare.

Jim,
I will polish your shoes and keep up with your pace.
Wherever and whenever, I will be by your side.
Because, forever and ever, and ever,

Brother and sister, we will always be.

Alice Yu, Grade 10
Little Flower Academy, BC

Volcanic Minds

twisted forms, creep from thoughts
like lightning bolts, electric watts?

ideas exploding
from minds unaware,
flowing red lava
I focus my stare.

molten red rock, hits cold blue water
my thoughts cool down, clean and proper.

chisel away
at the surface of brain,
I take what I please
use it for my gain.

the layers are thick, ideas warm and unused
ideas new and old, theorized, then excused.

the volcanic eruption that is my mind
is asleep, hibernation,
to erupt once again
flowing ideas, no explanation.

Eric Peterson, Grade 12
Notre Dame Des Grands Lacs School, ON

Snow

It's snowing;
It is neither black, nor beige,
Nor red, nor gray,
But white. The flakes are so small.   Alléluia!

It's winter;
It's snowing, and all the flakes are brothers.
They are white lace
Against a blue sky.   Alléluia!

In this cold, we light a fire,
And here we are, all alone, just the two of us.
Do we love one another?
Outside, it's so good.   Alléluia!

What? Yes? Be, my love!
I sing the Alléluia,
For the angels are
On this day favourable to me.   Alléluia!

Catherine Francine Pelletier, Grade 11
College Catholique Franco-Ouest, ON

The True Meaning of Life

Is life really about what you
Think it is?
Or is it just about what
You've made it to be?

Is it really about
Sex, drugs and rock'n roll?
Or is it truly about
Happiness, joy and peace?

And what is freedom anyway?
Have you not learned from your mistakes yet?
What is keeping you in chains?
Is it your past or your present?

If you search deep enough,
You are bound to know the answer.
If you stay still long enough,
He, who loved you first, may blow the answer in your ear.

Paul-Rémi Poulin, Grade 11
École Notre-Dame-des-Vertus, SK

I'm An...

I'm a lithium-ion rechargeable battery.
I energize my friends with motivation,
Help light them up on their darkest days.
I forgive the bad things you might have done to me
When I feel down or tired,
I go ahead, recharge myself and start up fresh again.
I work well together with a partner of the same type,
I also perform well alone.
I'm environmentally friendly and helpful to many people.
By getting rid of negative things, I create energy.
I have a hard exterior to protect myself.
I'm a lithium-ion rechargeable battery.

Dominic Leung, Grade 10
Burnaby North Secondary School, BC

Ode to My Computer

My computer is my tormentor,
its relentless perfection, its constant efficiency,
it keeps me from daydreaming.

My computer is my tormentor,
fatal errors, a money pit smug on my desk,
it is part of me.

My computer is my tormentor,
it swallows emails, it never gives up,
it directs my life.

My computer is my tormentor,
it reminds me of work to do, of youth lost,
of worse to come.

My computer is my tormentor,
a project machine, a graphing expert and time consumer,
a contradiction in time.

My computer is my tormentor,
its metal exterior, its pentium heart,
it is true to its nature.

Veronica Licursi, Grade 11
Villa Maria High School, QC

The Most Horrible Vision*

I just had the most horrible vision
Of a young man slowly dying
Now he's lying in a cold dark coffin
And everyone else is crying
There are so many people it could have been
So many people it wasn't
But it had to be him, it was him
Of them all time picked only one
They're all so strong so hard inside
And they accept all the condolences
Even when it isn't enough they smile
In an effort to break this silence
How old was that young man
We all know he was too young to die
What's considered the right age
When everyone else is too old to cry?
I had the most horrible vision
And then I learned it was real
Somebody, somebody not worth dying
And nobody around can deal
Nobody can feel

Sarah Jane Walsh, Grade 10
Chateauguay Valley Regional High School, QC
*Dedicated to Placid, who left us late November.
May you rest in peace.

A Fantasy Without Magic

A fantasy without magic is like,
A pirate without a ship.
A pie without a crust.
A dog without a tail.
It's possible, yet highly unlikely.

A fantasy without magic is like,
A cookie with no sugar.
A beach with no water.
A religion with no purpose.
It might have been tried, but nobody wants it.

A fantasy without magic is like,
A game without guidelines.
A farmer without land.
A song without music.
It's pointless to have one without the other.

A fantasy without magic is like,
Harmony without melody.
Joy without peace.
Insight without outlook.
Together, they can compose an incredible thing.

Carlee Lewis, Grade 10
Mennonite Educational Institute, BC

True Friend

True friend is a beacon of lasting hope,
always there to be with you as you cope.
Through the lonely times of highs and lows,
to bring you back from the world below.

True friend is an existing proof of light;
when needed the most, comes to make things right.
Swelling up with eager happiness,
never again should you feel lifeless.

True friend is a keen and patient ear;
talk it all out, because it will hear.
Advice and suggestion it will give,
please, refresh your memories, and live!

True friend is someone to hold on to;
keep in touch, no matter what you do.
A loyal friend is your second family,
someone you can trust for all eternity.

Don't let the image of your friend become a memory,
because a memory, sad or wonderful, will remain,
a memory.

Ingrid Liu, Grade 12
Semiahmoo Secondary School, BC

Dependence

It starts out as a sample.
Unaware that opportunities are ample.
So you let the peer pressure take hold.
Unaware the effects could be so cold.
Naively telling yourself it will just be this once.
The next thing you know it's been a couple of months.
You begin to realize that this is taking you nowhere.
The dependency kicks in and you suddenly don't care.
Everything pure starts fading away.
You think having a fix will make it okay.

You are overcome with feelings of guilt.
For shunning your loved ones with the walls that you've built.
There is only one way to get out of this mess.
And get rid of the root of most of your stress.

You have to have the strength and believe in yourself.
And leave the drug use to somebody else.

Lance Martin, Grade 12
Waweyekisik Education Centre, SK

Jealousy of the Mind

Vines twisted in knots,
Slicing through flesh.
Its vice on me.
Crushed bones, broken in half,
Thorns like
Poison ivy, seep into veins.
Its hold
Powerful, a monster's embrace.
Scales mutate,
Green as moss
Feeding on skin.
Eyes bulging, glaring —
Unattainable.
Urges,
Undesirable desires
Filling souls.
Nails claws,
Skin tears
Limb from limb;
I gave in.

Rachel Klar, Grade 12
Westmount Collegiate Institute, ON

Life's a Game

Life's a game
There are moments where you'll win
For some, it may be the moment of fame.
And others, it can be thrown in the bin
Soon it will come to an end.
No matter how good you are,
We must know,
One day it will end.
And some day we'll all lose.
What we don't know is,
When it'll end.

Katherine Pham, Grade 11
Ascension of Our Lord Secondary School, ON

Roadside Madden

A girl I met while walking
No shadow did she cast
To her I started talking
Complete I was at last
The girl of beauty spoke that day
I still know what she said
Young man I took your breath away
So much I'm almost dead
I caught my jaw before it fell
She started down the lane
The next day after that was hell
My heart pounded with pain
I love you whispered in her ear
Never seeing her is my biggest fear.

D.J. Cust, Grade 10
William Mason School, SK

Your Eyes

Looking into your eyes is like falling into a dream
Golden brown like the leaves of autumn,
Swirling freely in the wind.
Amber like a summer's sunset,
Filling the sky and clouds with brilliant gold.
They lighten my world,
Like the sun lightens my day.
When light reaches them,
It's like staring into the sky.
When only sometimes you get a cloudless night.
The twinkle in your eyes,
Is like the twinkle of the stars.
Staring down on us from above with their excepting stares.
When gazing into your eyes,
All time seems to drift away.
All worries seem to disappear,
With simply one glance.
If only I could always see these eyes,
Nothing else would matter.
Just only to blink.

Dylan Parsons, Grade 11
Sydenham High School, ON

Eternal Love

Knowledge can be learned and gained,
but it can be forgotten
Friends are a guidance and gift
but they can be lost
Wealth is inherited and worked for
but has no real meaning
Love comes from everywhere and everyone
and is not able to be sold or broken
Love is truly eternal,
for it is with you always
And as long as we live or remember
Our love will stay with you forever.

Sylvain Langlois, Grade 12
College Catholique Franco-Ouest, ON

A Place…a Thought…an Escape

I escape to a place, I escape through a thought.
When my mind's being flooded with thoughts that won't stop.
Put them on hold, and I swallow my rage,
Break the depression cage; put it down on a page.
Scribble sloppy sentences in seconds, construct a bar or two.
This place is close to me but it's far to you.
You don't know this place, and you don't know me.
Cause I can show my anger, but I'm scared to say I'm lonely.
Unthinkable thoughts flow with ease through my lead.
They explode on paper like they do in my head.
They burn and torture, setting flames to notebooks.
Recite it back, impeccable. So perfectly floats hooks.
Bring it all together, let it seep in my brain.
Controversial to you, but to me it's all the same.
Metaphors and multi's, devils and angels float in my mind
Another perfect verse you can quote and rewind.
Now it sits there, screaming at me.
But strangely, I'm still feeling badly.
I'm vomiting words so fast I'm starting to spin.
Finished this one, still mad, so I do it again.

Blake Naeth, Grade 10
Paradise Hill School, SK

Love

It lies beneath you,
Never in the open.
You wonder if it's real.
Should you take the chance?
Your heart might get broken.
That doesn't stop you.
You try to find it,
But never succeed.
It haunts you like a ghost,
When unexpected.
It's like a bird in the sky,
That can't be caught.
It passes by,
And may never return.
You're shocked of what you've found.
Everyone has it,
You just think nothing of it.
Many try to forget,
But can't.
Would something so real ever be found?

Brandi Mullen, Grade 10
Clearwater Secondary School, BC

Young Poets
Grades 7-8-9

Note: The Top Ten poems were finalized through an online voting system. Creative Communication's judges first picked out the top poems. These poems were then posted online. The final step involved thousands of students and teachers who registered as online judges and voted for the Top Ten poems. We hope you enjoy these selections.

Top Poem Grades 7-8-9

Non Existent Friend

So sweet you are; your words with no harm.
You're so permanently considered wonderful.
You simplify the meaning of charm.
Your glee so contagious and beautiful.

Far from perfect, you are, like us
But different all the same.
You were never meant to be like us.
You make our little world change.

You don't see things the way we do
The cliques, the fights, the letters.
Perhaps we don't see things the way you do
The light, the joy, your way is so much better.

We won't stop the hurting of each other.
We'll be hurtful 'till the end.
But you never hurt any one of us.
You're my non existent friend.

Aaron Cosgrove, Grade 8
St Stephen Middle School, NB

Top Poem Grades 7-8-9

Poster Image

Look at the girl in the poster.
Do you see? Look closer.
Skinny, not fat,
Pretty, all that.

She's not even real
It's all for the public's appeal
Putting pressure on teens
Like they've got to be queens.

Modern society
No more sobriety
I'm going crazy
And the future looks hazy

I see a girl crying because
The poster image is not what she does.
She is herself.
Personality and style don't come off a shelf.

Natasha Haskins, Grade 8
Archbishop Carney Secondary School, BC

Top Poem Grades 7-8-9

My Older Brother

You wanted to become everything,
Until you grew older,
And now you've decided,
You want to be a soldier.

Dad encourages,
Mom sort of does too,
Seems only I know,
How much you've got to lose.

All the nasty things I've said to you,
All the dirty things I've done,
But never once have I told you,
You are my number one.

I'll never get to talk to you,
Or see you for awhile,
I'll never hear your laugh again,
I'll never see your smile.

Hopefully that day will come,
When I let out a sigh of relief,
When you're standing in Mom's doorway,
Alive and all in one piece.

Meagan Holden, Grade 9
Lester B Pearson High School, ON

Top Poem Grades 7-8-9

I Remember

I remember my dad in Air Force blue, saying goodbye and I love you
I remember my dad going to fight, and my mom crying late at night
I remember, I remember
I remember Aunt Carole wearing black and white, waving as her ship sailed out of sight
I remember her letters from abroad, and asking for her safety in our prayers to God
I remember, I remember
I remember Paul in khaki and green, going off to join the fighting machine
I remember phone calls, there were so few, but he always had time to talk to me too
I remember I remember
I remember stories Grandma has told, of hiding the menfolk, from armies so cold
I remember Grandpa turning away, the memories too painful to recall that day
I remember, I remember
I remember scars on Great-Grandpa's arm, from when soldiers burned the family barn
I remember his face as he told his tale, his choice of fighting or going to jail
I remember, I remember
I remember the courage of men of war, and pray in the future we'll fight no more
I remember their bravery and their pride, but I wish so many did not have to die
I remember, I remember
I'll remember when I put on my blues, that to my country I must be true
I'll remember that I need to bring peace, progress in the future means fighting must cease
I'll remember, I'll remember

Malcolm Jones, Grade 8
St Peter Catholic High School, ON

Top Poem Grades 7-8-9

Music

Music, my gift
My opportunity to go somewhere
It's in my blood
Just like blue eyes run in a family
It's my talent, it's who I am, it's my outlet
Music calms my soul
Music is the chains that bind me, my only talent
The only thing that will get me somewhere
The only thing that will get me a real education
It shrinks my opportunities, it chains my soul
Blood and passion bleed through the chains.
Music, it is my curse, I have no choice
It follows me wherever I go
Practicing at every given moment, losing sleep
Deep purple bags grow larger under my eyes
Like a growing tumor
I have no choice it is my curse.
But how else can I calm my soul,
What will give me a sense of identity?
Music, my gift, my chains, my curse

Emily Kerkhof, Grade 9
FE Madill Secondary School, ON

Top Poem Grades 7-8-9

The Diversity of Happiness

Though happiness doesn't always come easily
It comes no matter where you are,
Either by winning the latest video game
Or the thought of a small meal tonight
On Christmas morning,
Or the day the enemy country surrenders.

Happiness can come in great loads,
Or tiny piles
In a package,
Or on a note that declares your freedom.

Even though one man's happiness might seem trivial,
Happiness cannot be judged
Nor can it be measured
However, when you have it
You know,
And you never want to let it go.

Madisen Neufeld, Grade 8
Menno Simons Christian School, AB

Top Poem Grades 7-8-9

Peace Comes at a Heavy Price*

In World War II, peace came at a heavy price; men died among sand as they died among ice
They died by the thousands, so many young lives; their nineteen year old eyes glimmering like knives
Every three seconds of those six dreadful years; another life was lost causing heartache and tears
Parents crying over their son's letter of fate; his death caused by Hitler and his choice to dictate

The Axis hungry for power, they conquered the land; from Pacific islands to North Africa's sand
They fought and they won lands they thought fine; until the forces of good decided to combine
The Allies was their choice of name; though from different countries, their hearts were all the same
Always they were there to fight; to defend the land for what was right

They did their duty, they answered their call; to unite the people, to unite them all
In the face of danger they stood their ground; those brave, brave men, they were honor bound
When chances were bad, when chances were good; they held their ground and there they stood
They were among the bravest of any and all; even when their comrades did rapidly fall

The Allies fought, and they fought; until a lesson was taught
On the very last Berlin street; Germany was forced to admit defeat
With Japan left as the last Axis standing; the war was ended with a weapon, its power outstanding
On August 6, that frightful day; death was carried out to many by the Enola Gay

After the carnage and horror were through; they were given shiny medals, maybe one or two
But oh let me tell you, that's not enough; what I'm about to tell you; let's just say it's tough
Peace was not cheap, in blood it was earned; their only hope, was that a lesson was learned
Always remember, never forget; the sacrifices made with no regret

Steven Cameron Noel, Grade 7
Sir John Thompson Catholic Jr High School, AB
*Dedicated to both the veterans and those who died protecting our freedom during WWII

Top Poem Grades 7-8-9

I Wish I Was Me

I wish I was a movie star,
going to all these places.
Singing everywhere I go,
staring at all the faces.
I wish I was an astronaut,
flying towards the stars.
Visiting different planets,
like Jupiter and Mars.
I wish I was a cowboy,
riding a horse in the West.
Catching all those bad guys,
that would be the best.
I wish I was a princess,
getting everything I want,
Going to places with the prince,
to the ball or a fancy restaurant.
I wish I was a lot of things
and if I thought of them carefully,
If I had to choose just one,
I'd say I wish I was me.

Natasha Raseta, Grade 8
Ecole L'Heritage, ON

Top Poem Grades 7-8-9

The Unrecognized Disease

They swish by me as I am not a part of reality,
Laughing in high, phony voices that resemble Barbie.
Swinging their purses, they display their phones and MP's,
Their manicured nails clicking away on the cell's keys.

Their accessorized hands flutter all about,
Trying to attract attention, no doubt!
They all are so skinny and petite,
I guess that's how they earn the VIP seat.

I admit, I am quite jealous,
I wish I was just as visible and glamorous.
Rather, I am awkward and out of place,
I have none of that natural grace.

I own no authoritative influence,
I am no one, nothing, just silence.
I am friendless, a loner,
It is as if I don't belong here, never did, never will, a foreigner.

Those girls have it all,
They are the royal dolls.
The only reason as to why to each other we are so contrary,
Is because of the common, yet unrecognized disease, called popularity.

Kosan Shafaque, Grade 8
Islamic Foundation School, ON

Top Poem Grades 7-8-9

Ink

The art of the poet
Requires a mission,
A goal, an objective, a task.
Heed all you hear, vanquish all of your fears,
And from time to time, just stop to ask.

The art of the poet
Requires a passion,
A hope to be harboured inside.
The thoughts and the letters, all mixed up together
And laced with a strong wisp of pride.

The art of the poet
Requires a yearning,
To demonstrate what you've been shown.
The poetic feelings, and literate dealings,
Will demonstrate how much you've grown.

The art of the poet
Requires a pen,
To record every thought that one thinks.
The words are such wonders, such beautiful thoughts
And captured forever in ink.

Brody Weld, Grade 8
Codrington Public School, ON

Changing Seasons: Fall

I take a step,
And enter fall
I walk further on
Into the orange forest
One look up
I see colors
Yellow, orange, red
Maybe green

Another step further,
Showers of colors
All I see

Secondly,
A cold breeze
I take the last gradual step
And enter winter

Amanda Zielinski, Grade 8
St Peter Catholic High School, ON

Christmas

Carolers,
Presents,
Stockings,
Family visits,
Anxiety,
Insomnia,
Christmas dinners,
Snowball fights,
No school!
Late nights,
Lame office parties,
Electronics sales,
Christmas specials
(Usually reruns),
Freezing cold,
Wood-smoke smells,
Fire places alight,
Scented candles,
Boy, I sure do love Christmas.

Riley Maillet, Grade 8
St Peter Catholic High School, ON

Like a Bird

Like a bird who flies
I want to steal my liberty

Like a bird that pierces the clouds
I want to pierce my dreams

Like a bird who learns to fly
I want to learn how to live my life

How can we live like a bird?

Frédérique Laroche, Grade 9
Ecole Secondaire Jean Grou, QC

Mankind: The Clueless

My heart throbs.
My soul aches.
My eyes bleed with tears.

I watch the ignorance of mankind pass by my window;
Sometimes stopping at my doorstep.
So clueless of what the world will be one day.
So unaware.

They don't ask questions; Not "Why?" or even "How?"
Their greed for fame and fortune is the only thing that keeps them content.
But do they not realize there will come a day when those things won't matter anymore?

They have strayed from what life used to be about: Love and compassion for humanity.
Truly, Mankind is clueless; Clueless for eternity.

Rezan Banki, Grade 9
Clarke Road Secondary School, ON

Remembrance

R espect
E ach of all the soldiers their
M emories will live on
E mbrace their souls in
M emory of the fallen comrades who fought for their country we
B race their memories so that they may live on
R espect the people that they were taken from
A nd
N ever let their memories fade away their
C ountries may be sad but we will remember
E ach of all the soldiers that served their life to do to save their
countries you should remember it's called Remembrance Day.

Emett Stoney, Grade 7
Nawigizigweyas Education Centre, SK

On This Island...

Way away from where I am now,
Sits an extraordinary island,
Shaped like the head of a cow.
It's full of trees and mountains like the countryside of Thailand.

Some interesting animals live here
There are definitely no bears, moose or deer.
Creatures like koala bears, huge lizards and some beautiful fish
However, they're so dangerous; you won't be able to find any on a silver dish.

All the humans that live on this island are great,
But, they are the only ones that can decide your fate.
Don't worry, they won't harm you,
They'll just give you a task you need to do.

The sunset on this island is worth dying for.
Purple, pink, orange, and blue are all colors in the sky,
But, a good night's rest can be found straight through that door.
So, when it's all over, it's time to say goodnight and goodbye.

Francesca Masella, Grade 7
The Study School, QC

Love

My love for you cannot compare
Like a bird soaring through the air
I refuse to stop thinking of you throughout the day
From when I wake up in the morn'
Until at night I pray
It is like the flames of one hundred suns
But without you my love
There will be no burning one
This poem is written from my heart it's true
And my heart will be given to only you
You complete my cries, my laughs, my fun
Because you are, for me the only one
Your eyes remind me of sparkling jewels
It makes me seem like a real fool
Your smile is that of pearls so white
I will not let you go without a fight
That is why I write my poem of love
Just because you are a living, human dove

Ken Cave, Grade 7
Macdonald High School, QC

Swinging

Pumping.
Forcing my legs,
To keep going.
Back and forth,
Back and forth,
Back and forth.
I can feel the tension,
Building up, waiting to explode.
Going high, higher, highest,
With the wind whipping my hair,
Blowing away the pain, the sorrow, the hurt.
I keep going, not wanting to stop,
But knowing, that I'll have to.
Seeing the sun fade,
I slow down
And collapse.
I'm out of breath, heaving hard.
I get up.
I'm weak, but free.
Then slowly,
Walk away.

Rachelle Grey, Grade 8
The Elms Junior and Middle School, ON

Finality

At the funeral of my grandpa
Who had died with my mom by his side
Calling my brother's name
I laid his soft scout's blanket over
His nice smooth coffin.
The funeral director had closed the casket
With just a click.

Isaac Sweeting, Grade 8
MacKenzie Secondary School, BC

The Wind

The wind is like a storm
Swaying through the night
Hitting little cars sitting
Giving us a fright

The wind is like the grass
Growing bigger and stronger every day that goes by
Not knowing when it'll get weaker
For the last time

The wind is like the river
Moving day and night
Knocking people out
Giving a scary sight

Robin Diederichs, Grade 7
St Anne School, SK

Remembrance Day

A soldier is running,
His heart fastly pacing
His gun to side, his mind ever racing
Then he sees the most horrible thing
A thing like what would make your heart sting
He saw a fellow comrade actually, his dearest friend
Step on an object that made his life end
That soldier was changed at that life-changing moment
He did not speak, talk or even make a comment
And that is why I feel I should say
We should not forget the things on Remembrance Day

Rasheed Chase, Grade 8
Macdonald High School, QC

I Am

I am an active boy who loves sports
I wonder if I can play in the NHL
I hear the sound of a stick hitting the ice
I see the crowd cheering me on
I want to be as good as Bobby Orr
I am an active boy who loves sports

I pretend I am David Beckam
I feel like I'm a star
I touch the FIFA World Cup
I worry that I will be wide on my kick
I cry when I lose in double overtime
I am an active boy who loves sports

I understand playing in the NBA takes skill
I say team work is number one!
I dream of being a good point guard like Steve Nash
I try to make my right hand lay-ups
I hope to make the basketball team
I am an active boy who loves sports

Alexandre Schryer, Grade 8
École secondaire Macdonald-Cartier, ON

Sophie-Émilie

S carce
O riginal
P ositive
H appy
I ntelligent
E nergetic

É nthusiastic
M erry
I rreplaceable
L ittle
I mportant
E xtraordinary

Sophie-Émilie Poulin-Lapierre, Grade 8
Collège Jésus-Marie de Sillery, QC

Marie Aude

M eticulous
A musing
R esourceful
I ntelligent
E nthusiastic

A lways smiling
U nusual
D ances well
E nergetic

Marie Aude des Loges-Cyrenne, Grade 8
Collège Jésus-Marie de Sillery, QC

Remembrance

R emember
E ndure
M edicine
E leventh hour
M arvelous
B rave
R espect
A stonishing
N urses
C eremony
E leventh of November

Letitia Desjarlais, Grade 7
Nawigizigweyas Education Centre, SK

The Joy of Winter

The fluffy white snow
fell tenderly to the ground
as children played some
entertaining winter games
some were making snowmen
others were playing tag
several were singing
some beautiful winter carols

What a Joy Winter brings.

Larry Wipf, Grade 7
Milford Colony School, AB

Life

Heavenly freedom
It's soul food
So many choices?
Love in a tub
Many you like.
The perfect place to be.

Ethan Frisse, Grade 8
MacKenzie Secondary School, BC

Alone

I stand alone, in the corner,
Trapped by invisible walls
Trapped by their pointing and laughing,
And I stand alone.

I am alone
Thoughts run through my head
Like a storm rolling over the prairies,
I am a reject, an outcast
Someone not wanted,
I think alone.

I am different alone
Like an oak tree in the desert,
Other than ordinary
I have different clothes
Different language, different thoughts
Different dreams, different answers,
I speak alone.

I dream alone of being accepted,
But their pointing and laughing
Breaks my dreams,
I cry alone.

Regan Van Walleghem, Grade 9
JA Cuddy Elementary School, MB

Sorry

I'm really sorry
for everything I've done
Please forgive me
'Cause you're so special, hun
You're so amazing
And the best person ever
I really want
to be with you forever.
You made me happy,
I made you sad
Just believe me
When I say I feel really bad.
I'll try my best to be
the best person ever for you
'Cause babe
I love you

Shannon O'Leary, Grade 8
St Peter Catholic High School, ON

This Heart of Mine

This heart of mine
Saw only the wrong light
Forgot to lighten
The rest of the room
And suddenly
The lights are opened
I see this dream
He comes to me
He torments me
Visits me in my sleep
I long for his presence
When I am awake
He hides in me
My thoughts are disturbed
He makes me crazy
It's all in my mind
I must be strong
And carry on
It's just a dream
But he feels so real
I can't forget this dream

Charlène Boutin, Grade 8
Ecole Golden Valley, QC

Winter

W hite beautiful snow
I nteresting
N utcrackers
T ime for hot chocolate
E xciting snow ball fights
R eally cold

Roxane Navert, Grade 7
Macdonald High School, QC

Answering the Call

Still as she lies in
the hospital bed,
Peacefully on her pillow
rests her head,
Family sits beside her,
Silent tears wash over their cheeks
Hoping that she will get better,
and never have this sickness again.

But then relief that the pain is over,
because last night

God called her home

Family and friends hold a funeral
While our beloved aunt rejoices with
the angels in heaven

At last.

Adina Kleinsasser, Grade 7
Milford Colony School, AB

Alone

When I look in the mirror
I see the inner pain
When people look at me
They see a big smile that can entertain
Inside out
It's not the same
Two different girls with the same name
On the outside I act as if everything is okay
But after, when I feel alone
I turn away
from the girl that used to smile and pretend to be okay
I get sad; sometimes mad
about the things I never had
Hope that someday,
Alone, I won't feel so sad…

Sandra Michelashvili, Grade 8
École Pierre-Brosseau, QC

The Day

One scorching day, I went outside,
Hopped on my bike and took a long ride.

I brought my enormous fishing pole out,
When I arrived at the bridge, there were fish swimming about.

I took a long time to tie on my jig,
cast it out, and caught something big!

I dipped in my net to scoop the fish up,
when I opened its mouth, it spat something up.

Jamie Felix, Grade 7
Milverton Public School, ON

My Other Half

I will hold you up when you are down,
Just as I know you would do for me.
I will give you a smile to replace your frown.
Without you where would I be?

Through my darkest days,
It gave me comfort to know,
That you were by my side,
Wherever my path may go.

You make me burst out with laughter,
And you comfort me when I am sad,
You are the greatest friend.
That a person could ever have.

Wherever we are,
Whatever we do,
We just have to remember,
We have a friendship so true.

Kelsey Lee, Grade 8
Montgomery Middle School, BC

Seasons Changing

The green leaves started changing
to oranges and lemon yellow,
as the warmth of the sun
turned into a cool breeze,
and I could hear the leaves laughing
as they fell to the ground,
which soon turned to be rock solid,
and I could feel the little white balls falling from the sky
as I flapped my wings and flew toward the warm weather,
like the geese in the sky.

Emily-Ann Butler, Grade 8
St Peter Catholic High School, ON

The Changes of Seasons

Snowflakes fall,
There's snow everywhere
I miss the summer so much.
I lie in bed with a hat on my head
It's too cold to wear nothing,
The summers were warm,
But the grass was wet for we had splashed in it
We wore our bathing suits for it was too hot in the heat.
The night gets weaker,
For there isn't any heat,
The power's gone out and I'm all alone
I hide under my blankets
I think of the good times
I swish my blankets off
For my parents have arrived home
I give them each a hug
They come to tuck me in…
I fall asleep and I dream of snowflakes
Winter isn't as bad as I thought…

Samantha Martin, Grade 7
Macdonald High School, QC

The Butterfly

There was a butterfly who was trying to fly
But his wings didn't want to try

Fighting against his own self
That was the hardest part for himself

The butterfly tried to fly
But his wings didn't want to try

Day after day, the butterfly tried
Unable, he closed his eyes and cried

Once when he woke up
He tried to spring up

And he won his own fight
He was like every other butterfly in flight

Marie-Eve Desjardins, Grade 9
Ecole Secondaire Jean Grou, QC

Snow

Little snow flakes fall from the skies
Upon my little eyes
So pretty and wonderful
Sparkly and beautiful

Different shapes
Different sizes
All in beautiful disguises
Lovely snow everywhere I go
For everyone to share
Carly Schneider, Grade 8
Macdonald High School, QC

The Small Very Timid Dragon!

It was a small very timid dragon
In the bottom of a dark place
Where millions of chains
were hung on him.

The small very timid dragon
had to find a manner
To rid him of his chains
which keeps him from his dreams.

The small very timid dragon
had to gather all the force of his soul
To succeed
To fulfill his dearest dream
Which was to be free
and be himself.
Mélissa Scarfone, Grade 9
Ecole Secondaire Jean Grou, QC

The Golden Arrow

High above the foliage,
a hawk,
wings by.
Its feathers splayed,
catching a cold updraft,
disappearing into the morning haze.
Early rays,
piercing the darkness,
setting the horizon ablaze.
Dawn is approaching.
The sun glistens off a brazen wing.
Senses alert,
keen eyes scanning,
the slightest movement detected.
The golden arrow,
precise aim,
instant death,
explosion of fur.
Intense hunger satisfied,
at least for now.
Joel Wismer, Grade 9
Mount Douglas Secondary School, BC

Unforgettable Past

I look at this flag and remember long ago,
How many lives were taken from the country.
I might be young, but I definitely know,
That men and women have suffered greatly,
To win the great battle,
That many have now forgotten.

Tears were shed and hearts were broken,
But all that didn't stop them from fighting,
Many must have prayed for victory so they could return home,
To their wives and children.
But some couldn't even see the rising of the sun for the very last time,
But the tears from their very own eyes at the thought of their family home all alone.

We know God heard the cries of many,
For he gave us the victory,
That many didn't believe would come and that many didn't live to see.
But God knew the ones that had died had done their duty,
And would be rewarded greatly.
And would never have to go through the pain that was caused.

Many tears are still shed today,
And broken hearts that can't be mended.
But remember let us not put it last… our Unforgettable Past.
Rachelle Wollman, Grade 8
Twilight Colony School, MB

My Heart

I think of you at night, while everyone's asleep.
I wonder if you really care, or are your feelings weak.

I never really could tell, and to this day I still believe,
That one day love will heal us, not you and me…but we.

We argue constantly, and when I finally think you're gone,
Once again you find some way, to make my hating you seem wrong.

The way you used to look at me, as I stood so far away,
But when I said I hated it, you really made my day.

I now know that when it comes to you, all my games are played,
Because I have no choice but realness. my lying pushed you away.

If you only knew, what it does to hear your voice.
My heart trembles at your appearance, and love is my only choice.

If loving you is wrong, I will never be right,
And I won't give up my heart, without pushing for a fight.

I hate to say this now, but you got me on my knees,
Praying for that special day…that you will fall in love with me
Brie McAuley, Grade 7
Huttonville School, ON

Somebody for You…

M agnificent, kind, smiling
A nd always sincere
R eliable, confident
I know how to keep secrets and I'm
A lways there for you

C an you choose me as a friend?
O r are you missing on something special
T ime for me to tell you my last request
E very day I want to be with you!

Maria Cote, Grade 8
Collège Jésus-Marie de Sillery, QC

The Party Hat

I was alone in my room, other than my dog, and I was upset.
He looked upset, too.
His eyes were droopy, and his ears hung low.
Sometimes, to cheer up, I dressed up.
Dresses and party hats.
So I tried it on Angus.
I got a dress with a blue and white checkered pattern,
and a party hat that was purple with coloured polka dots.
He barely struggled as I put the dress on him.
The hat got stuck in his floppy ears.
When I took the dress off,
we took a picture.
Whenever I see party hats in the store,
I think of them getting stuck
in Angus' floppy ears
all over again.

Emily Cameron, Grade 8
Nationview Public School, ON

Celebrate the Earth

Beginning with speak, stones shall listen.
Rivers run to greet and stars are lit in the eve.
All of everything, break out in celebration.
Singing commence, bring stars from the sky.
Rocks well with tears at a sad tune
and trees sway with an upbeat tempo.
Birds carry voices to heavens and above,
taking with them tales and songs.
To far corners the voices ring.
None can escape the melody and rhythm.
Everyone!
Rise in song and join.
Begin to dance whilst many hearts pound the beats.
Dance and sing round the stage.
Water slaps applause keeping in time.
Together sweep across the stage.
Fly and tangle and twirl all about.
Spin and turn, whisper and churn.
Wind soars spinning around, skipping around.
World dance along keeping time with the song.

Katie Uniacke, Grade 9
Bell High School, ON

Fall

Leaves are falling, soft as snowflakes
A spectrum of colors: gold, red and brown
Hissing and crackling underneath our feet
A colorful carpet on the ground.

Squirrels are harvesting; the birds fly south
Summer's warmth no more; winter's chill slowly stepping in.
The man in the moon watches in astonishment.
He knows autumn is here; the loveliest season of the year.

Sandra Konji, Grade 8
St Peter Catholic High School, ON

Rain

I hear the rain,
Seeming to wash away all my pain
Washing away my frustration,
I have found new motivation
I feel the rain
Washing away all my pain
Thunder booms behind me
I just want to be free
I race the wind
I don't want this feeling to end
Lightning flashes,
Thunder crashes
My spirits are lifted
My problems have drifted
I collapse to the ground
The rain is all around.

Acacia Grunsell, Grade 9
Peace Academy of Virtual Education, AB

My Excuse

I woke up this morning feeling brilliant.
I had finished my homework in an instant.
So I played games, on the computer and outside too,
All the way until my curfew.
But you see, there was just one tiny thing,
One very important tiny something.
I had an assignment due that day,
That I had forgotten to portray.
So I went to school not knowing what to do,
I was trying to think of something to argue.
An excuse! An excuse! That was it!
It didn't take me long to think up a plan,
I would say that my postman,
Came in my house, grabbed my assignment and ran.
That excuse didn't quite fool my teacher,
She sent me to the office of Ms. Principal Archer.
She gave me a detention
And scolded me for my bad action.
I learned my lesson and that was it,
The end of my excuses I admit.

Alexandra Landry, Grade 7
The Study School, QC

Soccer

S o much fun.
O vertime is too hard.
C ome over and practice.
C an you play soccer at the park with us.
E njoy yourself when you play.
R emember do not break the rules.

Gabriel Bérubé, Grade 7
Macdonald High School, QC

The Flower in the Rain

The flower needs water
to be able to grow
but not too much
because she can die
The flower is delicate,
sweet and shiny.

The flower needs beams of the sun
to be able to release its beauty
But when the sun hides
the rain comes there
and can affect the flower.

But the flower
thanks to its big strengths
was able to survive
against the rain.
This flower bud grew
and became a beautiful flower
filled with happiness.

Daniela Coca-Morales, Grade 9
Ecole Secondaire Jean Grou, QC

Sport

Life is like sports
You put on your gear
Step out on the playing field
You play
Maybe score a few and get scored on
But when the buzzer sounds
Win or lose
The game is over.

Brendan Doucet, Grade 8
MacKenzie Secondary School, BC

Global Warming

G reen house gases
L ess snow
O zone layer
B ad weather
A ll over the world
L arger storms

WARMING

Richard Lester, Grade 8
MacKenzie Secondary School, BC

It Speaks

The blue waves roar and
the hot sand speaks — now night and
not a sound is heard

Dylan Bridges, Grade 7
Chedoke Middle School, ON

Perfection

What is perfection?
But only a reflection
Smallest thighs
Bluest eyes
Puckered lips
Swaggering hips
Best of the best
Forget about the rest
Makeup hides
What's really inside
Surgery knives
Risking lives
Bleach her hair
And ruin what's there
Losing weight
Feeling faint
Not genuine
It's all a lie
What is perfection?
Well it's not my selection

Michelle Krahn, Grade 8
Alexander Forbes School, AB

The Broken Heart

My heart is broken
Broken in small pieces
Why did you break my heat
My heart is passioned for you

You are my sunshine
You keep me holding on
Because without you
I'm nothing

I want to be loved by you
Only you

Esther Schembre, Grade 9
Ecole Secondaire Jean Grou, QC

Audrey

A greeable
U nique
D aring
R esponsible
E nergetic
Y oung adult

Audrey Gagnon-Timchuck, Grade 8
Collège Jésus-Marie de Sillery, QC

When Petals Cry

The petals are crying,
they droop, colour fades
Unwanted, unwanted,
The conformity has pushed it to its limit,
Let it wait for the first drop of hope

The dew is dripping
glistens; shines
it cares, deeply cares,
the liquid is healing the withered,
the first drop of hope

The thorns were sharp,
but now are dull,
It wants to be different desperately,
hope is currently accompanied by joy

The flower's beauty startles the weak,
it's bright and smiles,
loved more by one, loved more by one,
the beauty longs to be shared,
shared throughout the hopeless.

Jillian Tranquilla, Grade 9
Menno Simons Christian School, AB

Every Three Months

Born in Red Deer,
That was okay
Moved to Edmonton
I thought I would burst.
Moved to Quesnel
My face went gloomier
Three months
Then to Prince George
And now I hate her.
Three months have passed
We move again,
Mackenzie's the town
We stay in for now.

Justice Ferguson, Grade 8
MacKenzie Secondary School, BC

Hide from Everything

Warm and making us cheerful
what's more wonderful than the sun

Strong and imposing
only one thing can put it aside

making us down and sad
what's more depressive than the clouds

just like humans
nobody can hide from everything

Liliane Vanier, Grade 9
Ecole Secondaire Jean Grou, QC

The Twister

The twister. Howling winds, swirling, twisting,
and spinning. Terror. The scream increases as
the storm comes closer. A wild roar begins,
as the eye of the storm passes overhead.
Wind rips shingles from rooftops, the
siding from houses, and cars from
driveways. Trailers fly through
the air, buildings are crushed,
like matchboxes underfoot.
Then, silence. People
tentatively emerge
from the ruins,
to survey the
damage.
Shock
sets
in.

Jonathan Hallett, Grade 9
St George's School, BC

Remembrance Day

War is sad
War is blood shed and pain
War is death and destruction
War is a fight over land or freedom.

Hear the cries of sons, brother and fathers
War brings famine, death and sadness
That's why we should remember those who risked their lives
For our freedom today.

Gage Teer, Grade 7
Bayview Elementary School, BC

Sunsets in Summer

I sit here watching,
as the sun slowly sinks behind the clouds.
The deep oranges and purples dance in the sky.
As if they are dancing to music.
A fiesta miles above.
When it's over,
the day's heat slowly escapes.
After abandoning me,
leaving me wondering,
will it ever come back?
Or is it lost forever?
It returns at dawn,
the great ball of fire floating in the sky.
The whole earth has simply come alive again.
I dream of one day,
I will sit in this exact spot
with my children,
to share with them,
the Earth's natural beauty.

Taylor Ace, Grade 8
Nationview Public School, ON

Halloween Night

I see many things this Halloween
I see friends trick-or-treating with candy to eat.
I see witches and ghosts, dim in the light
I see many things this Halloween night.

I hear many things this Halloween
I hear bats and black cats, and I'm ready to scream.
I hear Frankenstein, Dracula, ready to bite
I hear many things this Halloween night.

I really love this Halloween
Though it's dark and nothing can be seen.
Even though some things give me a fright
I really love this Halloween night.

Georgia Takacsy, Grade 7
The Study School, QC

The Hunt

His eyes fixed,
His ears twitched,
He moved in a crouch,
Slow and low,
His tail flicked,

His eyes moved,
Muscles tensed,
The mouse was there by the fence,

Ears flattened as he pounced,
The mouse squealed and,
Ran round and round,
He landed perfectly on the mouse,
feeling proud he headed back to his cathouse.

Megan Dumas, Grade 8
Kootenay Discovery School, BC

Remembrance Day

As the great soldiers fought with pride and might,
Trying to ignore their hunger and pain.
Through the endless days and the sleepless nights,
Making their beds on the cold rough terrain.

The soldiers are strangers to those in need,
Their uniforms speak loudly for great hope.
With every death comes a woeful plead,
With every fight it takes more to cope.

This is why there is a Remembrance Day,
So the soldiers will not be forgotten.
The ultimate cost for freedom they pay,
With the lives lost of brave women and men.

Poppies are to thank those you'll never know,
Allowing a peace for others to grow.

Cameron Anderson, Grade 7
100 Mile House Elementary School, BC

What Is a Friend?

Someone who is loyal
They're there when you need them
Fun to be with
Helpful in the time of need
Stand up for you
Get help when you're hurt
Someone to go fishing with
A good listener
Someone to talk to
Someone to just hang out with
That is a friend

Matt Bancroft, Grade 7
Milverton Public School, ON

Death

Death is everywhere
in the ground
and in the sky
it can be found
underwater
or on land
it comes and goes
you try to run
and have some fun
but it doesn't work
he comes around
anyway

Tyler Boyle, Grade 8
MacKenzie Secondary School, BC

Weather Outside

Freezing cold wind
Whistles through the air
Frost covers the hills
Whiteness conceals the Earth
Pristine soft fluffy flakes
Fall from the gray
and misty sky
To land on the white hard ground
forming a white blanket

The fresh winter scene
Fills the cold air outside
As the wind sways the
covered white trees back and forth
Temperature continuously dropping
Let it snow! Let it snow!

Debbie Kleinsasser, Grade 7
Milford Colony School, AB

Summer Fishing

Icy, cold, dark water
Nice, soft breeze of the fresh air
Down the river, summer fishing

Mitchell Boertien, Grade 7
Milverton Public School, ON

Loving a Horse

Horses can be free and wild,
But something holds them back, it is love, and it makes them mild.

A bond with a horse,
Is a beautiful thing,
It is an awesome force.

Loving a horse is heartwarming,
If that horse loves you back,
You'll feel as if you want to sing.

Stephanie Melsted, Grade 7
Riverton Early Middle Years School, MB

Never Forgot

Music fills the house as tears fill her eyes.
She can't take many more of all these good byes.
Broken promises millions of lies.
A kiss on the cheek and one final goodbye.
She's kept it together she stayed full of will.
But honey she's just fallin' even farther down that hill.
Her mother's abuse and her friends cruel words,
With no one to confide with no where to turn.
She wears her scars like the bruises on her ego.
She can't remember when it started it was so long ago.
Help her find her way give her someone to confide in too.
Can she rely on someone? Could she trust in you?
Years from now with a husband and kids.
They'll be playing outside and see what she hid.
The scars on her wrists the pain in her eyes,
They'll ask where it came from who caused it and why…
With no answer she'll simply brush them off.
With a broken heart for lying and remembering why she tried but never forgot…

Jolene Perron, Grade 8
St Bernard Separate School, ON

Do You Wonder?

Do you ever wonder when time will really cave in?
When the planets will align for the work you've done?
When you try so hard for something, but you become a beggar?
It's like your life is perfect, polished glass.
But the only reason you live is for it to shatter?
Do you ever see the stars, and think there is no hope?
But your heart replies by smiling, and falling in love with the seconds?
Its like you fall in love, and try everything to please that special person.
When they turn around and crush you, by saying they hate you.

Do you ever wonder if there is space to climb free, and live in a new sanctuary?
Where you can regain, and finally get what you deserve?
There is, and it is waiting for you.
Close your eyes….
Think with faith…
Trust God.

Do you ever wonder?

Josiah Sinanan, Grade 8
Heritage Christian Academy, AB

War

In the cold they lay sleeping, Night and Day
Poppies bloom before long closed eyes they look
Above, birds happily fly as they say.
"We are the dead who's lives raging war took.

Our families cry beside the new-made graves
Larks fly high above their heads, singing gay.
People remember us, the few, the Brave
Who fought for the freedoms they have today

The soldiers who lived would say we are blessed
to live here this day. They remember us
the ones who were killed and forever rest
Under some poppies and a great white cross

Remember, in the midst of everything
We are the ones, that lived, and died, to win."

Gideon Wipf, Grade 8
Milford Colony School, AB

Birthday

Year after year it comes back once again, ever so slowly,
Like the sand, trickling out of its hourglass
You want time to stop, to enjoy once again its pleasures and yet
Time moves forward, one day at a time.
You are changing, things are changing around you but
You have no control over them.
You are no longer a child, but an adult,
Yearning to go back to your childhood,
You are grown, struggling with life's dilemmas,
Trying to get through life's obstacles, one day at a time.
A happy occasion but ever so brutal,
Leaving us with the pain of time, not having enough of it
The possibility of not fulfilling it,
Aging every year,
A happy birthday does not seem possible anymore.

Vanessa Tammaro, Grade 8
Macdonald High School, QC

The Trouble with Boys

My hopes and dreams have shattered
My love was taken away

All because a boy broke my heart today
He messed with my heart

Then he threw it away, he caught my eye
But then he looked away

But he left me feeling
A feeling of rejection

I don't know what to do; I don't know what to say
Except a boy broke my heart today.

Kayla Fehr, Grade 8
La Crete Public School, AB

The Love in My Heart

Since I met him
I hope and dreamed
I trust this love
So I always dream
But hear me now
With my emotions uptight
and my little heart broken
Because all the words I say about my lover.
My lover who fills me with hatred
The person who succeeded
To catch my heart
And to give me
All the good moments of laughter…
Now makes me suffer
I hope one day to be happy…
Now all is deserted
My suffering will always be there
Because this person I love the most
Created this suffering

Jessica Larivière, Grade 9
Ecole Secondaire Jean Grou, QC

The Circle of Life

It doesn't matter how much you try
You will one day die
Even if you try to flee
Death is written in your destiny

Death will always be there
But you can live a wonderful life with people you care
You don't have to be afraid
Because if you have love
All you problems will fade

Life is tough but death is rough
Everything will one day end
Except family and friends
Unfortunately every life ends

Vinh Tran, Grade 9
Ecole Secondaire Jean Grou, QC

I Belong in This World

I belong in this world.
My life was born in this world
I really don't care if people tease me
or I don't care if they hit me
and I don't care for other people
who disrespect me.
I only care for the people who respect me
for I will always belong in this world.
People who respect other people
belong in this world
so I belong in this world.

Karen Machiskinic, Grade 8
Nawigizigweyas Education Centre, SK

Winter

Winter nights get oh so dark,
to see our way we light a spark.

Mom is paying off the bills,
while me and friends slide down big hills.

Santa comes with a HO! HO! HO!
while little children sip hot cocoa

Christmas trees we decorate,
And all our calendars are up to date.

The place we freeze is our fingers and toes,
and frostbite hits us on the nose

Now ladies and gentlemen I got to go,
But I shall finish with a pile of snow.

Krystal McCaughan Kleefeld, Grade 7
Macdonald High School, QC

The Dentist

Going to the dentist I always hate,
I don't know what they're sticking in my mouth.
I know that tooth decay would be my fate,
But I'd rather just take a trip down south.

I see all the tools he uses in there,
And they usually give me a fright.
I'm going tomorrow which is not fair,
I'll definitely be worried tonight.

But afterwards it does kind of feel good,
To get the dentist appointment all done.
But that numbing feeling bugs me; it should,
So I just complain to my Dad and Mom.

Really, That's it? Wow it went by so fast.
The dentist is only bad while it lasts.

Rachel Atkinson, Grade 7
Milverton Public School, ON

The River of Dreams

Gliding down the swift flowing river,
The splash of the water makes me quiver.
Down the river, as I gaze into the sky,
I think of the things that make me cry.
Leaves on the surrounding trees, dance to the ground,
There is nobody in sight to make a sound.
I float under the small, stone bridge,
Which takes me over the beautiful ridge.
Suddenly the rapids come into sight,
I wake up, and turn the boat with all of my might.
I sigh and sadly I realize that the river of dreams was over.

Rosalyn Desa, Grade 7
Immaculate Conception, BC

The Jewelry

On this beautiful day of sunshine,
the jewelry shines splendorous and
impressed all buyers.
After many years,
one day the beautiful jewelry was lost in the chest
cast away and in the dark.

Josiane Beaudoin, Grade 9
Ecole Secondaire Jean Grou, QC

What About?

In the beginning, everything was good
But what about the day when everything went wrong
This singing bird is in a happy mood
But that day changed when we didn't hear a song
Trapped in his branch the bird can't get out
"Every man for himself" the tree said so loud
He needs to grow, he can't stay
But he can't go, he has no way
He is screaming for help with all his breath
But what about him if people don't care
Maybe the baby bird thinking about death
Like this people's mind will be fair
This world may be real
Things may be free
But the best thing he could do, is dream
About the day when he will spread his wings
About that day when he will release
Bad side it's what they see
But what about me?

Alexandra Kouacou Boulom, Grade 9
Ecole Secondaire Jean Grou, QC

The True Colours of Autumn

I was a leaf, old, yet with such impeccable beauty,
crimson, sunshine on daisies.
Though I remember when I was fresh and first inhaled,
the sweet fragrant scent of the air around me,
and felt the morning sunshine hit me,
and wrap its arms around me,
as I embraced the feeling of life.
But the bitter cold swept through,
and rushed all around me while singing its sickly sweet song
reminding us of its imminence.
And that's when it happened,
I was swept away
and I flowed through the violent wind,
who took me wherever it desired.
Soon I was imprisoned, stuck on the hard ground
and got buried in layers of diamond white snow, and became
a part of everything.
I am now the earth, the very ground you walk on,
the lucky four-leaf clover you pick,
I am
everything.

Michelle Briere, Grade 8
St Peter Catholic High School, ON

Different Colors

The new girl, different girl,
heads off to school.
The crowd stares in awe as she walks past,
Some say things that are quite cruel.
She is hoping this day will be her last!

The teachers do not want her in their classes,
all except one teacher who made a difference.
She didn't care if her student was black,
and because of this her life was put at such expense.

This young girl no longer sat alone.
What was so different about her for others to despise?
She was finally able to walk home,
her face she hoped they would recognize!

This new girl, different girl,
may have stayed the same,
but it was history that would change,
all around the world!

Stephanie Squires, Grade 8
The Elms Junior and Middle School, ON

Morning Greeting

Beautiful golden sun rising at dawn
Glowing
Round and dazzling
Turning the sky bright orange
Providing light and warmth
Cheerfully greeting creation
Birds respond joyfully in melody
Plants respond by lifting their heads
People respond in happy chatter
All creation welcoming a new morn
Delighted!

William Kim, Grade 8
British Columbia Christian Academy, BC

Voice

I am something far greater than flesh and bone
I am stronger than the voice that stands alone
I wish to speak what was spoken before
I wish to hear what you never ignore
I only ponder when I am taught
I only know things that were already sought
I the voice who stands alone
I the people who listen in silence
Must stand together minds alike
Yet different, unique with no dislike
To teachings of power that thought provokes
Taught with no sense 'til you read the cheat sheet
Then sense returns to it's rightful place
In mind set which only this which is known

Vicki Trask, Grade 9
Westmount Charter School, AB

War and Peace

As soldiers cry silently, enemies
have no mercy, and keep on shooting them
the war would have gone on for centuries
but one side gave up, the war is now stemmed

The women cry for hours and hours
thinking of the lost sons and husbands they
have lost in the war, these men were no cowards
hope fighting may come to an end someday.

Parents cry, thinking of their families
that they lost to battle and will never
see or meet or talk with them anymore
families will always miss them and will cry their hearts out.

Always remember how brave they were and fought
there will be hope that we don't get caught.

Rebecca Hofer, Grade 7
Milford Colony School, AB

Our Canoe

I skim along in my canoe.
Floating, while not touching the water,
watching the beauty of the trees dancing on the water.
Between my parents,
laughing at the silly things my dad says.
We laugh as we almost tip the canoe.
Being here,
alone with them.
Makes me so happy,
no one can crush my happiness.
The ripples.
We watch as they surround us,
circling around.
While we get out,
we hear a loon call,
how beautiful.
Looking at the water,
I see the reflection of the sky.
Looking at the lake,
I will always remember,
beauty.

Nicole Hallam, Grade 8
Nationview Public School, ON

What He Had Expected

One day, I wrote a poem about a boat
My teacher told me it wasn't at my level
He blew up like a steaming kettle
This fact made me feel like I had no talent
Like a colourless painter's pallet
I wrote this poem hoping he would accept it
Hoping it would be what he had expected
I ask you now, is this at my level?

Victoria Clifford, Grade 7
École Notre-Dame-des-Vertus, SK

Life

To start life, you have to live life,
To live life, you have learn life,
To learn life, you have to believe in life,
To believe in life, you have to love life,
To love life, you need an open mind.

Simone Hunt, Grade 8
Laurelwood Public School, ON

Mr. Know-It-All

This boy was truly a know-it-all,
He thought he was the best,
He won every spelling bee,
And got an A on every test.

This boy was really a teacher's pet,
He had no other friend,
He sat down at lunch and ate alone,
With nothing to regret.

One day the boy received his test,
He was expecting his weekly A,
But suddenly, anxiety gripped him,
Something was underway.

The boy had never got an F before,
He had not received his A,
He said he studied really hard,
So what was there more to say?

The boy was no longer a know-it-all,
He was no longer the best,
He didn't win every spelling bee,
And didn't get an A on every test.

Christina Tammaro, Grade 8
Macdonald High School, QC

Christmas Time

The snow is snowing.
Christmas is near,
Everyone is shopping far and near.
Jack Frost is frosting up the land.
Frosty is chilling.
The trees are glistening.
The houses are shining bright.
The holly is jolly.
Churches are filling.
Carols are singing.
The children are playing.
People are skating.
Time is singing.
Bells are ringing.
Rudolph is leading
Santa with goodies.
For the good girls and boys

April Crevier, Grade 7
Macdonald High School, QC

Without You

Thinking, wondering, trying to figure it out.
Making mistakes, isn't that what life's all about.
Making you happy, that's what I'm trying to do.
Suffering the pain, that's how I'll get through to you.

Knowing life is nothing *without* you,
knowing that I'll never be with you.
Trying to carry on without you.
But I'll never know unless you take me through,
I just want you to know that I'm nothing without you.

L.O.V.E., that's the definition of you and me.
You're trying to make us history but I think we are meant to be.
I think people are able to see,
see why me and you need to be.
But all you want to make us is history,
that's what you think of you and me.

I try to face it all but I'm not strong enough, strong enough without you.
I can't do what everyone says,
I'm not the guy you think I am.
Without you,
this isn't true and I can't go on with my life knowing that we can't continue!

Elias Abou-Assaly, Grade 8
St Peter Catholic High School, ON

Edward Brave

'Tis time again, when moon is full and evil fills the night
When deathly screams could pierce the air and make you pray for light
And as you pass the misty yard where corpses rot in graves
Your mind may wander off to thoughts of long lost Edward Brave

For Edward Brave was once a man who stole from buried dead
And it was neither man nor beast that Edward Brave did dread
The only thing that Edward feared, though no one had he told
The only thing that Edward feared were those from whom he stole

They came to him inside his head as Edward slept at night
They asked him for the things he took, but he refused their plight
And as the corpses in his dreams were not repaid their debts
With Edward they grew angry, and turned requests to threats

Then one night, when the moon was full, and Edward went to bed
The corpses came to him once more, but not inside his head
They visited his house at dusk, risen from the grave
They took the things he stole from them, and then took Edward Brave

And at that time, when moon is full and evil fills the night
When deathly screams do pierce the air and make you pray for light
And when you pass the misty yard where corpses rot in graves
Remember what those corpses did to long lost Edward Brave

Danny Hamilton, Grade 9
Bradford District High School, ON

I See You Through My Blind Eyes

I see you…
the memory from since the moment we have met,
all of it, has just flashed in front of my eyes.
To see, it is such an ironic word for me to use.
But you, you are the one who has turned the darkness
in my lonely world to a bright sky.
Everything we have gone through, I can feel;
your voice, your laughter, I can hear;
and I can see.
Your face and your everything are vividly imprinted in my mind.
I see you…

Moonlight Miracle, Grade 8
J N Burnett Secondary School, BC

Chicks with Sticks

Ringette, a game just for girls
But we're more like pretty young pearls
A game played with wooden sticks
On the ice, we look so slick.

We grab onto that round blue ring
While we twirl and swirl and swing
Speed skating like a carnivore
So we can shoot with strength and score.

Whether we win or whether we lose
We will never get the give-up blues
With all our teamwork and persistence
This should lead us to excellence.

Catch the spirit and play ringette
The fun of it, you'll never forget
You'll laugh, you'll skate, you'll get your kicks
This amazing game of chicks with sticks.

Amanda Kost, Grade 7
The Study School, QC

One Last Kiss

I sit, here, on this hard and dusty floor
I look back and front, and then I look no more.
I lie, here, in a broken shatter
Don't bother; I don't matter.
I crouch, here, over my dead body
And hold my hand, its soaked and bloody.
I kneel, here, and pray just one more time
This life, it is no longer mine.
I let go, here, to something I don't want to hold
I never listened, to what I had been told.
I cry, here, because I've lost it all
My hand slips, and I just let it fall.
I stand, here, and slowly turn away
Oh well, I shan't live another day.
I walk, away, into a dark abyss
I turn to you, I blow you one last kiss.

Shelby Verspeek, Grade 9
Portage Collegiate Institute, MB

When I Need You

Snow covered trees surround me
The frozen river stands still
Looking up, I see majestic mountains
And clear skies above

I can see my breath in front of me
And rub my cold hands to keep warm
Not bothering to wipe the tears on my face
I crumple to a heap on the soft snow

Why have you abandoned me?
Especially when I needed you most!
When things are as hopeless as can be
And everyone else has left me

As if in return, the skies open up
And send soft, fluffy snow down on me
With renewed strength, and a comforting voice
I stand up and continue my trek

Pausing here and there to catch my breath
My eyes are opened to the beauty surrounding me
Through the hardships ahead, good times and bad
I know you'll be along side to help me

Christina Lukianiuk, Grade 8
British Columbia Christian Academy, BC

Words of Wisdom

Rappers sometimes say words of truth
Gang violence, street crimes and talk of us youth
Public speakers are addressing that we must care
About those who speak nothing but insults and swears

Our deepest fear is that this is us
All bubbled up with hatred and punching fists
Truth is what we fear and denial is what we seek
Telling fibs about others, when we're the weak

Then there's knowledge from the wise
And courage from the brave
Listening to their thoughts
When words of wisdom are what we crave

Just to be able to cough up the right
Instead of spitting out the wrong
Who's going to tell us what's to be done
When they are struggling and are on the run

For the best; or somewhat near
Is the direction, in which they steer
May unload a dark path
Though in the end they'll pass that wrath

Abbas Abbas, Grade 8
John English Junior and Middle School, ON

Remember

"Remember the good times" that was the last thing he said to her, then he was gone. From then on she was thinking about what he had meant, was it remember the times we laughed, the times we cried, the times we shared our secrets that no one else knew or did he mean the times we wished the moments would never end. All of a sudden she knew what he meant, she ran as fast as she could, back to the place where he stood and whispered, "I remembered the good times, and it was just too hard to let you go."

Megan Holden, Grade 7
Milverton Public School, ON

The Fairy

A faint little tapping noise, like small fingers upon a windowpane,
Is heard by a cricket awakening from a long slumber.
A tiny fairy scampers across the wet grass, freshly kissed by the morning dew.
She laughs a light and beautiful laugh
As the tall blades of grass tickle her bare feet.
This creature, so minuscule and delicate makes her way towards the pond with care.
Her hair, like silk is long and golden,
Dainty feet and dainty hands,
A crown and dress made from the petals of a buttercup she has.
As sweet as honey and as good as gold,
She is Princess Buttercup, the most beautiful creature you ever will encounter.
She turns her tiny head, not aware of being observed,
And spreads her lovely yellow wings.
She flies to the edge of the water and splashes her rosy face with cool water.
Then once again she spreads her wonderful fairy wings,
Then vanishes out of sight for a moment.
And reappears and perches herself upon the highest branch of a great oak tree.
She admires her vast and beautiful kingdom,
Tilts her lovely head and wonders, who could be more content?
To break the silence of the peaceful moment and in response to her query,
The entire forest awakes: The birds sing a happy tune and the sun rises before her eyes.

Samantha Backman, Grade 7
The Study School, QC

In the Absence of Humanity

Cloaked under the shadows of early dawn, I forget the faces of who will soon be gone,
I and I'm regretting now, the choice I've made, I've killed much more than I have saved.

I see ghosts of people with dissipated minds, dangerously balanced on the thinnest of lines,
I'm watching stars being shot from the sky, and bombs counting down the last minute in time.

I hear nothing but blood pounding in my ears, a silent world that drowned in tears,
My mind's askew and my gun is loaded, as I catalogue the hearts that have exploded.

I taste the blood of those I've killed, whispered screams, and mortar spilled,
Crying for those who shot me first, I'm surprised to find how much guilt can hurt.

In the absence of humanity, the world splits at its seams, smothering peace under the grave of our dreams,
There's too much smoke, its getting hard to see, nobody cries for the casualties of peace.

I cross my heart and hold my breath, fear burns much colder than my death,
People are killed, still bowed in prayer, pleading for hope that isn't there.

The fire tears through and the world seems to stop, shocked expressions on bodies that drop,
The flame subsides, only irony burns, I'm writing to you from a world that never learns.

Emma Armstrong, Grade 7
Jack Miner Public School, ON

Having a Heart Is:
Knowing how to respect others
Thinking about other people and not only yourself

Having a heart is also
being able to help the people around you

Having a good heart is knowing how to forgive

Even with our highs and our lows
our frustration and our problems

We should be able to make it through all of it
But mostly, a heart should be able to love without hesitating

And having a bad heart can come back
to get us in the end
Nadia Sabir, Grade 9
Ecole Secondaire Jean Grou, QC

Amour
Love is like a flower,
It blossoms into something beautiful over time.
Real love has real valor,
And it will last for a lifetime.

Friendship is often the history before love,
Expressed in many ways.
As well it is a dove,
The magic in a daze.

Devotion is the glue,
That always brings the bond closer.
It has the strength to break through,
To make everything better.

If this is the contents of love,
Then love is truly the most extraordinary thing.
With it you can rise above,
All that is fading.

Chloé Anassis, Grade 7
The Study School, QC

Space
Space is vast and full of nothingness
Space is large and humungous,
It has lots of stars and planets,
Galaxies and asteroids made of granite,
Astronauts go to the moon,
And plan to go to mars in 2022,
Mercury, Venus, Earth, Mars,
Jupiter, Saturn, Uranus, Neptune and Pluto,
Are planets they'll go to tomorrow.
Allan Huot, Grade 8
Macdonald High School, QC

To the End...
A true friend,
Will be here to the end.

Even thought you may fight,
Everything will be all right.

When you experience great sorrow,
Because of her it will be better tomorrow.

When she is blue,
You help her through.

You both hang on,
Even when you don't get along.

And when you are lost in the night,
Together you find the light.

This is a true friend,
And she will be here to the end.
Emily Starczala, Grade 9
St Benedict Catholic Secondary School, ON

Life's Blossoms
They bloom as in spring and make life so colorful,
They make your heart sing,
There is always a place in your heart for a flower

For a flower is like a child
The child grows into someone who makes a difference
A flower blooms into something beautiful
They both affect the world greatly

A flower brings peace and colors into the world
A child brings excitement and love
Every flower has a unique pattern
And every child has a personality all its own

Each petal has a different pattern
And each face has a special glow
Each flower has a particular place in life
Each child has a different destiny
And each can be what they were meant to be
Beautiful
Kayla Smith, Grade 9
FE Madill Secondary School, ON

Life Is...
Life is...
Something you should spend happily,
A thing that can be taken away at anytime,
An adventure
Something that no one can change,
Sometimes unfair.
Amna Fatima, Grade 8
North Kipling Junior and Middle School, ON

We Could

We open our eyes
But nothing's in sight,
We try to make peace
But only put up a fight.
We try to give
But only take away,
We try to speak
But have nothing to say.
We try to feel happy
But only feel rage,
We try to set free
But only to cage.
We try to understand
But nothing's understood,
We try so hard
But if we try harder, we could.

Vanessa Mignelli, Grade 8
Blessed Trinity Catholic School, ON

Fear

Fear is a wall,
there's no way around,
it's too high to climb.
The wall goes on forever.
However,
there is a door,
but it's locked.
Facing your fear is the key.
If you don't face,
your fear,
it will corner you,
forever.
When you get through,
the wall,
it disappears until,
a new fear develops.

Heather Veitch, Grade 7
William G Davis Public School, ON

My Mysterious Lover

When I see you
I can't go towards you
I want to tell you
I love you

When I meet you
I can't talk with you
I don't know if I can tell you
I love you

When I talk with you
I can't look at you
Now I'll tell you
I love you

Andréa Turbide, Grade 8
Collège Jésus-Marie de Sillery, QC

Do You Really Understand?

Everybody has a loved one that passes away
Helpless we are to know
But do you understand?
People say, "I'm sorry to hear that."
They give you a hug and then get back to their regular schedule.
But do they really understand?
Do they know how we feel?
Drowning, heart broken, sometimes very insecure.
We know that there's no one on this earth that can ever replace them.
All we need is a very comforting atmosphere.
All we have to hang on to is memories.
But the question is
Do you really understand?

Jolise Pornan-Roe, Grade 8
Menno Simons Christian School, AB

Fall

There was a cold brisk wind outside,
I looked down and saw everyone falling down.
Soon I was with everyone else.
Then the wind blew me onto the path.
The people walking their dogs kept trampling on top of me.
After a month or so, I looked up and saw the first snowflake of winter,
falling down towards me.

Bradley Murphy, Grade 8
St Peter Catholic High School, ON

I Miss You

when I sit alone in my room, for some reason I think of you.
I see your face just like you were here, then I burst into tears.
Then I go to give you a hug and kiss before you disappear into the light of mist…
In my dreams it's the same thing you turn around and just ignore me,
If I had just one wish, I would wish to give my Grande-pa one last kiss…

Kayla Fleury, Grade 8
Pontiac Public High School, QC

Floating Along the River Bed

The beautiful river is calm with clear skies
With forests' roots reaching into the calm river, blowing in the wind
Green mountains in the distance, reaching as far as the eye can see
Reaching far beyond the horizon, and high above the clouds
Dawn is awakening, with birds in the sky, the trees, the water
Chirping and singing their praises to mother nature, with high spirits
Natives float along the river bed, praising nature, embracing nature
Listening to the earth speak to them, listening to the voice of the wind
Men strengthen their sails as the wind goes against them, along the river bed
Commander holds his sword to the sky, men wait for his command
Passing by mountain, forest, nature, ignoring the beauty and river passing by
Not alone on the river bed, skies above, water below, spirits of the water
Along the river, all eyes on them, looking, examining
Natives float along the river bed, not noticing the English men
They look along the horizon, stare across the mountains
Looking into the heart of the forest
Floating along the river bed

Chelsea Forster, Grade 8
British Columbia Christian Academy, BC

If Only I Had Listened

I had a childhood friend, who had to move away,
We'd make each other laugh and I wished that she could stay
The years went by fast, then she called me one day,
To say we should meet, she was just a mile away.

We met at a bar, "Have a few drinks" I said,
But she simply refused and bought a soda instead.
We must have been there for hours and as I chugged away,
She said that I should stop and we really shouldn't stay.

But I merely ignored her and bought another glass,
And kept drinking away, like a car being filled with gas.
When I felt we should go, she said she should drive,
But I stubbornly insisted because I felt so alive.

Not aware of her fear, I jammed my foot on the throttle,
With one hand on the wheel and the other holding a bottle.
But then there was a crash and I was lying on the ground,
I felt the pain of surgery, but there was a new pain that I found.

The surgeon then apologized and said my friend had died,
I only wished that I'd agreed to let her give me a ride.
So I visit her grave, feeling heartbroken and regretful,
She'd still be alive today, had I driven sober and careful.

Samantha Deeley, Grade 7
Macdonald High School, QC

A Garden of Hopes

Her tears are the rose's rain,
We do not see this long lost child.
Her rose grows in a garden,
All thorny and wild.

The way out is concealed by emerald green vines.
She sits waiting lonely and silent.
Hidden behind the wall of lies,
Waiting hopeful and tolerant.

The sun dries the flood of tears,
Saves the rose from death's grasp.
While the wind blows away her fears,
Trying to forget a horrible past.

Dreaming of a safe home to keep,
Waiting patiently she falls asleep.

Marissa Majek, Grade 8
Victoria School of Performing and Visual Arts, AB

The Leaf

Attached to a tree
I sway in the wind
waiting for something to happen
along comes a breeze and carries me away
to the place that I have forgotten

Alexis Smart, Grade 9
F E Osborne School, AB

Crystallized Music Box

The warmth has long since faded,
The optimism frozen,
The loving pulse stopped.
A cracking heart in a crystallized music box.
It lies within a castle of ice,
Silently calling out to the world it knows is beyond the walls,
But no one can breach the doors…

My only comfort is the slowly disappearing lullaby of memories.

Christina Black, Grade 9
Henry G Izatt Middle School, MB

Grizzly Bear

He turns his head to see a camera.
Glancing at him the grizzly runs.
Fear and anger tear through his mind.
He runs.
There is no place to hide him.
He can hear voices yelling.
He rips through a small village and doesn't notice.
Soon, he is chased,
His claws scraping against the raw earth.
No one can stop him.
Ropes grip him.
Guns are shot.
Now there is not grizzly in a cage,
Only bodies from a hopeless fight.

Caitlyn Jerome, Grade 9
FE Madill Secondary School, ON

Nature

The sun breathes but a whisper of light through the trees
It is fall, standing in my grandfather's maple bush
I stare at the magical world of colours and smells
There are ashes at my feet
His, my grandfather's
He is part of nature again
Has he always been?
Am I not now?
Alive I lay in the grass
It enfolds my body
Mother Earth wanting to protect me
Above, clouds like fluffy cotton balls
Dance in the breeze that tickles my face
Here, I cry gently, lazily
I feel Nature, Nature is God
God is Nature
I am Nature, I am God
The cycle of Nature continues
Grandfather rest well
You are with God as you have always been
In this part of paradise, your maple bush

Abram Mazal, Grade 8
École secondaire Macdonald-Cartier, ON

A Hole in One
Hit it off the tee
It is soaring through the air
Plop, it's in the hole.
Jennifer Gibbs, Grade 8
MacKenzie Secondary School, BC

Katie
She is wind,
Flying free and wild.
She is a wild fire,
Tearing up the pasture.
She is silk,
Soft on my fingers.
She is a friend,
Listening when no one else will.
She is a puppy,
Spirited and full of spunk.
She is lightning,
Striking with hoof here and tooth there.
She is a gentle nudge
When we walk around the pasture.
Stephanie Clemmer, Grade 7
Milverton Public School, ON

Skateboarding
When you skateboard
You slide the rail.
This is called a grind.
There are lots of grinds.

There are names for grinds
Like 50-50, 5-0, board slide,
Nose slide, tail slide too.
Also nose blunt, nose grind

A feeble, smith grind, dark slide,
Is a board slide but on the grip tape.
And there are way more.

I like to skateboard
But I don't know how to grind.
Devin Douglas Zagozewski, Grade 7
Riverton Early Middle Years School, MB

Marianne
M ellow
A musing
R adiant
I ntelligent
A greeable
N atural
N ice
E nergetic
Marianne Croteau, Grade 8
Collège Jésus-Marie de Sillery, QC

I Am a Redneck
I am the feather to a bird.
I am the hunters to Canada.
I am the hoof to a horse.
I am Homer to the Simpsons.
I am the snow to Alaska.
I am the fur to a fox.
I am a potato to the couch.
I am the banana to a split.
I am the stink to garbage.
I am the red in fire.
I am the blue to the sky.
I am boxes to bums.
I am dirt to the road.
I am color to paint.
I am blood to the body.
I am the "A" in awesome.
I am the nails in houses.
I am the road to cars.
I am a zipper to a sleeping bag.
I am a redneck, and I am necessary!
Chet Paslawski, Grade 9
33 Central, SK

Thanksgiving
Thanksgiving is,
a day to thank God for the harvest,
To talk with our family,
to catch up on what we've missed,
An occasion,
to be helpful to people who can't afford
to celebrate this special day.
Meagan Leduc, Grade 8
St Peter Catholic High School, ON

Up in the Sky
Up in the sky
The dove thought that she wasn't so high
So she started to fly
all the way up in the sky.

She felt so shy
because of the wind,
who was so, so high.

The dove started to cry,
the wind started to get so powerful
that the dove got weak
all the way up in the sky.

But the dove started to think
if I believe in myself I'll become stronger
and I will fly so high
that I will be higher than the wind
up in the sky.
Vanessa Olan Carpio, Grade 9
Ecole Secondaire Jean Grou, QC

We Are One
Out in the pasture
Through the gate
Standing in the stirrups
Cantering back home
Just me and Duster
We are one
One object, moving with each other
Leaving our troubles behind
Passing Andy and Crystal
Leaving them behind
Feeling the wind in our hair
Hearing only our heartbeats
Echoing in our ears
A race against time it seems
As we canter on
Cantering on home
We are one
One object
Moving with each other
Leaving our troubles behind
We are one.
Sini Bales, Grade 8
School of Hope, AB

Moms
Moms love to do,
What they think is best for you.
They always love you with all their heart,
Even when you're far apart.
Desiree Watson, Grade 7
Milverton Public School, ON

In My Head
So dim and yet so clear
So far and yet so near
So low and yet so high
I could almost touch the sky

So dark and yet so light
So day and yet so night
So nice and yet so not
So cold and yet so hot

So joyful and yet so depressed
So naked and yet so dressed
So bitter and yet so sweet
So messy and yet so neat

So black and yet so white
So heavy and yet so light
So alive and yet so dead…

Is this all just in my head?
Miranda Heathers, Grade 7
Milverton Public School, ON

Imaginary Place

She sits quietly in a small room
Staring at the blank wall
All alone with nobody left to save her
Hidden away from the rest of the world
Trying not to cry
She looks at her battered sneakers
She's tired and hungry
And inside she feels dead
Her spirit still lives yet it is going to break soon,

Okay, so that's not really true
She's actually sitting in a huge room
Staring at the stain glass windows
More alone then she has ever been
Her world is hidden away from her
Trying not to cry
She looks at her polished black dress shoes
She's sad and lonely
And she knows her mother isn't only dead on the inside
Her spirit has already broken
Followed by her fragile heart.

Somerdaye Duncan, Grade 7
Bayview Public School, ON

Christmas Time

The leaves are gone
The trees are bare
Snow has arrived here and there
Time for giving time for taking
And always remember the celebrating
So get together with your family and friends
To make many memories before it ends
Make the most of it while it lasts
And never forget about the past

Sabrina Lazier, Grade 8
Macdonald High School, QC

Winter

Winter is a lot of fun,
You get to jump, build things and run.
We can drink hot chocolate,
That is extremely great.

You can put in some marshmallows
We can share with friends and fellows.
After snowball fights and other snow things,
In the snow we make lots of rings.

It may be cold or even freezing,
But only the taggers are wheezing.
It is a wonderful time of year,
After I play I look in the mirror.

Brooke Henry, Grade 7
Riverton Early Middle Years School, MB

The Time

It is sad to think
Of all the things I could have learned or done
But time passed by me
And I grew up too quickly

It is sad to leave the past
But time does not give me a choice
Time is not that fair
Time is the one that separates us

I am sad to know
That maybe I will not have as much time as I need
That time flies
And still it goes

Morgane Bazinet, Grade 8
Collège Jésus-Marie de Sillery, QC

Autumn Memories

When the birds fly way down south,
When the wind rustles through the uniquely colored leaves,
Autumn is here.
When you feel the gusts of wind blowing through your hair,
When it's time to pull out those warm winter jackets,
Autumn is here.
When the forests look like paintings,
When long mountain hikes are almost essential,
You know autumn is here.
Apple picking in apple orchards,
Pumpkin carving for that special Halloween night,
That is autumn spirit.
When nothing cheers you up more than sitting by a toasty fire,
When using socks and slippers too,
that of course is autumn love.
For now is the time for pies and jams,
Now is the time for giving thanks,
…Now is the time for autumn.
Savor these precious moments,
Because autumn is,
And always will be, a season of joy.

Emma Durham, Grade 7
The Study School, QC

Hope Upon a Star*

Tonight I wish upon a star,
For Madeleine McCann, wherever you are.
I hope that, Madeleine, you know,
Our hearts are with you, wherever you go.
And your family is dearly missing you,
Tonight they'll be hoping and praying for you too.
We are all anxious, but we won't lose hope,
So no matter how hard it is to cope,
Don't worry, don't be sad,
You'll soon be back with your mom and your dad.

Rachel Bromberg, Grade 7
Pleasantville Public School, ON
*Dedicated to Madeleine McCann, missing since 5/03/07

Farewell, for Now

If only they could see
How hard it is to leave behind
The warmth from the sun
The trickle and splash of water
The breeze that runs through my hair

Farewell, for now
To the country where I was born
To the land where I grew up in
To the place where I started a family
I will miss thee greatly

But I will not say goodbye
For goodbye means goodbye forever
My spirit is still within my country
But my body has entered a new world

Until that day, that joyous day
When my body reunites with my spirit
Farewell, for now

Candice Harris, Grade 9
Woburn Collegiate Institute, ON

Life and Death

Life
Fun, amusing
Living, loving, laughing
Jumping, spinning, young, old
Losing, leaving, breaking
Dark, gone
Death

Jillian Main, Grade 8
Campbellton Middle School, NB

Basketball

I heard something about the ball who
wanted to keep his dreams

When he had a dream he jumped up

In general his life was simple
he joked with friends and family
he went to school
but he had difficulty
keeping his dreams

So in this world when
you have a dream
you have a reason to live

And the ball knew this
Every time he had a dream
he jump up…
he jumped up in the basket.

Rosela Altenor, Grade 9
Ecole Secondaire Jean Grou, QC

Doubt

The rest of the world fades away once I step onto the ice.
It feels smooth as I skate around our end.
I watch as the other team does the same.
They'll be hard to beat, but we can do it.
I look over at my own team, the familiar faces that share a familiar passion.

I wonder. What emotions will this game hold?
Happiness, we'll most likely score the first goal.
Frustration, how come I try so hard, but I can never play like her?
I watch her raise it perfectly and score.

I get nervous waiting for the pre-game practice to end, and the game to begin.
The whistle blows. We do a pre-game cheer.
The game has begun. I'm on the first shift of the game.
I miss the first pass, but determined not to miss another.
Seconds later, I'm battling in their corner.
I get a split second, and pass the puck to the slot.
My line mate scores. I head back to the bench and sit down.
I feel a tap on my shoulder.
"Good job" My coach tells me. I feel a sense of happiness.

My questions of doubt reenter my mind.
I push them away, and step onto,
That smooth surface once again.

Katie Beach, Grade 8
Nationview Public School, ON

Canada

Canada, my home sweet home, the lovely place where I was born,
Home to all of nature's gifts, and to winter's cold and snowy drifts.

Place to where maple is found, and nice people are all around,
Luscious apples await to be picked, to later on be picnicked.

The land where Aboriginals once stood, the latest ancestors of manhood,
Who incredibly marked our history, due to their skill and creativity.

Where lies the St. Lawrence River, that never stops to quiver,
In the shimmery glowing night, or the sunshine that's always bright.

Where music is golden, and always open,
To anyone who wishes, to dance to different valses.

The home to multicultural faces, of all different ages,
Where democracy lives, and justice forgives.

Origin of fun winter activities, where you fulfill such duties,
Like skiing, skating, and sledding, where the season fun is just beginning.

Canada, my home sweet home, the lovely place where I was born,
Where I have grown up, and will always worship.

Sabrina Roy, Grade 7
The Study School, QC

Fall

Leaves high and low on the tree
start loosening their grip as the cold draws near.
Letting go from the tree, falling with many colours
of red, yellow, and brown.
The wind guiding them with it's breath
sending them blowing every which way.
Some swirling towards the ground.
The leaves were colliding with soft touches
as they passed by, clinging to each other
not to lose each other in the blizzard of leaves.
The leaves spinning towards the ground
landed on the ground with a smooth, soft landing.

Timothy Monfils, Grade 8
St Peter Catholic High School, ON

The Mind

Questions make us believe
There's something out there we don't know
Questions are secrets we search
Knowing answers are wrong
For being someone that people don't expect you to be
And make them live what's called an evolution.
You turn around making a revolution.
You open your eyes to see the one you love has left
Saying to you it's just an illusion
So is life what it's meant to be?
Air is not meant to be seen
For breathing air that's clean
Good solutions have been seen.

Nicolay Cano Escamilla, Grade 9
Ecole Secondaire Jean Grou, QC

The Tears Only Come at Night

The tears only come at night,
You were my way out.
You'd hold me so close, so tight.
I was your world,
You always told me it would get better,
Always proud to know I was your girl.
Never had to fight for me; knew I'd be there
You always told me you couldn't open your eyes
So I helped you see the door was ever shut
You could always leave; instead you held on to me.
That day finally came,
The day I never wanted to meet.
The day you told me you didn't want me
That you didn't love me.
Sometimes the tears come
But only at night.
You were my way out
You always held me so close, and so tight.
So I'd wipe my tear away,
Only while I sleep
So I shut my eyes.

Amber Vaughan, Grade 8
Macdonald High School, QC

War

War kills innocent villagers
With no regrets torching their homes
Killing their families for no reason
Shooting down anyone who has a weapon
Doesn't matter if it's defending or for killing
Blowing up supplies and food
Leaving them stranded
Tearing up their streets
Using bombs and land mines

Is this gonna bring peace or just more war?

Andrew Hall, Grade 7
Bayview Elementary School, BC

Thanks for Being My Sister*

Thanks for being my sister,
I just want you to know,
That we may fight and bicker,
But we love each other so.

Thanks for being my sister,
We like to wear that silly friendship hat,
We'll make it through each and every day,
With the help of our cat.

Thanks for being my sister,
We share a special bond,
Not so much like peanut butter and jam,
But more like sludge from a pond.

Thanks for being my sister,
Even though you're forced to,
And you have no choice,
Together we can always praise the Lord,
By and by, through and through.

Nicolette Gignac, Grade 8
Pine View Public School, ON
*Dedicated to my only sister Jackie

The Beautiful Sea

As I sit down by the shore,
I watch the waves crash and roar.
The sand is as white as the oyster's pearl,
underneath the waves that curl.
I hear the clamor from the seagulls above,
while crew members shout "goodbye" to their loves.
The sun's beautiful, steaming rays,
had most definitely caught my gaze.
I feel a breeze flow through my hair,
while the fish, birds, and people stare.
They stare not at me,
but at the beautiful sea.

Amanda Styrczula-King, Grade 8
Macdonald High School, QC

Remembrance Day

R emember all the soldiers that sacrificed their lives in war
E nd all wars!!
M others and fathers and other relatives that passed away
E ager to get out of the army
M achine guns soldiers got shot by
B ravery is what you must have when you go to war
R emember the men and women who fought for our country
A rmory is where they keep their guns
N urses helping the injured soldiers
C uts and bullet wounds of the soldiers
E nded lives of friends, parents, grandparents and others

D efend our country so people will be happy and safe
A rmy is dangerous, but if you're in, you can't say "No"
Y do we have to fight? Can't we talk things out?

Chris Brown, Grade 7
Bayview Elementary School, BC

Like a Flaming Tree

A white fence near a fruit ranch
some orange and yellow maple leaves
falling down from the maple branch
like a flaming tree
There are some green leaves
changing to the maple leaves
like a colourful silk curtain
It's a quiet place
that nobody went
It's a beautiful place
that everybody chant

Harry Jeong, Grade 8
British Columbia Christian Academy, BC

Homework

I'm sick of homework, make it stop
I'd rather watch TV with chips and pop
Doing homework all alone
I'd rather be talking on the phone
At the table with a blank stare
I'd rather be working on my hair
Working quietly without a peep
I'd rather be getting my beauty sleep
I have so much homework it will make you sick
I'd rather be listening to my music
All the writing, thinking and reading
I'd rather stuff my face eating
All this homework open wide
I'd rather be free, playing outside
There's lots of things I'd rather do
But homework is important too
I could not do it, not hold my end of the trade
But then I'll fail my seventh grade
Sure, I'd have time to climb a tree
But my mom would probably kill me.

Chantal Laforge, Grade 7
École Notre-Dame-des-Vertus, SK

Two Way Ahead of Him

Little train ran his life on one rail
But one day little train arrived in front of two rails

He didn't know which way to take
Not knowing where it was going to take him

He thought about it night and day
He had to find the good way

He had to make a choice
He had to listen to his heart

That's what he did
And he doesn't regret it!

Kloé Therrien, Grade 9
Ecole Secondaire Jean Grou, QC

Someday

One day we will all be gone
but we all still have to stay strong
Cause if we give up hope we will be lost
Lost in ourselves and in every way
We will all be gone someday
But enjoy it till that day comes
Be grateful for what you have
Be grateful for you Creator
Because if you don't you would have nothing
We all rely on something but on what?
For food and water that's all we need
So why do people have to be greedy?
Some people have everything
Some people have nothing
So be kind and give some of your everything
To those unfortunate people
Who are happy with nothing.

Cory Gentes, Grade 9
Gladys Cook Educational Centre, MB

Heartbroken

It hurts when you're heartbroken
It feels like a part of you has been stolen
What's happening to me every day,
I keep getting my heart taken away.
All these things seem to happen in a blink of an eye
All the things I know, I start to cry
It's hard when you have it all on your mind
But it's all you will ever find.
Months and months will be passing by.
You will be in pain most of that time.
When you think, you will start to cry.
Once you let go it will be fine.

Francis Beaulieu, Grade 9
Gladys Cook Educational Centre, MB

Lovers

Two hearts combining to become one,
That's the feeling of love for some.
Having the feeling of being on cloud 9,
And receiving letters that say,
Forever you will be mine.
Marking the calendar for the 14th of February,
And being impatient for the anniversary,
Going out for candlelight dinners,
And getting the romantic lovebird jitters.
Dancing under the moonlight rays,
Always remembering the wonderful days.

Marjan Faqiri, Grade 8
The Elms Junior and Middle School, ON

My Grandma*

My Grandma is a mother hen,
Compassionately caring for her children and grandchildren.

My Grandma is a chef,
Cooking our delicious Christmas dinners.

My Grandma is a workhorse,
Doing chores and helping out every day.

My Grandma is an Einstein,
Having helped her kids with their tedious homework.

My Grandma is a bright, sunny day,
Everyone loves and cherishes her!

Kirstie Carter, Grade 7
Milverton Public School, ON
*Dedicated to my Grandma, who passed away June 10, 2007.

Drift Away

We used to have good times
Playing games and making rhymes
All that stuff little girls do
But one day you said shoo
You had your new friends you didn't need me
You were caught up in your popularity
Every now and then we would have fun and play together
Like a roller coaster up and down, enemies then friends forever
Yes, you were not the best friend you could have been
In fact you were sometimes snobby and mean

You were supposed to be my best friend
Super close and tight till the end
But something happened one day you had to leave me
Now I am all alone and broken as you can see
Ever since you moved away
There's been something I've wanted to say
That every minute of every day
You slowly drift away.

Dakotah Cable, Grade 7
Cranberry Portage Elementary School, MB

Young Love

Love's definition is just plain confusion
You're young and still full of delusion
This special person enters your heart
All kinds of feelings, can't even imagine where to start
They'll smile at you and you'll smile right back
While frightened you may have a heart attack
They make you laugh with a simple remark
Love is everything special including a spark

Aimee Colcomb, Grade 7
Macdonald High School, QC

I Am From

I am from laughs at the park and my brother's football games
From my mom's lasagna and my dad's bacon and eggs
From volleyball to being with friends
I am from Christmas get-togethers and gifts
From birthday cards and swimming quickly
I am from lakes and oceans
From camping and burning fires
I am from love and peace
From toy trucks and piles of dirt
I am from pizza and pickles
From cakes with icing
I am from braces to nice teeth
From bullying to beat
I am from hate and anger
From mother and father
I am from blue skies and clouds
From this is where I'm from

Jessica Leigh Hurst-Voeltz, Grade 9
Captain Meares Elementary Secondary School, BC

I Am

I am not one person. I am four.
Inside of me is a spirit
That tells me the truth
When I deny it to myself.
I am not an individual I am one part of a larger body
That fights against and for the wishes of the brain.
I am not a teenager.
I am a child, clutching the hand of my Father.
I am not one heart.
I am two, one afraid of death
The other longing for it.
I am not alone.
My thoughts are shared with the spirits inside me.
I am not a warrior.
But I must fight for what I believe in.
I long to leave battle, but I know all too well my duty.
I am not perfect. But I still love, and am loved.
I am not unhappy.
Never truly unhappy. Never.
I am blessed.
I am a child of God.

Laura McGugan, Grade 9
FE Madill Secondary School, ON

The Hidden Star

There was once a star
hidden by a cloud.
The star had a beautiful personality
and large dreams
unfortunately, the star
could not show.
What it suffered
which had much sorrow
because of the cloud
that hid its sorrow
and its suffering
then nobody could notice
that the star was not
in its normal state.

Isabelle Bossé, Grade 9
Ecole Secondaire Jean Grou, QC

Winter

Starts as little flakes of white
Then there's plenty of fresh powder.
Everyone gets to enjoy it
Then spring comes — vibrant yellow
The sun comes out, the snow melts
The fun is over.

Cory Gratton, Grade 8
MacKenzie Secondary School, BC

Sports

S uper fun.
P lay to win.
O ccasionally my team loses.
R icochet shots go in the net.
T he game is over.
S uper game, hard effort.

Dominic Perron, Grade 7
Macdonald High School, QC

Love Sometimes Hurts...

I never knew when I wished to have you
It would soon come true
I'm here now with my heart broken
It leaves me with hesitance
If I should give love one more chance
I look deep down in the ocean
I'll never get wet
It's safe (here)
No danger
Should I take the chance
I should now open myself to the pain
The waves that are washing over me
But the truth is I don't think I will ever
Get over where you've left me
You were my one true love
And now you're gone forever

Marina Lynn MacNeil, Grade 8
Macdonald High School, QC

Tribute to a Lady

Lady Jane's story, it is truly sad,
Her father wanted money, and did the very bad,
He married her away, to those who wanted power,
But it was not him, but she, who went to London's tower,
For her cousin had died, and her guardian was keen,
And so it was, that she became queen,
The real queen came, and Jane was sent,
To London Tower, where she must repent,
Because of her father, Jane had committed treason,
She took a place that was not hers, and Mary thought this reason,
To have her killed, and laid to rest,
For she had rebelled, and Mary thought it best,
So Jane climbed the scaffold, and said a little speech,
I'm sorry! Let me live! — that was her beseech,
But no knight in shining armour, upon a gallant steed,
Would help poor Lady Jane, and have it she be freed,
Because she was Protestant, her body could not be laid,
Alongside the other queens, to whom no one gave aid,
Lady Jane is long gone, her name no longer spoken,
But Edward remembered her always, and forever kept her token.

Laura McKay, Grade 9
Carberry Collegiate, MB

The Human Herd

The breeze is blowing in my face, you'll feel it on your human race,
How sad and sorrowful you felt, let all those feelings freeze and melt.
Forget about the awful times, of wars, of fights, and all the crimes,
Let them scatter, one by one,
The pain that was caused, the horror that's been done,
Throw out the old, start with the new, because years you live, only a few,
And celebrate the great and best, and do not think about the rest,
What's done is done, it's over now, but you may hear a single meow,
A daring whisper to your ease, a moment that you cannot seize,
A memory has again come, but it's nothing but a single hum,
No worries come into your mind, the thoughts of it are small and blind.
Unless it all comes back to life, it's not a spoon now, it's a knife,
A sharp one, yes so sharp indeed, it started from a tiny seed,
And grew into a horrid fight, now, we have to cry good night,
The cruel and fowl have now come back, and now our hearts will again crack,
Our peaceful world will burst to flames,
We'll live like pictures without frames,
Our life will never be complete, we'll fight with everyone we meet,
Then daylight saves us all again, there's sunny days, no pouring rain,
And with happiness we say these words, we have faith in human herds.

Anna Farbis, Grade 7
St Timothy Separate School, ON

Peace

Peace is like glue,
Holding all of the puzzle pieces together.
Each part with its own unique role,
Harmony, tolerance, compromise and acceptance.
They all make the puzzle complete,
The world's a canvas and we're the paintbrushes that makes it a better place.

Julia Chau, Grade 7
Christ the King Catholic Elementary School, ON

The Power of Love
Love is a bond that is, hard to break
It is made up of special powers that is not fake,

Love will always remain
It's like your heart has a stain,

It is something special that happens to everyone
Love never loses it always has won,

If you still don't understand what love means
Just look into, your heart and everything will be seen.

Sanan Samadi, Grade 7
Chedoke Middle School, ON

Ascend
Dream a dream that's worth dreaming,
Hold close to you, those who are precious.
Have faith within yourself.
Kindness and confidence run through
These veins.

Stand strong!
You shall prevail!
The battle has passed but the war lingers on…
Steady my lead shall seek your truth.
The past behind and the future is dawning;
Follow your heart for it
Brightens the way.

The golden sun sets the skies ablaze,
The moon cools the air;
Stars shining brightly,
With glowering, starry,
Glares.

Meghan Garrioch, Grade 8
St Peter Catholic High School, ON

The Sunflower
Yesterday, the sunflower was standing tall
Facing east towards the light
with her yellow petals she smiled back at the sun

But today the sun is out
The clouds are in
The rain is pouring
And the wind is blowing

With each blow
She sways from left to right
Bends a little but doesn't break
Through it all, she remains strong

For tomorrow is another day
And the sun will shine again

Déborah Apollon-Roy, Grade 9
Ecole Secondaire Jean Grou, QC

Fireman*
Glowing like the sun
Flames blossoming like flowers
Licking at the pages like snakes' tongues
Heat rising like hatred.

Burning down libraries
Dowsing houses in kerosene
Watching the flames jump up the building
Arresting the criminals.

Burning history
Abolishing ideas
Destroying religion
Turning dreams into ash.

Enforcing the law
"All books shall be burnt"
And there is joy in fire
Kindling the vision of a perfect world.

So is the way of the fireman
Light one page
Then light the rest
Until all books are gone…

Daniel Goldenberg, Grade 9
Sir Robert Borden High School, ON
*Dedicated to Ray Bradbury's, "Fahrenheit 451"

The Little Boy Sitting Across
The little girl,
sitting on the sidewalk.
Wouldn't stop mocking,
the little boy sitting across.

The boy had brown skin and short brown hair,
but looked aware,
of the situation.
He was from a different nation.

He realized that the little girl,
was laughing at him because of his race,
he then had a sad face.
Why would people do that he thought?

Does it make them feel better?
Her sweater,
it's the same colour!

Shouldn't everybody be equal,
we're not different!
Isn't that kind of general.

Chloé Espiard, Grade 7
The Study School, QC

As You Were

A silent wind
Brushed the trees of their crystal
The deer pranced on the white ground
And continue on
A grizzly slumbers in his cave
All is normal in the mid of winter.
Kristen Brousseau, Grade 8
MacKenzie Secondary School, BC

Fire

When you hear a crackle
or smell a puff of smoke,
you quickly snatch the children,
and fly out that door to escape.

Then standing in the bitter cold,
not knowing where to go.
Father announces quickly,
run, run you must go.

Standing at the warm barn heaters
waiting for the trucks to come.
Calling so that everyone is here,
and then you realize you forgot one.

You quickly run to the house,
Knowing it's too late.
Always wondering why
your sister did not come.
Mary Martin, Grade 7
Milverton Public School, ON

The Canvas

I sat staring at the canvas,
Spread white on wooden frame,
With paints for a purpose,
Which I hoped was to paint.

With loyal brush in hand,
And a mind pleasantly blank,
My wavering strokes tempt;
But still my hand is faulty,
For my creativity was unkempt.

I sat staring at surface
Bleached taunting white,
As it snickered at my pace.
For if ever one called forever,
It'd be to my brush to canvas' lace.

I stood staring at the canvas,
Spread on wooden frame,
I packed away the paints;
Tomorrow is another day.
Daegan Sit, Grade 9
Bayview Secondary School, ON

The Birds

A bird is like a kite
flying in the wind
dipping and diving
catching a breeze.

A bird is like an airplane
soaring through the sky
flying into the wind
looking for a place to land

A bird is like a musical
singing away sweetly
no really high or low notes
emptying his breath with sound.
Stuart Symenuk, Grade 7
St Anne School, SK

Soccer

I'm a ball, I get kicked lots.
And I get kicked really hard sometimes
from lots of people, sometimes I'm
really happy because the people kick me
in the net and I get surprised because
the people scream because they
score, and I'm happy too, I get kicked
really hard and sometimes not hard,
they do tricks on me too, and they go
to the goalie and they try to score on
him, and if they do they scream again
my ears full.
Bernard Siemens, Grade 7
Riverton Early Middle Years School, MB

The Shoe

Life is a shoe.
First it fits perfectly
and keeps your feet warm and dry.
Then your feet grow.
The laces fray,
the shoes rip.
You can never wear them again.
Garrett Lewis, Grade 8
MacKenzie Secondary School, BC

Invisible Confession

I am invisible to you
No matter what I do
There is nothing I can say
To make you look my way
No matter how hard I try
You make me want to cry
My heart is now broken
From words unspoken
Amanda Taylor, Grade 9
Dryden High School, ON

Love

My love for you is strong
It may last long
You are but a simple stranger
so we might not be together
We are set to be a blind date
so we could be soul mates
I tried to get to your heart
But I had no success
And then I started to cry
Unexpectedly you also tried
I cried louder and louder
Then you took me into your arms
and you held me tighter
You said that you would be there for me
So I looked into your deep blue eyes
And they showed no lies.
Now I trust you forever
With no doubts whatsoever
For it brings happiness to us both
So say your good-byes
To the loneliness that was once there.
Chung Tina See, Grade 7
École Pierre-Brosseau, QC

Camille

C urious
A musing
M arvellous
I ntelligent
L ogical
L oyal
E nergetic
Camille Brunet-Asselin, Grade 8
Collège Jésus-Marie de Sillery, QC

Inside

Inside a bubble that somebody blew,
I am that wall that you see through,
Away from space, I'm trapped inside,
There is no room, no room inside.
Inside a star that everybody sees,
They see the sparkle but can't see me,
Away from land, I'm trapped inside,
I'm sorry I did it, sorry I lied.
Inside a song that nobody hears,
It's only me wet from tears,
Away from grace, I'm trapped inside,
I'm floating away to the other side.
Inside my soul that you reach through,
I am that ghost that stays with you,
Away from them, I watch you sleep,
I visit your dreams, in peace so deep.
Inside a bubble that somebody blew,
I am your angel, that somebody is you!
April Nickerson, Grade 8
Senator Riley School, AB

Snowfall

Crunch, crunch, crunch.
I'm taking in deep breaths,
I have sore legs and feet.

I came just for the thrill of hearing the man say,
"Ready, set, push!"
Down to the bottom as I look up at the sky,
I'm realizing that I couldn't be doing this without the soft,
white flakes of snow.

I curve slightly around the corner.
Slowing down,
Slowing down,
Stop.

As I stand there I slowly open my mouth,
Feeling the snow fall gently upon me.
It starts to turn into a liquid,
That flows like a stream down the back of my throat.

Still looking to the sky,
I say to myself,
"Maybe just one more time."

Brodie Geurkink, Grade 8
Nationview Public School, ON

Obsession

As the sun sets and the world fades to black
The moon shines brightly outside my window…
As I dream, I hear your voice,
It whispers sweet nothings inside my head
But this is all an illusion…
A very precious illusion indeed.

Keep talking.
Calm the monsters that gnaw at my heart
This is only a carefully crafted hallucination,
A mere glitch in my head,
But I still depend on your voice.
Please, tell me I'm the only one.

Pull me deeper into the abyss
I'll follow you anywhere…
Just promise me you won't leave.

The sun begins to rise with brilliant fiery rays
My eyes flutter open,
I realize that my dream has evaporated into the bright sky
I am wounded by your sudden departure
But I shall wait for the moon to shine again
So that your presence may intoxicate me some more.

Kristen Ho, Grade 8
Churchill Heights Public School, ON

Cars

Cars
Fast, sleek
Aerodynamic, exotic, modern
German, European, American, Italian
Turbo, custom, curvy, race car, competition
Tuner, muscle, NASCAR, car drivers
Classic, popular, enthusiastic
Nitrous, horse power
Cars

Raza Qadri, Grade 7
New Horizons School, AB

The Scar

Ran as fast as I can around the house,
like I was a maniac jacked up on Mountain Dew,

But then…
BAM,

I smacked my head on the corner of the brick fireplace.

I was down, bawling my eyes out,
blood coming out of my right eyebrow.

All I could think of was if my mom was coming to help me.
No stitches,
just a lot of Band-Aids,
Kleenex and a tiny scar.

Blue and black eye.

People ask, "How did you get that?"
I say "hit my head on the corner of the brick fireplace."

Stewart McKelvie, Grade 8
Nationview Public School, ON

Beneath the White Crosses

Shouts and cries echo in the still night sky.
Guns boom and soldier after soldier falls
to the ground, dead, while larks gracefully fly
Eruption of earth, another voice calls

Another soldier is called up to God
One, who will never see daylight again
But he is now under the cold damp sod
With many fields of young and worthy men

Poppies blooming beside the white crosses
Where now beloved ones peacefully lay
Wives, now still thinking of their great losses
They will never wake, and there they will stay

Now everybody, start to recognize
the terror in war and its sacrifice

Lorna Kleinsasser, Grade 8
Milford Colony School, AB

Christmas Wish

She sat there so lonely and quiet
not uttering a sound,
And when I asked her
There was only silence found
The tears ran silently
Abrupt and wet
As the girl choked out the words
"Christmas, with Daddy."

The sobs now come freely
As she shook with grief
I guessed for an answer
"Dad," she whispers in a weep

Days later the news came
The poor, sweet little girl
Was killed in an accident
Her Christmas wish
Was answered at last.

Linda Wipf, Grade 7
Milford Colony School, AB

Melody

M ellow
E njoyable
L ovable
O ne of a kind
D ecent
Y outhful

Melody Poulin, Grade 8
Collège Jésus-Marie de Sillery, QC

Isabelle

I rreplaceable
S entimental
A musing
B reezy
E nergetic
L adylike
L ittle
E nthusiastic

Isabelle Hinse, Grade 8
Collège Jésus-Marie de Sillery, QC

Hockey

I love playing hockey.
I'm going top speed.
I glide to the net.
The wind freezes the sweat to my face.
I can hear sticks hitting the ice
Waiting for the perfect pass.
The crowd chanting.
Whistles blowing.
It's the best time of my life.

Corey Stone, Grade 8
Nationview Public School, ON

JFK

Is he here yet? We've been here all morning,
now all smell salty, sweat stinging my nose,
I swallow hard, as we get to see John Kennedy.
The parade is about to start,
I peer out to seek John Kennedy's limo,
it's out in the distance, soon it will reach here!
The noon sun dries my lips, I lick them to wet, but my throat is sandpaper.
Here he is! The president is here!

Everyone's smiling, joy swells in me,
Kennedy is here, he is smiling, waving,
people all forget the heat, for the president is here!

A lone bullet sings through the sky silencing all the joy.
The silence then erupts into chaos.
I go into shock, my mind trying to understand just what happened.
The president's been shot, is he dead?
Oh God, everyone around me is panicking,
I stand here, mind reeling I can't believe it — the president has been shot.

Everyone swarming, I swallow hard, my heart fluttering,
I hear women screaming, babies crying, sirens wailing, eee-ooo eee-ooo.
All I can do is stand here, the same phrase going on and on,
The president is dead.

Kevin Comeau, Grade 8
Fallingbrook Public School, ON

Fight for Silver

You're standing there, staring down your opponent.
You feel a little frightened,
so you bite your lip so he won't notice.
You start to feel a little unwell,
and think that maybe you're not as good as everybody else.
Your hearts pounding like a bass drum,
as the other two fighters step out of the ring.

It's so close; you don't even know who wins.
Before the judge calls the winners, you start to feel a little discouraged,
that you probably didn't win. Then he calls your name,
and it's all you can do not to jump up and sprint over.

As you're standing there,
with that heavy silver medal around your neck.
You realize that everyone is watching you. You're exhausted,
but no one can see it because of how happy and excited you look.
That's when you realize, you just came second over hundreds of people.
That's when the huge sense of accomplishment kicks in.
You feel indestructible.

Then it's off to the next ring, to stare down someone else.
And this time, win gold.

Andrew Havekes, Grade 8
Nationview Public School, ON

Christmas

Every year on Christmas Day
Your toy nutcrackers come and play
Santa comes to all the good little boys and girls
To put some toys under the tree that twirls
You'll hear the reindeers' hooves on your roof
But then they'll disappear with a "poof"
You'd better watch out of the snow, coming down fast
But you can catch the snowflakes while they last
The jingle bells are ringing,
While the choir is singing,
Rudolph's nose will shine through the night,
While the other reindeer put up a fight
You'll receive a lot of presents,
Being better treated than a peasant
The Jews will celebrate Hanukkah
With a bunch of lit up candles,
Christmas is almost over
New Year's Day is right around the corner
Christmas is now gone
But you can still be number one!

Scott Tucker, Grade 8
Macdonald High School, QC

Friction

This is friction
We don't need an alibi
We are surely not ashamed
And I salute your teary eyes
Although this feeling is unnamed
For now I'll call it friction
Let it drag on once again
Let it drag on forever
And I know you're reading my mind
Because we're sure it's now or never
And now I salute friction
Euphoric sadness cracks your lips
And then escapes a silent howl
Because I think that we both know
These butterflies are just for now
So I cling on to friction
You have put me in a trance
There's nothing more about this day
Please stay with me, won't you come back?
And then you took my heart away
And with it, you took friction

Kendall Wooding, Grade 9
Argyle Secondary School, BC

The Life on Earth

A life where you've never seen a war
A life, a perfect life where you just see the peace
A life where you see love and not violence
A life where everybody is gentle
A life like this is the life I want to live

Fleurilien Michael, Grade 9
Ecole Secondaire Jean Grou, QC

What Christmas Means to Me

White snow falling from a dark, cloudy sky
Carolers singing hymns of praise while passing by
The Salvation Army going door to door
Yes, Christmas time is here once more

Encountering smiles everywhere you go
Saying "hello" to people, even those you don't know
No matter where you walk, there's snow and ice
It's all very surreal, but very nice

The true meaning of Christmas is neglected by us
We just make this special time seem like a fuss
It's all about cooking and cleaning and buying gifts
Away from Christmas's true meaning do our intents drift

Now the lights are shining and the tree is up
But somehow, it feels as though it's not enough
Because Christmas isn't about the latest fashion trends
It's a time to spend with family and friends

A time to love and a time to care
A time to give, to receive and a time to share
A time to be happy and carefree
That's what Christmas means to me

Brent Nuevo, Grade 7
St Anne French Immersion School, ON

Bamboo and Water

Ponds reflect the early rays of the sun,
And reflections bounce off the surface.
The giant panda eats his bamboo by the pond.

Black and white,
His paws slowly climb up the stem.
He nibbles quietly,
Like the rest of the forest around him.

Soon this sight will be gone.
Waters black,
And pandas gone.
Who do we blame?
Who is the cause?
We must blame ourselves.

It was we who cut down trees.
It was we who polluted the water,
And we are the cause of extinction.

Stop polluting.
Stop destroying.
Just save.

Eric Kavcic, Grade 8
St Peter Catholic High School, ON

I Remember

I remember it was a miraculous day with hardly any wind and a perfect temperature.
I remember looking across the vast ocean for miles like a flying bird.
And overseeing the wave crests break as they moved up the beach like snow being pushed by the plow.
I remember the warm breeze against my face as I came down like a comet comes to earth.
I remember smelling the salty air as it blew in off the ocean like when a car passes you fast.
I remember the sound of crabs scurrying along the rocks like dice hitting a board.
And the crunch of dead seaweed like corn flakes lying on the ground.
I remember that as the best time of my life like winning an award at the Olympics.
But I will still come to have many more glorious memories.

Jamie McConnery, Grade 9
Eric Graves Memorial Jr High School, NS

Memories

Memories pull at my heart, yet I cannot remember.
Time stretches, yet I cannot see the memories I hold so dear.
Your image fades, first the clothes, then the color, now the face.
Why I can't remember, I don't know.
Why I try, I will never know.
But I know that you must stay.
What you did I cannot say, just that you will come.
To save me from this path, maybe you will come to deprive me of my life.
I don't know, just that you will come.
Half of me waits in anticipation, half of me waits in fear.
I must wait to see, while my life drags on.
Only you can change it. You can sculpt the once beautiful sculpture to what it was before. Or you can destroy it. I don't care;
just sweep me away to a land of wonder and beauty, or to the oblivion that we all must face.
Just take me away, I don't care. Save me from this life I chose, I try so hard to save the memories so I can see what you did,
look, and act like so maybe, just maybe someday, I can leave what I chose.
Come I'm not afraid, take me far away.

Melissa Reid, Grade 8
Red Wing School, SK

If Only

Staring out my window I wonder what would happen If I never knew you
My heart wouldn't be broken my eyes wouldn't be crying my soul wouldn't be yearning for you
Sometimes I wish I never met you I wish I never spoke to you
If I never laid my eyes on you I wouldn't be feeling this way and my heart wouldn't be in pieces
My love wouldn't be tainted and my mind wouldn't be stained with thoughts of you
I hope one day I'll forget the pain I feel and move on stop thinking of you and just move on with my life
Then I think to myself I wouldn't be who I am if I didn't know you I wouldn't have felt true love
I know the pain hurts but sometimes I feel it was all worth it
You showed me how to love you showed me how to care
You showed me how to open my heart and let you in
You showed me so much I can't help but to say thank you
You were so many things to me so many names you could have
My armor my love my soul my heart my everything
You kept out the hurt and brought in love
You loved me constantly you were dear to my heart I can't see my life without you
I know you leaving broke my heart and I know it broke yours too
I don't care that you left I don't care that you're gone
I don't care that you made me promises my heart doesn't care for that
I care that you care I care that you care enough to promise the promises I'll never forget
My heart cares for you my heart only loves you my heart is with no one else but you
You are my love and my life and I can't wait for you to come back

Deborah Bryan, Grade 9
Woburn Collegiate Institute, ON

Disguise

Disguise,
magical, mysterious secret,
you hide behind the mask, the cape, or the hood,
praying that no one notices your existence,
and sometimes, to your contentment, they don't

Disguise,
others may shudder at its display,
and though they may not know it,
the person behind it is also trembling,
due to what they've become

Disguise,
agonizing time enclosed with bottled up feelings,
but you cannot reveal yourself,
you may not disclose what is going on,
for fear of the inquiries of others

My disguise,
my magical, mysterious secret,
my agonizing time amidst my feelings,
but why am I allowing this to happen?
What have I to conceal?

Kristie Jones, Grade 8
St Peter Catholic High School, ON

Lost One

I'm down here while you're up there somewhere
Wondering why you had to die
It made me cry saying goodbye
I'm living in pain
It's driving me insane

I'm like a leaf with lots of grief
Without it's tree no one remembers me
I remember the love that we once shared
I'm writing this poem to let you know I cared

I miss you Mom why'd you have to go
For what it means to lose you no one will ever know
I'm trapped in pain
That I can't explain

I feel the world closing in
For all the sin I let begin
I'm writing this poem from deep down in my heart
Cause all the memories and times shared, it all fell apart

Peace is yours dear Mom, it's so sweet to breathe your name
As in life I loved you, so in death I do the same

Adrian Murdock, Grade 9
Gladys Cook Educational Centre, MB

Perfection

The ideal image, the flawless form;
The formula refined by millennia reborn;
A being that becomes but does not conform…
When crafted by gentle and loving hands
And aged by Time's forever-flowing sands,
Begets its own tale, a tempting dance…
Of loving admiration and blessed design;
Modest elegance and beauty divine;
A token of innocence and Love's true ensign…
Of shapely curves, and rounded shapes;
Molded with wisdom, a classical make;
Twisted by trends, and never to fade…
Of a heavenly model, by the Gods themselves;
Hardened by Fire that Earth could not quell;
And chiseled by Water the Wind itself impels…
But alas and alack, dear friend, it's true
That such Perfection will never make its debut;
For this world and its assets will always lay askew.
And yet…might it be a gift that these are the lives we lead?
May we find true perfection…in the perfectly flawed?

Maggie Cheung, Grade 9
Woburn Collegiate Institute, ON

Love

Realization
Pursue
Rejection
Fear
Acceptance
Doubt
Love
All

Lindsie Green, Grade 9
Francis Libermann Catholic High School, ON

Storm

Darkness fills the sky, making it black
Thunder arrives, causing a loud crack
The leaves whisper secrets to those who are near
The wind howls loudly for all to hear
The rain pounds on the ground
Making sounds, so profound
The thunder is shouting
The water is spouting
It begins to hail
The wind continues to wail
While the thunder and lightning have ceased
The power of the storm has decreased
And the hail slows
As the water flows
The wind becomes less violent
The storm is pretty silent
When the last drop of rain falls to the soil
That marks the end of the storm's turmoil

Jasmin Risk, Grade 9
Elboya Elementary and Jr High School, AB

Just Me

I'm just me
But no one seems to see
And I can't help being shy
With all those people passing by
And I try to make friends
But in the end
I look like a fool
And people think I'm uncool
So why can't anybody see
That I'm just being me

Jessica McGibbon, Grade 9
North Hastings High School, ON

Winter Joy

White crystals, falling, blanketing,
frozen earth, insulating.
Children playing, sledding.
Rosy hands, cocoa holding.
Happy smiles, people meeting.
Frostbitten noses, snowmen making.
Frozen ice, skating.

Sidewalk shoveling, hockey playing.
with the sky pouring it's soul.
Making the Earth white and lofty.
Shouts of joy fill the air
  as the Earth transforms.

Rachel Wipf, Grade 8
Milford Colony School, AB

Life

Life can be happy,
Life can be sad.

Life could be good,
Or it can be bad.

Life has been boring,
But it also has been fun.

Life can be dark,
Or as bright as the sun.

Life has hate,
Life has love.

Life can be grey,
Or as white as a dove.

Life can be short,
Life can be long

But life is beautiful,
Just like a song!

Paige Henry, Grade 7
Riverton Early Middle Years School, MB

The Change of Seasons

The ground is white,
The whole world is smiling in delight.
Christmas time is around the corner,
All families gather together with aunts, uncles and cousin Warner.
As the snow starts to melt and the leaves begin to bloom,
We all get ready with our buckets, mops and brooms.
We are all done with spring cleaning,
And all children are singing.
Outdoor sports are beginning,
Parents and siblings will forever be cheering.
As summer slowly comes to an end,
The beginning of autumn starts to mend.
We are all admiring the colors of the leaves that are so deep,
But we are all definitely enjoying the extra hour of sleep!

Jordana Serero, Grade 7
The Study School, QC

Left Behind

I sit at my computer and stare.
Just waiting, alone, for someone to care.
No messages come up, no one calls me on my phone.
Time passes by as I sit here alone.
My heart is aching there's nothing inside.
I just need a friend to be beside.
I wish things were different now, back to the way they used to be.
When I mattered to people, or so it had seemed to me.
Those people I thought would be there forever,
At the first sign of change they did what they said they would never.
They moved on, found new friends and didn't need me anymore.
But change is change — All is fair in love and in war.
I still love them now, even though gone,
It's a shame I was the only one who couldn't move on.
I might burst any second, the tears are so hard to fight.
I put on an act at school and cry myself to sleep every night.
I'm at my lowest point but I still refuse to break,
as I continue to live this life that's so ridiculously fake.
I'm trying to live in the past, and still remember those days of laughter.
So tell me again what ever happened to living happily ever after?

Elise Rossignol, Grade 8
St Peter Catholic High School, ON

The Earth Lady

She grows an apple on a tree and takes a juicy bite,
her dark, forest green, robe dragging gently on the ground.
Golden radiant hair dancing in the wind,
She rides a noble steed beautiful white and grey.
In the woods is where she lives and takes in the beauty around her.
Creating young trees that whisper their thanks for life,
and flowers coming to greet
She goes to see her favorite tree to sit on its delicate branches.
Birds and squirrels sing their song and circle around their leader.
Rabbits gather and the lady says her story,
Animals' eyes shining like stars at the fascinating tale.
They ask her name and she tells them, the Earth Lady.

Alyssa Poisson, Grade 8
Macdonald High School, QC

Friends Forever

Friends forever and ever
Friends for always

Good friends would be more special
than a diamond would be

Friends come and go,
New friends, old friends; what matters is
they are all your friends.

They are your friends, friends forever.
Friends are always in your heart
even though they might be very far

Never forget your friends, your friends forever
We all have friends, good friends

Fateha Aslam, Grade 7
Macdonald High School, QC

Life and Death

Life is powerful,
life is strong
it's like a long melodious song.
It's a wonderful thing,
a wonderful sight,
it's like having superhuman might.
It's great,
it leaps
it's something that you'll always want to keep.
But it's not going to last as long as you'd want,
because the grim reaper is soon gonna haunt.

Taylor Dunne, Grade 8
Burnaby Mountain Secondary School, BC

Babies

You're the ones that demand attention,
But give us back so much affection.
Without knowing it you brighten our days and lives,
As you grow and suddenly reach your fives.
Oh, what happiness you bring to us,
With that great big smile or tired fuss.
You are loving, generous and special people to us all,
You are the light at the end of the tunnel,
Your inner and outer beauty,
Outshines us all.
When you grow up and become older,
The mothers become sadder and sadder.
Their baby has gone,
Their childhood is done,
It is now time for them all to move on.
Babies are to be thanked,
And never spanked,
For teaching us what really matters.
Oh, how very important you are to us!

Sabrina Nolan, Grade 7
The Study School, QC

I Imagine…

Christmas is coming,
everyone is gonna be drumming.
If there is lots of snow this year,
people will be full of cheer.

Christmas holidays are like relaxing in the pool,
kids don't have to follow any rule of the school.
The snow is going to be very shiny,
the icicles will seem to be very tiny.

This is going to be the best Christmas ever,
a time to remember this forever…

Sahiban Katari, Grade 7
Pleasantville Public School, ON

Rowing

Rowing all alone
In my old white kayak
In the middle of the sea

I look to my right
I see the beautiful sunset
Leaving tracks of yellow and red

I also see the mountains
Covering the sun as it goes home
Shining a mysterious blue

I look down into the water
I see the fish swimming
In the yellow and red water

Rowing all alone
In the middle of the sea
Would you like to join me?

Michelle Choi, Grade 8
British Columbia Christian Academy, BC

All My Hope

A boy sat alone in a hospital bed,
the knowledge of cancer clear in his head.
That night he heard a voice in his sleep
that said, "please child do not weep,
do not worry do not grieve,
you will be fine if you believe."
He knew surely, it must be a dream
for he was sitting with an angel by a stream.
She said, "I must leave now but please know
God is with you wherever you go."
When he woke he called his family near
and told them quietly he no longer feared
the things that would happen the things that would be
"Because," he said, "God is with me."

Amber Kortekaas, Grade 8
St Peter Catholic High School, ON

Lime Green

Lime green is so awesome,
It is as awesome as a possum.
I love limes and I love green.
Them put together is the best color I have ever seen.

Lime green is so shiny and bright,
The color lime green is really light.
I will never like a color as much,
Cause lime green gives me the magic touch.

I like the way it blinds your eyes,
It can hurt so much it will make you cry.
It is the best color ever.
I will love it forever and ever.

Taylor-Rae Johannesson, Grade 7
Riverton Early Middle Years School, MB

Pain

Pain, pain is like a darkness,
It surrounds our every move,
If you let it consume you,
It won't be long before it breaks loose.

In living life we know,
Not all things go our way,
But you can't keep living in that moment,
Just live your life day by day.

Take the hardships and the easy ones,
The low points and the high,
It will take your body without sympathy,
Feels like your hands and feet are tied.

Drowning in the sorrow of your self pain,
Wanting the strength you lack before you pay the price,
Pain isn't a game you can win or lose at,
You decide your fate without a dice.

Pain, pain is like a darkness,
It surrounds our every move,
If you let it consume you,
It won't be long before it breaks loose.

Sarah Newman, Grade 7
Milverton Public School, ON

War

Yesterday a man came to my door,
He told me my dad had died in the war.
I cried and cried,
I could not stop if I tried.
I cried myself to sleep,
and now again today I am starting to weep.
I hope this horrible war soon ends,
So no one else loses a parent again.

Rosina Filice, Grade 7
Nativity of Our Lord Catholic School, ON

I Shall Never Forget

Meeting you was destiny, I swear, it was fate
No matter what everyone else says, it was no mistake

Like the sun, you enlightened my life
In you poured, filling me
Sharing, your own love and joy

Like a soft white tissue, you touched upon my face
Brushed away all my tears; silenced all my cries

Like a best friend, you assured me
That you'd always be there
Promising to move through life, hand in hand with mine

Like a soldier armed for battle, you rescued me from my depths
Slaying away all my dragons; demolishing all my fears

Like a teacher, you taught me to
Smile, laugh, and love
You gave me a reason to enjoy life
That reason, is you

Meeting you was destiny, I swear it was fate
Although you're no longer a part of me, it was no mistake.

Cynthia Sritharan, Grade 9
Woburn Collegiate Institute, ON

Skeleton Hill

There is this hill you see.
Where many people flee.

Many people sell their soul,
To find the riches of gold.

Opened graves have been found,
From the people way, way down.

The shrilling cry of murdered souls,
That try to come up from the deep dark holes.

The devil creeps around,
Looking for souls to drown.

People who walk at night,
See the weary sights.

They tap you on the shoulder,
And your heart grows colder.

This is your life if you don't have Jesus right.

Laura Martens, Grade 8
La Crete Public School, AB

The Crow's Call

Beyond the yellow fringe
of darkness and day
lay the perfectly still brick house.
While shards of twilight gold
broke below on the sparkling stream.

Squirrels, furry balls
danced up and down.
While one by one rotting acorns
rolled down the darkening hill.

The moonlight caressed the dimming land,
and enigmatic screams pierced
the silence of the night.

The squirrels jumped
and below was heard,
the plaintive calls
of raven crows.

Then silence
And the quiet of night.

Benedict Leung, Grade 9
St George's School, BC

Labels

I wish we could put it all behind us
I wish we could see people as gold instead of rust
We all have labels that are used too often
Sometimes I wonder how and when

What are in the minds of the perfects?
Are they really wrecks?
What will become of the geeks?
Will they succeed?

And what will happen to that one girl?
The girl who is friendly yet shy
The girl who everyone confides
The girl who stands all alone in the hall
Her confidence and self esteem seems so tall

Whatever her secret is remember this
Next time you want to call someone stupid our a jerk
Shut up and sit down because that's not how it works

Some people call it high school
Some people call it cool
I call it bullying
Because I'm that girl

Jennifer Parkinson, Grade 8
British Columbia Christian Academy, BC

Life

It's right in front of you
You miss it for a bigger picture
You miss if for something you can buy
And then disappointed when you can't
But think
Just think how lucky you are,
Think of those who lost theirs,
Think of those who don't have one
Think of how lucky you are,
To have a life
So don't take for granted how much you have
Be thankful for what you have

Sonja Hilton, Grade 7
Elkford Secondary School, BC

Addressed to Unknown

So I'm here in this room,
Writing this poem for you,
But you have no clue,
Of what I'm going through.
Yes, you are one of my good friends,
But our friendship is starting to bend.
Do you really care for me like I care for you?
Will you actually stay up late to help me too?
When will you finally see
That you're hurting me so badly?
Do you see these tears that I cry?
Just tell me the truth, you don't need to lie.
Do you even want me to be your friend?
Or was this all just pretend?
I just don't know what to do,
To make you like me as a friend too.
And just so you know,
These words are honestly from my heart and soul.
I really do love and care for you,
But I still haven't seen that you feel the same way too.

Allena Nguyen, Grade 9
Little Flower Academy, BC

Fading Star

This fading star in the starry sky
wants to shine brightly but is too shy
Even if he tried really hard
he would only end up as a falling star

No matter how much time flows by
he would continue to try
Because deep down inside him
he strongly believed in his dream

He doesn't know how long he will last
but he can't forget all the burdens of his past
A long time ago he lost his way
but he will find the right path one day

Kenny Siriphong-Savejvong, Grade 9
Ecole Secondaire Jean Grou, QC

A Friendship Is Stopped!

When I sleep
I dream of a nice friendship
but when I have nightmares
I see the end of a friendship.

One day they said
A flower can't fade
The world can't stop
A friend can't be lost.

But the world doesn't stop.
Sometimes flowers fade.
This friendship is lost.

Sara Tummillo, Grade 9
Ecole Secondaire Jean Grou, QC

Marie-Michelle

M ajestic
A musing
R eliable
I ntelligent
E asygoing
M agnificent
I rreplaceable
C andid
H elpful
E nthusiastic
L adylike
L ittle
E ager

Marie-Michèlle Methot, Grade 8
Collège Jésus-Marie de Sillery, QC

Handle Bars

I grip the handle bars,
with my little hands.
I start going slowly,
knowing my dad's right there holding on.

I begin pedaling faster, and faster,
As my dad says 1, 2, 3, and let's go!
I pedal twice,
then collapse to the ground.

As I get up,
I brush the rocks off my knee.
I try again,
knowing if I keep trying,
I will succeed.

I pedal twice more,
then a third,
going quicker, and quicker,
till I fall again.

Colton Stitt, Grade 8
Nationview Public School, ON

If Only They Knew

This world isn't perfect, if only they knew,
This world isn't perfect, like me and like you,
this world isn't perfect, but there are things we can do,
This world isn't perfect, if only they knew.

School and homework, and teachers, and tests,
These are the things that kids these days dread.
If only they knew that some child out there,
Has never been taught, do you think that's fair?

They all complain about their different troubles.
Their money, their friends, their jobs, and their lovers.
If only they thought of everyone else,
This world could be a much better place.

Money, and gold, and parties and cars
These are the things that mean the world to some,
If only they knew that so many out there
Went to bed with no food, and had no clothes to wear.

All the people who don't wear the "right" clothes, or don't have the "right" looks,
They are the ones, who know what their life's really worth,
All those who listen and their love they do show.
Those are the people who truly do know.

Mishel Ukhanov, Grade 8
Laurelwood Public School, ON

True Love's First Kiss

When you know someone special
That you would give your heart and soul to
Their company is everything you could want
But still you ask what more do I need?

All you need is that special someone to make your day go as planned
The one that knows your every need
The one who needs your love in return
They think of you in every way
And still love you after making mistakes
You're everything a girl could want
So why do you choose not to show love
The girl you're crazy about feels the same way

When the moment is right
The clean ice-cold breeze blows across your face
Winter's surroundings: fluffy white snowflakes gently falling
The beautiful scent of her perfume dancing on the tip of your nose
Looking deeply into her blazing blue eyes
And slowly do you touch feeling warmth
And then the kiss that makes you love her more

Amanda Gadwa, Grade 9
Kehewin Community Education Centre, AB

The Gaping Hole

The gaping hole in my chest
Throbbed as I slowly
Made my way through
The crowd of laughing posers.
The last thread of my sanity
Snapped and I was
Sprawled on the cold, hard floor of
Depression. I couldn't yell. I
Couldn't cry. I had become a
Hollow shell.
Indestructible.
Insults could not even scratch the surface of my
Lifeless casing. Nothing could possibly make me feel
Any worse than I did right then.
I finally had an advantage over those
Pathetic wannabes.
Nothing more could be taken from me.

Rachel Bruce, Grade 7
Willoughby Elementary School, BC

Sea Shell

There was a sea shell, by the shore
I was looking, but I never found more.
I wondered where all the sea shells had gone.
I kept looking, but I didn't see one all night long.
The only one I found was special.
The color was a sweet caramel.
It looks like someone drew on it with skill.
It means so much to me and always will
This sea shell will be mine forever.
Will I give it away? Never!

Kaeleigh Muir, Grade 8
Macdonald High School, QC

The Darkened Trail

All in pain, he stood weeping,
mournful and sadly keeping.
A gift from Death has touched a friend,
twisted in grief, his heart won't mend.

Shadow lay upon the ground,
the loss of a friend he surely found.
Betrayal, distrust shall be his mates,
followed by the voice of hate.

The heavens overtaken by darkened night,
amongst his foes he shall fight.
Thoughts of vengeance full he ate,
all in pain, yet he will wait.

As Shadow rises and begins to creep,
mournful voices begin to peep.
It's all in darkness that he will wake,
to set his own true darkened fate.

Laura Waltenbury, Grade 9
Nicholson Catholic College, ON

Their Souls Will Live Forever On

They lit our lives like a burning fire,
They fought for freedom and our hearts' desire,
They gave us courage, they gave us hope,
They led us up a slippery slope.
They fought through wind, rain and sleet,
They kept our souls and hearts complete,
They kept our dreams up, soaring high,
They left us with a silent good-bye.
They moved us with a burning sorrow,
They touched our hearts and left to go,
With their courage we shall carry on,
Their souls will live,
Forever on.

Nirushi Kuhathasan, Grade 9
Middlefield Collegiate Institute, ON

The Question of Columbine

Which way to go
Do you side with faith or choose your life
What would you do?
A gun is held against your head,
A question asked, Do you believe in God?
How do you choose?

A yes will end your life
But how will life go on if you chose yourself
The time is ticking away
A no is your ticket out of this mess
But will your life be a bigger mess if you lie to the gunman?
The thoughts rush past

How do you know
You won't die either way,
Oh the questions you would like to ask
You need to answer right away
But what if you chose the wrong path?
You'll take your chances and follow your heart

You look into the gunman's eyes
You know your answer, you give him your response:
I believe in God

Sonya Dyck, Grade 7
Milverton Public School, ON

Life Is Hard

Every time you come you have to do the same things
Sometimes you just want to get away
And wish for a better day.
Sometimes I just want to get down and pray
While trying to figure out a way

Shanique Morris, Grade 8
École Pierre-Brosseau, QC

The Walk of the Ant

An ant walked a long path.
To find something to change his life.
But facing the world,
What can an at do?
Except to learn how to carry,
Carry all the weight of his world.
And this little ant walks
a long path,
Never sure to find
What it is searching for.

Dérick Beaudoin-Résolus, Grade 9
Ecole Secondaire Jean Grou, QC

Love

The warmth of your touch
The sincerity of your words
The glow in your bright eyes
I could love no one else like I love you.
Your smile makes me melt
Your hair makes me weak.
The way you show me you care
And how you're always there
You always speak to me
In sweet honesty and truth
And those are the reasons
I so dearly love you.

Matthew Good, Grade 7
Macdonald High School, QC

Friend's Death

Her hand goes limp,
As limp as an imps,
She opens her eyes,
As she slowly lies,
Upon her friends bed.

She loosens her jaw,
Opens her maw,
Her eyes close,
The wind blows,
Her hair wildly flies,
As she lies,
On her friends bed,
Now she is dead.

Her friend cries,
As she lies,
Dead upon the bed,
She lowers her head,
Whispers goodbye,
She keeps an eye,
On her best friend,
Who was with her at the end.

Camryn Coughlan, Grade 7
George Bonner Middle School, BC

Airplanes

Through the air, the airplanes fly,
Deeply into the fresh blue sky.

Flying along the bumpy sky blue,
Up in the air, that airplane flew.

Flying in the air, the big jet flies,
In the air, in the bright blue skies.

Carter Comeau, Grade 7
Riverton Early Middle Years School, MB

The Game I Love

I step on the ice
and I start to glide,
I can feel the hard smooth ice
under my skate,
and see my breath
in the cold winter air.

I can feel the puck
moving back and forth on my stick,
making a swoosh noise every time.
I see the puck
flying through the air
after I shoot.

And when the puck
goes in the net,
my confidence
goes way up,
and I feel like
I'm on top of the world,
and nobody can take it away, not ever.

This game, this game I love, is my life.

Spencer Corkery, Grade 8
Nationview Public School, ON

The Night Sky

Look up
And wonder
At the mystery,
And majesty,
Of the night sky.
Stars sit there,
Winking,
To tell the world,
They're all right.
The moon,
Watches.
A tolerant,
And caring,
Mother,
Of us all.

Rianna Janke, Grade 8
School of Hope, AB

Tears

Tears are like rain drops
they are the same
because they are both feelings
and words that can't be spoken

Chelsea Gore, Grade 9
Johnston Heights Secondary School, BC

Fly

Everybody wants to fly,
To fly in a blue sky,
Like a beautiful butterfly,
Everybody loves to dream,
To dream that they fly,
Like a beautiful butterfly,
Be happy like you are,
And you will fly in the sky,
Like a beautiful butterfly.

Maxime Brochu, Grade 9
École Pierre-Brosseau, QC

We Remember

You lay in peace where you are,
The horror you've been through,
You gave your life for your country
Our minds are now with you.

Even though you have a family,
You knew what you had to do,
Your little girls will never know,
The hero that was you.

She never wanted you to go,
That place so far away,
Even though you did what's right,
She wants you here today.

We wear the poppy just for you,
We're thankful for what you've done,
We wish that war was over,
'Cause dying is no fun.

Stephanie Barre, Grade 8
St Ambrose School, AB

Game Time

"Buzz" the horn blows
The cheer goes up One, Two, Three
They line up and the puck drops,
BOOM!
Striding down the ice, Shhk, Shhk
"Tweeet"
Penalty shot
A "Pting" off the cross bar
No Goal

Brodie Moulding, Grade 8
MacKenzie Secondary School, BC

The Big Game

Entering the arena you can feel the excitement.
The roar of the crowd.
Getting dressed, listening to the rock and roll music.
All pumped up!

Stepping onto the ice.
The home crowd cheering so loud,
they are like raising the roof.
Supporting everyone on the ice.

The first blow of the whistle.
The big game is finally starting.
The home team gets the puck, they go end to end,
and score the first goal!

But with five minutes left the visitors tie
the game at one all.
Then the home team, with 20 seconds left,
scores an amazing shorthanded goal!

And the winners of the Stanley Cup Finals is the
wonderful Ottawa Senators.

Scott Ropp, Grade 7
Milverton Public School, ON

Snowflakes

Walking ice-paved streets in the dead of night.
Snowflakes drift freely through the cold night air,
They soak the sky with patterns, silver-white,
Spiraling down to land on soft dark hair,

They dance, without a care, without a word,
Snowflakes still falling from heavens above.
The wind whips around, burning their faces
But they have no hats, no scarves, not a glove.

The cold does not phase their frostbitten skin,
As their ice-cold fingertips intertwine,
One moment lips touch before walking on
They walk past frozen trees, line after line

The wind picks up, fast as lightning it runs,
Trees scream out as their branches are broken.
Numb fingers trace the outline of her neck,
Their words of love linger there unspoken,

She's wrapped in arms strong enough to break her.
In the distance a wolf howls and cries,
Although she is frozen straight through to her bones,
She can't look away from his still blue eyes.

Taylor Newlands, Grade 9
Earl Haig Secondary School, ON

Fooled

I've been fooled
My eyes are wide open
But they are helplessly shielded by lies
I knew this would happen
Yet I didn't see this coming
If my eyes are so wide open,
didn't even blink,
How do you think,
I didn't notice this?
I wonder too
If only I knew
How one with perfect vision
Could be so hopelessly blind
So mistaken
I was wrong
I know
But you don't
There's a surprise hidden behind my eyes.

Magdalena Banka, Grade 7
Immaculate Conception, BC

I Wish Love Could See

I was stupid to have thought I loved you
Now that you're gone, I can see what went on
I can see I was wrong

I could fill these pages with hate and disgust
But it's not all for you
They're aimed mostly at me

I am finally in a relationship
So different from the ones I knew
I'm mature now and smarter too

You are nothing
You gave up on everything
And I gave up on you

Love is blind, but I can see you

Alanah White, Grade 9
Eric Graves Memorial Jr High School, NS

Fall Changes

Fall comes around
Every year the same time
The season won't hesitate
To show its early signs
A sole yellow leaf
Overtaken by green
Like the new kid in a crowded playground
Trying to fit in,
Pretty soon the tree will be covered with colours
Flickering in the cool fall nights
Until it's gone.

Lucca Arsenault-Verrelli, Grade 8
St Peter Catholic High School, ON

Jump, Spin, Go!!!!

As I glide across the ice,
in my new skates
the sharp, shiny blade,
gets caught in an invisible crack,
I stumble,
then fall,
My knee is throbbing,
but I get back up to try again,
This time I manage to miss the crack,
I jump,
then spin,
As I land I fall down *again*
I'm determined to get this right,
I try again, and again,
Now I'm beginning to realize,
that enormous blisters,
are growing on the back of my ankles,
I give up for the day,
but I promise you,
that I'm gonna try again tomorrow.

Emily Peters, Grade 8
Nationview Public School, ON

Where My Soul Resides

At Milford I will always stay
Until I reach my dying day
I cannot leave it, it's my home
It's worth writing into this poem
I love my colony Milford
Everywhere I go
I love my colony Milford
And they all love me so
Milford is my colony
Milford, my soul's nation
Milford is a beautiful place
A wonderful habitation
At Milford I will age and die
At Milford in my grave I'll lie

Sarah Kleinsasser, Grade 7
Milford Colony School, AB

Kittens

Kitten warm cuddly.
Cute and fuzzy.
Sitting around the fire
Purring softly.
Through the night.
They love to eat.
They love to sleep.
They also love to leap
From couch to couch.
They love to be played with.
That is the way
Kittens love to live.

Brittany Thomas, Grade 7
Macdonald High School, QC

The Flight of Destiny

Innocent people board the plane,
Unaware they will never touch ground again,
A woman looks out the window of a tower,
There is a plane,
She screams and runs down the stairs,
She made it to the bottom floor,
Almost to the doors,
There are people crying and screaming all around,
The plane and the tower collide,
Suddenly all life is taken from her,
Reporters swarm,
Mothers cry,
Husbands weep,
Children scream,
Once again uncertain destiny claims the life of yet, another victim.

Madison Galloway, Grade 8
Vincent Massey School, AB

Up at My Cottage

We have a cottage at Forest Lake, my mom calls it our family escape
I made a treehouse just for me,
Look up and you will see,
It has a ladder you have to climb to come inside, I really don't mind
The little chipmunks stop their play and look up at me as if to say
"I wish we had a house built that way"
My dad cut down trees to build the floor and I did the rest, I wanted more
I dragged the wood across the yard, hammering until my hands were numb
Making sure it was perfectly done
I called to my mom to come and see, "Use the stairs, they will hold you"
She had a worried look that she would fall through!
She smiled proudly and said to me
"I would sleep out here without any cares,
If it wasn't for the big black bears"
I clean up my nails and put my hammer away
For winter is coming but not to stay
I'll be back in the spring on a sunny day
to sit high in my treehouse and watch the chipmunks at play.

Skyler O'Boyle, Grade 7
Macdonald High School, QC

The Era in Fall

There's a time for everything during the fall season.
There's a time for the brilliant sun to smile on people,
There's a time for the wind to blow with the cloudy, moody skies.
There's a time for a crackling of the dead multicolourful,
elegant and ravishing leaves — Crackle, Crackle
falling and joining together as one whole family
There's a time for the rainbow of colours to come
From separate, unique backgrounds
Brown, beige, marigold and red represent different cultures
They lead to calm, amicable, depressing times
There will be a time that the fall season will abolish,
But there will be a time that the fall season will come
just around the corner!

Elizabeth Gyamfi, Grade 8
St Peter Catholic High School, ON

Fantasy

I dreamt I had delightful wings,
Like the ones gracefully perched on a blue jay,
And I could fly away.
I dreamt I wore a pirate hat,
And I had a hook for a hand.
I sailed a massive ship,
And traveled the world for plunder.

I dreamt I had stunning long hair,
And a breathtaking frock made of silk.
I sat with a straight back,
On my lovely throne
Like a true princess would.

I could dream everlastingly
Of knights and dragons,
Of kings and queens,
Of the village of fairy tale,
And of the neighbourhood of fantasy.

Alas,
I must awake someday.

Bianca Rakheja, Grade 7
Miss Edgar's and Miss Cramp's School, QC

The Man

The man I thought would never grow old,
the one I looked up to but never told.
I used to think he had a heart carved from gold
until he made mine tear at the fold.
The man I prayed would live forever
turned out to be gone, swept away like a feather.

P. H., Grade 9
Nanaimo District Secondary School, BC

A Broken Pencil

A broken pencil
When I think of it
It reminds me of me
At least it seems
Every day my heart cries out
In every way it's shattered
But almost all the pieces are lost or confined
The rest just don't know what to do
Most of the time I feel lost
And broken like a pencil
I'm crooked in many ways
And I'm scared to reveal myself
I'm broken in lots of ways
Some cannot be fixed
I wish I knew what to do, but I don't
So when I think of it
In lots of ways
I am a broken pencil

Louie Beardy, Grade 9
Gladys Cook Educational Centre, MB

A Tree Is Life

A tree is Life.
It starts as a seed, then sapling,
Then it keeps growing older and stronger.

A tree is Strength.
It stands over us, through everything,
Tall, strong and very courageous.

A tree is Courage,
Protecting us from harm,
Sturdy, stable and wise.

A tree is Wisdom,
Telling us its many stories,
Kind, old and free.

A tree is Freedom,
Reaching towards the endless sky,
Curious, reaching, living.

A tree is Life,
With all its strength, courage,
Wisdom and freedom.
A tree is you and me.

Alison Moore, Grade 7
Jack Miner Public School, ON

God and Science

Is religion or science true?
Why do two easy choices,
Affect our lives so much.
Science gives us proof.
It is easy to choose science.
Religion is based on assumptions.
It might be make believe,
Like Santa Claus or the Easter bunny.
Science gives us a false sense of knowing,
But religion is fulfilling.
It gives us something to believe,
It gives our lives meaning.

Science has us viewed as apes along with proof.
Even though it is ugly, it might be the truth.
It is the truth like fire burns.
Religion has no proof,
But it is prettier than us being apes.
It is prettier like a puppy to a hairy spider.
This is the hardest choice of our lives,
It gives us freedom or leaves us with questions.
Choice is not always easy.

Christian Gomes, Grade 9
St Benedict Catholic Secondary School, ON

The Heart Who Will Survive
Did you ever hear about a heart
that got hurt by a lying knife.

A knife that always said whatever
the heart wanted to hear.

Until one day, she realized
that it was all a lie

The only thing she felt then
was pain and miser

But by living her life day by day
That heart forgot all about the suffering
The knife had put her through.

She now learned how to grow stronger
with a new mystery. lover
Lisa Grande, Grade 9
Ecole Secondaire Jean Grou, QC

The Pencil's Fight
Far away on the blank
there's a pencil who creates
From his art you can see
the amazing liberty
But somehow an eraser
always erases his secret art
but the written stick never gives up
With his dream he keeps his will
and he screams his victory
With his hope he writes and writes
but like always it disappears
He continues until he loses all hope
With his dream he keeps his will
and he screams again his victory
And with a "pop"
His opponent disappears
like his skill
Jean-Philippe Corbeil, Grade 9
Ecole Secondaire Jean Grou, QC

Dragon
This is a dragon
Eyes burning with fire
Body coated in scales and muscles
Breath of fire
The creatures of myths
This is a dragon
The iron will to win
Wings as far as the eye can see
Claws as thick as trees
This is a dragon
Can you handle it's roar of thunder
Charles Kitts, Grade 7
School of Hope, AB

The Greatest Pain
Most people don't realize
The one pain is losing
the one person you trust.
The one soul you believe in.
The one you love.

The instant you hear it.
The moment it hits you.
You've realized it,
You've experienced the moment of,
The greatest pain.
Samantha Lamothe, Grade 7
Macdonald High School, QC

The Four Seasons
Summer, winter, spring, fall,
There is a way to enjoy them all.

Summer, it is so much fun,
You can swim and play under the sun.

Winter is great for tobogganing,
'Tis the season to laugh and sing.

Spring is when the flowers sprout,
It is a happy season without any doubt.

Fall is such a pretty time,
The colours are all at their prime.

The four seasons are really great,
Some you may love, some you may hate.

All four seasons are very fine
At any given day or time.
Carson Deshevy-Renouf, Grade 7
St Peter's School, ON

The Friendship Is Precious
The friendship is loyal
Beautiful, faithful
I'm scared of losing it with you

The friendship is pure

When I knew
I lost your friendship

I received the arrow
That broke my heart

The friendship is precious
We don't have to lost it
Betty Cardoso-Correia, Grade 9
Ecole Secondaire Jean Grou, QC

It Will Be Ok
There's no worry, don't need to tear.
You don't have to live your life in fear.
Let there be life beyond the dead,
and may no regret fill the head.
I am ok and so shall you be.
A better place is what I see.
I watch over you and enjoy my day.
So I've come to say it will be ok.
Jacqueline Cappadocia, Grade 7
Pleasantville Public School, ON

Natacha
N ice
A musing
T houghtful
A utonomous
C almness
H appy
A ffectionate
Natacha Maciagowski, Grade 8
Collège Jésus-Marie de Sillery, QC

Angel of Confusion
The very first time I saw you
I loved your hair and smile
Every time I heard your voice
I would listen a little while
When you walked in the room
A smile grew on my face
Whenever you were absent
I'd cry at your empty place
You made me feel so special
Not like others did
But sometimes that happiness
You somehow got rid
For you said you liked me
Then said it wasn't true
Now I don't know the answer
And I don't know what to do
Because of this confusion
I really want to know
Tell me all the truth
So the painful unknown will go
Tatiana Kopchuk, Grade 7
St Kevin School, AB

Winter
W hite snow
I nteresting
N ever hot
T iny snowflakes on my face
E xciting
R eally cold…brrrr
Sabrina Savage, Grade 7
Macdonald High School, QC

A Book

A book is like a portal
Taunting us to jump in
Waiting for us to open the book and flip the pages

A book is like a bomb that just went off in my head
Filling it up with a lot of ideas

A book is like a soaring dove flying gracefully
On the page
As it goes it soars and I realize I just finished the book!!!

Amanda Derksen, Grade 7
St Anne School, SK

Undisturbable Peace

Looking around as you walk
down the stony path you see many things.
A tree
bending over to tell another
a secret, passing
it on and on through the forest
sometimes you can hear the trees
trying to tell you their secret.
Even the wind tries to get into your head.
Looking at the border fence seeing the sun rising above it
it's like it's the sun's job to watch over the campers.
Yet, the fence is so far away,
it could take miles and miles to get there.
The path under your feet slowly blends into the grass.
The best part of this journey is the feeling of the shade
from the leaves on your face as you walk under the trees.
It's like the trees are pushing away the darkness
and make room for the light to shine through.

Paige Muzychka, Grade 8
Menno Simons Christian School, AB

Me

This is me,
What more can I say
I have lots of friends,
The type you can keep until the end,
I have my moods,
Sometimes depressed yet always happy,
I'll always have a smile upon my face,
Some may like me yet others may not,
To me it means nothing I obviously forgot,
I am not perfect, and will never be,
But I still have dreams that I wish to succeed,
Some words put me down but I'll always fight,
For my friends will never see me teary-eyed,
I'll try my best to make people happy,
And I'll never give up on whatever's happening,
I encourage the ones who need me the most.
And I will not ask for anything in return,
I am someone you shouldn't forget,
And this is how my poem will end.

Amanda Fincken, Grade 8
Macdonald High School, QC

A Winter Blizzard

Children are laughing from left to right.
Everyone is thinking, Oh what a beautiful sight.
But suddenly roars in a huge gust of snow.
The tree branches are swaying, how much it must blow!
The next day was Christmas and everyone knew.
That the blizzard had passed and all came through.
The swings and slides were covered in snow.
The children are gasping and shouting Oh No!
The children all thought of what to do.
Suddenly and idea just came through!
The children built towers are high as nobody would know.
Rapidly they fired their canons of snow!
Along came Santa exclaiming, HO HO HO!

Sebastian Adugalski, Grade 7
Immaculate Conception, BC

Skies of Time

When I am little, before I fall to sleep
I look out my window
And see the sky, so dark, so deep

I grow a bit older, and as I crawl into my bed
I look out that very window
And see lights of orange instead

I am all grown up now, but I cannot rest
For I see outside my same window
A billboard with the words: "Buying Is The Best"

I lay up and wonder, until all hours of the night
What if my grandchildren grow up
To only see the city's lights?

What if they never have the pleasure
To see the birds, up soaring high
Or never get to see the stars that lit my childhood's sky?

Gennesse Walker-Scace, Grade 9
Penetanguishene Secondary School, ON

Spring Is Here

The blazing sun is constantly shining
The visible clouds are slowly combining
Flowers of paradise are awakening and blooming
The animals are finding spaces for rooming

Large shadows are looming on the canyon wall
The last drops of snow wave goodbye as they fall
The birds fly along the breeze in the sky
Plants once were dead raise themselves high

The ice melts away leaving water behind
The cold sea calms to waves all aligned
The trees are bare with branches of sorrow
But shaking with happiness the leaves by tomorrow!

Ruha Bhatti, Grade 9
Erindale Secondary School, ON

Again
The sun splashes us with light,
And the clouds showers us with rain.
As the wind blows past,
Life will grow again.
Mammals give birth,
Reptiles lay eggs,
The cycle starts again.
The eagles will glide,
The crawling will hide,
The cycle starts again.
Peacocks will mate,
The season's not late,
The cycle starts again.
The young ones all grow,
They, too, will grow old,
And the cycle starts again.
The sun will always rise,
Until the last all dies,
For, it will explode.
But for those other worlds,
The cycle starts again.

Shannon Guo, Grade 7
Dundas Central School, ON

A Great Man…*
He was a great man,
Although he had never confronted a law,
Never ended a war,
Composed a symphony,
Or written a world famous novel,
As he had wished in his youth.

He was still greater than that,
He was certainly no war general,
Or close to a great politician,
He was greater than a famous
composer,
Or prize winning novelist,

Which makes him still a great man!

Allicia Finch, Grade 7
Dalmeny High School, SK
*Dedicated to my grandpa
Edward Schick 9/01/06*

When We Go Out to Play
Every summer the sun shines bright
Look up above, the birds are in flight.

We run in the fields below,
Hand in hand, toe in toe.

What a beautiful summer day,
When we go out to play.

Rachel Martin, Grade 7
Milverton Public School, ON

Alzheimer's*
They call it the slow way of saying goodbye
All I ask of you is to try.
Try to be brave, try to be strong
I keep hoping nothing is wrong.
As you become weak
As you can no longer speak
As you get thin
I think that what has happened is a sin
Each day a struggle, each day a pain
Until the news they told us, hit me like a train.
Forty-eight hours left
That's what they expect
But, I knew that you were strong
And the doctors would be wrong
Since the news, 60 hours had passed
That's how long you had last
Today your spirit left this Earth, but Alzheimer's took you from us first
I love you Grandma so dearly,
I hoped I showed that very clearly.
I'll cherish that last smile on your face, and that one last embrace
You are and always will be loved…

Amanda Baldo, Grade 8
St Peter Catholic High School, ON
Dedicated to Betty Baldo, rest peacefully.

Fear
Stuck in a world,
So full of fears,
In the corner, people lay curled,
So many tears,
Streaming down scared cheeks.
Wondering if it's the end,
Of counting your weeks.
For yourself, you must fend.

You wonder if you'll live or die,
Because you don't have much money,
And all you want to do is cry.
When you look up in the sky, it's not even sunny,
But through all of the pain and misery, you realize,
That you have a family, so loving and kind,
With hearts so big in size,
That's when you notice that fear, is all in the mind.

So you must overcome,
What is troubling you inside,
Then you think everyone has some
Kind of fear that makes them want to hide,
And when you do finally overcome the fear, your heart is full of pride.

Ashley Stuart, Grade 9
Lockeport Regional High School, NS

War

Guns booming, shouts, cries echo through the night,
Barely heard larks fly as soldiers fall, dead
Stumbling men fall and cry, while missiles fly
Dazed, shocked and confused comrades bury dead.

Soldiers are very brave to fight bloody war,
Some die, some barely alive, and all are very brave,
Men's bodies are bleeding, uniforms torn
When soldiers shoot the wrong they fill grave.

And now some lie under poppy-filled fields
With families at home crying their heart out,
For fathers and sons who fought and died,
Will they ever get over this depart.

Now we should be grateful, for sacrifice,
For freedom and lives that brought us a rise.

Dave Hofer, Grade 8
Milford Colony School, AB

These Dark Brown Eyes

I look into these dark brown eyes
and I see the fire that burns inside.
They burn with pride, passion and a glow,
and when these eyes are on the track,
they burst out and don't look back.
They keep on pushing until the end,
and once they cross that finish line
They explode like fireworks, these dark brown eyes.

Julianne Lamarche, Grade 8
St Peter Catholic High School, ON

Invisible Heart, Invisible You

A room full of nothing,
Space emptied of everything but you,
and no matter how close I get to finding you,
I'll get farther from knowing you
I attempt to reach out to you
I hear every breath you take
Every beat your empty heart almost doesn't make.
Through open eyes, fixated on you,
I glimpse the outline of your shadow.
But still, I look right through you.
And all I see in the mirror behind you is myself.
Could it be that you don't exist?
Or could you be so hollow
It takes but one glance to see right through
Your invisible heart
And right through you the door handle grips my gaze.
But I wouldn't dare move,
You've always been the first to go.
Take your leave, I'll take mine
Without one look back, I'll follow through,
away from the solid path that led me to this invisible you.

Shamina Kallu, Grade 9
Delview Secondary School, BC

My Love

It all started when we glanced at each other
You reversed my heart and you know it
A wind of love is our history; it was born not to stop
Our love grows day by day

I let you enter my heart and fill it
All I want to be is the girl
Falling asleep in your arms
I will not care about anything else

Telling the sky not to be blue
Well, it's like telling me
Not to be in love with you
The truth is I can't stop thinking about you

There's no place that I'd rather be
Than right here with you
I look at your beautiful smile
Sends me in a fit of desire

Without you by my side
I don't know if I'm still alive
If I can breathe and if I can speak
I know that I will love you forever

Bianca Vachon, Grade 8
Macdonald High School, QC

Dirt Road

I'm walking along no name streets
Searching frantically and finding nothing
Everything is still, unmoving
It starts to rain and skies are turning grey
Signs are appearing and I'm becoming confused
Where do I go?
I'm so far from where I started and so far from the end
Mistakes are all around me
I tried to get somewhere but I got lost
I hear a voice ask me
Who are you?
I cannot answer because I do not know
I hold my head and cry
Minutes turn into hours and I'm still lost
I sit down and listen to the silence
I hear birds on an empty road, chirping into the wind
I stand and walk along the road
It's filled with dirt and grime but it feels right, more relaxed
The storm is passing and the sun is appearing
The dirt road seems long but I am willing to take the journey
Because in the end, I might be found.

Andrea Vulic, Grade 8
Nativity of Our Lord Catholic School, ON

A Sunset's Goodbye

A sunset goes down for its good night sleep
It goes down slowly
Without a peep
You hear in the distance a chirp and a sigh
The birds must be coming
For their good night's lie

The deer and the bear close their eyes tight
Yet they can't go to sleep cause of the sight
They open their eyes to this breathtaking scene
In one moment or two

It's…
GONE!
The sirens are going and the sky turns black
I hide downstairs
And wait

When I think it's over I go outside
And see the bombs have destroyed where the animals lie
I think to myself…
Why can't we get along?

Jacqueline Orr, Grade 7
The Study School, QC

A Wild Ride

I grabbed the reins,
and began walking down the trails.
As the instructor shows me,
and tells me to do something.

Every time I try to teach star
what to do,
As in slow down
or go faster,
I know he understands me.

As I'm walking through the trails
and through the trees.
Learning how to make him turn left or right,
or how to let him know exactly what I'm
trying to teach him.

Now the time has come,
and my lessons are over,
wishing I could have more time.

I will be back again tomorrow,
I promise.

Chantal Markell, Grade 8
Nationview Public School, ON

Seasons

Springtime is a colourful, happy time
newborns wander around in the fresh air
flowers bloom every colour you can think of
making people happy

Summer's green and rainy
children swimming in the cool blue lakes
people watch
the beautiful grass and trees

Fall's leaves falling
looks like it's raining
all sorts of colourful leaves
lying on the ground

Winters glistening snow
laying fluffy on the earth
looks like the stars
twinkling in the sky.

John Hofer, Grade 7
Milford Colony School, AB

In the Black of Night

In the black of night
Comes the dreams of many
The dreams whisper, the nightmares scream.
As night goes on
The owls hoot and wolves howl.
No one sees.

Stacey Hillyard, Grade 8
MacKenzie Secondary School, BC

Don't Leave

Why now? Why me?
Oh, why can't you see
That I still need you, I still want you.
Don't leave me here, alone with my fear.
Why can't you stay a little longer?
Why can't you see that I need you?
Why can't you be a little stronger?
Why can't you let your heart lead you?
My tears fall, on this page.
All the world is a stage —
We're the actors, we're the factors.
We all play a part, and yours broke my heart.
Why did you have to make me think
That I could have all I wanted?
I saw my happiness, I stood at the brink,
And now all my dreams are haunted.
Make your choice — raise your voice —
You're at the door — wait no more —
Please…don't leave me here.
Don't leave.
Please.

Samantha Morin, Grade 8
St Joseph Catholic High School, ON

Who Knew?

She's braver than Spider-Man,
And braver than Superman
No one's braver than her.
But when push comes to shove,
And she has to shine.
She doesn't know what she can do.
She has to live up to her expectations,
Everyone counts on her to be the best,
Honestly, her ego's too big for herself.
When the time comes to show what she's got,
She should have walked the walk,
Instead of talking the talk.
And this comes to show you
That TALK is bigger than ACTION,
If you can't live up to what you say,
Then you might as well not talk at all.
Everyone will recognize you when the word goes out,
Everyone knows,
So live up to your expectations
And if you don't
Expect to have a great big fall.

Ashley Stendel, Grade 7
The Study School, QC

Shadows

Shadows crawling across the room,
Marking the places filled with gloom.
They're in the closet, on the door,
Crawling to you across the floor.

Dancing monsters, gruesome ghouls,
Screaming spirits, bloody duels;
These things all go on in your room,
On the night of the full moon.

With the approach of the banshee song,
The werewolves come to howl along,
And soon, your once peaceful domain
Is filled with the cries of their horrid strain.

You're encased by fear, surrounded by pain,
But under your covers, there is no gain.
Because you don't even realize that the ghosts and the howls
Were all caused by a fear of shadows.

The ghost was a leaf, the banshee a dress,
The spirit the wind, and the ghoul a clothes mess
The darkness the light switch, the house is the moan
The werewolf your dog, and the shadow your own.

Rachel Pigden, Grade 7
Tosorontio Central Public School, ON

Hammer and Heart of Ice

She gave him her heart
a heart hard like ice
She loves him ad he betrayed her love to her.
She promised to love him
as long as she lived
He was the only one who she wanted to be next to.

He didn't' see how
She loved him
He chose to take a hammer
and to break her heart in 1,000 pieces
and her heart can only be repaired
by the one who destroyed it.

Jennifer Debrosse, Grade 9
Ecole Secondaire Jean Grou, QC

My Brother

He is a pigsty
Never cleans up after himself
He is an empty bank
Owes me a lot of money
He is a trouble master
Breaking rules
He is a people person
Always has a group of friends
He is a sliver
You can't get rid of him
He is a typical teenager
Getting into trouble, bugging his sister
Big brother
Knowing that his job is done when I get mad

Stacey Kuepfer, Grade 7
Milverton Public School, ON

The Test

Pencil in hand, I think, I choose, I guess
Digits are like wet jeans, head is like a throbbing heart
I read, I frown, I worry
Two minutes pass, three minutes pass, lose track of time

Cheat, cheat, cheat, this word fills my mind
Should I? Shouldn't I? I can't choose
Clenched teeth, darting eyes, desperate boy
Peer over shoulder, I look, I copy, I cheat

One answer down, three to go
I read, I sigh, I cheat
The cycle continues
Last question, I don't know the answer

I hope, I pray, I search
I look, I see, I copy
I get caught cheating,
I cheat, I fail

T.K. Jeong, Grade 9
St George's School, BC

Football

Fall, family and football
Changing colours, falling leaves,
Time to pick the football team.
Winning pass, fumbles and falls,
Green grass stains on my knees,
Sun is gleaming through the forest.
Laughter, smiles, high five's all around.
That's fall, family and football.

Fall, family and football
Feeling the leather football in my hands,
Trying to score a winning pass,
Touchdowns make the team cheer high.
Catching the ball means everything
Everyone loves to win
Especially when it's your team
That's fall, family and football.

Sarah Chippior, Grade 8
St Peter Catholic High School, ON

Hope

Hope is miracles, courage and belief,
Belief that there will be no more grief.
Hope is not given like a gift,
Hope is created from the heart
And it gives you a lift.

H ope
O vercoming obstacles
P ower
E nding your grief

Mackenzie Popoff, Grade 7
Kamsack Comprehensive Institute, SK

Fall

The leaves are changing colour
And floating to the ground
I'm looking out the window
My face without a frown

It is my favourite season
I'd say I like it the best
Everyone should agree
It is above the rest

I jump into piles of leaves
And throw them everywhere
I do all I please
With the wind in my hair

It's now getting dark
A smile spreads over my face
I will grab a few beautiful leaves
And put them on my fireplace

Breanne Ridyard, Grade 8
St Peter Catholic High School, ON

The Labyrinth of Life

In this labyrinth of lies and deception only a true friend can help you;
In this labyrinth of lies and deception only a foe can wear a fake smile;
In this labyrinth of lies and deception only envy can hurt you;
In this labyrinth of lies and deception only you can be you;
This is the labyrinth of life.

Kahentanoron Sarah Beaver, Grade 8
Ratihente High School, QC

Man's Destructive Invention: Global Warming

It has come, finally come; it has finally come to working.
From the industrial age to our present cities, it was sixty years in the making.
We denied it, said it wasn't true, but the truth is we resisted.
But now it's here, visible, and no more can we say it never existed.
Summers are getting warm and long, winters short and frail.
All this shows that global warming will go off the scale.
Plants and animals will disappear; species gone forever.
If we want to save the world, now's the time to be clever.
Glaciers melting, sea levels rising;
Soon New York and Tokyo will be drowning.
But we're still doing it — spewing pollution,
Don't we know we're adding to the destruction?
The time to change is now, not tomorrow, not later,
As we continue to stall, Mother Nature looks at us as a traitor.
Is it too late? Can we save the world we know?
Will this mistake be the final blow?
Whatever we do, global warming must not continue to climb.
Whatever we do, it must be sublime.
Whatever we do, this is the time.

Kawin Ethayarajh, Grade 7
Churchill Heights Public School, ON

Two Different Worlds

He walks into the room, everyone's eyes on him
To my belief, he comes and sits with me, he grabs my hands
I just melt, his hands are so comforting, reassuring
He looks into my eyes, time just seems to stop
I pinch myself, to make sure I'm not dreaming

I wish time would stop, so this would never have to end
But this will only last for so long because we have to get back to our worlds.
No one would ever accept us together
I want to tell him how I feel about him so bad
Just so he knows
Because I know he feels the same way
But we cannot be, never
We will never be

Even though I always wonder what more there could be between us
I'm afraid to find out
Because I know it won't happen
We are from two different worlds it won't work
But it will always be my dream
And maybe someday when worlds accept each other
Maybe that day my dream will come true

Lauren Mulholland, Grade 9
FE Madill Secondary School, ON

Christmas

Christmas time is almost here
it's the time of cheer
lots of presents everywhere

You must be crazy not to celebrate
the food everyone makes is great
ice cream and milkshakes is what's best, hurray!

If you try to stop yourself
hide them behind a shelf
that will be lots of help

open your presents before it's time, the suspense will go away
but that will ruin Christmas day
the best day of all the days

Justin Senior, Grade 8
Macdonald High School, QC

Why

I sit on my chair and watch the world go by
Wondering why oh why.
Is there a point to life?
What is the world? What does it mean to live?
Why is there school? Why do we learn?
I'm so confused on what to do.
Do I stay or go? Do I talk or do I walk?
Am I living my life right or wrong?
Is there a way to live?
Do all my friends feel the same way?
Do they wonder why we fight?
Is there a point to love or hate?
I see people doing wrong.
I care for them, but should I just go along?
Do I tell them to stop or support their decisions?
It is hard to know for many reasons.
Do I look to the future or focus on the present?
I'm confused, so I sit on my chair and watch the world go by
Wondering why oh why.

Jessica Ferguson, Grade 8
Macdonald High School, QC

Am I Good Enough

School, family, friends, life
Am I good enough
Will I pass every class
Will I memorize every move
Feeling empty, alone, unloved, unworthy
Expectations fill the air
I am a great one they all say
What would they do if they knew the real me
The one who feels, who cries, who laughs,
The one who wonders…
I know the real me, but am I good enough…
…yes I am

Ariah Leroux, Grade 7
Macdonald High School, QC

A Tribute to Him

My eyes catch a glimpse of that front page headline
The words I repeat sends a quiver up my spine
"Boy From The Congo 13 Is Now Dead"
I read on and realize it's because of what he said

He'd spoken of his life and how when he was young
Soldiers came and the words they had sung
Were of hate and death and of wars which never end
Then they forced this poor boy to shoot his best friend

I think of all the lives lost in war
Numbers too high for us to ignore
Yet those numbers aren't people that you and I know
They're just statistics, they pass and go

But this story I read in the paper today
Is somebody real and we know now he lays
We live on this planet we are all much the same
He made a difference, not for fortune and fame

I cannot believe it, my body fills with rage
How can this happen to someone my age?
It seems far far away yet it's so close to home
A tribute to him is why I made this poem.

Lauren Bingeman, Grade 8
Laurelwood Public School, ON

Juno Beach

60 seconds to the beach.
You've been training for several years,
To hide away your feelings and your tears.
40 seconds to the beach.
The first wave of soldiers has landed on the beach,
The blood they spill will forever teach.
20 seconds to the beach.
The task that lies ahead,
Is to establish a beachhead.
10 seconds to the beach.
You're supposed to be a machine,
The images will forever be seen.
5 seconds to the beach.
For some their lives will flash before their eyes,
They will forever make a final sacrifice.
The ramp drops onto soft, red sand,
It's time for us to make a stand.
We need to brave our fears,
And conceal our inner tears.
For the brothers that were stranded upon the beach,
You will forever teach, as you rest on Juno Beach.

Dan Tweedle, Grade 9
Grimsby Secondary School, ON

Cinderella

Cinderella dressed in rags, went downstairs to pack her bags
She was going to the ball, if she finished scrubbing halls
When she got downstairs however; she wasn't able to tell whether
Her siblings left without her or, they wouldn't let her out the door

She went into her room and sighed, hid her face, began to cry
But as her teardrops hit the floor; she saw someone in the frame of the door
Cinderella then looked up, saw the fairy and dropped her cup
Immediately she bent down, but stopped when she saw she now wore a gown

Her hair and her shoes had changed as well, the slippers were made of glass, she could tell
A pumpkin turned into a coach, "You have till midnight, at the most"
Ella went and had some fun, and she caught the eye of someone
The prince decided to take a chance, he went up to Ella and asked her to dance

Ella now was in such awe; she started dancing, and she saw
Her sister's jealous faces true; until the clock struck quarter-to
It dawned on her as the clock struck twelve, she was doomed, as they say, she was back to herself
As fast as she could, she ran back to her coach, but it was no longer "the pumpkin with the most"

She ran down the stairs, her slipper remained, the prince found it then while he held back the pain
Then creating a search, he set out to find, the lovely girl who left it behind
After two weeks work, he came to a house; with three lovely daughters, and a pet mouse
The third girl fit perfectly into the shoe, and they went to the castle to start off anew

Devon Jones, Grade 7
Bayview Public School, ON

Home

I'm going home.
Where is home?
An odd shaped building made of bricks?
Or maybe a music store, emotions pouring out, with rhythm?
Maybe a friend's house, your not close to any of your relatives
Maybe a park, no one to tell you not to swing too high, or slide down too fast.
Maybe a laundry room, the washing machine so loud no one can hear you scream.
Maybe a computer room, you can type all your needing to release.
Maybe school, all you focus on is historic dead guys and foreign languages you'll never understand.
Maybe in a hospital, you remember that these people are suffering worse than you.
Maybe in a younger sibling's nursery, you remember how simple life was when you understood nothing.
Maybe in a cemetery wishing you were with that loved one.
Or maybe in your mother's arms, You can cry forever and you know she won't make fun of your pain.
As long as you can be somewhere, without a care in the world.
It's home.

Alessia Mastrorillo, Grade 7
St Clare Catholic Elementary School, ON

A Day at the Beach

The water splashing in my face as I run into the nice cold water. Feeling free for the first time in a long time. The cold sand going all over my leg as I kick down my sandcastle for the third time. The water from the beach tickling my toes as I try to reenter the lake. Being dried off by the sun's burning rays. Feeling the coziness of my towel as I lay down to rest.

Josh DeHaan, Grade 7
Milverton Public School, ON

Memories

I'm moving away to another place
Where I will be an unknown face.
A shadow in society
Where my only friend I'll have, is me.

I lie on my bed and drift away
To another time with brighter days.
These happy thoughts fill me with glee
These thoughts are all my memories.

Our great big deck and the big ol' trees.
The buzzing of the bumble bees.
The calming wind that blew at night
That soothed my soul and took the fright.

And then of course, there's all my friends
The good times I had with them are without end.
Those people I've known for so long
Push me forward and keep me strong.

I know that soon I'll meet new friends
And there'll be happiness without end
And soon new memories there will be
For Mom and Dad and even me.

Brent Cosgrove, Grade 9
Elizabeth Sutherland School, NS

Cheated on You

I don't let you get to where you're going to
You know I only do what I want to
Well you heard I'm a heart breaker
And you feel a little sicker
But what I'm getting to makes you lonely
When the guys ask what your problem man
You only shake your head and move on
On Sunday you only pass by
But on the way you hear the singing
And you just can't go any further
You walk inside and there I stand
In my wedding dress but with another man
And the sight you see is too much for you
I cheated on you I see that now
I used to think I was too good for you, but
You were the better part of me
I am without you now
Without you forever and ever
You told me I would always be a part of you
Now that I can see
You will always be a part of me.

Joyce Neustaeter, Grade 8
La Crete Public School, AB

White

Blankness,
Like when I'm with you
I don't know what to say.
So I say nothing so that I don't mess things up.
But you wonder why I never say anything.
Blurry,
like my mind when I'm with you.
Blank not thinking of anything but you and what not to say.
And how beautiful you are in your dress,
But you think of why I never say anything.
You,
Perfect for me but my mind is white.
Blurry like a snow storm I see the words but I don't say them.
I'm too scared to mess things up
I don't want you to leave.

Tyler Smith, Grade 9
FE Madill Secondary School, ON

9/11

As I watch the news about 9/11
A hijacked plane crashes
You see the sadness in my eyes
As I watch the Twin Towers stumble down
And turn to ashes
Thousands of people turn into angels
I cannot believe this is real
How could someone plan such a disgrace
At this moment, I feel like crying

Take away our fears
Wipe away our tears
Send us peace
In this world full of jealousy
That's all we ask for is PEACE

Bianca Théberge, Grade 8
Macdonald High School, QC

As the Sun Rises

As the sun rises, it's orange and yellow.
It sings a song, like the soft song of a cello.
Across the ocean where it never ever ends
Straight and flat until it looks like it bends.
This sight that I see, just look take a glance.
The beauty of it all can put you in a trance.
Out of the nothing come clouds dark and grey.
That means only one thing, a storm's coming today.
Who knew the ocean could make such a wave.
To be caught in this storm, it could take you to your grave.
As the storm started to stop and decay.
Out of the clouds shot a bright sunray.
All is now stilled, all is now calm.
No need to be afraid the oceans back in your palm.
Back to the beginning where the sun rises its rays
It will continue like this for the rest of its days.

Jillian Clary, Grade 8
École Notre-Dame-des-Vertus, SK

The World

A world of pain, sorrow, and death
Hiding behind a cheerful mask
Confusion strikes one player
As hate engulfs his life
Ever searching for the one
The one who inflicted all this suffering
This is not just a game
Not so innocent as people think
Oblivious to the world around them
They play
As evil still walks the lands
The terror of death approaches
Fear surfaces
Bloody screams in the background
Welcome to the world

Kelly Thieson, Grade 9
Rosslyn School, AB

Camille

C urious
A rtistic
M agical
I ntelligent
L iving it up
L adylike
E ager

Camille V. Dutil, Grade 8
Collège Jésus-Marie de Sillery, QC

Stage Fright

The butterflies in your tummy
The knot you can't get out
A person inside you yelling
Wanting to scream and shout

Your mouth hanging wide open
Your body frozen like ice
The monster kicking inside you
That isn't very nice

Wanting to run away
And hide under your bed
Feeling very dizzy
Like someone hit you in the head

You want to disappear
Vanish on the spot
Feeling very thirsty
Sweaty and hot

I know how you feel
So I'll give you some advice
Think in a positive way
And don't be so uptight

Irene De Souza, Grade 7
Immaculate Conception, BC

Be Who You Are

The world washes away,
waiting for your wounds to wake.
Only to waste the full insanity of them,
by destroying all those who try to help.
When we look into their eyes we see the truth,
but we know we can't handle it so we walk away in despise.
Not enjoying what we did but we live with it.

In our minds,
we handle it our way.
Not the right way but our way.
Those who don't like it are the ones who don't understand.
What you have to go through they're on the outside looking in.

You fall for others, insane ways.
Due to those on the outside thinking you're the bad guy.
That's when it's enough, and you awake a new person.
What has happened cannot control your life
because when you make it control you,
You only hurt yourself.

Just rise to your feet and tell yourself:
"What you say and what you do, cannot affect me, I am who I am."

Ben Elliott, Grade 7
William G Davis Public School, ON

Questions for You

The environment loves us
she cradles us in her leafy vegetation
she provides natural shelters
she whispers sweet advice with the all-knowing breeze
she is our home
The environment loves us
Do you show your love for her?

We never noticed the environment's cry for help
We never noticed her more frequent temper tantrums
We never noticed her stinging tears of rain that fell from the skies
We never noticed her fever rising
The environment is sick
How can you save her?

You know she's worth it
You know she is ill
You can't let her suffer anymore or we'll all have to pay the price
So stand together and do your part
How many doctors will it take?
None
It will take all of Human kind!

Amy Muzik, Grade 8
St Peter Catholic High School, ON

Natural Flaw

Oh! What a tragic site the world has become
For it has become a breathing nightmare for some
We may believe we live in a blissful place
However, the world is masked away from our face
With wars and battles contaminating a city
Without a thought of the insanity
The world we consume today
Was not the one from the dreams of yesterday
With people, accepting the lack of respect
And not caring about what is the effect
But again
I hear from some
Oh! What a tragic site the world has become

Besma Chowdhury, Grade 8
The Elms Junior and Middle School, ON

The Bear

As the sun rose
And the night fell
My heart spun with excitement and joy
It was coming out of its cave!
The battle began
My eyes shone like they had never shone before
I grabbed my note book
Bite
I drew endlessly…
There was blood on my paper
As the sun was sinking
I hit, it swiped its claws
My soul rose towards the sky
Night began
All that was left was a drawing
Of a mother bear and her cub

Kylee Seto, Grade 7
Ecole Rose-des-Vents, BC

Figure Skating Is My Favorite Sport

Figure skating is my favorite sport,
It certainly is the best sport for me,
When you get new skates you can get a sore,
When you land a big jump you'll shout with glee.

I love to do a lot of skills and dance,
In dance I always do the "canasta,"
When I land a big jump I want to prance,
When I look out to the stands I see Ma.

I always love to do lots of free skate
I get really excited to land jumps
When I do a perfect spin it's like fate
When I land big jumps I get goose bumps.

Figure skating is my favorite sport
It certainly is the best sport for me.

Kristine Everett, Grade 7
Riverton Early Middle Years School, MB

Your Memory

You came one day, and said to me
That you were going far, far away
You were leaving me here all alone
With no one to share the rest of my life.
I looked back on the many past days
When you'd come by, just like today
We'd go together, for long walks in the woods
Which seemed tame then, but very frightening now.
We'd go swimming in the nearby creek
Then lie on our backs to watch the moon rise
And count the stars which shone brightly above
Till we heard my mother calling, it was time to come home.
We'd run through the wheat fields on my farm
The wind blowing our hair back till we could run no more
The wheat still stands, but it's no longer welcoming
I can't go running through it without you.
Now that you're gone, I've nothing left to do
But sit here alone, and try to keep from missing you.
I often lie awake, till deep into the night
Wondering if there is someone else, but I know that no one
Could ever take your place.

Kathy Waldner, Grade 9
Twilight Colony School, MB

Politicians

The politicians had a lot of power
The dictators caused lots of trouble
Poverty was all around and
War resurfaced again and again

The dictators caused lots of trouble
Killing innocents, causing confusion
War resurfaced again and again
Many were harmed and countless were lost

Killing innocents, causing confusion
Malevolent dictators ruled the world
Many were harmed and countless were lost
Closed in their fists was the power to harm

Malevolent dictators ruled the world
Believing themselves to be the almighty God
Closed in their fists was the power to harm
Forgetting that God was watching them, forever and ever

Believing themselves to be the almighty God
They had the passion for power over all
Forgetting that God was watching them, forever and ever
One day they fell, and with them their power

Roshan Bagga, Grade 9
St George's School, BC

Global Warming

Global warming,
Nobody likes it
It threatens so many things
No more white Christmases
Everything is getting greener and greener
Warmer and warmer

All because of pollution
What we really really have to do
To stop this awful thing is stop pollution
So please Canada
Let's stop global warming.

Dario Armas, Grade 8
Macdonald High School, QC

A Moment

This feeling inside me,
is hard to describe.
With everyone watching,
its something I hide.

I want to communicate,
I want to share.
But every time I try,
I start to shed tears.

My world goes black,
my heart gets cold.
Now I realize,
there's no hand to hold.

The earth below me,
soon seems to fade.
As time goes by,
all things change.

Emyle Wong-Hoffman, Grade 9
Burnaby South Secondary School, BC

My Camp!

Beautiful, calm lake
filled with fish so great.
Lots of animals big and small.
Deer, frogs and baby bald eagles,
look around see the trees,
filled with birds, bats and a
whole lot of bees.
Listen, hear the wind and the
sound of humming bird
wings!
At night hear the chirp of the
almighty bullfrog saying hi.
Bye for now great woods so deep.

Chelsey Whalen, Grade 8
Elizabeth Sutherland School, NS

Parting from Your Homeland

Have you had your homeland crushed,
Like Iraq or South Vietnam?
The complete environment airbrushed,
With acid and napalm.

Cities in destruction,
Homeless by the roads.
We keep good care of our children,
While our living room explodes.

We have nowhere else to go,
Whatever will we do?
Leaving the country in sorrow,
Here from the airplane view.

Now we've reached Canada,
A place of endless peace.
The life of a new era,
And the beauty of the geese.

Mehwar Raza, Grade 7
Beverley Heights Middle School, ON

Love

Love is like a box of roses
It's all about the way it poses
When you get it in your heart
When it leaves you fall apart
But never forget if you are true
That your heart will never leave you
But if you do any cheating
Your heart will be beating
And it's all about the time you spend
Until you die at the end
Love is a wonderful thing
Please don't let it be a fling

Sheldon Houle, Grade 9
Gladys Cook Educational Centre, MB

Feelings

Happiness is yellow like the sun,
It stays bright even at night

Excitement is red like a bull,
It can't be trapped inside

Peace is white like the clouds,
it floats gently in the sky

Disappointment is gray like fog,
It never goes away

Anger is red like a burning fire,
It's like being denied your deepest desire

Hazen Phillips, Grade 7
St Anne School, SK

Rosalie

R adiant
O riginal
S entimental
A good worker
L adylike
I ntelligent
E nergetic

Rosalie Boutin, Grade 8
Collège Jésus-Marie de Sillery, QC

Forgive and Forget

Forgetting
the past
Forgiving
each other
Let's try to
make things right,
and reunite
with each other.
The love deep inside
runs and collides
The day you came into my heart
it finally started a spark.
Forgiving and forgetting
is all you have to do.
Be with me
so my dreams come true!

Tiana Yu, Grade 7
Menno Simons Christian School, AB

My Game

I examine the ball
it's small white and round
with little dimples all over.
I drop the ball
I feel the grass on my hands
as I set the ball up
I can feel that little breeze,
pushing on my face.
I reach to the bag
grab the club
I can feel the grip rubbing
between my hands
as I prepare to swing...

The grass is white now
the little white ball
with dimples all over
sits in the dark building
gently waiting
for the green grass
to come again.

Jared Stewart, Grade 8
Nationview Public School, ON

My Cat

My cat is gentle and very sweet;
She eats candy while she walks down the street.
And when she comes home,
She goes straight to sleep.

My cat's no trouble when it comes to food;
A tin of tuna is always good.
She eats it all up in one single bite,
And then she runs off out of sight.

Later, I find her under my bed,
Waiting for me to pet her all up.
I kiss her good night
And turn off the lights.

I wake up in the morning to see
That she is sleeping next to me.
She's all warm and cuddly,
So I pull her close to me.

She starts to purr
When I sing to her,
And then we get up
Hungry for breakfast.

Malika Karasek-Bereza, Grade 7
The Study School, QC

Perfection

So close, within grasp
Laughing shyly, taunting, daunting on and on
Longing for perfection
Work so very hard
Striving and pushing mental stress
And breaking apart into an awful mess
Perfection is so close but a mile away
Perfection is something causing unbelievable loss of rest
You see your imperfections every day
Live with them, think of them
Every second of every single day
Imperfection is living imperfect
But perfection, is simply being perfect
Perfection taunts you in the mirrors
Perfection laughs at you in your marks
Perfection drives and drives you hard
Tests your limits then rips you apart
Society magazines tell you this
Perfection is the only thing on the list
But life tells you another thing
That being perfect isn't what you're missing

Alannah O'Neill, Grade 9
Arnprior District High School, ON

Pain

Anger is a feeling.
Once you feel anger, you feel pain.
Once you feel pain, you feel hurt.
Once you feel hurt, you feel sad.
Once you feel sad, you feel hurt.
You hurt because others hurt you.
But does that give you the right to hurt others?
Why do we do it?
We do it because of pain.
But once you learn to forgive.
I believe you get a second chance to live.
Listen to what I say,
Because most of us had to learn the hard way.

Faron Henderson, Grade 9
Gladys Cook Educational Centre, MB

How Do They Do It?

I've never seen the things you have lived.
I can't imagine the pain of seeing a friend die of hunger.
When I am in my cozy bed,
You are in a small mud shelter,
When I take the bus to school,
You walk a mile looking for breakfast,
When I don't want to do the dishes,
You would go to bed hungry,
When I die at the age of 91,
You die of hunger at the age of 10,
When I complain something is too hard,
Or when I give up,
At the end of the day,
When I thank the Lord for all of my blessings,
I realize…
I couldn't last a day in your life.

Katie Mulvihill, Grade 7
St Augustine Elementary Jr High School, AB

Just Fine

When I look at me
I like what I see
And I know I shouldn't change
But all I hear is that I don't look good
And that's hard to take
Then when I look back
I've seen how I've changed
I shouldn't let anybody tell me how to dress
I know I shouldn't change my life for anybody.
Just for me
And now I know
When I'm walking down the street
And people are looking at me
They probably don't like me
But I won't change my life for anybody
But me
Because I'm just fine.

Malika Spooner, Grade 8
École Pierre-Brosseau, QC

Pencil's Love

Did you hear about the pencil
that writes every day
his love for another

His poem was beautiful
But one day an eraser came
an he won the heart of the other

The shock was terrible
after this day
The pencil's life became miserable
Then he threw his poems away...

David Bergeron, Grade 9
Ecole Secondaire Jean Grou, QC

The Hunt

Cradling his shiny new gun
He entered a world of green
The coarse mat of pine needles
Muffling his footsteps.

Moving steadily to the north
He spots a deer
Just over the next rise.
Its ears prick, its nose wiggles
As it raises its head
Sensing his presence.

While the deer runs away
With bounding leaps
The last and dwindling rays of sun
Filter through the lush canopy
To the still forest floor below.

An uneasy silence grips the forest
As darkening shadows lengthen
And creep from tree to tree
The weary hunter turns and trudges back
To his dark but cozy cabin.

Ryan Weber, Grade 7
Milverton Public School, ON

An Autumn Breeze

The leaves fall in an Autumn breeze
cracking when I step
a colourful carpet under my feet

The trees fall asleep
along with the bears
for winter is coming

The cold starts
For winter is near
and the white blanket begins its descent.

Kevin Donoghue, Grade 8
St Peter Catholic High School, ON

Why?

He asked if we could talk,
So we walked to a quiet spot.
With no one around but me and him.
My stomach started turning,
As I try not to cry.
I see his mouth open,
To speak the words that will end everything.
My heart started pounding,
When he said those two words,
Those horrifying words.
"It's over."
He hugged me and said,
"I'm sorry we just can't be together."
The he walked away.
As he walked away, all I could think, was all the good times we had together,
His great look,
And those stunning eyes.
When I saw his smile in my head,
I started to cry.
Then I wondered why?
Why was it over between me and him.

Ayla Gibeault, Grade 8
Lillian Berg Public School, ON

Remember

You are moving from a place, you've lived for many years,
Please, don't be sad because I've shed so many tears.
Remember all the bad times, and all the good times we've been through,
I just want to let you know that, I *will* miss you!
Remember all the funny things and all that awesome stuff,
You were always with me, though the situation was tough.
Remember when in youth group, when you would make me smile?
You really made that night rock, and through the whole week while!
When you leave us, have fun, when you go from the place not here today,
Please just remember that, your friendships are here to stay!

Hillary Freeman, Grade 9
St Benedict Catholic Secondary School, ON

Little Spirit

You rest upon the graceful wings of my white messenger birds
You linger in long summer shadows
Winking at me every time I turn
If I dare to look, you quickly vanish
Funny little sprite!
I know you still see me:
You leave ripples in the still ponds that I dream of at night
You glide along the moonbeams that brush by my hands while I write
Reading my secrets
Jack Frost spins by my window
Leaving traces of your reflection on the glass
My numb fingers trace the fine lines
You make me laugh,
Funny little sprite!
Skipping, spinning, dancing with me
Tickling my bare toes.

Sasha M. Fergusson, Grade 7
Tyee Elementary School, BC

Remembrance Day

Some families may have lost many relatives
While away at war
Some soldiers had to watch their friends for family
Struggles when they had been shot.

Remembrance Day is remember
Those who fought for us
The people who put their lives at risk
To save their country and families.
Jaleena Greene, Grade 7
Bayview Elementary School, BC

Mom

Smooth, pure, sand under my feet
A big rock with moss all over it
Loud waves violently crashing against the sand
The mist is rolling in, the fog,
my life is a mystery

I sit on this big rock, my feet in the sand,
My toes wet from the salty water,
A clear, beautiful voice fills my ears,
Big strong trees surround me

The voice has stopped, all that can be heard is the waves now
I want to stay here forever,
Forever, here on my rock,
Please don't leave me, memories

Staring at the strong, dangerous ocean
I am thinking of you
Are you thinking of me?

I feel you here with me
Please stay here
Don't leave me again.
Sarah Smith, Grade 8
British Columbia Christian Academy, BC

Sirens

Voices under the blue water,
Calling seductively to the sailor.
By this they slaughter,
Worse than the meanest jailer.

Honest sailor, deceitful pirate.
None of these men will be spared.
For the women's beauty will call to them,
For these women are the dark sea's gem.

They are the Sirens
The voices that lead men to drown,
To dance forever,
With the daughters of the deep ocean's crown.
Deanna Gardner, Grade 9
Pleasant Valley Secondary School, BC

I Am From...

I am from the shadows and spotlights of my own imagination,
The dark times, the light times, the sorrow and the joy,
Of my ever-changing, mood-shifting life.
This is where I am from.
I am from welfare and charity,
The good deeds and generosity of my fellow man,
I am from what seems to be luck, but may be fate,
And I am from my never-changing, ever-loving family.
This is where I am from.
I am from creativity, joy within poverty, peace in times of need.
I am from all that I ever needed,
All that anyone ever needed,
All that the world will ever really need,
Love is where I am from.
I am from looking back,
Looking back to where I am from,
And now I see, that even if this "luck" had not occurred,
Even if we had not become independent,
This poem would be the same,
Not one word would be different,
Especially the line "Love is where I am from."
Aaron Onstad, Grade 8
Burnaby North Secondary School, BC

Seasons

Seasons change and people grow,
We aren't the same friends that we used to know.
Our heads are now held proudly high,
When we used to just sit and cry.

We now won't eat to be the right size,
And all that we can think about are cute guys.
A long time ago we ate all that junk food,
And thought that boys were just icky and rude.

Our second home is now the mall,
We dress each day as if we are going to a ball.
We used to not like going shopping,
And only needed clothes fit for hopping.

We now have reputations to keep,
We can never be seen publicly to weep,
A long time ago no one cared,
And all of us really shared.

Now I remember and really miss,
Our old times' carelessness,
I wish I had it all again,
But shopping *is* nice now and then!
Morgan Sutherland-Deveen, Grade 8
St Peter Catholic High School, ON

I Am

I Am
one that is not whom he wishes to be
but who he has to be
I am
one who stands out,
even if it seems I fit in.
I feel as though I'm lost, with no sense of direction
because my view is always changing.
Is my glass half empty or half full?
I do not know if I'm being looked up to
or down upon.
I struggle to find myself.
But that is who I have to be,
at least for now.

Zac Douglas, Grade 9
FE Madill Secondary School, ON

Fear of Night

In the darkness of the night,
I think about, and look out for light,
In my dreams, it shines so bright,
And often takes away my fright.

Horrid creatures lurk at night,
But if they see the shining light,
In the darkness, oh so bright,
They will retreat, eyes filled with fright.

The darkness will be gone, with the night,
The sun will rise, and shed its light,
I'll look ahead, my life shines bright,
In my heart, no trace of fright.

Then once again, will come the night,
I'll look forward to the morning light,
But until then, the angels bright,
Will keep me safe, I'll sleep, no fright.

Lauren Wong, Grade 8
Mother Teresa Catholic High School, ON

To a Friend

You have the nicest eyes
Brown and open
You have the best voice
It's measured and calm
You have the best ears
Perfect for listening to what I say
You understand me the most
With your intelligent mind
We share all kinds of secrets
Hiding under the blankets in the dark
Completely unafraid since we were together
You are my best friend
And you know the best way to make me smile.

Maggie Brooks, Grade 9
Lester B Pearson Catholic High School, ON

Immune

Mirrors were created ages ago,
For some it was essential
For some others, it was their worst enemy
My eyes couldn't avoid them
I hated myself

Wanting to look like someone else was my biggest wish
Crying was selfish
Living was fair
Hurting myself wasn't worthwhile

I realized that people were dying
While I was crying
Crying for not finding myself pretty was ridiculous

In the end, I started thanking God
For giving me the chance to live this life
In having a good health and a beloved family
I started enjoying it
Instead of wasting it in being sad.

"Life is too short to be lived this way"

Imane Bouymaj, Grade 9
Ecole Secondaire Jean Grou, QC

Peace

Suspending and exciting,
But always ends,
Ups and downs happening!
With good time and good friends

But what we take for granted,
Has its ways to stop,
We have our environment,
Sizzling ready to pop!

Health Decreasing
Lives being taken
People hurting the innocent
Dead, Families Shaken

So now is time to take a stand,
Be the best you can,
Help those around you
Start think about them stop thinking me!

So next time you're asked
"What do you want for the holidays?"
Think and say, "Mom, I want world peace,"

Salma Hees, Grade 8
The Elms Junior and Middle School, ON

Run Through the Jungle

Danger with every step,
Relatives so distant.
Home, away from the smoke and destruction.
Home.
Zeros scream overhead.
Screaming everywhere,
Screaming.
We are all part of the death machine, Relentless.
War is just oil on the gears.
With every explosion up ahead,
A hero is born,
And a hero lost.
Mud and silt,
Another skin.
Shells blazing,
A mother's kin.
It looms ahead,
Like an 18 wheeler on your doorstep.
Freedom that is,
Freedom.
It's what we strive for — Freedom.

Brad McClenaghan, Grade 9
FE Madill Secondary School, ON

Life

The beauty with life can be great
But life can also be really bad

Life can go the way you want it to go but
If you throw your dreams away you won't have a life
You want!

Life can make you Happy
And life can make you sad

If you smile you will be happy
If you frown you will be sad or mad
God made us to be happy and cheerful

You can make your life fun
Or you can make your life boring
The way you feel makes your day

Life can be short, life can be long
Life can be dull, life can be jolly
Life can be bright, life can be dark
Life is like the sun
Life is everything
I love life!

Stacy Irvine, Grade 7
Riverton Early Middle Years School, MB

Loud

A rooster cock-a-doodle doing through the morning sky.
A Harley Davidson screaming through the streets.
A band noisily playing to their tune.
A jet loudly blowing through the sky.
And me
A blasting slap shot soaring into the goal.

Thomas Schnitzler, Grade 7
St Anne School, SK

Fall

Fall comes and fall goes,
but when it's here it's a beautiful time.
Orange and yellow leaves soon ready to fall,
soon to join the others on the ground.

Fall indeed is a beautiful time,
Colourful leaves everywhere on the ground,
For kids to pile them up,
into gigantic hills,
to jump in and have fun.

All the animals getting ready for winter,
gathering and storing food.
Chipmunks and squirrels everywhere trying to gather food,
before it's too late when winter comes.

Fall would soon end,
so sad as it went by so fast,
And all the leaves soon to be covered,
in a big sheet of snow.

Jordan Malette, Grade 8
St Peter Catholic High School, ON

Day Dreamer

I hear the noise "please remain seated"
the announcer said.
The riders in the back row
SCREAMING I am SHAKING.
My arm hair standing up.
The motion of the coaster started the lift hill launching
me straight up 40 mph like blood rushing through my body.

And out of no where I drop 95' straight down.
The wild turns and half loops.
Threw me to the edge of my seat,
right into a tunnel with a silent stop and a big awkward silence.
I open my eyes and count one, two, we shot off.
I saw the other people,
out of the corner of my eye.
The coaster stopped
or did it?
In the sound of my ear, "son, it's time to get on"
I slightly open my eyes.
I'm such a day dreamer.

Corbin Hagerman, Grade 8
William G Davis Public School, ON

Candle

As I sit on the table alone,
I dread the day when I'll be lit.
The family gathers as I moan,
I'm going to die where I sit.

The little girl grabs the red lighter,
the boy grabs the loud ringing phone,
I sit on the table a fighter,
yet wishing to be all alone.

After she lights my waxy long wick
I throw a tantrum with my flame.
They don't notice, not even a lick.
I sat there 'til the snuffer came.

As he graciously put out my fire,
I whispered a thank you to him.
They all left and I began to tire,
once again I'm in the room, dim.

Kayla Kanwischer, Grade 7
Kanwischer Home School, AB

If I Was a Boy

As I gaze into the mirror
I find myself looking
staring, wondering
why this is happening to me.
I am not a little boy
that one played with toy cars,
or pretend I was a super hero.
I am not the little boy who
wanted to start school
that played with my dad
or played in the mud.
Still…
I don't notice my feeling,
my growing,
and my talking.
I'm a young man
I can feel it
still…
I am the one playing with toy cars
pretend I am a super hero,
and playing with my dad.

Nicole Arnold, Grade 8
Chaplin School, SK

Audrey

A mazing
U ncomplicated
D etermined
R esponsible
E arnest
Y é yé

Audrey Imbeault, Grade 8
Collège Jésus-Marie de Sillery, QC

How It Begins

You begin your day at the end of the world,
Your step may change the guilt of all,
So don't follow.

The crowds throw themselves away
Believe in you, you can make it through the pain,
Changing is harder
When you're told numerous lies.
Scars and bruises all hurt,
Sigh and agree and you might as well throw your life away.

Melissa Nadeau, Grade 8
MacKenzie Secondary School, BC

Pearl

The water was so calm, its surface looked like floating silk;
A pearl sat in her palm, a round and perfect drop of milk.

It glowed quite royally, exquisite with a magic shine;
'Twas nature's little miracle that made her life so fine.

The gentle lap of waves on sand at night lulled her to sleep
On her small piece of promised land that lay for her to keep.

The sun sent golden rays of light from sunrise straight to dusk;
The moon and stars shone faithfully, like friends she'd always trust.

The wafting scent of salty air and gentle kiss of breeze
Brought roses to her cheeks and made her happy and at ease.

But yet, among the wonders that surround this little girl
The miracle that she loves most is you, her lucky pearl.

Elisabeth Farquhar, Grade 8
Villa Maria High School, QC

Dreams

You cannot touch or feel dreams,
You cannot hear or talk to dreams,
But what you can do, is imagine them.

Dreams are things you imagine, they could be good or bad.
Your dream could be about winning your first medal, or about a beautiful shining sun.
But it could also be about a thunderstorm, or a dreadful war.

Dreams are magical things that transport you to a different world.
They let you express yourself, or share your emotions.
They make you cry, laugh, smile, get mad, or anything you can think of.

You can dream about the craziest thing, and you would think it's real.
You always believe what's in your dream,
But you don't believe what is actually real.

Dreams wait for you at night,
They wait for you in your cozy bed,
They wait for you wherever you fall asleep, to create another magical moment.

Caroline Najjar, Grade 7
The Study School, QC

Someday

I cannot hear your laughter,
I cannot see your smile.
I wish that we could talk again
If only for a while.

I know you're watching over me,
Seeing everything I do.
And though you'll always be with me,
I'll always be missing you.

You taught me that life is much too short,
And at anytime could end.
But know that no matter where you are,
You will always be my friend.

And when it's time for me to go,
You'll be there to show me the way.
I wish that you could still be here,
But I'll see you again, someday.

Crystal Kowalski, Grade 7
Englefeld School, SK

A Stars

A star dreams about something
that can make it shine when she's in the sky

But the star I am doesn't want
to be in the sky

I wanna be with you because
I think you can make me shine

Stephanie Debrosse, Grade 9
Ecole Secondaire Jean Grou, QC

Why?

Why is it that when someone dies, we mourn their death,
instead of celebrating their life?
Why is it that when you have the chance to say good bye,
you always say, see you later?

Why do we always wait until the last minute to say goodbye?
When in reality the person we are saying goodbye to,
may already be gone.

Why is it that we never realize what we have,
until it is gone?
Why do we always do this not only to us,
but to everyone else?

Why? We are afraid that if we say goodbye, it will end.
We are afraid of reality, even though we live it every day.
We don't want to realize that the end has come,
we may never get it back.

Hayley Leonard, Grade 9
Eric Graves Memorial Jr High School, NS

Lexy

She bounds out of the truck,
she's excited to see me, I smile.
"Hey Lexy!" I yell,
she races past, I laugh
you can stand in her way, go right ahead,
she won't bump into you.
She's a black, and shiny blur.
I get dizzy just watching her.
You can't stop her
wait a while, until she's calmer, and less energized.
"Lexy!" I call, and she comes, running freely,
with her ears flapping in the wind, with me waiting,
and watching.
She makes me happy,
she's a huge mound of energy,
she sits down beside me, finally exhausted,
as I'm watching her intently, petting her,
while she pants heavily.
She's my dog,
she's Lexy, and I love her,
as much as she is energetic.

Erin van Winden, Grade 8
Nationview Public School, ON

Untitled

I was very nice with this friend
I remember that her father hated me for some reasons
I heard that she can't see me anymore
I saw her father yelling at her
I worried that she was punished
I thought "I can't see her anymore"
But, I want to change.

I am worried
I think that I am going to explode
I need to try to not see her
I try to talk to her on the phone
I feel bad
I forgive her father for that
Now I can change

I will forget her
I choose to tell her
I dream to be with her
I hope that it will happen
I predict it will happen
I know that it will happen

I will change

Ahmad Khalaf, Grade 8
École Pierre-Brosseau, QC

Why Should It Matter?

If snowflakes are different shapes
Why should it matter?
If footprints are different sizes
Why should it matter?
If evergreens are different heights
Why should it matter?
If rainbows are different colors
Why should it matter?
Then if people are different
Shapes, sizes, heights, and colors
Why should it matter?

Olivia Pei, Grade 8
College Avenue Public School, ON

Early Morning Snow

Dawn finally breaks,
The sky's clear as can be.
There's snow on the ground
As far as you see.
The air's deathly cold,
And the snow's a foot deep.
It's still early morning,
But none are asleep.
The children laugh gaily;
The adults lounge around.
Breakfast is forgotten;
Outside there's hardly a sound.
The earth seems peaceful,
Quiet, and such,
Until the children come out;
No spot's left untouched.
The clouds return
And the snow starts to flow.
Tomorrow we'll have some more
Early morning snow.

Emilia Pierson, Grade 7
Keystone Academy, BC

Western Cowboy

Riding through the lonely plains
Shifting in the saddle, pulling the reigns
"Hurry up" My boots dig in his sides
Pain pushing him to lazy strides.

The sensitive horse trots all day long
Throughout it all stays very calm
My pet, my babe, my western horse
I love you when you round the course.

I've won medals for his beauty
I think my horse is a total cutie
To tell him "thank you" carrots will do
Hay bales and green grass he loves too.

Levi Kleinsasser, Grade 7
Milford Colony School, AB

Pizza

"That will be 30 minutes,"
answers the voice on the other line.
My mouth waters as we wait.
It starts to feel like years.
At last my mom says "let's go."

We watch him pull the pizza
out of the oven,
the cheese sizzling.
The aroma devastates me as I get closer.
At last he hands it to us.

I open the box
and take a piece,
the flavour, so intense.
I could taste everything at once.
No pizza will ever taste like this.

Devin Fraser, Grade 8
Nationview Public School, ON

Freedom Wears No Shoes

Freedom wears no shoes,
She runs swift on agile feet.
When imprisoned she can't move.
Her feet are chained,
Until some great battle frees her,
And freedom runs again.

Kalisse Van Dellen, Grade 8
Home School, AB

See Them Again

It starts off so good,
getting by as much as we could.
Watching them being taken away,
there's nothing left for me to say,
God I wish they never left this way.
I'm trying to be strong,
but yet everything feels so wrong.
Sitting in my room,
thinking of the good times and bad,
I never thought I could feel so sad.
Wishing I could hear their voice,
hold their hand,
give them a hug,
or see them smile.
I already know that won't be
happening for a while.
Thinking about them every day,
knowing that they're happy and
having fun in their new home.
Makes me so happy, and helps
me count the day till I see them again.

Tori Poirier, Grade 9
FE Madill Secondary School, ON

Fall

The third season
The time between summer and winter
The time of preparation
The beginning of school
The ending of warmth
And the beginning of something new

Christopher Sayyeau, Grade 8
St Peter Catholic High School, ON

Time

Time will freeze,
then the world,
will end,
life will stop,
thoughts and memories,
will cease,
existence never happened,
hope is slipping,
disappearing,
worry is flowing,
silently, speed accumulates,
velocity is always,
before impact,
wondering what's happening,
screaming with rage,
with fear,
disappointment is creeping,
through thoughts.
The end is near.
The end is here.

Sheryl Robitaille, Grade 8
Ecole intermediaire Sacre-Coeur, ON

Candle in the Wind

Like pain on a heart
Is the wind on a candle
Pain will break
And wind will blow away

As the candle is burning
It's almost dying
And as my heart is beating
You are leaving

If my heart was a candle
The wind wouldn't blow its fire away
'cause the power of love
would not make it fade

Don't leave me alone
I'm scared in the dark
The fire is out
And I have too many doubts

Sara Filion, Grade 9
Ecole Secondaire Jean Grou, QC

Fear

It was November the 7th
My friend's birthday.
Her house was up the street
So I walked.
The snow lightly fell, the moon shone, the wind whistled
I was only across the street from my house
When a car sped past me
Slammed on the brakes and sped backwards toward me
I was scared, I was terrified
I was only twelve —
And I was all alone
I started to run
Car almost hit me
I never ran faster,
Ran up my stairs
In the door
Screamed at my parents
They ran outside
I was crying
I was shaking
The car was gone!

Chelsa Gelsinger, Grade 8
MacKenzie Secondary School, BC

Feelings

Feelings you have
Not created by you but by God
Who gave you these feelings for a reason
These are the feelings you have

Feelings of caring
Watching over someone you care about
Taking care of what they do
Helping when someone needs it

Feelings of having faith
Giving your life to God in His hands
Letting someone do something that he or she can do
Putting life at a risk with God on your side

Feelings of forgiveness
Heart of saying "It's all right"
Knowing that someone didn't mean it
Having no grudge against someone

Feelings of anger
Something that everyone has
But cannot be controlled easily
But only with God's help you can overcome it

Adeline Teh, Grade 8
British Columbia Christian Academy, BC

Love

Love is easy to fall into
Yet so hard to fall out of
Sometimes your heart can be like a battle field.
Fighting for love
They say love lasts forever
Yet forever seems to end
Love isn't always what you think it will be
It can hurt you in so many ways
But at the same time
Make you feel unexplainable
Every time your heart breaks it always takes
A little bit of everything you've gained

Bryanne Lacombe Gobeil, Grade 7
Macdonald High School, QC

Slipping Away

Like two dark clouds on a stormy night
My thoughts clashing like thunder with all its might
I sit in the corner, questions echoing off the wall
Feeling as if sucked into a dark abyss; a long deep fall.

Gray creeping in, staining the carefree days
Standing alone on a forked path, going two different ways
The ground fails around me; I'm hanging by a thread
Everyone's long gone since; so far ahead.

A blood red knife bluntly strikes the sky
My footsteps pick up dust, the world heaves a sigh
One step into oblivion, the land vast and stricken
A net cast in the shadows; secrets woven.

One tip of a domino, all else follows
One mistake after another, weeping after our own woes
One miscalculated measure, one daunting dismay
All else crumbles, slowly slipping away.

Annie Tseng, Grade 9
Burnaby Central Secondary School, BC

Nick Woods

Ever since I was a child
I have always heard how relaxing golf is
Just the whole idea of the perfect swing
What that is or how you do the perfect swing
I don't know
So I thought I would try
After 5 minutes of golf
I was kicking and screaming my lungs out.
Now as I look back on those memories
I see the steps I have taken
To get to the perfect swing
Just feeling the golf club slicing through the air
As I smash that #3 Titleists golf ball
At 120 mph
Out of the bunker
At Sandy row golf course
Then hearing the soft faint sound
Of the swoosh as the golf ball passes into the 6th hole

Nicholas Maheux, Grade 8
Nationview Public School, ON

Love

What is love?
Is it romance?
Is it two people getting together?
I can't tell.
I have never felt love.
I went out with plenty of boys.
None show me love.
Have you felt love?

Diamond Peeace, Grade 7
Nawigizigweyas Education Centre, SK

Dreamer

My life is now shattered,
My education is tattered,
My tries to please have faltered.

I could try to make life better,
I could work so much harder.

But, no instead, I dream through the day,
I dream the long day away,
And I cannot stop this terrible way.

I do nothing in this wretched life,
But dream of living without strife.

I am the dreamer,
Dreamer of the impossible,
And the dreams that never come true.

Michelle Au Yeung, Grade 9
Hugh McRoberts Secondary School, BC

Better Off*

You are my best friend,
No matter what I said.
You were always there for me,
Even when I told you not to be.
One day you moved away,
And my heart had to pay.
You were off to a different school,
And I was stuck the fool.
I sat at home,
All alone,
Because you didn't live down the street,
And weren't in my bus seat.
Meeting you,
Was the best thing I could do.
And letting you go,
Just came to show,
That you're better where you are.
Yet no matter how far,
'Til the end,
You will always be…my best friend.

Bobbie Gaucher, Grade 8
Macdonald High School, QC
*Dedicated to Bryan Shane

Something About Love

We all know that love is the perfect way to get hurt
And we all learned that someone who wasn't supposed to hurt you
Probably will
We also know that good-byes will always hurt
Memories, good or bad will always bring tears
And there is no word who can't replace those feelings.
To the world you may be just one person
But to one person you may be the whole world
This person will break your heart one day
That's why you don't make someone your everything
Because when they've gone
You've got nothing.

Marjorie Gonzalez Ortiz, Grade 9
Ecole Secondaire Jean Grou, QC

Clouds

We are the   We are the
People walking across the sky,
                             The bringers of rain and snow,
We are clouds   We are clouds
                             Who rise from earth, rivers,
And sea
                             From which we came,
We return to   We return to
As we let the rain
                             Fall
                             And the snow
Drift
Down to the ground so low   Down to the ground so low
Beneath us,
                             To lands of men
And of mountains of fire
                             Never to spew their molten contents
To the outside world again
                             Yet as we die, we bear the knowledge
That we will some day
Journey across the sky once more   Journey across the sky once more

Xuanyu An, Grade 7
Northridge Public School, ON

90 Minutes of a Soccer Game

I hear people insulting each other, I see a fight and I smell salty blood.
I see the referee giving out red cards. I feel my heartbeat,
the adrenaline from the anger and the heat coming out of my body.

I hear and see the crowds cheering. I see the soccer ball,
I see the net and I feel the eagerness to score.

I feel the soccer ball on my hurting foot from kicking the ball so much,
I see the soccer players shouting "pass the ball!" I see and smell the grass.

I smell sweat, I hear the whistle and I taste the ice cold water,
and the sour orange juice. My work here is done.

Crimson Jo, Grade 7
St Maurice School, MB

Child of Redeem

I
led
the t
hree wis
emen to a king, a babe of Royalty. He
came to Earth to save all men. Are
n't you blessed, you three wisem
en, you met this child of redeem,
and that is why you were born aga
in. Now I feel blessed, because I am
the Christmas star   and I was picked
to lead you   to this bab
y Je   sus.

Tabitha Kleinsasser, Grade 8
Milford Colony School, AB

Eraser Rain

Here comes the rain
The eraser rain
It falls and washes away the pain
Come unstoppable eraser rain
Erase the hate and erase the pain
Leave an empty frame
Eraser rain
If you can survive the rain
You will see the sun again
Here comes the unstoppable eraser rain

Kaleb Kemp, Grade 8
Captain Meares Elementary Secondary School, BC

Pretty Girl

Love can sometimes be like magic
But magic can sometimes be an illusion.
Things aren't always what they seem

Not all scars show and not all wounds heal
Sometimes you can't see the pain someone feels.

She puckers her lips with her ruby lipstick
Makes up her eyes
She's almost done with her disguise.
Today she tried something new
She tied her hair up just for you.

You walk by her and still don't care
Pretty girl, just wants some care
Scared girl, it's okay
Because tomorrow will be another day
Distant girl, who's out of sight

Go home and pray tonight
Because tomorrow will have a different light
For this boy will want to stay.

Theodora Matsoukas, Grade 8
Macdonald High School, QC

How Much You Mean to Me

Every time you say,
You want to end your life,
I just pray to get me through the night,
And I just hope that you will be all right,

Cause you always know that it's not too late,
It's never too late,
I think of you every day,
All I want is for you to be okay,
And I hope not to have to pay one day,

As we walk hand-in-hand,
Time slips by like grains of sand,
When we're apart I dream of you,
Hoping that you do too,

Love is fragile, love is blind,
Look at us two of a kind,
As we reach our destination,
I pause and turn in expectation,

No one knows how much you mean to me,
That's the way love should be.

Jeffrey Huberdeau, Grade 9
Gladys Cook Educational Centre, MB

Trixie

Here lies Trixie
She had a friend named Dixie
Once I had a little grey kitty,
She was so adorable and pretty

Big eyes and always wore a smile
She played and then took a nap for a while

Trixie was always so much fun
Trixie loved everyone

One day a man poisoned her
And we were so sad because there was no cure

I cried very hard
All my friends gave me a card

One day I went to the super-mart
And realized that she will always be in our heart

Kisses, hugs, and laughs, too
She had plenty more to give to you

Desarae Bilinski, Grade 7
Riverton Early Middle Years School, MB

The Amazon Rainforest
The mighty Amazon Rainforest is green and bold
Some of her trees are quite old
Her leafs are silk
She is Mother Nature and has a heart of gold
The Amazon basin is her sorrow which flows down her cheeks
We take her bounty and never give back as the lumberjacks cut down her children
Her trees are towers that cut through the air and into the sky
Her plants and flowers are like gold because they're small and valuable
I want to save her from her sorrow but what can I do I'm just a kid.

Jordan Madden, Grade 8
Macdonald High School, QC

Liberty's Dessert
Freedom
What does it really mean?
The dictionary defines it as a state in which somebody is able to act and live as he or she chooses,
Without being subject to any undue restraints or restrictions.
But what happened to the real meaning?
The days where we could run free in the fields of sunflowers,
And laugh out loud as our soles were tickled by the grass under our feet.
The days where love was love, and nothing else.
The days where every day of life meant something, another day to accomplish your goals.
Where is that now?
Where can we run free? In filthy city streets?
Whom can we love openly? Those who end up bitter enemies?
How can we live freely, when there's no longer any truth in this Godforsaken world?
It's a simple-to-pronounce seven letter word.
Why is it so hard for me to acquire?
I want my piece of sweet freedom.
I want my liberty with a cherry on top.
No strings attached, no genetically modified fruit.
My destiny wasn't written in the stars, because I've got the pen and book at hand.
And liberation is my ink.
So fire away, world.

Linda Luarasi, Grade 9
Northern Secondary School, ON

Mistakes
Frankly I don't know what to say, I won't cry over you today.
I know that you used me for that, I know that for a fact.
I stand clear from this path; I just can't see us like that.
Consider yourself lucky, that I'm here either way.
I'll stand on top of the planet and watch the stars fade away.
I found a rope on the moon, and I'll see you soon.
Your gift from outer space is getting strangled away from this disgusting place.
No need to lie sweetie, I finally figured you out.
You have changed and I hope you rearrange that when you're alone, I'll be fine on my own.
Don't come running to me ever again, there's a slim chance that I'll let you back in.
This time I'm not wrong, so please count me as long gone.
You had me at hello, but sorry I'll never come back.
This was your mistake, and it's not my fault if you feel heartache.
Think before you act, that's all I'll say about that.

Kimberly Kearns, Grade 9
Ritchie School, AB

Rescue

I got a sudden phone call,
from my sister last summer.
I was told about a horse,
that had been starved.
I rushed to this creature,
as quick as possible.
When I saw him,
I was speechless.
He walked out of a barnyard,
with no grass,
no shelter,
no clean water.
There was mud half way to his knees.
I gently brushed my hand across his nose,
where scars were left from a halter,
that had grown into his face.
I gently pet across his stomach,
where his ribs were showing.
I cleaned him up,
I took him home,
to a place where he belongs.

Taylor Houghton, Grade 8
Nationview Public School, ON

No! No! No! How Could This Happen?

I'm in my fort
It's made of wood.
It's kind of dangerous
But who really cares
So long as it's fun!

One night there's a thunder storm
Ka boom a crack of lightning fills the sky,
The rain flies down faster and faster
Bigger and bigger then it stops.

I go to my fort
Worried about it,
I hurried down the road
On my four-wheeler.

I'm there in a minute and a half
I walk through the forest,
Once I'm there I see the roof
OH NO! It collapsed.

I'm frustrated and angry
Because it took me forever to build,
But I grabbed my tools and I started it again.

Daniel Lillico, Grade 8
Nationview Public School, ON

The Walk

The leaves rustle on the ground
and the trees sway
with the now tamed wind.

I walk down the path,
him beside me.
His collar jingles.

Street lights flicker
on and off.
And then,

Darkness.
Silence.
Our footsteps are the only sudden noises.

More footsteps
but this time, not ours.
We are not alone.

Lexie Ward, Grade 8
Balmoral Drive Senior Public School, ON

Fall Leaves

The leaves paint the road.
As frost covers the window,
Fall is in the air.

Lauren Darvell, Grade 8
Balmoral Drive Senior Public School, ON

Planet Earth

The world is our home and not our garbage
But why do we keep it so dirty.

We throw away garbage on the ground
We can't even keep it clean.

People waste and can't even recycle
We get worse and worse.

If it were your home or your friends
Wouldn't you keep it clean.

We drive cars but it's not really helping
Why can't we all drive hybrids.

The Earth gives us life and we should be thankful
But all we do is answer back with destructions.

Why are we so mean with the Earth
If it were our friend we would respect him.

So all I'm trying to say is keep Earth clean
As it was your home.

Nicolas Gosselin, Grade 8
Macdonald High School, QC

Flooded Rivers

Machetes swing,
Rivers run red,
Not enough graves.
To bury the dead,
Innocent children,
Crying out in the night,
Why are they victims
Of this terrible fight!

Millions of people without a home,
Doomed throughout their country to roam.
Orphans left behind,
Destruction everywhere,
They wonder why,
People don't care!

Power and greed,
Invites people to kill.
While the world watches,
It won't stop till,
YOU TAKE ACTION!

Tashpreet Dhanoa, Grade 8
The Elms Junior and Middle School, ON

Bryan's Blunder in Buffalo

Did you see the Leafs game last night?
Oh, it made me close my eyes in fright.
We were winning one to zero,
When Bryan McCabe decided to be a hero.

He took the puck into his own zone,
And what he did made me groan.
He took a shot at his own net,
And he scored! Something that I will never forget.

Scoring the goal to tie the game,
Made him completely to blame.
It was a pretty good shot,
Too bad he shot it in his own slot.

What he did nearly made me cry,
All I could do was stare at the TV and sigh.
And to think that he is the highest paid player on the team,
All he does is make me scream.

Maybe I'm not being very fair,
After the game, he wasn't exactly walking on air.
Do you think Toronto will get rid of him,
If he plays like that, his chances of staying are very slim.

Rehaan Khan, Grade 9
Delphi Secondary Alternative School, ON

Hockey

My sharp blades hit the ice,
The wind blew in my face as I whisked
Down the frozen surface!
My stick hit the cold shiny ice,
The wicked fast puck came to me!
There were 5 seconds left in the last period.
I blasted the puck...
The arena went silent.
The puck hit the back of the worn out net,
It was in!
The extremely loud buzzer went off,
The crowd went wild!!

Amber Davies, Grade 7
Riverton Early Middle Years School, MB

My Love and Heart for You

My love for you
is like the beautiful doves soaring through the sky
My heart for you
is like the center of a delicious blueberry pie
My love for you
is like sparkling wires
My heart for you
is like the desire of a wood burning fire
My love for you
is like a blooming flower
My love and heart or you
is no longer here
now that you have disappeared

Stephanie Chicoine, Grade 7
Macdonald High School, QC

Hockey

Hockey is an awesome game,
Make it to the hall of fame.
Sizzling shots and amazing saves,
All set up by the perfect plays
In he comes on a clear breakaway!
Will he deke or will he shoot away?
Fans holding their breath and on their feet
Can you spot one empty seat?
The player dekes and makes the goalie flop.
The all-star is robbed! What a sensational stop!
The clock winds down and still a tie
Looks like we're headed to overtime.
No one scored; to a shootout we go!
The fans are tense in every row!
The first four score and fifth player misses,
This shot decides on which team wins it.
Montreal scores; they've won hockey's prize!
Lord Stanley's cup is in their eyes.
Congratulations! My dad and I cheer!
I just can't wait till hockey next year!

Bryan Glasgow, Grade 7
Macdonald High School, QC

Friends

When I need a shoulder to cry on
You're there for me my friend
When I need to get something out
You always have the ear to lend

From boys to school to gossip to fads
We've talked about it all
And I know that whatever comes my way
You'll pick me up after I fall

Tragedy to happiness we've been there together
There's nothing we haven't done
Going to the park at 9:00 P.M.
Just to watch the setting sun

Staying up late just to talk about nothing
Or seeing if we'll beat our record again
Countless smiles and tears from laugher
I owe it all to you my friend

Kelsey AuCoin, Grade 9
St Matthew High School, ON

Inside a Book

Inside a book is a far off land, with magical
places and beautiful gardens, you can go everywhere in a book.
Inside a book you can travel to the sea, a forest, even space!
Anywhere you want to go you can go in a book.
Inside a book you can meet different people, a wizard, a witch,
a magical fairy, anyone you want to see you can read in a book.

Elizabeth Kocur, Grade 7
St Anne School, SK

I Love You...

Those three breathless words
Mean so much.
It's the undiscovering mystery
In our hearts,
That makes us feel like there's hope.
Maybe some day, when we aren't looking,
A rose will blossom and we can unleash
The affection that's been waiting
To be found.
Hark! Thy heart soars with freedom,
Breathlessly filled with passion.
Hope was on our side
Every step we took.
The most soothing sound,
Fills the air with despair.
The moment he whispered "I Love You,"
an enchanting yet magical
Tale was born.
The end of an adventure,
The beginning of a new journey.

Jaclyn Miles, Grade 9
Aurora High School, ON

I Am

I am a young Canadian girl who loves to hunt
I wonder if there will be a grouse around the next corner
I hear the rustle of the leaves as something moves in the bush
I see a shadow behind the trees
I want to shoot the grouse hiding nearby
I am a young Canadian girl who loves to hunt

I pretend I am the hunter of old trying to feed my family
I feel the trees closing in on me as it gets darker
I touch the clouds from the top of the mountain
I worry that I may get lost in the bush
I cry when I miss my target
I am a young Canadian girl who loves to hunt

I understand that I am part of nature
I say I am part of the cycle of life
I dream of hunting the caribou of northern Quebec
I try to help others understand my passion
I hope to pass my heritage on to my children
I am a young Canadian girl who loves to hunt

Kaytlin Dowdall, Grade 8
École secondaire Macdonald-Cartier, ON

Paradise

When the waves hit the shore,
And the sun sets on the horizon,
When the blue herons soar over the lake,
I am in paradise

When the leaves turn to gold,
And they fall to the ground,
When the night turns cold,
I am in paradise

When the first snowfall covers the ground,
And the grass fades away,
When the cardinals sing,
I am in paradise

When the snow starts to melt,
And the marigolds bloom,
When the robins return from the south,
I am in paradise

Sarah Tomaszewski, Grade 8
St Peter Catholic High School, ON

Tornado

It sounded like a train coming down the tracks.
The sky was pitch dark of purple and black.
It whirled and hurled all around me.
But then all of the sudden it stopped.
It was like the air after a rainfall.
Like nothing had ever happened.
Fallen trees and branches.
Everywhere damage.
The tornado.

Lindy Bancroft, Grade 7
Milverton Public School, ON

Rainy Day

Sitting in front of the window
With a book and a cup of tea
Listening to the drum of rain
Over the sound of distant music
And the cat's quiet purring.

In the corner is the fireplace
The fire now only a small flame
But its heat still warms the room
The burning wood giving off a sweet smokey smell
Giving the room a sense of comfort.

The softness of my sweater against my skin
Cool mist breeze against my face
Frost tingeing the windowpane
The fur on my cat's back tickles my feet
Gives this rainy day a melancholy feeling.

Katherine Wesselius, Grade 8
Mackenzie Middle School, MB

Different

I may be different from you; and you
May be different from I but we are all,
All and all but also through and through,
But we are not for when you have to call
Upon me, you use words that break me down,
This is where I go hide and my heart cries,
And when our gazes meet, that's when I frown
And my soul and spirit lies down and dies.
So go ahead and call me anything,
Because you know I will not run away,
For even though you treat me like nothing,
For my sadness is leaving at the bay.
So when you call me a different name,
It shows how much you can bring me my fame.

Kabrina Duquette, Grade 9
Midland Secondary School, ON

Colors of the Wind

Colors of the wind could never be seen
In other ways of saying
No one would be looking
At the colors of the wind that nobody had seen

I've tried to see what it would look like?
And wouldn't it be just a plain white book
A book that tells a story that was never told
Colors of the wind what magic do you hold?

Inside my heart I feel something
Something that gives Life to living
It's wind isn't it? No it's air
But there's a similarity they both are fair.

Symon Ernest Hernandez, Grade 7
École Notre-Dame-des-Vertus, SK

Life

Have you ever felt that society has no place for you
Like everything is happening without you
As if the world is turning but no one really cares
And like you are the only one
Who is trying to make a difference in this world.
Life is like an ocean and we are all like tiny shrimp
Even if we try to make life better
There will always be someone
Bigger than you
that will put you down and tell you that you are not good enough.
Life is filled with People
who say they want to fix things but don't start.
Poverty,
Racism,
Pollution,
Global Warming.
Everything possible is happening but
No one really cares enough to do something about it
But I guess that's just life.

Emily Lubkiwski, Grade 7
École Notre-Dame-des-Vertus, SK

Scared and Alone

You hear the voices loud and clear
and you feel your body fill with fear
you feel so scared and so alone
you know that all you have to do is pick up the phone
there's people here to help you through
those long scary nights that confuse you
they know what to do to make things right
so you don't have to go alone in this fight
you need to know that you're not to blame
but the people that hurt you should be ashamed
you are beautiful inside and out
so there's no need to scream and shout
so make your life worth every day
so that some day you'll be able to say
that no matter what happens you've got people that love you
and would do anything it took to see you smile
and they'll always make your life worth while
they are the people that make sure you're not scared and alone
because you'll always have them to turn to

Ashleigh Znidaric, Grade 9
St Benedict Catholic Secondary School, ON

Young Poets
Grades 4-5-6

Note: The Top Ten poems were finalized through an online voting system. Creative Communication's judges first picked out the top poems. These poems were then posted online. The final step involved thousands of students and teachers who registered as online judges and voted for the Top Ten poems. We hope you enjoy these selections.

Top Poem Grades 4-5-6

Winter Has Come

I woke up this morning,
There was a blanket of snow,
I can't see the grass,
Oh, where did it go?
The trees are all bare,
No leaves to be seen,
And now everything's white,
Instead of all green.
The wind is strong now,
It blows and blows,
It shakes the branches,
And whips the snow.
Flakes rest on the branches,
Of the bare trees,
And now the strong wind,
Is just a light breeze.
These are the things
I love about winter,
From a hot chocolate,
To a cold snowy blizzard.

Michelle Brooke, Grade 5
Forest Hill Public School, ON

Top Poem Grades 4-5-6

Halloween Night

The black black cat
Creeps across the fence
As the wolves howl at the moon
All of a sudden

BOO!!
Candy races into
Trick-or-treaters bags of silk
Chocolate brown
Cherry red, lemon lime yellow
Mango orange chips, cans of pop,
chocolate bars
Billions of treats
At the dead of
night
f
a
l
l
Everyone goes to bed!

Mikayla Shay Cliffe, Grade 4
Avondale School, AB

Top Poem Grades 4-5-6

About May

May I learn to plant a garden
May I fly up to the sky
May I watch the buzzing bees
As they busily buzz by
May I feel the whirling wind
As it brushes right by me
May I feel the falling raindrops
And climb up all the trees
May I hear the wind and rain
Each and every single day
May I have lots of fun in spring
Because it is time for…
MAY!!

Emily DesRoches, Grade 6
Hampton Middle School, NB

Top Poem Grades 4-5-6

Autumn Leaves

When fall is coming they fall from trees,
old and ancient graceful leaves
as they float down silently creating peace,
a smell in the air of autumn leaves
and amidst the war, the blood and the violence
the crunch of the leaves will never silence.

Dillon Dong, Grade 6
Holy Cross School, ON

Top Poem Grades 4-5-6

Remembrance Day

Remembrance Day is all about war
All the people that survived and those who did not.
It takes courage to leave your family
Thinking it may be the last time you see them.

Remembrance Day is a time when
We honor those who went to war,
Remember those who fought for our country
And all the people who died helping to save others.

Remembrance Day is about Flanders Fields
That's where the poppies grow
To show respect we wear poppies in November
Remembrance Day is important to our country.

Melissa Kowatski, Grade 6
Bayview Elementary School, BC

Top Poem Grades 4-5-6

Mud Puddles

I went out walking and what did I see?
A great big beautiful apple tree
And there just happened to be
The best looking mud puddle staring at me.

I smiled and laughed and jumped up high
I landed in the middle with a great big sigh
I was swishing and splashing my feet
Playing in a mud puddle is sure hard to beat.

Edith-Anne McGrath-McCoy, Grade 6
Bayview Elementary School, BC

Top Poem Grades 4-5-6

Growing Up

As I look back at pictures of my younger years,
I smile and laugh and sometimes shed tears.
I like to see what's changed and how I've grown,
What's different since I've moved away from home.

My childhood was a laughable one,
I was like a wild chimpanzee, always having fun.
But as I've grown up now, others have too
Some of them still living and others gone, making me blue.

I've gotten more responsible, mature as well,
I've gotten more advice from experiences, in which I tell.
I'm like a young cheetah cub, becoming a mother,
Like a young child trying to act like another.

I still make mistakes and do things I regret,
Because growing up is like being best friends with someone you've just met.
I'll always remember how much fun I had being little,
And I'll get through growing up like a challenging, but great riddle.

Maggie Rendulich, Grade 6
St Catherine Elementary School, AB

Top Poem Grades 4-5-6

Halloween!

Witches riding on their brooms
Mummies rising from their tombs!
Trick or Treating here and there.
Monsters running everywhere!
Kids are screaming and running with fear…
"Come on guys the monster is here!"
Candy falling on the ground
Chocolate scattered all around!
Halloween what a fright…
Monsters still will roam the night!!!

Jasmine Rowe, Grade 6
King George Public School, ON

Top Poem Grades 4-5-6

Remembrance Day

Remembrance Day is when we remember,
The soldiers who fought in the war.
The mothers, fathers, sons and daughters,
hearts were very sore.

Soldiers fought in harsh conditions,
in freezing cold and burning hot.
As soldiers met their enemies,
some died, some lived and some were caught.

The women worked hard to keep their lives on track.
Working at home and at jobs, until the men came back.
Children helped too, as they did chores and they shared.
Children gave food, clothes, and shelter to show that they cared.

People at home received news bad and good.
Helping each other whenever they could.
Soldiers fought hard so we could be free.
I'll never forget what they did for me.

Jack Stevenson, Grade 5
Forest Hill Public School, ON

Top Poem Grades 4-5-6

A Different Me

When I'm on a horse I'm a different me,
It's just my own world and my world is carefree.
When it's raining out my life is not my own,
I'm in a different body, in a different home.
When I'm in my bed dreaming I am anything,
I'm a famous rock star singing all that I can sing.
When I'm sitting watching television and lazing around,
I feel like I'm on a mountaintop gazing down upon the ground.
When I'm sitting bored looking out the window when I'm in the car,
I'm really soaring up in the sky going wide and far.
And when I'm riding on my bike the wind blowing in my face,
It feels like I'm an olympic biker winning the race.
But when I come back to reality and my fantasies are done,
I'm just plain old me, but that can still be fun.

Laura Wells, Grade 6
Holly Meadows Elementary School, ON

Christmas

C hildren laughing, playing, having fun
H appy faces everywhere
R eceiving gifts on this day
I n the snow loving the day
S inging carols house to house
T ime to have fun on this day
M agical times will appear
A fter sleeping
S anta Claus is here

Sarah Veloo, Grade 6
Dr F D Sinclair Elementary School, BC

A Full Moon Shines

A full moon shines
On this dark and scary night.
Its eerie glow
Is the only source of light.
I must admit that
I'm getting quite a fright.
So many things
That might leap out and bite.
But then again
It's Halloween tonight.

Kately Nikiforuk, Grade 6
Edgemont School, AB

Thanksgiving

T ime to be giving
H aving a harvest
A ll the apple pie
N o one in the family is left out
K eeping thanks from your family
S tuffing in the turkey
G ather all the thanks
I give thanks for the freedom
V ery pretty mayflowers
I love the colours of the fall leaves
N othing to be forgotten
G reat Thanksgiving dinner

Carley Gottschalk, Grade 5
Muskoka Falls Public School, ON

All About Me

V ery enjoyable
I 'll tease you
N ot very good in spelling
A clumsy person
Y es it's me, Vinay!

S occer fan
I hate liars
D oesn't like homework
H ardworking
U nforgettable, Vinay!

Vinay Sidhu, Grade 5
Dr F D Sinclair Elementary School, BC

AA Flak Cannons

A ir born divisions
A ssault on German strongholds

F ighting with fierce aggression
L ooking at allies on ground
A ttacking with no mercy
K illing ruthlessly, everywhere a thick silhouette of blood

C racks of thundering artillery fire
A wards and medals with a dull shine
N o more gruesome warfare
N one say a word
O nly for a small while
N urses and medics rush to save the lives of soldiers
S herman tanks slowly rolling up the ghastly beaches of D-day

Caleb Gibbons, Grade 6
Falmouth District School, NS

Amazon

The hot sun beating down on me.
As we boat through the disgusting sticky swamp.
We pass by berry bushes with the largest juiciest berries I have ever seen.
Those thick dark green anacondas curled up in the brown gross mud.
I see the fuzzy monkeys making funny noises.
Whipping through the trees; are striped tigers.
There are those alligators and crocodiles, with their bumpy, spiky, scaly skin.
Those monkeys swinging on those furry long vines.
All that dirty salty water pushing against the boat.
I see those beautiful, fascinating flowers all around.
I wish I was at the Amazon, the foggy mysterious Amazon.

Dalton Dyck, Grade 4
Margaret Wooding School, AB

I Am

I am an imaginative girl who believes in magic
I wonder if fairies really dance in rings of toadstools
I hear tiny pixie bells ringing at midnight
I see merchildren darting through colorful seaweed
I want all patients to be cured of their health problems
I am an imaginative girl who believes in magic

I pretend to have fairy wings and flit through the sun-dappled trees
I feel happy when I see a lush, green meadow filled with unicorns below me
I touch the silky rainbow mane of a pure white mare
I worry about the safety of all poor children in Africa
I cry for all the poverty and sorrow in the world
I am an imaginative girl who believes in magic

I understand that one day death will take me
I say magical creatures do still exist
I dream that the magnificent power of the white unicorn is surging through my body
I try my best in everything I do
I hope that one day I will meet the magical creatures I have mentioned
I am an imaginative girl who believes in magic

Sarah Morin, Grade 6
St Elizabeth Ann Seton School, ON

Josh Rubin

Josh
Fun, comical, clever, kind
Son of Irene and Howard
Lover of dogs, cats and food
Who feels happy, sad and mad
Who needs a sister, comfy socks, and a new basketball net
Who fears cockroaches, spiders and beetles
Who gives charity, happiness and laughs
Who would like to see Niagara Falls, Sean Paul and Morocco
Resident of Montreal, Canada
Rubin

Josh Rubin, Grade 4
Ecole Akiva, QC

Rebecca Weill

Rebecca
Encouraging, thoughtful, graceful, picky
Sister of Sacha
Lover of figure skating, arts and crafts and animals
Who feels lovable, joyful and angry
Who needs her mom, clothes, good health
Who fears darkness, being deserted, death
Who gives hope, happiness, love
Who would like to see Miley Cyrus, Egypt and London
Resident of Quebec, Canada
Weill

Rebecca Weill, Grade 4
Ecole Akiva, QC

Nature's Blessings

January brings the snow
People line up their shovels row by row.
February brings the rain
People take shelter again and again.
March brings the shrill
I think I just felt a chill.
April brings beautiful buds
Then the bears have cubs.

May brings little foals
It's time to dig holes.
June brings summer break
Go to the beach and have a milk shake.
July brings low winds
Let's go fishing and see little fins.

August brings sheaves of corn
Thank you God harvest has shorn.
September brings the chill
Hockey season is in the will.
October brings pumpkins
Halloween is erupting.
November and December bring a sleet
Little stockings and chilly feet.

Aaron Manicom, Grade 5
St Noel Chabanel Catholic Elementary School, ON

Summer Holiday

S ummer holidays are sunny and warm.
U nder the umbrella that saves us from the heat.
M y friends all come and play with me!
M y family and I have fun together.
E veryone has a great time.
R emember the fun times during summer.

H ot breezy days in the summer time heat.
O h! The living is easy!
L icking ice cream on a delightful day.
I f only it would last forever!
D own by the sea the waves crash.
A lways be prepared for an exciting day.
Y ou never know what the day will be like.

George Athitakis, Grade 5
Castlebridge Public School, ON

Cooking

I cooked pancakes as tough as feet.
I cooked a stew I wouldn't eat.
I baked a wedding cake as slimy as a snake.
I made spaghetti you eat with a rake.
I cooked an apple pie
If you eat it, you will die.
I made an ice cream sundae
If you eat it, you won't live to Monday.

Brandon Wannamaker, Grade 6
Uniacke District School, NS

Christmas

Christmas colors everywhere
Decorations here and there
Christmas lights in the night
Sitting outside by the moonlight

Listening to music all night long
Listening to my favorite song
Jesus Christ was born on Christmas day
We sing Christmas carols every which way

We celebrate Jesus Christ's birth
Being with our families is the best thing on earth
Opening presents on Christmas morning
That is what Christmas is all about!!!!!!

Alecia Hobson, Grade 6
Uniacke District School, NS

War

War is sad
Blood shades over friends
Soldiers losing lives to save their country
They stand up strong until the end
And they lose their lives to save you and your friends
And every year, we remember those who died.

Brandon McAlinden, Grade 6
Bayview Elementary School, BC

Holly

I love Holly so much.
She is the best thing on earth.

Every time I think about her,
Or see her,
When I'm sick, sad, or mad,
I feel happy.

Holly has the cutest smile,
But she is very paranoid,
Every time she hears a thump,
She swings her head to where the noise
Came from.

I think it's hilarious when she drools…
Oh yeah, I forgot to tell you,
She, Holly,
Is a cat.

Benjamin Galbraith, Grade 6
Uniacke District School, NS

Smile

S parkling
M arvelous mouth
I t has lots of teeth
L oving lips
E verybody has one

Bryanne MacDonald, Grade 4
Linsford Park School, AB

Thanksgiving

T hankful for what we have.
H arvest winter vegetables.
A corns that squirrels gather.
N ow baseball playoffs start.
K ind to one another.
S haring food with others.
G ive our thanks to God.
I nviting friends over.
V iewing beautiful scenery.
I love pumpkin pie.
N ew settlers arrived a Plymouth Rock.
G ourds are used to decorate.

McKinnley Matthews, Grade 5
Muskoka Falls Public School, ON

All About Me

I am born in a family that has problems.
There is money that flies away
and sickness at the hospital
and a book of dreams.
And a best friend.
I do my things at school
and I do my best.

Sarah St-Pierre, Grade 5
Ste-Foy Elementary School, QC

The Shores of Beausoleil Island

My favourite place are the shores of Beausoleil Island.
The sun shimmers on the water like sparkling diamonds.
The scent of majestic pines is carried by the gentle breeze.
Schools of minnows playfully skip across the water,
As a lurking bass springs up and gulps them down.
Basking turtles scurry off a rock with a splash,
As a heron lands near them.
As I put my feet in the refreshing clear water,
I feel a silky snake swiftly slither against my leg while searching for his dinner.
I hope Beausoleil's magnificent creatures will always live in harmony.

Ryan Jackson, Grade 5
Forest Hill Public School, ON

My Favorite Place

My favorite place is a tree in my backyard
I dart out of my house and I scramble up this tree
When I scramble up it I feel the ragged bark and the smooth leaves
I smell the soft scent of chlorophyll and fresh dew on grass
I see all the nature around me frolicking and flying
Some squirrels screech at me while I sit on my branch
As the day passes I will change limbs
Some birds will come to the bird feeder underneath me
Soon I will descend the tree by climbing down the trunk
As the sun sets with brilliance like amber colored embers
I smell dinner and scamper in but I know I'll be back tomorrow

Connor Hadley, Grade 5
Forest Hill Public School, ON

Friendship Foes

They hate each other one minute, and get into a big fight.
Two seconds later the quarrel is over, and everything's all right.

It's a whirlwind of emotions, whatever can we do?
Girls that are supposed to be friends, but also act like enemies too.

We just need to remember that all pals sometimes get mad,
But don't throw away the friendship, because that would be really sad.

Genuine friends stick together, and choose to work their problems out.
That's the meaning of true friendship, of that there is no doubt!

Kennedy Neustaeter, Grade 4
Linsford Park School, AB

The Deck at the Cottage

My favourite place is sitting on the deck at the cottage
I can hear the loons laughing loudly while they play in the water
I can see the sun setting slowly in the pinkish red sky
The fresh smell of cedar in my new deck chair calms me
I can hardly wait to go water skiing when the wind settles down
When the wind stops blowing the water is so clam, it looks like a mirror
There is nothing like the feeling of gliding on top of calm water
Watching the silky smooth slalom spray launch into the sky
As I let go of the handle and slowly sink into the gentle water
I look forward to another evening on my deck on a sunny summer day

Robert Andrews, Grade 5
Forest Hill Public School, ON

My Evil Teddy Bear

My evil teddy bear woke me up last night,
He told me something that gave me quite a fright,

He whispered in my ear and said what I shall not speak,
What he said haunted me for a very long week,

And now when I look into his dark evil eyes,
I miss the cheerful side in his colorful bow tie.

So tonight when I go to bed that frightful little stare,
Will be put across my evil teddy bear!

Alyse Mercey, Grade 6
Credit Meadows Elementary School, ON

September

September September what beautiful leaves.
The deep golden yellows are the color of trees.

Mother Nature watches squirrels
gathering chestnut brown treasures.
Where do they hide them?
In a secret place where nobody knows but me.

September September come to me.
My favourite season is here.

Megan Gladue, Grade 4
Avondale School, AB

My Life

Brandes
Weird, interesting, loyal, honorable
Sister of Austin and Morgan
Lover of relatives, sports and babies
Who feels excited, thrilled and under the weather
Who needs love, friendship and peace
Who fears needles, weapons and nightmares
Who gives happiness, effort and friendship
Who would like to see peace, the Dead Sea and Israel
Resident of Canada
Tecks-Bleuer

Brandes Tecks-Bleuer, Grade 4
Ecole Akiva, QC

Just Imagine

Just imagine a world with peace.
With happiness and without violence
Imagine a world with honour.
Imagine a world with love
Without senseless death or pain
Only kindness to stop the menacing reign.
Imagine a world without anger or greed
To help the people in need.
Imagine a world with a hurt free environment.
Just imagine a world as loving as Jesus' heart to live in!

Quentin MacSpurren, Grade 6
St Philip School, AB

That Old Hat

That old hat I found in a heap of mess
Color lost and faded
That old hat so elegant, sophisticated and dusty
So thick and warm
That old hat, dull and colorless
But priceless to me
That old hat was my grandfather's
Given to me on his deathbed.

Patrick MacMillan, Grade 6
Uniacke District School, NS

The Ones We Will Always Remember

Lest we forget,
The terrible threat,
The ones we will always remember,
Went off to the war,
Came back with less more,
The tears that will haunt us forever.
Now there they lie,
A twinkle in their eye,
The ones we will always remember.

Mikayla Rancourt, Grade 4
Vanway Elementary School, BC

The Power of a Poppy

As the deadly guns shot into the dark night,
Brave men fought for what was right.

A poppy sprung up over a lowly grave,
To honor a soldier who was very brave.

Soon poppies began to grow everywhere,
To cover the dead with a blanket of care.

So today when you see that little red flower,
Think of it as a symbol of remembering power!

Taryn Barnes, Grade 4
Linsford Park School, AB

Matthew Spotted Bull

Matthew

Helpful boy, trustful, athletic, playful
Son of Russell and Rayanna
Lover of bike riding
Who feels happy and angry
Who needs fun and money
Who gives friendship and time
Who fears ghosts and people yelling at you
Who likes to wear army pants and Indian t-shirts
Who would like to see Disneyland and LA
Resident of Nanaimo

Spotted Bull

Matthew Spotted Bull, Grade 4
Bayview Elementary School, BC

Page 197

Falling Leaves
with vibrant colours,
they hang on tree branches,
waiting to flutter
Ciaron Costello, Grade 5
Nativity of Our Lord Catholic School, ON

Trees, Sun and Birds
Blow wind through the trees,
Blow wind with the breeze.
Blow wind and never stop,
So blow wind blow.

Sun shine through the day,
Sun shine while I play.
Sun shine every day,
So shine sun shine.

Fly birds through the sky,
Fly birds by and by.
With every swerve and dive you make,
Fly birds Fly.

Hannah Cho, Grade 5
Norseman Junior and Middle School, ON

Delicious
Delicious is…
A triple chocolate four layer cake,
A strawberry vanilla milkshake.
A platter of mashed potatoes,
A juicy meal in Barbados.
A cheese Quesadilla with sour cream,
Maybe afternoon tea with the Queen.
And me,
Munching it all in my delightful dream
Haley Jackalin, Grade 6
Queen of All Saints Elementary School, BC

Clean Your Room
Clean your room my mother yelled
but I cleaned it just last year
so there I was locked in my room
I'll never do it alive I wailed
I'm going to get a knife, she joked
I got bored and looked around
wow, this place is dirty, I thought
better start to pick up
when done, I suddenly realized
hey, isn't that what I should have
done before?
Courtney Allen, Grade 6
Hampton Middle School, NB

I Am
I am a monkey that eats flies.
I am a frog that eats bananas.
I am a bear that eats grass.
I am a cow that eats berries.
Rebecca Ouellette, Grade 5
Ecole les Cypres, AB

Christmas
Winter is here I can't wait to see,
The white snow on my feet.
Christmas is fun the kids think,
Everyone is on the ice rink.
Santa's in the sky waving,
While the kids are sleeping.
There's joy in the house,
Every girl and boy is happy.
All families are laughing,
While they are eating.
Hurray! It's Christmas.
Sanjam Gill, Grade 6
Dr F D Sinclair Elementary School, BC

Morris Lee
As high as the gigantic mountain.
As low as you and me.
As slow as the tall pouring fountain.
Came the death of Morris Lee
For one Friday night I know,
Poor Morris was sick in bed
We called the doctor Evan Snow
And quickly the doctor said,
"Let the boy be near the fire"
"Make sure he's safe and all warm"
"His fever is getting quite higher"
"Don't let him wear clothes torn"
With that the doctor was gone,
Morris slowly opened his eyes,
and said at the crack of dawn
"Do you think I am going to die?"
As high as the gigantic Mountain
As low as you and me.
As slow as the tall pouring fountain
Came the death of Morris Lee.
Good bye Morris Lee.
Myka Hangdaan, Grade 6
Miller's Grove School, ON

Dragon
D angerous
R eally scary
A mazingly powerful jaws
G reat, strong flying wings
O ut of sight awesome fire
N ever bother a dragon
Tyler Tarrington, Grade 4
Linsford Park School, AB

The True Meaning of Christmas
The true meaning of Christmas,
Is to have happiness and joy,
it is not about missing classes,
it is not about getting lots of toys.

The true meaning of Christmas,
is to love and care,
always remember,
never to swear.

The true meaning of Christmas,
is always be nice,
even to people,
whom you don't really like.

The true meaning of Christmas,
is about family and friends
who gather around to talk and eat
after having fun they go to sleep.

The true meaning of Christmas,
is that Jesus was born,
to save all people
from everlasting doom.
Michelle Basinang, Grade 5
Dr F D Sinclair Elementary School, BC

Autumn
Leaves leaves fall
from the brown trees
they float down to the ground
swaying and dancing as they go

Some are yellow
Others are still green

Some are soft
While some are hard and crunchy
Under my feet
Dakota Alstad, Grade 4
Avondale School, AB

Getting Sick
Getting sick isn't fun
To stay home, and not play in the sun,

Chicken pox and tummy aches,
What more does it take?

Moans and groans
Fill up the home,

Please get me out of here!!
"Another day, dear."
Nicole Bernardo, Grade 6
William G Davis Public School, ON

Love

Love is bright
It is a flame in the dark
With patience it will lighten
Love is never wrong
It will find you and you will love
will succeed and win your satisfaction
With it you can feel the things you never felt before
That's Love

Fatima Fatima, Grade 6
Dr F D Sinclair Elementary School, BC

Stop Bullying

You should stop bullying, here is why,
Bullying is horrible and makes you want to cry.
Every time you get bullied, you feel you want to hide,
But everyone can help you, let's all stop the tide.
It's very sad indeed, as everyone can see,
We can all put a stop to it, just follow me.

Teodor Zetko, Grade 4
Nativity of Our Lord Catholic School, ON

Graceful Water

Running, flowing, stream, reflection … river
People, fun, hat, summer … beach
Rock, splashing, fish swimming, canoeing, kayaking … cottage
Items wash up from water, sailing, cruises, dock … bay
Soap, bubbles, water everywhere, toys … bath
Winter canal, snow, hail … winter water
River,
    beach,
        cottage,
            bay,
                bath,
                    winter water
                      … graceful water

Joshua Wagamese, Grade 6
Holy Cross School, ON

Flowing

Snow, Snow they are flowing.
Out of the sky just like a waterfall.
Flowing from up high the little patterns from the sky.
Beautiful little things floating from the sky.
Tiny delicate flakes coming from up high.
Flowing from so far from so far.
Above flowing from the cloud the snow is magical appearing.
Out of the sky you can think it will never stop.
Flowing from up high all the snow gathering together.
Joining to each other snow come on
down meet one another.
Come make some friends snow come on down
sprinkle around the town.
Flutter on down when someone sleds down the hill.
Swoosh in the air make some more friends.

Alexa Thompson, Grade 6
St Anne School, SK

Inside a Pop Machine

Inside a pop machine there are gold ramps
that take your coin to the small bubble men.
Inside a pop machine the bubble men choose
the pop that you would like and put it on a little conveyor belt.
Inside a pop machine the belt carries it through
a snowy land to make the pop cold.
Then the pop falls into the little slot for you to drink.

Ben Grummett, Grade 6
St Anne School, SK

My Other Side

She screams
She destroys
She ties my shoe laces together
She makes a mess
She says words backwards,
Like instead of saying silly pig she says "pilly sig"
Oh my, what will I do with my other side?

Amy Baker, Grade 6
Ecole les Cypres, AB

Water Ways

Floats gracefully to shore
Joyfully it won't bore you

A salty smell that stings your cut
The smooth shell that washes to shore

How it tastes refreshing on a hot summer's day

Wherever it might be in a pond, lake or sea
You can find it no matter where you go
You'll see.

Santana Bellantoni, Grade 6
Holy Cross School, ON

Leaves

L eaves are lovely
E ven in the summer
A t the time of fall the leaves change colour
V ery beautiful leaves
E very one loves to play in the leaves
S ee people cleaning up the leaves

Jay Sweeney, Grade 6
Holy Cross School, ON

The Withered Willow

The wind flowing through the withered branches,
Creatures advancing running in an avalanche,
Hate flowing through the damp stagnant air,
all of the torches light up in a glowing flare,

Creatures attack by night but only to die again,
All in the field of the withered willow.

Matthew Delosada, Grade 6
Devon Gardens Elementary School, BC

Read

Read it's a lot of fun
Reading is great for you
You can read about castles
And lots of other stuff too
So come and read
The more you read the smarter you get
You can read fiction and nonfiction too

Austin Bennett, Grade 5
Chiganois Elementary School, NS

Basketball

B all
A net
S ome tall players
K eep trying
E veryone plays
T ake a turn
B ounce the ball
A round the gym
L ose
L ike to play

Dale Vincent, Grade 6
New Germany Elementary School, NS

Riding Free

As I ride around the ring,
The morning birds begin to sing.

I feel as though I'm flying,
Like a star that's brightly shining.

When I jump it's like I soar,
As if I'm human no more.

Along the track it's dusty,
Making my shirt look rusty.

Wild and bouncing is my hair,
But I don't really care.

When I ride I'm free,
And as happy as can be.

Amelia George, Grade 6
Uniacke District School, NS

Clam Shell

Its brown rays are
Like a rainbow with no color
The bright yellow spots shine
Like stars in the dark night sky
The purple and white swirling together
Is like a misty ocean breeze filling the air
The scrape of purple stands out
Like the healing wounds in life

Alina Quarin, Grade 5
Ranch Park Elementary School, BC

Rebecca Nadler

Rebecca
Joyful, caring, hilarious, energetic
Daughter of Phil and Karen
Lover of wildlife, video games and her family
Who feels excited, jumpy and happy
Who needs her sister to stop bothering her, a dog and a new video game
Who fears lightning, needles and forgetting her work
Who gives kindness, attention and friendship
Who'd like to see a penguin, hockey game and a Pokemon movie
Resident of Montreal
Nadler

Rebecca Nadler, Grade 4
Ecole Akiva, QC

The Football Legend Buzzsaw

B oy, this kid is a really hard hitter!
U nknown of his name we call him buzz.
Z oo is probably where he's from because he's like an animal.
Z izzzz is all you hear when he hits the QB!
S ee him on the field for one split second and then you get knocked down!
A ll around you hear "Go Buzz"
W ho is this monster? Why it's me!

Shawn Rizk, Grade 6
St Anne French Immersion School, ON

My Favourite Place

My favourite place is on a hill
I watch the frisky wave's glisten from the sun's rays
I can almost feel the gentle paws of chipmunks scurrying away from me

As the leaves blow around me I can hear the outside crust crackle
I watch the sun slowly slide over the cliff
As I observe the sparrows swooping at the mosquitoes
It darkens and animals scurry away as the star-filled sky replaced the golden sun

My mom invites me in for my dinner
As I walk down the path to my cottage I observe bunnies bounding towards the hill
And spy on snakes slithering silently threw the grass
As I walk towards my cottage I know I would be back tomorrow.

Sara Johnston, Grade 5
Forest Hill Public School, ON

Sophie Waxlax

Sophie
Accommodating, exquisite, stylish, delicate
Daughter of John and Jody
Lover of computers, television, and reading
Who feels shy, cheerful, and serious
Who needs a lock on my door, a bigger closet, and my own bathroom.
Who fears snakes, spiders and sharks.
Who gives clothes, money and love.
Who would like to see Italy, Russia and Germany
Resident of Montreal, Quebec, Canada.
Waxlax

Sophie Waxlax, Grade 4
Ecole Akiva, QC

Christmas

Snow is very beautiful
It's a good time of the year
All the kids are happy
Because it's Christmas time
When the children are asleep
Santa comes down the chimney
and puts presents under your Christmas tree

Tayten Cunningham, Grade 5
Dr F D Sinclair Elementary School, BC

Flowers

A flower is like a new world,
It's opening for the first time.

The center is so pretty,
It looks like a lemon or a lime.

When the petals blossom,
You know it's spring.

Sometimes if you sit in a patch of flowers,
You can imagine anything.

If a flower dies,
There's nothing inside.

Flowers are a lot like humans,
So go and plant one outside.

Felicia Licht, Grade 6
Credit Meadows Elementary School, ON

Oak Tree

The wind blows gently through the rustling trees,
and the leaves fall slowly to the ground.
The grass that grows in the fields beyond,
is disturbed by a mighty pound.
A tree has fallen in the peaceful woods,
frightening every creature.
The great oak tree has died,
at once, quietly and peacefully.
Sorrow creeps around every nook and cranny,
filling all creatures with sadness.
All who remember the great oak tree,
are filled with beauty, courage and happiness.

Hannah Cummings, Grade 6
Hampton Middle School, NB

Flowers

In the spring, flowers grow.
The wind makes the colorful petals blow.
The rain and the sun help them bloom
In the winter the flowers are doomed.
Some of the flowers grow in spring.
Joy to the gardener the blooms will bring.

Zachery Durley, Grade 6
Hampton Middle School, NB

Our War Heroes

The soldiers were happy,
Joyful and glad,
but now they are dirty,
cold and sad.
In the trenches so far from home,
they feel cold, wet and alone.
Since poppies grew in Flanders Field that day,
they represent our soldiers who have died,
and who are living today.
They made peace so we could be free.
They risked their lives for you and me.
Thank you to the soldiers who were great people.
we will come and praise you under the church steeple.

Ava Sturm, Grade 5
West Richmond Education Centre, NS

December

Winter time is here.
That means Christmas is near.
Christmas trees and colorful lights.
Candy canes and hot cocoa.
Gingerbread houses and turkey dinners galore.

Cold noses and warm hearts.
Snowmen snowball fights and forts that are cold
That's what winter has in store.

Nikita VanVessem, Grade 6
Uniacke District School, NS

Saving the Species

Dew is glistening on the leaves,
The grass is rustling underneath their feet.
The skies above are blue and clear,
And all life is waking from its slumber.

Butterflies and birds alike,
Are fluttering between the trees.
Woodland creatures are awakening,
And lights are seen in the distance.

But suddenly an odd scent is caught,
And all creatures panic and hide.
An unlucky pheasant is too slow,
And a shot reverberates all around.

The pheasant is unfortunate,
But there are many of its kind.
What if, by accident or even worse,
A lone animal in its species is shot and killed?

I hope, like I know many others do,
That we can save the endangered species.
The Earth is our home,
But remember, it's the animal's home too.

Kirstin Webb, Grade 6
Sir William Osler Elementary School, ON

Joy

The summer breeze by the ocean
carries joy with a sweet singing voice

The rolling waves of turquoise and cyan
bring joy with each ripple

The warming sand of crushed crystals
creates joy with every footstep

Joy comes as a flash of silver light
in any place, at any time

Aromas of the lilacs, lilies and roses
in the summertime immerse you in joy

The gentle touch of a heartfelt kiss
enchants you, with feelings of joy

The feeling of the deepest love,
travels to the heart, in showers of joy

Friends are joy.
Family is joy.
Love is joy.
Samantha Nicole Stahlke, Grade 6
Jack Miner Public School, ON

Golfing

Golf
Double Bogey
Hole in one
Big ended gold club
Ball
James Varner, Grade 5
New Germany Elementary School, NS

Everyone Can Be Heroes

Anyone can be a hero
You don't need super power
Even you can be a hero
Help others
They will think you are a hero
If you have a kind heart,
If you care,
You might think just helping,
Will not be a hero
But people who have been helped
Will never forget
You don't have to be famous,
You don't have to be the strongest,
There are lot of ways you can help other
Just care for others and,
look inside your heart,
I believe you can be a hero.
Aye Oo, Grade 6
Dr F D Sinclair Elementary School, BC

Summer

Oh Summer, Oh Summer, how can I compare you to anything sweet?
For your fun, warm days sweep me right off my feet.
Swinging on swings, splashing in the pool,
Hooray! For I am off school!
Although you won't last, I'll have fun while I can.
Maybe I'll ride my bike with my good friend.
Even though I'm a boy, and you are a season, we are much alike, and I have a reason!
You like to have fun, and so do I!
Any person who's ever had summer knows it's fun and knows why!
James Epp, Grade 6
Riverheights School, MB

Anger

The piercing eyes of the most evil demonic being,
Ripping at your insides like a twisting wall of flames.
The most fiery scarlet screams its name,
The most orchestral boom of crescendo blares,
Burning and raging until joy is a pile of ashes,
Even the smallest demonstration of ignorance will ignite it like a match,
It is a shapeless form, twisting and contracting in an endless void.
ANGER IS THE FIRE IN THE SOUL
Laura Parent, Grade 6
Jack Miner Public School, ON

Christmas Lights

One reason I like winter is for all the Christmas lights
And watching all the snow come down on the very first Christmas Night.

I see the twinkling lights flicker yellow, blue and red
These are the images going 'round inside my head.

Each year we set up the Christmas tree and listen to Christmas songs
Strung up around are Christmas lights we're dancing all along.
Madison Lacroix, Grade 6
Ecole les Cypres, AB

My Tattletale Twin

Since I have the misfortune to have a twin,
It seems that at school, I can never win.

My tattletale sister will always rat me out,
Of that there is certainly, not any doubt.

Once when my locker was far from clean,
My irritating sister, started to scream.

She had to go and tell every single person that I know,
I was so mad that like a volcano, I wanted to blow!

But instead I cleaned up my horrific mess,
And to my dad I did confess.

Now I'm just waiting to tell, when my sister does something wrong,
Knowing her as I do…that shouldn't take too long!
James Comer, Grade 4
Linsford Park School, AB

Growing Up

As I lay in the Pet Store like a person in a casket,
Seeing strange people walk in,
Hoping to see my mom again,
Each day I pray to see at least a picture of her.

One year has passed.
I see all of my cuter littler mates go,
And I am left behind.
Sometimes I feel as ugly as a rat.

Each day I get older.
My hair starts to turn gray as an African elephant.
I can feel my brittle bones creak.
Hip dysplasia is all I am thinking of.

But now as I lay in a cage,
I shall pray for another day,
Of which I will cherish every second.
Still pondering if I shall see my mom again.

Austin Furber, Grade 6
St Catherine Elementary School, AB

My Life Is Nature

My school is nature, nature is my life.
My life is my family, my family is my love.
My love is fun, fun is my friend…
My friend is English, English is my passion.
My passion is for animals, animals are endangered.
Endangered is the planet, the planet where I live.
I live in Canada, Canada is my country.
My country is forest, forest is trees.
Trees are water, water is me.
I am my language, my language is French.
French is Quebec, Quebec is a province.
A province of quality and good as food.
Food is our land, our land is rich.
Rich is our culture, our culture is fantastic.
Fantastic is the word to describe my life!

Daphne Savoie, Grade 6
Ecole Marie Anne, QC

My Favourite Place Outside

My favourite place is my tree
The touch of the sticky sap sticking to my hand
The sound of wind whistling through the branches
How the squirrels are nibbling on nuts
Woodpeckers peck away as their loud sound seems like a
Drill drilling a tree, obnoxious to most,
Yet musically beautiful on our old, old tree
The smell of the prickly pine pinches my nose
this is my favourite because it is peaceful and private
I can see all the different colours of the different seasons
This is my favourite place outside.
I know I'll be back some other day.

Devyn Small, Grade 5
Forest Hill Public School, ON

Just Imagine…

Just imagine all war put to an end!
Everyone could be a friend.
No more bombing or shooting a gun,
So innocent children of all countries can have some fun.
To wake up each day with smiling eyes!
Knowing that there's clear blue skies!
Bright gleaming faces all around square, oval, heart and round.
With warm pounding hearts, we'll all live in tranquility.
Peace is our weapon of immunity!
Love and peace everywhere.
Hugs, kisses and lots of care.
No more fearful horror like we have now.
Just imagine…WOW!

Sydney MacDonald, Grade 6
St Philip School, AB

Remembrance Day

Remembrance Day is about remembering
The men and women who fought in the war
To remember the people who risked their lives
To save their country and their family.

Did they fight because they wanted to
Or did they fight because they had to?
The war might go on for years
Soldiers that fought in the war
Are fighting for Peace.

Meagan Sampson, Grade 6
Bayview Elementary School, BC

Living Dead

I am dead but living on
Haunting everyone that is not gone.
Heaven took me in the but the underworld still wants me.
I am stuck between because the Devil is so mean.
I am dead but living on.

Kain Smith, Grade 6
William G Davis Public School, ON

Michael Wyse

Michael

Smart, athletic, fast, a soccer player
Son of Mike and Kora
Lover of playing soccer and canoe racing
Who feels happy and lucky
Who needs fun and friends
Who gives time and respect
Who fears bears and crazy drivers
Who likes to wear shorts and under armour shirts
Who would like to see Hawaii
Resident of Nanaimo

Wyse

Michael Wyse, Grade 4
Bayview Elementary School, BC

Thumb-Sucker

I am a boy who likes to run.
I also like to suck my thumb.
My friends always giggle
throughout the day.
Just because I suck my poor thumb.

Savana-Mae Cameron, Grade 4
Ecole les Cypres, AB

Love of Light

Darkness surrounds me when I am sad
But will not take over my love of light.

For when a smile is upon my face
The sun is out full and bright

Life is a beautiful thing
If you don't let the dark time take over

You just have to brighten it up
With a little lucky clover

Jennifer Moore, Grade 6
Hampton Middle School, NB

Music

The sound of music
Always cheers me up
It gets me pumped
It gets me motivated
Music is my passion
Although I don't play
I will always like it
I like rap music
I like hip-hop music
Nothing except for one thing
Will stand in the way
Of me listening to my favourite songs.

Anthony Pollock, Grade 6
St Anne French Immersion School, ON

Colourful Leaves

L eaves are quickly falling.
E mpty bare tree.
A ll the leaves have fallen.
V ery crunchy leaves.
E ach leaf is colourful.
S kies are filled with colourful leaves.

Dylan Archer, Grade 4
Avondale School, AB

Cupid Island

On the water she wants a kiss
He's so nervous he might miss
She still waits for that kiss.

Abigail Doucette, Grade 5
New Germany Elementary School, NS

Fire

Orange, yellow, red
colours of the flames burning
brightly shining lights.

Chris DeGoutiere, Grade 5
Bayview Elementary School, BC

Spirits

My papa is there for me,
and I am there for him.
Our love for each other
is still here.
He is a spirit that leads
my path to the future.

Sidney Wright, Grade 6
William G Davis Public School, ON

Zelda 4

"Zelda" is a hard, gray cube.
I use my thumbs
To make her use her bow and arrow.
She tries to use her magic.
She sees dragons.
Old dragons
In the high sky.
Zelda protects the world
From evil.

Dylan Raftus, Grade 6
Uniacke District School, NS

Feeling Blue

All you can do
When I'm feeling blue
Is take me for a walk in the park
It's all you can do

It's probably not because of you
That I'm feeling blue
Maybe my mood
A friend or two

When I'm feeling blue
You'll feel it too
Ignore my faces
It's all you can do

I slept not well
Maybe that rings a bell
Heard some bad news
My elbow won't swell

All you can do
When I'm feeling blue
Is take me for a walk in the park
It's all you can do

Michal Coret, Grade 6
Charles Beaudoin Public School, ON

Fireworks!!!

Fireworks they go
Boom! Crash! Boom!
Pretty pictures
Pretty colors
Very bright
In the night sky
Disappearing
Slowly over
The water
Shouting
From a boat
"I love fireworks!"
Boom! Crash! Boom!
FIREWORKS!!!

Anika Cajan, Grade 6
St Anne French Immersion School, ON

My Name Is…

J umping jaguar
A crobatic armadillo
R unning raccoon
E ating elephant
D ancing dog

I cy iguana
Z ippy zebra
O rdinary otter
N aughty newt

And that is my name!

Jared Izon, Grade 4
Bayview Elementary School, BC

Snow

Snow is cold and fun
Not allowed throwing snowballs
Making snowmen smile

Malyssa Mack, Grade 5
Bayview Elementary School, BC

Thanksgiving

T urning winter in the leaves
H aving a cornucopia of vegetables
A very good dinner I will eat
N ice knitted clothes for winter
K now everything is nice and neat
S aving leftovers for later
G iving greetings and eating
I ce cream for dessert
V ery good turkey
I ce and frost is forming
N ice treats for me to eat
G iving, sharing and caring

Connor Payton, Grade 5
Muskoka Falls Public School, ON

Love

Love is like a friend, it can care about you,
And some drift apart, you need someone
Who will stay, loyal to your heart
It runs away you look and look again,
And when you find it, it's love to come again!
But is love as simple as you think NO!
Love is hard to find,
But keep it in your heart and in your mind
Love is something that will come when...
You find the right one!

Heather Snow, Grade 6
Hampton Middle School, NB

Autumn/Fall

Orange, yellow, red leaves
Having fun candy please!

Migration, for birds,
Hibernation for animals,

Shiver it's getting colder,
Mom says come in Grandma's one year older,

Halloween's coming kids are pleased.

Camilla Ryther, Grade 5
St Noel Chabanel Catholic Elementary School, ON

What Is Green?

Green is like the wet grass from a field.
Green is like a strong sweet peppermint.
Green is like the morning dew on a spring leaf.
Green is like the big watermelon on the vine.
Green is like the long swinging vine in the forest.
Green is like the fake bushy clown wig.
Green is like the mushy Play Dough between my fingers.
Green is like the flower just about to bloom.

What is green you ask?
Green is all these things!

Matthew Douglass, Grade 4
Bayview Public School, ON

On Remembrance Day

On Remembrance Day
We stay
And remember those
Who left their homes
Day and night
They fought for what's right
Even in the rain
They found a way to work through the pain
That's why we stay
On Remembrance Day

Chantelle Halliday, Grade 6
Walnut Road Elementary School, BC

Water

Wavy, slippery, splashing
Dancing everywhere
Spring, fall and summer just began
Soft, silent, salty
Soaking up the sea
Plants, animals and people feel like they're free!

Connor Godin, Grade 6
Holy Cross School, ON

Spirit Girl

She stares upon her world,
Far from her now.
As far away as one could be.
She's close but too far to reach.
It's changed so much since she last roamed,
On the dirt and swam in the water.
She is a spirit girl.

Victoria Mitchell, Grade 6
Nellie McClung School, AB

Autumn Autumn

Autumn is great
Autumn is cold like a morning breeze.
The trees turn chestnut brown.
The leaves turn cherry red and lemon yellow
The French green grass turns into crystal white snow.

Autumn Autumn

Kids love autumn
It's very fun
Kids pounce in the leaves
off the trampoline.
The parents love autumn too
because the kids are gone
and the parents have peace and quiet.

Palmer Boucher, Grade 4
Avondale School, AB

Ponies

All sizes of ponies big, medium, large
All kinds of colored ponies
Pure white, light brown, gray, white with polka dot
Pure black

Ponies smell nice, look nice too
Fresh cut green grass tastes good for the ponies
Love to be patted behind the ear
Big ponies are good to ride and jump

Ponies have big hooves
Ponies have big shiny manes
Big, small ponies are all nice
Ponies are good to have on farms

Sarah Moore, Grade 6
Uniacke District School, NS

Friends

Friends are here, friends are there,
Friends are everywhere,
friends are near,
When you drop a tear,
Friends stay close,
When you need them the most,
They give you a part,
In their hearts,
When you're spirits need a lift,
Your friendship is a gift,
Friends are like night,
Or like birds in flight,
When our friendship stays,
It brightens up our days,
When I'm in the pond,
She's underground,
So lets give a cheer,
To our best musketeers,
Though friends may not be forever,
And they may not end up together,
They're still one of a kind.

Nahili Taha, Grade 6
Islamic Foundation School, ON

Water

Smooth, slippery, salty, splashing
Ocean.

Wet, waves, whooshing, warmth
Beach.

Bubbles, blue, beach
Fun.

Sand, seagulls, splashing, silence
Enjoyable.

Playing, private, personal
Fountain.

Adria Burri, Grade 6
Holy Cross School, ON

Remembrance

R emember people who died
E nemies fighting
M en at war
E ager to save their country
M any families cried at home
B elieve God is with them
R emorse for the men
A dmire the brave
N ever ending
C ourage to fight
E ncourage with prayer

Katie Bleick, Grade 4
Linsford Park School, AB

My Self-Portrait

My hair is like the tall green grass that blows in the breeze.
My eyes are like the round berries that glow in the sunshine.
My fingers are like the little skinny branches on a big tree.
My heart is like the warmest core in the big bright sun.
It is as red as the blood flowing down my hot cheeks.
It has love and compassion in it.
One part of my body is special, and it is my warm, loving heart.
I am thankful for the body I have been given, especially my heart.

Keiko Pan, Grade 5
Blakeburn Elementary School, BC

Peace

If peace never stopped there would be no war.
There would be no fights.
If guns stopped shooting people and killing,
If there was no killing there would be no wars, there would be peace.

If there was no bullying,
If there was more love,
If there were only nice words,
People are like Jesus, and there is peace.

Sweat running down your neck…
Guns yelling out shells and bullets then
Soldiers screaming their heads off.
Peace is like Heaven,
But the thing I like the most is when the sun rises and the war is over,
The glow fills my heart.

That is peace.

Dallas Stinn, Grade 6
St Catherine Elementary School, AB

Unpopular

You don't understand my sorrow, my sadness or my woe
The feeling of being free, I will never really know
You don't understand why I'm down, because no one will raise me up high
No one ever looks at me and I don't even know why
They'd rather stare at nail polish on their tiny fingertips
And stare in the mirror putting glossy lipstick on their lips
They are tigers gnawing at my head
But when the teachers are around, they're like little sheep in bed
You don't understand my anguish, my grief or my despair
The endless torment of being left out, no one will even care
You don't understand my pain, or extreme hurt I feel inside
I want to run away and hide
They are burning up inside of me and tearing out my soul
In this play I have no part, I do not have a role
One laugh, one snicker, one giggle to my face
No where to go, I can't hide in one place
So this is her school yard diary
I hope you'd realize
How their world really feels
And how it feels to lose your pride

Joelle Mariano, Grade 6
Immaculate Conception, BC

Peace

A world without wars, fighting or spying,
Blue skies above no one is crying,
Love, friendship and care in everyone's heart,
And this is what we wish would start.

Of course this really is fantasy,
For everyone because you see,
Not everyone knows the goodness of peace,
How everything would be calm like the seas.

Gunshots, cannons and shooting is what,
Many people today have only got,
No family, no friends, no love,
They need peace, peace like a dove.

So that is why we wish for peace,
Peace, peace is what we seek,
So everyone could enjoy life,
And not be worried, for they have light.

Megan Bourassa, Grade 6
Immaculate Conception, BC

A Snowy Christmas

Snow flakes falling on the ground,
Cold, nice and round
Lovely shapes dropping from the sky,
With a light breeze passing by
Kids sliding on their sleds
People relaxing on their beds,
Families laying down beside the fireplace
And drinking hot chocolate with marshmallows,
During a snowy day.
Children making snowmen,
running home for a carrot nose.
People decorating the Christmas tree,
the bright yellow star on the very top.
A wonderful snowy day!

Emma Blagojevic, Grade 5
Dr F D Sinclair Elementary School, BC

If Heaven Was?

If heaven was an hour it would be twilight,
When the fireflies start their dancing on the lawn.

If heaven was a train, it sure would be a fast one
And if heaven was a tear, it would be my last one.

And everything you wanted is out there waiting
And everyone you wanted is still alive.

Don't cry a tear for them now,
There comes a time we all must say good-bye
And if that's what heaven's made of
I ain't afraid to die.

Akeysha McGrath, Grade 6
Bayview Elementary School, BC

The Moose That Got Loose

The goose had a moose that got loose —
He didn't know what to do.
The goose said, "That moose can't run very fast,
So where could he be?
Is he here? Is he there?
Oh, where could he be?
Is he North? Is he South?
Oh, where could he be?
He could be up, he could be down,
He could be anywhere around!
He could be at Ben's or at Mary's.
Oh, where could he be?
Wait a minute…I see him now,
Over there behind that tree!"

Nyrée Rainville, Grade 5
Ecole les Cypres, AB

The Leaves

The leaves are dancing, leaves are swaying,
the leaves are everywhere!
There's mixed red, green, brown, orange, dark yellow —
all sorts of colors!

The sun is shining on the leaves, lemon yellow.
The leaves are dancing, the leaves are swaying
and even hovering off the ground!

As the leaves are soaring and floating
they're also spinning and twirling.
Some leaves are falling softly and heavily.
Some leaves are falling madly and eagerly.

Some are only falling calmly down.
While the wind is blowing,
the leaves are scattering and flying away for fall!

Joshuah Bunyan, Grade 4
Avondale School, AB

Imagine

Let your imagination soar on its own two wings,
Let it speak out, and listen as it sings.
Let a thousand skies, lead its way,
Let a single smile make its day.
Let a happy person, make it grow,
Let a single speck, make it all show.
Imagine…
Let a blade of grass, brighten up its day,
Let it be free, but don't always let it get its way.
Let a soaring heron, fly above its head,
Let it watch, as a snake starts to shed.
Let a crowing rooster, make it all believe,
Let it do this all, and never will it deceive…
Imagine…

Emily Kovach, Grade 6
Central Public School, ON

My Favorite Pine Tree

My favorite place is my pine tree. I let my dog out, and my cats are outside. I run to my pine tree in my back yard. I can hear the trees rustling in the distances. The chipmunks scattering, and the birds singing their soft melodies. The needles falling softly on the ground. I feel the bumpy bark on my soft hands. The sharp needles poking into my soft sore hands. When I look down I can see the ground cover in the leaves. Then I look up just to see the great birds soaring in the sky. I look to my left and I can see the simmering, sunny sun that is breaking through onto my face. A needle falls onto my head, I look at it and it looks like an icicle. When I start climbing down I hope that tomorrow I can come back to my pine tree.

Kara Stephan, Grade 5
Forest Hill Public School, ON

Georgina Life Switch

The day is coming, the day is coming. My parents are moving me and my brothers far far away. I have to leave my house, my friends, my city, my school, and all the things I care about the most, what I took for granted, I have to leave behind.

I asked my parents if I could live with one of my friends. I told them I would call them every day and visit them all the time. But "NO" THAT would be breaking our family up. Like I care I said to them. But they still up and moved me. The last day of school sad and cold as ice. Whenever I saw one of my friends they would cry and then I would too.

My new house is not a home it's just a house. I'll never get used to it. My new school is different. The new school has very strange rules.

I'm sad my friends are gone I have to make new ones. I'm crying every night, home sick I think. I feel as though I don't belong. My mom tells me no one likes change but sometimes it's for the best.

Now I agree with her a little bit just a little bit. I will still miss my old life. I just had to learn these things happen in life.

Jordan Lee Vickaryous-Remenda, Grade 6
St Anne School, SK

A Poppy Brings Peace

Trumpets boom over the country, as rays from the sun glisten over the mountains and shine over the lush green ground.
The calmness ends when the sky darkens and the country is filled with many men and tanks.
Planes fly across the sky, boats fill the seas and mighty winds howl over the mountains.
The country is engulfed with many lights that brighten the sky and seas with darkness raining above.

Bombs from planes rain down in terror!
Torpedoes from boats brighten the seas!
Rifles bring death to all these who live!
Until one surrenders, and calmness is restored.

The once lush green ground is now where all those who have perished lie,
Where many crosses cry to the raining bombs and rifles that had lit the sky,
That have brought them to what they are on the dark red ground,
For those that have lived fear and sadness is all that remains.

Now towns, cities, and countries all dark and put to waste,
Peace and happiness is nowhere to be seen,
The only thing around is sadness in the wasteland where the bombs boomed and the rifles shot the crying soldiers.
Until a single poppy bloomed by the crosses where the soldiers lay in peace.

Ben Clarke, Grade 6
St Catherine Elementary School, AB

Autumn

Autumn brings leaves falling, children laughing walking in the pine fresh forest.
The wind howls whistling through my hair, running faster and faster in my little blue vest.
It is autumn, it is cold but FUNNER than ever!!!

Niamh Donnelly, Grade 5
St Noel Chabanel Catholic Elementary School, ON

Winter

Winter has finally come,
school has almost gone out
the children can play,
finally, snow has come back
kids have some fun,
kids can make snowmen,
have snowball fights,
make forts,
with their family and friends
moms and dads give you hot chocolate,
kids wish not to go back to school
let the snow stay,
forever to play all day long,
so that we can't go back to school for the rest of the year.

Rita Seng, Grade 6
Dr F D Sinclair Elementary School, BC

Talent

If you decided that, you have no talent or greatness,
You decided wrong,
And I will help you excel your image upon this,
In this poem, that will get you and your talent along.

Oh, the joy of the talent giving,
It could not come to you at first,
But soon an alarm in your mind will be ringing,
It will feel like an excitement burst.

To find your talent it will never hurt,
You don't have to look through the burning earth's core,
To find that fulfilling excitement burst,
You have to free yourself and you don't have to do anymore.

Let your talent be like a pamphlet
Guiding you through the way,
Don't give up and soon your talent,
Will feel like a sun-filled ray.

Have your talent open your soul,
And have it deeply excel your mind,
Climb up your growing spiritual pole,
At the top, it would be your talent that you find.

Angelica Poversky, Grade 4
Tomekichi Homma Elementary School, BC

Shadow

He hates the shade.
I love the shade.
He hates the water.
I love the water.
He hates the dark.
I hate the dark too.
Now we both have something in common!

Bobbie Cooper, Grade 6
Ecole les Cypres, AB

Dancing

Swirling colours all around me.
Dazzling lights above my head.
To get this special feeling there is no fee.
I'm in my own world where no one can pull me out.
Can you guess what I'm doing?
I know you can! I have no doubt.
That you could guess I'm DANCING!

Madison Pelham, Grade 6
Hampton Middle School, NB

My Favorite Place

My favorite place is a sandy beach at my cottage,
Where I like to sit, at sunset and read a book.

When I sit there I hear the peaceful waves,
Gently lapping against the shore,
Splashing the rocks and getting me wet.

And the seagulls squawking from the rocks above,
Hoping I will feed them.

The crimson sun is slowly setting past the water,
Tossing golden strips of light on the sand,
Making it sparkle.

The water is a deep, sea green,
And I see the last sailboats, coming in for the night,
Looking like coloured shark fins,
Poking out of the water.

The warm smell of the golden sand,
The chilly wet smell of the water,
And the tasty scent of dinner surrounds me.

As I climb up the steep rocks to my cottage,
I wish to come again next year.

Jessica Rapson, Grade 5
Forest Hill Public School, ON

Big Beehive

My favourite place is Big Beehive
The terrain is rocky and jagged.
Where it is cold every day
I hear running water as I jump rock to rock.

We stumble through the soft slippery snow
A little squirrel scurries to find food.
There is a lake, which is as clear as glass
The colour of the lake is green as an emerald.

The sight of snow reminds me of winter
When we get to the top the sight is wonderful
As if it was painted
I hike down knowing I just saw an awesome sight.

Riley Parker, Grade 5
Forest Hill Public School, ON

Christmas Holidays

C hristmas is a holiday
H olly above your door
R elatives come to visit
I am happy to have people who love me
S taying happy with your family
T ime to play in the snow
M aking presents with love
A t a house nice and warm
S anta brings you gifts

H olidays are the best
O ne of the greatest days is Christmas
L ying in bed waiting for Santa
I hope I get lots of presents
D ancing to special music
A lways be good or Santa won't come
Y ou and your family together
S inging Christmas carols

Jasmeet Deol, Grade 5
Dr F D Sinclair Elementary School, BC

Water

As water touches my tongue
It is wet and salty
The waterfall is crystal clear
Shimmery, sparkling
Making rushing bubbles
Through the mist

But water is not all good
It is daring
Slippery
And messy to mess with
Also expensive
Hard to buy

It might be alarming just think
Soft, fun
And it might tickle toes
As you're walking
By the ocean

When you see
That graceful fountain frozen
Think, it is worth the trouble!
Water will come again.

Jacqueline Mudie, Grade 6
Holy Cross School, ON

Snow

S oft
N ever melts in the cold, cold winter
O h how I love to play in the snow
W hite wonder falling from the sky

Max Ohlmann, Grade 4
Linsford Park School, AB

Reading

Silence fills the room.
The only sound is turning pages.
The story pulls you in,
Hauls you out of this world,
And into another.

Your eyes begin to ache,
From focusing for long stretches of time.
STOP! That's it! No more!
But this story's so good…

Mallory Kroll, Grade 6
Uniacke District School, NS

The Wii

You wave it, you swish it,
you turn it, you churn it.
All of these and more.
You click it, you tap it,
you press it, you hold it.
In some games there is gore.
You buy it, you play it,
you like it, you love it.
So you can play some more.
It's fun, it's cool,
it's new, it's cheap.
The Wii is so hard core!

Daniel Tarek Meisels Mandour, Grade 5
Ste-Foy Elementary School, QC

Chase

It's nearly Chase's birthday,
A black and white Collie,
He's the blonde of the house,
A puppy who is jolly.

While Dad and I play air hockey,
Chase barks, watching the puck,
I hit the puck hard
It flings up, I yell, "Dad duck!"

He loves to be out in the day,
Jumping in the snow like a bunny,
Rolling around as we play
He is worth the money.

Jacob Beaulieu, Grade 6
Uniacke District School, NS

Grass

It is so green and…
It is so bright and …
It moves from side to side
Because the wind blows
Cold in the winter.

Garret McAlinden, Grade 5
Bayview Elementary School, BC

Webkinz…

Webkinz are my favorite.
I always wanted one.

Then I got a black lab.
It was lots of fun.

Next I got a little kinz.
Coco is her name.

Now I can go on the computer,
And play a lot of games.

Samantha King, Grade 6
Uniacke District School, NS

Candy

Candy, candy
Sweet candy.
Melt in your mouth
With desire.
Soft, hard
Tasty, gooey
Some are green
Pink, yellow
All the colors
Of the rainbow
Candy is the coolest
Thing in the world

Kyra Paige Bonagofsky, Grade 4
Margaret Wooding School, AB

A Goose, a Loon, and a Hare

A goose, a loon, and a hare
Spent the day at the fair
They ate so much pie
They thought they would die
Next time they would share

Cam Jensen, Grade 6
St Anne School, SK

Silence and Sorrow

I stand here in silence remembering you,
Deep in my heart I feel so blue.

Today is another Remembrance Day,
My thoughts are of a battlefield far away.

All day long the brave men fought,
The air rings out with a loud gun shot.

Soldiers run, collapse and yell,
Death and blood shed is a terrible smell.

So much devastation, how could this be?
To end war forever is my fervent plea!

Alexa Gordon, Grade 4
Linsford Park School, AB

Autumn

A utumn is when there's leaves
U ndoing summer things
T reats on Halloween
U se care watch out for things
M oms and dads playing with you
N ot the day yet but soon

Sebastian Corallo, Grade 5
St Noel Chabanel Catholic Elementary School, ON

Christmas Eve

It's Christmas Eve! Hooray, Hooray!
The cookies are set out
Chocolate chip, they are,
A carrot for Rudolph.

The tree is lit up
All bright and sparkling
Presents —
Big ones, little ones, shiny ones, dull ones.

We go to bed, it's late at night.
It's snowing heavily,
Finally, a white Christmas.

Alex Williams, Grade 6
Uniacke District School, NS

Remembrance Day

In Flanders fields the poppies grow,
Between the crosses row by row,
Make us remember that ones that fought in war,
Some still come door to door.

I'll wear a poppy as red as can be,
To show that I remember those who fought for me.
Thinking of the men that fought in the war,
Thousands died and saw so much gore.

So kids, please play without fighting.
Remember to share your games and toys.
Be kind and thoughtful,
To all girls and boys.

On the 11th day at the 11th hour of every Remembrance Day
we should all remember the men that fought and died for us.

Ben Maurice, Grade 5
Forest Hill Public School, ON

Snow Angels

Snow angels from the heavens above,
They come in peace to spread their love,
Even though the angels are white,
Their souls are beautiful, happy and bright,
They bear their love into the night,
To let you know they'll be all right.

Shannon O'Donohue, Grade 4
Sioux Mountain School, ON

Snowflakes

S nowflakes are sprinkling to the earth
N ew Year's day is on the way
O n the ground snow angels look wonderful
W ind is rushing through my brown hair
I ce skating on the cold ice
N ot a single drop of rain falling
G littering snow is on the freezing ground

Inderjeet Dhaliwal, Grade 5
Dr F D Sinclair Elementary School, BC

Love

Love is a four letter word,
meaning many things.
Love means holding someone close,
not pushing them away.
Love means spending time with family,
sharing with a friend,
or giving someone a smile.
Love is a four letter word meaning many things,
but most of all it means you and me.

Justine Sprague, Grade 6
St Anne French Immersion School, ON

Football

Football is the time of day
To sit back, relax and watch us play
Watch us for that long hour
Just sit back there on the tower
I always have the ball in my hand to hold
At the end of the season, I hope to get a trophy of gold.

I don't want to ruin the day
If my Dad gets disappointed what will he say?
Sitting up there and don't think it's lame
For me this is a wonderful game!

Tiger Haire, Grade 6
Bayview Elementary School, BC

Christmas!

I like to sit by the warm cozy fireplace.
We make yummy gingerbread houses.

I love to go skating with my family.
At school we make winter crafts.

I help my mom decorate the tree.
Before I go to bed I hang my stocking.

I play with my friends out in the snow.
Just waiting for turkey, carrots, turnips, potatoes…yummy!

Can't wait 'til Christmas morning,
All the gifts under the tree.

Mallory Collier, Grade 6
Uniacke District School, NS

Leaves

L eaves are soft and smooth.
E xciting to jump in.
A nd crunchy to walk on.
V ivid and colourful.
E nchanting and beautiful.
S ummer ends and leaves fall.

Adam O'Brien, Grade 6
Holy Cross School, ON

Remembrance Day

R emember the soldiers
E veryone respects
M embers of Canada who fought for us
E very country tries to survive
M any people sacrifice
B attle keeps raging on
R ed poppies grow
A re larks still bravely singing?
N ow they lie in Flanders fields
C rosses sitting row on row
E ach are now resting in peace

D ead but brave these people lay
A gain the guns still shooting
Y oung and old still fighting for freedom

Mary Liamzon, Grade 5
Dr F D Sinclair Elementary School, BC

Snow

Snow is fluffy
snow is white
snow is fun
to play in,
make a
snowman or
make a snow angel,
Snow is always fun
play in it for hours or five minutes
trust me it will be fun.
Have a snowball fight,
get all wet
who cares it's for the fun
so come on
enjoy
it only comes once a year.

Rayan Makhdumi, Grade 5
Dr F D Sinclair Elementary School, BC

Dream Beach

Swing in the hammock
Rest under windy palm trees
Dig into the sand
Dive into the clear blue sea
Scuba dive deep in the sea.

BreAnne Snyder, Grade 5
New Germany Elementary School, NS

Heart Breaker

With war wandering wildly throughout the world
With lives leaving us day by day
Our love for life becomes as hard as clay
An undying wish the soldiers come home is what the devastated families pray.

Their pulsing sadness was like being pricked with a thorn
With their pins and badges all rusted and worn
Their jackets and hats all ripped and torn.

Every day the children cry, "where is daddy?"
"My dears he is on his way home," is what the scared and lonely mothers moan.

As we all know they are battling at war
They're fighting for honor, their country and more
We are all hoping for the fighting to cease
So that everyone around us can live in a world of peace.

Hannah Jackson, Grade 6
St Philip School, AB

Just Imagine

Just imagine anything.
Anything at all.
Just imagine being able to walk on water.
Just imagine a little boy sitting in a corner listening to
His parents fight a pointless war.
Just imagine a wilted flower spending its last moments on Earth
Accompanied only by bitterness and sorrow.
Just imagine the happiness of a couple in the hospital
With their newborn child.
Just imagine millions of brave people fighting an endless battle.
Just imagine a lone heart beating to the rhythm of silence.
Just imagine all of your dreams coming true, with all your questions answered.
Just imagine thinking you've mastered all of science,
Just to discover something more.
Just imagine.
Anything at all.

Madison Nelson, Grade 6
St Philip School, AB

Jake Pringle

Jake

Smart, athletic, in shape, funny
Son of Grant and Lana
Lover of lacrosse, biking, skateboarding and chilling with friends
Who feels happy and energetic
Who needs family and friends
Who gives love and friendship
Who fears losing loved ones and death
Who likes to wear shorts and muscle shirts
Who would like to see Hollywood and Hawaii
Resident of Nanaimo

Pringle

Jake Pringle, Grade 4
Bayview Elementary School, BC

Friendship

Friendship is about
All the ups and downs

It's about all the smiles
Laughs, and frowns

You're always together
Laughing with each other

A friend always understands
You always walk together hand in hand

Friendship will last forever
And if forever ends
You'll still be with each other
Issa Cahoy, Grade 6
St Anne French Immersion School, ON

When I Was Younger

When I was younger,
My sister was bossy
But now that I'm older,
I play with her very nicely

When I was younger,
I knew addition
But now that I'm older,
I know division

When I was younger,
I had a gameboy
But now that I'm older,
I have a DS.

When I was younger,
I needed naps during the day
But now that I'm older,
I only sleep at night
Matthew Stendel, Grade 4
Ecole Akiva, QC

On a Snowy Day

On a snowy day
I like to play,
When snowflakes fall
gently from the sky.
Building a snowman is so much fun
But when a frosty breeze passes by,
I like to sit by the fire with hot cocoa,
Relaxing on the warm couch,
I couldn't feel much better.
A warm and cozy bed,
Makes me fall into a dreamy sleep.
Kiran Rashid, Grade 5
Dr F D Sinclair Elementary School, BC

Rover

On a big sunny hillside,
Way down in the clover
Sits a little dog Rover.
He ran from home,
To be alone,
On the big and sunny hillside.

A fly buzzed by,
A froggy croaked,
And Rover moped.
His brothers and sisters;
They were too small,
His friends; they did not call.

His father; he was bad,
His mother; she was sad,
At the badness of his dad.
There in the bushes,
A fox came out,
And began to pout.

What a sad day for Rover!
Raquel Miller, Grade 4
Riverdale School, MB

Autumn

In the fall
The leaves drop from the trees
Like rain comes down
From the sky
So beautiful
Green, yellow and red leaves
Your kids may want to rake the leaves
And jump into the huge pile
And have a terrific time
There are a lot of good things
About fall
That I can't explain.
Justice Bursey, Grade 4
Avondale School, AB

Flowers

Flower
So beautiful
Lots of colors
It is breath taking
Plant
Vanessa Ernst, Grade 5
New Germany Elementary School, NS

Golf

You can drive the golf ball
In the hole it will fall
A hole in one it is called.
Daniel Lohnes, Grade 5
New Germany Elementary School, NS

Thinking

I think,
over and over again.
About life,
about me,
about him.
I'm in class,
thinking, thinking,
what will happen next?
Next?
I never thought about next.
He is just there,
in the class,
in the halls,
out at recess.
He's just part of the scenery,
going along with life,
like nothing's going on.
Thinking, thinking.
Brandi Baker, Grade 6
St Anne French Immersion School, ON

Flowers

There are many types
Roses, sunflowers, tulips
They're good for a gift
Rodney Seward, Grade 5
Bayview Elementary School, BC

Trains

I like trains very much,
models are my favorite,
I watch them go everywhere,
Diesel engines roaring loud.

Real trains are very big,
And also very loud,
Pulling cars everywhere through cities,
Every train is different.

The engines grunt and groan,
When they transport crates,
Every train has a whistle,
Even some model trains.
Christopher Wannamaker, Grade 6
Uniacke District School, NS

Winter

W ind is rushing through my hair
I ce skating on the cold winter ice
N ew Year's is coming
T rees are decorated
E veryone is playing outside
R ed and green are colours of Christmas
Charndeep Lottay, Grade 5
Dr F D Sinclair Elementary School, BC

Snow

Snow has fallen all around
It covers the ground.
So it can't be found,
When snow has fallen
All you can think
Is X-mas is coming quick as a wink.
For kids
It's playing with snowballs
Snowmen.
For grown-ups
It's shoveling
Or staying in bed.

Magen Patey, Grade 6
Uniacke District School, NS

Winter

In the winter time
the ground is covered
in a white blanket of snow
the trees are bare
the birds have flown.

Families are happy
filled with Christmas spirit
bells are jingling
in the crisp morning air.

In the day and through the night
the snow falls so softly
and in the morning kids awaken
their hearts full of excitement.

Deer are chewing the last green off trees
squirrels eat the nuts they've stored
birds fly south to a warmer place
while winter works its magic.

Kayla Parsons, Grade 6
Uniacke District School, NS

Layla Rice

Layla

Smart, creative, pretty and talented
Daughter of Jen and Dad
Lover of singing and dancing
Who feels shy and excited
Who needs a baby-sitter and excitement
Who gives time and friendship
Who fears cougars and spiders
Who likes to wear tank tops and skirts
Who would like to see Hollywood
Resident of B.C.

Rice

Layla Rice, Grade 4
Bayview Elementary School, BC

Wonderful Water

Swooshing and swishing
solid and smooth or splashy and see through
thirst quenching and refreshing
dangerous, with waves the size of mountains that are about to collapse
quiet, peaceful, water

Russell Stuart, Grade 6
Holy Cross School, ON

So Little Time

So little time to walk, to talk, to think, to breathe.
I feel like I'm in a deep trance. With people and places.
Malls, halls, stores, streets. It's all such a bore to me. You see?
People going in and out.
I wanna scream. I wanna shout!
I just wanna jump into a sparkling river and float until the sun goes down.
Where no one is there to sing and dance.
It really irritates me to see people walking on the streets.
Skipping, talking, laughing, calling.
Another thing I hate to see is little children on TV
No clothes, no food, imagine their mood.
It takes very little to kill someone's spirit. It's just really low.
They have so little need. To shop, to stop, to read.
Truthfully, all they can really do is plead!
There are friends who sometimes have your back.
But to keep your secrets is what they lack.
When they hurt you, you only see in white and black.
Your feelings are bottled, your minds jam-packed!
As I write this poem, I like to think,
At least I have my family.
The ones I love.

Kieran Bryk, Grade 6
Uniacke District School, NS

The Shining Star Shimmering

The stars up above fly through the sky like a dove
They jettison through the night following a destiny without a fright.
Up in the sky they fly so high towering in our black sky
They see the world through gleaming eyes
Through clouds of smoke we can be one before they're done
Which would be great!
We can watch the people from the air,
With the gentle wind in our hair,
Oh that would be great!
If only that could be real!
It would be a great deal!
You would shine like a star
You would never get far
From the world below
To watch and gleam at the odd fellow
From the heavens above this all a dream
Because the stars are leaving the day is erasing the night
And when the day fades away again
Our fantasies become real from now and then
And soon our dreams begin again.

Audrey-Anne St-Denis, Grade 6
St Philip School, AB

Freedom

Every person on this earth doesn't have freedom
Some don't have anyone to love them,
They get sold for slavery, money and work
They don't get toys, games or to run around free,
Some will work until forced to flee.
It's not just kids, it's adults too
Women who milk cows that go moo.
Men who work all day with hard, heavy bricks
And little kids who pick up firewood sticks.
This is a day of a working family,
Who works all day for little money.
You are so lucky to get anything you want,
Just go to the grocery store to get what you need
Candy, chocolate, chips and gum,
Little kids in Africa think please Mum.
If you see a UNICEF donor, donate to the kids who need money.
Now you do see,
The day of a typical, poor family.
I hope if you hear on the phone,
Someone say will you please donate today?
Say yes, I will donate and say Hooray!

Amritpal Minhas, Grade 6
Dr F D Sinclair Elementary School, BC

Fall

Fall is an awesome season,
And I have a good reason.

When the leaves change, take a look,
It's like a scene out of a book.

Fall is when the wood stove is on,
And when a blanket of frost covers the lawn.

It is fall when the hot weather bids farewell,
And the pumpkins and cornstalks start to sell.

Fall is the time the birds fly away,
But don't worry, they'll be back another day.

It is fall and these memories I'll keep,
Soon Canada has a long winter sleep.

Grace Carline, Grade 6
Hampton Middle School, NB

Dove

A dove is as white as the snow,
Flying up above, it glides gracefully in the sky.
It soars in the air swiftly and high.
It floats in the brisk night flow.
Don't you ever wonder why? Why, oh why, it flies so high?
When you look around you will see it go by.
Symbolizing peace and love, the dove has a magnificent glow.

Stephanie Ang, Grade 4
Immaculate Conception, BC

Fall

Leaves are falling off a tree
Giving work and fun to thee
Grass is covered by the frost
Lots of people being lost

Sweets! Candy! Trick or Treat
Put away the soccer cleat
Extra layers of jackets
Lots of big harvest baskets
This is the month of the rosary
Do lots and lots of prayers for Mary
Turkey's cook'n in the ovens
Saying hello to lots of cousins
Bears and chipmunks hibernate
Birds and insects migrate

Pumpkins are given scary looks
Now it's cold so read some books
Armies fought the World War I
Survivors of that're almost none
Poppies from the war will yield
Growing in the Flanders Field

Joseph Gino Boem, Grade 5
St Noel Chabanel Catholic Elementary School, ON

Spencer Meltzer

Spencer
Motor-mouthed, hilarious, athletic, nuts
Brother of Ariella and Elijah
Lover of sports, food and television
Who feels awesome, there should be more sports and weird
Who needs less homework, more recess and more fun
Who fears big needles, giant spiders and bad people
Who gives kindness, fairness and sportsmanship
Who would like to see the Habs win the Stanley Cup,
Hawaii and my own amusement park
Resident of Montreal, Quebec Canada
Meltzer

Spencer Meltzer, Grade 4
Ecole Akiva, QC

Thanksgiving

T hanks for what we have, not for what we want,
H unting for turkeys to eat for dinner.
A corns falling off, colored leaves and trees.
N o school it's a holiday.
K nowing everyone, you know.
S itting by the fireplace.
G athering with friends and family.
I eat lots of pumpkin pie.
V ery big appetites.
I love my family.
N ature outside.
G athering with nice people for dinner.

Courtney Steiger, Grade 4
Muskoka Falls Public School, ON

Thanksgiving

T urkey in the oven.
H aving fun with my family.
A corns.
N o more swimming.
K nowing my family loves me.
S quash is yummy.
G ravy to put on the turkey.
I like Thanksgiving.
V ery good meal.
I was full after dinner.
N ice season.
G rateful.

Deklan Henshaw, Grade 4
Muskoka Falls Public School, ON

Mom/Dad

Mom
loving, caring
cleaning, working, organizing.
My mom and dad love me,
loving, caring
Dad

Ferna Lafond, Grade 6
St Anne School, SK

Leaves

L eaves are colourful
E erie on Halloween
A n autumn breeze
V ery crunchy when dry
E arthbound
S cattered on the ground

Matthew Allan, Grade 6
Holy Cross School, ON

Water

You can swim in it
It can melt from snow and ice
It is in the sky

Trevor Crichton, Grade 5
Bayview Elementary School, BC

Emotions

Scared is pale like
white animal that runs through
your brain and gets you awake.
Jealousy is like black blood that makes
the darker side of you.
Sad is just like blue water
making your eyes red.
Anger is like red hot peppers
making your tongue all bitter.
Lazy is orange like video games
screaming and calling you!

Peter Hiemstra, Grade 6
St Anne School, SK

Daisy

People are tearing apart the land,
Not being taken care of,
Instead of rising, I am falling,
Doing whatever I can to survive,
I can't survive alone.
Now all that's left of me
Is a brown stem,
And a faded,
Yellow circle!

Sandra Papo, Grade 6
William G Davis Public School, ON

Fall

Fall is something to enjoy
in the Autumn sun.
The leaves how they dance
around the enchanted wind
in a spot that gleams through the air.
In the morning I was torn
that I was waken.
When it's day we can play.
When it's lunch we invite
people to have some punch.
In the evening we see
people leaving.
At night we are all
out of sight.

Ivan Galay, Grade 5
Dr F D Sinclair Elementary School, BC

Fall

Fall is beautiful,
Fall is fun.
Fall is colorful,
Under the fading sun.

The weather outside,
Is getting so cold.
It's time to wear a jacket.
I'm always told.

Outside in the leaves,
I want to play,
For I know soon,
They will blow away.

Allison Raitz, Grade 4
Linsford Park School, AB

No Smoking

Smoking stinks it's gross
It smells, it repels, it's bad
It is disgusting

Drake Belajac, Grade 6
New Germany Elementary School, NS

My Dad

I love my dad —
he's so kind and dear,
When I'm sad,
he lets me cry in his ear.
He's so sincere.
He's always near.
But best of all, he thinks being a dad
is the best career!

Haley Ticknor, Grade 5
Forest Hill Public School, ON

Despair

Despair is a menacing thundercloud
Drifting slowly across dark skies
Despair is the drip-drip dripping
Of rain, off a shingled roof
Despair is the ceaseless pound
Of waves against the shore
Despair is the cloudy, stormy sky
Over deep, dark dreary waters
Despair is a murky, clouded sea
Despair is utter absence
A poverty…
Of hope

Timothy Gadanidis, Grade 6
Jack Miner Public School, ON

Mom and Dad

Mom
Beautiful, careful
Loving, caring, sharing
Flowers, kids, sports, TV
Working, playing, coaching
Strong, tough
Dad

Josée Jantz, Grade 4
Ecole les Cypres, AB

Hockey

Early morning practices
get me out of bed.
I am at the rink at 6:00 am
charged and ready to go!!
When my blades hit the ice
That's when I shine.

Mat Savidant, Grade 6
Hampton Middle School, NB

Peace

P assionate about friendship
E nd all wars
A lways give people food and a home
C aring about others
E veryone needs love

Dayton Coulthard, Grade 4
Bayview Elementary School, BC

The End

Peace is a beautiful thing that flies through the air,
Although it isn't always here.
It is opposite all around the globe.

Black and darkness screaming at your face,
With skies of hatred and defeat.

Bang! Yells the rifle that echoes through my head
I cannot do anything to stop this except for just one thing…
To pray and hope.

Juan Pablo Sanchez, Grade 6
St Catherine Elementary School, AB

Fall Leaves

Red, green, orange, yellow and crispy brown
leaves fall from the sky down, down, down

Fall leaves fall

Cherry red, olive green, pumpkin orange,
banana yellow and café brown leaves fall
from the chestnut brown trees

Fall leaves fall

Prancing and dancing from the trees
leaves fall from the sky
many crunchy some crispy and smooth
other chewed and broken into *Few*!

Fall leaves fall

Jared Robinson, Grade 4
Avondale School, AB

Horrible Memories

Soldiers go to war one by one
They are fighting for our freedom
People we all remember will go down in history
Guns, bombs, and killing machines
Destroy everything in their path
People sadly lay in Flanders Fields.
As soon as the war has begun
People run back to their families,
Like they're coming back from school.
But they will always have a memory of
The horrible things that happened in the war,
Forever…
Things these soldiers won't let go,
War is over and soon you will be lying in bed.
These horrible memories forget them please,
Help your people they're in need.
Forget these awful memories,
People need you, serve them please.
These horrible memories are fantasies.

Arslan Bhatti, Grade 5
Dr F D Sinclair Elementary School, BC

We Remember

We remember the men who died in the war,
The gunshots, the bombs, and fighting galore.

Soldiers fought for us and put their lives in harm's way,
So that we could enjoy freedom and peace here today.

I will remember the sacrifice the veterans made,
For it is a debt that can never truly be repaid!

Kailey Green, Grade 4
Linsford Park School, AB

Halloween

It's Halloween It's Halloween.

With the crisp wind softly blowing,
children are dressing up in costumes
as the warm afternoon changes into
the cool brisk night.

After it is pitch black
children pack the café brown streets.
The poppy red and peach orange golden yellow
arid shriveled leaves are getting crushed
to little tiny bits as children run and stomp over them
going house to house.

After an hour or two the street drains
'til there's nothing but silence
Kids fall into bed so tired they drift to sleep
dreaming about candy.

Elijah Woods, Grade 4
Avondale School, AB

Why I Like Winter

Winter has come and spread its wonders
Giving it to those who are the founders
Everything is covered in a sheet of snow
Oh what a glorious glow

The roofs are filled with snow
When the wind will come the snow will blow
I wish the snow could stay
But when the sun comes up the snow will melt away

We say goodbye to the sun
For now, it's time for some fun
We run in the snow
And play as we go

We wait for the winter holidays
When they come we go outside to play
When I go outdoors I nearly freeze
Since there is such a cold breeze

Aishah Mohammed, Grade 6
Dr F D Sinclair Elementary School, BC

Just a Dream!

Dreaming…
Thunder, lightning
Storms, windy, frightening sight
Terrible, miserable, scared…
WAKE UP!!!

Jessica Bantog, Grade 4
Immaculate Conception, BC

Fun

We have a lot of fun,
In the deep white snow,
We all stand in a row,
And count to number three,
And fall down with the wind,
Like a heavy large ton.

Gabriela Neufeld, Grade 6
Riverdale School, MB

Cenotaph

C annon fire
E ntire division
N o end to war
O is for the "O' Canada"
T he day we wear a poppy
A day we remember
P oppies in Flanders Fields
H appy for victory

Ashton Kenny, Grade 6
Falmouth District School, NS

Spring

Spring time
Lots of flowers
A restart to nature
Warm, joyful, cheerful, feelings
Sunshine

Jolee Tung, Grade 5
Mulgrave School, BC

Water

Water drips and drips
Every time you take a sip
Water is a tool on a hot summer day
To keep you cool
It's the colour of nothing
If you know what I mean
Water, water, water
Save the precious water
Save each drop
'Cause that's what you've got
There's plenty of water for you and me
But don't waste it
Or we won't have any
Now that's water to me

Denis Nolasco, Grade 6
Holy Cross School, ON

Ryan Kalisky

Ryan
Humorous, chatter box, kind, clever
Son of Lorne and Debbie
Lover of sports, television and computers
Who feels that he doesn't like school, loves sports and is a very good athlete.
Who needs a dog, a brother and a new pair of socks.
Who fears jail, thieves and guns.
Who gives friendship, respect and kindness.
Who would like to see the Habs win, a cure for cancer and world peace.
Resident of Montreal, Quebec, Canada
Kalisky

Ryan Kalisky, Grade 4
Ecole Akiva, QC

Drizzling of Rain

Rain drizzles and drips across my window,
And I am cooped up inside my room.
I hear the pitter patter of the rain beating on the roof above me,
But my eyes stare out the unclear window.
Inside the room I feel as if there was no excitement or no life.

I tried to concentrate through the fogged up glass,
Then my heart beats fast with delight.
Outdoors it was beautiful as the sunflowers swayed wildly side to side,
The mice crawled through the glistening fields,
the grass digging into their fur.

A large truck rumbles and crunches along the dirt and gravel road,
the rain trails behind the tracks of the rusty vehicle.
The mighty small insects are gripping tight on the leaves of the large plants,
being careful not to be washed up by the rain.
The skies might have been grey, but the atmosphere was full of light.

I reached out and covered the window with its curtains.
What I had just witnessed outside was wonderful,
It filled what seemed as a gloomy day with excitement.
Rain was definitely a magical part of nature,
And I was truly thankful for rain.

Caroline Wojnas, Grade 6
Sir William Osler Elementary School, ON

Benjamin Lazare

Athletic, friendly, smart, tall
Son of Mark and Jo-ann
Lover of soccer, hockey, video games
Who feels he doesn't need homework, and reading, piano lessons
Who needs sleep, sports. TV
Who fears anacondas, robbers, terrorists
Who gives help, effort, friendship
Who would like to see all sport players, Maurice Richard, Ronaldinoh
Resident of Westmount, Montreal, Quebec
Lazare.

Benjamin Lazare, Grade 4
Ecole Akiva, QC

Falling Leaves

Let the leaves hug you,
Let them beat upon your head softly,
Let the leaves quietly whisper you a secret.
They make a little pile for you to jump in,
They make a beautiful fall scene,
The leaves might leave an imprint on your sidewalk,
But I still love them!

Sophia Quesada, Grade 4
Immaculate Conception, BC

Being Free

Our tails dance around like leaves
As our manes blow in the morning breeze
Our hooves hit the ground
As we prance around
I'm happy to run again
Instead of being cooped up in a pen
The expressions in our faces are full of delight
As my face shines in the glowing sunlight
Our legs getting tired as we run
But we have so much fun
The ground is getting worn out from all the prancing
My feet too are getting worn out from all our dancing
We are so tired of running
But we can't sit down nor lounge around
Only when the sun goes down
Do we finally stop prancing around

Danielle Barrett, Grade 5
Ranch Park Elementary School, BC

Remembrance

On August 16th, 2004
They left that very day for war
Many fought many died
We hung our head and there we cried
We remember the soldiers every day
For the poppies we wear and where they lay

Taylor Bumstead, Grade 5
St Noel Chabanel Catholic Elementary School, ON

Thanksgiving

T ime for giving.
H aving dinner with family.
A utumn is here.
N ature is changing.
K indness is spreading.
S haring a great meal.
G iving thanks for all we have.
I ce cream is for dessert.
V ery happy to see family.
I f you go inside you smell a delightful aroma.
N othing beats my grandma's cooking.
G etting to see family and friends.

Jessica Sherlock, Grade 5
Muskoka Falls Public School, ON

Hope

The hope that's darting around in the air,
There is one last piece of hope left somewhere,
I need to hope in the peacefulness of the hour,
Or my heart will slowly start to devour,
I have to wish upon a star,
And maybe I will make it just that far,
The hidden destiny that lies miles away,
I have to reach it quickly or it will slowly decay,
My life always parts in different directions,
My hope always crosses tricky intersections,
My heart sometimes will be cold and sour,
My hope will always be filled with power.

Marina Meredith, Grade 6
Queen of All Saints Elementary School, BC

I Pray to You

Dear Lord please help me
Through this very hard time
So that I will have the strength
To move on and be fine.

I know I cannot do anything
To make her be OK,
But if I pray to you,
I'm helping in some way

She is not breathing normally
I'm getting really scared
If she only knew
How very much I cared.

I don't want to see her die
This is something that can wait
For she has a life
That is loving and great.

As she takes her last breaths
I finish up my prayer
Lord please take care of her
And that I will love her, even if she's up there.

Madeleine Wong, Grade 6
Immaculate Conception, BC

The Best Season for Kids, Do You Know What It Is?

Summer is the greatest season
All kids do is play
sports and games and other things too
And they are never blue
They do it into the night
I wish that their parents did too
I love Summer and
I hope you do
Because if you don't
Shame on you

Harman Dhillon, Grade 6
Dr F D Sinclair Elementary School, BC

Carnivore/Herbivore

Carnivore
vicious deadly
terrify intimidate devour
predator flesh prey vegetation
shudder scurry amble
amiable harmless
Herbivore
Adam Murray, Grade 5
Forest Hill Public School, ON

Snow Is…

Slippery crystals
Cold, white flakes
Wet ice
Deep to walk in
Making forts
Fun when the powers off

That's what snow is!
Taylor Anderson, Grade 4
Bayview Elementary School, BC

Skiing

I have a backpack.
I am skiing down a hill.
I lost my hand poles.
I start rolling down the hill.
I crashed into a snow bank.
Brandan Beeler, Grade 6
New Germany Elementary School, NS

Fire/Water

Fire
Crimson, searing
Flickering, glistening, crackling
Campfire, brightness, ocean, darkness
Crashing, sparkling, rumbling
Aqua, freezing
Water
Kirin Rastogi, Grade 5
Forest Hill Public School, ON

Sunset

Sunset glows in the air
To let the flowers grow
And so it does not rain on us
But if it does,
You need an umbrella.

If the sun comes up,
Then at night it goes down
And in the morning
The sun will come up again
Until the end.
Carri-Lynn Daniels, Grade 5
Bayview Elementary School, BC

Caitlin Cooper

Caitlin
Drama queen, quacious, fun, comic
Daughter of Jill and Regan
Lover of my mom, my dog and Miley Cyrus
Who feels that Israel should be peaceful, exhausted and hyper
Who needs love, electronics and my mom
Who fears small places, certain animals and kidnapping
Who gives love, laughs and brain teasers
Who would like to see Miley Cyrus, Melrose Ave., Broadway plays
Resident of Montreal Quebec.
Cooper
Caitlin Cooper, Grade 4
Ecole Akiva, QC

Just Imagine Colour

Imagine colour
The bright yellow of the sun the deep blue of the ocean
The orange of a crackling fire the light purple of a blossoming flower
Just imagine the beautiful green of a spring day full of harmony and peace

Now imagine all that gone
The yellow bed of fall leaves now becomes a crunchy grey patch of sadness

Now imagine all that gone
The blue of the beautiful clear sky now becomes a grey pool of despair

Now imagine all that gone
The orange of ripe pumpkins waiting for harvest now becomes a grey field of sorrow

Now imagine all that gone
The purple of the darkest grape on the vine now becomes as tiny as a dot of grey grief

Now imagine all that gone
The green of lush plants asking for our admiration
Now becomes like soiled string, hanging from helpless hands

Just imagine an unhappy grey mass of oppression or poverty or war
Unimaginable!
Wendy Lafferty, Grade 6
St Philip School, AB

My Favourite Place

My favourite place is at the campsite.
I hear the water crashing against the rocks.
The fire's colours of yellow and orange are just like the beautiful sunset over the water.
I smell the smoke from the charred logs burning in the fire.
The trees appear black and grey against the midnight sky.
The leaves blow in the wind, while others crackle under my feet.
The rain begins to fall on my shoulders and I am suddenly cold.
I maneuver to the tent pitched nearby,
Drop to my knees and crawl into my waiting sleeping bag.
I feel wrapped within wonderful warmth,
Then fall asleep effortlessly to the sound of my family slumbering.
Spencer James Mason, Grade 5
Forest Hill Public School, ON

Feelings

Happiness is yellow like the bright and glowing sun,
Shining up in the sky,
Waiting, just waiting, for happy people to come.
Misery is black, dark like the night sky,
It waits for day to end,
To take away all joy.
Sorrow is blue,
Like lightning striking through the sky,
Making people cry.
Anger is orange like burning, scorching flames,
For when your anger peaks,
Those flames start to burn inside you.
And when those flames burn inside you,
You seem to desire nothing more,
Then burn down the person
That started these flames inside you.
Curiosity is green like the leaves on trees
Which seems to be all you see,
When exploring in the forests,
In which there is only beauty
That only you can see.

Taylor Sokul, Grade 6
St Anne School, SK

Imagine

Imagine you were at seas in a boat
Just dumped off and left to float
Left to sit there and cry
And so you think o'my

Imagine you were locked in a tower
With nothing not even a shower
So when you think of escape
You look to the window but you're surrounded by lake

Imagine a boy with a smile so wide
When his mom saw it she always cried
As he smiled his teeth were so white
They were just like a light

Imagine a world full of love
Where no one would push and no one would shove
With no more fighting and no more war
All that stuff will go out the door

Josh Matear, Grade 6
St Philip School, AB

I Love My Family

F rom the bottom of my heart there's
A family of mine, who I love
M ay not be perfect but
I still,
L ove my mom my dad, every one of them
Y oung to old, aunt to uncle, grandma to grandpa

Katie Rotchin, Grade 4
Ecole Akiva, QC

Blind

A story about a girl who had no sight,
Who always worked with all her might.
Despite living her life being called "blind,"
Her nature was extremely kind.
Her life filled with sorrow never saw a smile,
But she kept on looking mile after mile.
One sudden day,
"A car hit her" is all that I can say.
She ended up on a patient bed,
Her face so pale her wounds so red.
She suddenly fell fast asleep,
And indeed it was deep.
She flashed back to all her times,
The nasty horns and the sweet chimes.
The day she was born, she had eyesight, she could see,
The day she was blind, which happened when she was three.
The love of her parents which was forever lost,
Echoed in her mind,
Until her eyes, just like her parents, closed forever.
She had died in her sleep.

Slesha Sharma, Grade 6
Wismer Public School, ON

My Four Wheeler

I have a four wheeler that is muddy and red.
I have a gray helmet that I wear on my head.

I start up my engine and off I go,
Over the hills and down the road slow.

I stop at my cousin's and he comes for a ride.
We go through the trails riding side by side.

We get back home, and put my four wheeler in the shed.
I am so tired I go straight to bed.

I wake up in the morning and wash my bike,
Because my mom might take me again tonight.

Zachary Gallant, Grade 6
Hampton Middle School, NB

Martin Luther King Jr.

M artin is a great person.
A ll the people thanked him
R eally they did
T he people enjoy the freedom now
I n the old times he saved mostly the colored people
N ow in the new times lots of people are still mean

K eep on helping your brothers
I n the hotel you got killed for no reason
N ow people felt sorry
G reat things happen after you were gone

Diana Thambiaiah, Grade 5
Dr F D Sinclair Elementary School, BC

Snow Is...

Cold frozen snowmen
Wet slippery snowballs
Icy wet igloos
Snowy hills for snow boarding
Slippery ice for hockey
Deep snow to walk in

That's what snow is!
Kyle Rattlesnake, Grade 4
Bayview Elementary School, BC

Why, Why, Why

Why do we get up?
Why do we get dressed?
Why do we do our hair?
Why do we exist?

Why do we drive our cars?
Why do we take the train?
Why do we get on the bus?
This is driving me insane!

Why do we eat fruit?
Why do we eat meat?
Why do we eat vegetables?
Why in the world, do we eat?

I guess we'll never know,
Unless we look for it.
But I'm pretty lazy.
So do it yourself,
I quit!
Eric Hicks, Grade 6
St Anne French Immersion School, ON

Rain

Water from the sky
The grass will grow when it rains
Really tall and green
Jeremy White, Grade 5
Bayview Elementary School, BC

War Is Nothing

War is nothing we can stop.
It's incredibly strong.
Nothing can stop it only death.
On November 11th is Remembrance Day.
Understanding the sacrifice.
No one should fight with guns.
Dads that can't see their babies.
Everyone who died in war.
Do not point guns at other people.
Roger Matheson, Grade 5
Chiganois Elementary School, NS

One Halloween

There are lots of
Drifting leaves
And scary things.
Like jack-o'-lanterns
And pumpkins and costumes.
But it's to spend time
With your family
And having fun.
Brayden Jarvis, Grade 4
Avondale School, AB

O Earth

O Lord
for my friends
I thank You

O Sun
for the power
I thank you

O Earth
for the blood
I thank you

O Sun
for the warmth
I thank you

O Sea
for the water
I thank you
Jacob Ferdinand, Grade 4
Chiganois Elementary School, NS

Day and Night

It was a beautiful night
Until sun and moon had a fight
All night and day,
They just didn't like to play,
So it was both dark and light.
Dominique Zwicker, Grade 6
New Germany Elementary School, NS

Water

Salty, blue, wavy
An ocean
Clear, sprinkling, sparkling
A peaceful fountain
Blue, chlorine, cold
A swimming pool
Blue, man made, life
An aquarium
Refreshing, wet, cold
Drinking fountain
Nicholas Smail-Raina, Grade 6
Holy Cross School, ON

Darkness

The shadow of people,
An alley at night,
It might scare you,
but don't be afraid.
There is nothing inside,
Face your fears,
and go inside.
Nothing will hurt you,
Just try not to cry.
Just try to face,
The darkness inside.
Mark Fram, Grade 6
William G Davis Public School, ON

Thanksgiving

T he wonderful season
H ave a good Thanksgiving
A re the leaves red yet
N ice meal
K indness is very nice to give to others
S tuff is good
G reat turkey
I am thankful for family
V ery tender turkey
I love stuffing
N ow is fall
G ood day and happy Thanksgiving
Sam White, Grade 5
Muskoka Falls Public School, ON

When I Was

When I was zero
My mom was my hero
When I was one
I was fun
When I was two
I was blue
When I was three
I climbed a tree
When I was four
I wanted more
When I was five
I felt alive
When I was six
I loved lipstick
When I was seven
I wished I was eleven
When I was eight
I was so great
When I was nine
Everything was mine
Now I'm ten I wish I were one again
Abbi Oakford, Grade 5
Hythe Elementary School, AB

My Best Friend

You're so awesome, you make my heart blossom.
You're so nice and always precise.
You're so kind, my smile you will find.
You're so pretty and always so witty.
You're so funny, you make my day sunny.
You're so caring and yet so daring.
You're so honest, your memories are fondest.
You're so fair and light as air.
You're my best friend, a gift I would send.
These are the things that I like about you.
You're my best friend, loyal and true.

Kailyn Smith, Grade 6
Immaculate Conception, BC

Should War Take This Land

In the forests green and dark
Stood tall nature's silent sentinels.
Through these trees on boughs brown or grey
Nature's smaller critters live and play.

In the center of the forest great
Stood the proud, noble ancient birch,
With many exquisite birds roosting there
Nuzzled on branch silver, grey and fair.

What would this be should war take this land?
A battlefield of despair it would become.
Gone would be the peace of this land.
Throw down your arms!

Should war take this land? What is the cost?
While, perpetual poverty! And many lives lost!
What is worse than that? This must be removed!
Throw down your arms!

In this forest dark and ravishing,
God's creatures are tranquil and happy.
Under the boughs that are green, peace is there.
For this I beg you, throw down your arms!

Josh Stang, Grade 6
St Philip School, AB

Autumn

Leaves are falling from the trees
And dancing in the sky
Their many colours are wonderful
In the autumn sky.
The windy breeze blows the
Autumn leaves around to fall on the ground.
The little children come and
Throw the leaves up high
To see them in the autumn sky.

Kaela Palmer-Leclerc, Grade 5
St Noel Chabanel Catholic Elementary School, ON

When I Was Younger

When I was younger,
I had cancer
But now that I'm older,
I have been cancer free for two years!

When I was younger,
I used to call "Elmo" "Emlo"
But now that I'm older,
I don't even care about that show.

When I was younger,
I used to think the moon was green cheese,
But now that I'm older,
I know it's a satellite.

When I was younger,
I used to think I was a movie star
But now that I'm older,
I know I'm too young to be one!

Jake Shtern, Grade 4
Ecole Akiva, QC

Halloween Candy

H alloween is spooky
A great time to have fun with everybody
L ighting up all the jack-o-lanterns
L ots of candy in your tummy
O uch! eat so many treats and get a tummy ache
W hen it is scary it's Halloween
E veryone gets together
E ntering door to door
N asty and spooky costumes

C andy is the best treat you can get on Halloween
A lot of fun going trick-or-treating
N ot so much candy left
D ie to get more TREATS
Y ummy food to eat

Rajdeep Dhaliwal, Grade 5
Dr F D Sinclair Elementary School, BC

Friendship

Fate was kind and you were sent
To be my trusted friend
I'll stand by you till the end
Because that's what friends should do

All I can say
I want you to stay
You have been so dear to me
Our friendship means so much to me

Love loyalty and honesty are the true keys
To Be My Best Friend

Moaz Barakat, Grade 6
William G Davis Public School, ON

Dancing

I love to move
I love to groove
I like to twirl and spin around
Let my cold feet touch the ground
I love to jump I like to hop
I never ever want to stop
I like to be silly
I like to dance funny
I like to be me
and let my body break free
my arms are swinging in the air
my legs are moving everywhere
I giggle and I wiggle
I tumble, I fall
I get back up and do it again
sweat slides off my face
I can't stop
there's no time to wait

Elizabeth Campbell, Grade 6
Uniacke District School, NS

Snow Bird

It cries to its sigh
It whispers to its shadow
It shrieks to its echo

Omar Salemohamed, Grade 5
Mulgrave School, BC

Water

Water falls, water falling
into the stream.
Fish laying newborns
then disappearing
in the moving water.

Cedric Taylor, Grade 6
Bayview Elementary School, BC

Fall Is Coming

Lightning thrashing
Rain falling
Leaves blowing
Animals running for cover
Owls watching your every move
Everyone heading to bed
To wait for this storm to go away
Twenty-four hours later:
Everyone wakes up and notices that
the rains stopped.
The kids run outside and jump
in the mud puddles
Wheeeeeeeee!!
Then something fills the air
It's the smell of turkey
Then the kids run in and eat!

Brandon Nichol, Grade 4
Avondale School, AB

Little Fingers and Tiny Toes

Little fingers, tiny toes.
Beautiful eyes and a cute button nose.
I remember waiting, excitedly thinking about,
How I would take care of you without a doubt.
Before you came into our hearts
Our family had only 4 parts
Mom, Dad, Ky, and me
And now we'd have another one to love so tenderly!
I remember wanting to go and see you enter this world.
Feeling flustered about whether I wanted a boy or another girl.
On one hand a brother would be another adventure to take.
But with a sister we would know the right decisions to make.
Well on Thursday at 12 midnight
We found out we'd have another set of nails to paint.
Weighing 5 pounds and a beautiful young baby girl,
Another delicate, precious pearl!
I am so glad that I'll be here to watch over you
And to say to you every night how much, "I LOVE YOU!"

Tayler Tabernero, Grade 6
Immaculate Conception, BC

Zachary Wagman

Kind, humorous, playful, sportive
Son of Jeffrey and Carole
Lover of computers, television and pasta
Who feels happy, cool and excited
Who needs friends, entertainment and less homework
Who fears spiders, needles and blood
Who gives friendship, love and happiness
Who would like to see his own airplane, good marks and Vegas
Resident of Canada
Wagman

Zachary Wagman, Grade 4
Ecole Akiva, QC

Mackenzie's Garden

My friend's backyard is my favourite place to be.
It is peaceful there
With the rainbow of flowers that warms my heart.
Splashes of purple, yellow and red awaken my senses.
The blooms with their fantastic familiar fragrance
Is as comforting as a hug.
Bending down to enjoy the scents, the flowers brush against my nose
Like a soft blanket of fleece.
I can almost hear the delicate movement of the butterfly's wings
As it flutters from flower to flower.
I scan around the garden and see the gate.
It makes me wonder what is on the other side.
Anticipation builds as I make my way toward the entry
When suddenly my name is called to go home.
I reluctantly retreat
My mind still racing with possibilities.

Sydney Burns, Grade 5
Forest Hill Public School, ON

Remember

The soldiers fought for peace
And love as bloodshed across the land.
They battled for respect and relinquished their lives for us.
Poppies never die as they bloom in the sky.

Jacob Burella, Grade 5
St Noel Chabanel Catholic Elementary School, ON

The Cockle Shell

The inside is as smooth as a pearl
The top is as bumpy as a coral reef
Inside as shiny as the sea sparkling in the sun
Its black polka dots are as black as the depths of the sea

Felitche Hutchinson, Grade 5
Ranch Park Elementary School, BC

Feathers and Snowflakes

Feathers are soft like a snowflake in the sky,
they float in the air swiftly and high,
they are white and smooth in the windy air,
they are small and pretty as they beautifully fly away.

Genevieve Trinidad, Grade 4
Immaculate Conception, BC

Penguins

Black and white all over
Making nests and things
Making sounds like ork and zings.
Penguins are very cool but they may not like school.

Camille Saunders, Grade 5
Ecole Saint-Christophe, AB

Just Imagine

Just imagine that you're as beautiful as a soaring dove;
Your heart is filled with peace and love;
You're a dove that is soaring free;
It makes you wonder who you want to be;
Just imagine.

Just imagine that you're as strong as an oak tree:
Standing proud and peering over me;
It makes you wonder if you're who you want to be;
Just imagine.

Just imagine you're a wild dog that's running free;
Running over hills to come to me;
You're a wild dog that's bold and free;
It makes you wonder if you're who you want to be;
Just imagine.

Whether you're as beautiful as a soaring dove;
As strong as an oak tree;
Or running free like a wild dog;
It all makes you wonder,
If you are who you want to be.

Mikaila Wodynski, Grade 6
St Philip School, AB

Feelings

Anger is like thunder shouting through the white sky.
Happiness is like yellow bananas, always smiling back at you.
Confusion is like dark blue raindrops, scattered everywhere.
Lazy is black, as you're lying in your bed.
Frustration is like red Doritos, burning your tongue with heat.

Cole Reid, Grade 6
St Anne School, SK

Blessing

B e happy for all the things you have
L et your heart lead you to the future
E very day you should be thankful
S elfishness is not a good way to solve problems
S elf defense is a good way to protect you
I am thankful for my family
N ever hurt someone physically or in feelings
G reat blessings happen every day.

Angela Mercieca, Grade 5
St Noel Chabanel Catholic Elementary School, ON

Why Do Good Men Die

Soldiers march, brave and bold their story to be retold.
Woman weep, children cry, evil vultures fly high.
Grim faced they march over the ground
which many shall not march over again.
Shots rang out, soldiers died,
soldiers lied,
never to stand again.
The ground drank the blood of fallen men that day,
their spirit here to stay,
people still cry to the sky,
where fallen men do fly.
Why, did good men, kind men die,
to fly, to rest in the sky,
forever more?
Why?

Jacob Green, Grade 6
John Ross Robertson Jr Public School, ON

Thanksgiving

T hankful for family and friends.
H appy people all around.
A utumn begins.
N ot a neglected person.
K indness spread all around.
S tuffing in the turkey.
G iving feels good!
I love my family.
V acation!
I love the celebration!
N ever be mean.
G reen leaves turn orange, red, and yellow.

Maggie Slaughter, Grade 5
Muskoka Falls Public School, ON

Tall and Small

She's tall, I'm small, I try to look through her,
What's inside, what's she thinking? I'd give anything to know.
She calls me names, I keep them tucked in, this has got to stop.
I want to flash back, I think I can I hope I can, I don't.
For sticks and stones will break my bones but names will never hurt me.

Emma Vossen, Grade 6
Immaculate Conception, BC

Halloween

Halloween is my favorite time to play all day! You get candy have fun and you get cavities. But you get to see friends trick-or-treating! And different costumes, but sometimes you have to wait a little longer because it is on a school day. Jack-o-lanterns full of light, Halloween decorations everywhere you go! No wonder they call it a holiday because it's so much fun!!! If only it was more than once a year. Candy apples, sugar, gummy bears, fudge, apples, it is so much fun. There's so much to do at Halloween.

Jill Robicheau, Grade 4
Pictou Elementary School, NS

Horses

Horses are an animal that don't just lay around. They run free with their manes flapping up and down. They're happy as can be. Some are friendly some are vicious so watch their back feet. Horses are animals that cost a lot of cash. Once you get it you fall in love. It's hard to say good-bye. Riding on their back running so free, bareback riding up and down the beach sand flying all over the place is such a joy. The end of the day you put them away knowing you will ride again tomorrow.

Sam Currie, Grade 5
Chiganois Elementary School, NS

What Is Life?

Did you ever imagine life as God's wonderful creations?
A creation like the welcoming sun rising over the horizon.
Followed by stupendous, sparkling stars in the midnight sky.
A collage at spring time of colorful flowers blooming in the fields.

Just imagine life is also like starting a journey up an all-terrain mountain.
As years go by you get closer and closer to the top of the fountain.
Life is a pathway of many turns, you never know which one to choose.
Some pathways lead to the dark, eerie midnight forest and some
may lead to the remarkable, panoramic mountain view.
Sometimes we intend to get lost in our highly-difficult world.

Our life is like a search for the key to success and well being.
Life is as difficult as finding the missing puzzle pieces to finish your life successfully.

As the years go by, you have one miniature step left to the top of the mountain.
Just imagine ending your life is like finishing your difficult journey up the all-terrain mountain,
to reach the beginning of eternal life in Heaven.

Anna Mikolajczak, Grade 6
St Philip School, AB

I Am From

I am from a dream of destiny and fantasy where adventure is like no other kind,
where there's bubble gum rainbows and cotton candy sundaes floating in the clouds,
I am from a world of graceful dolphins and a place where you can swim and play all day long,
I am from the ocean where I listen to the waves of the sea and the creatures of the deep,
I am from a place where if life gives you crayons you color your own world,
I am from a place where everything is free and life will never end.

Safiyyah Figaro, Grade 6
Chedoke Middle School, ON

Haunted

H ot chocolate is delicious on cold days
A ghost flies in the distance
U nder the blankets I'm freezing
N o one could cheer me up when I hurt my leg
T oday there was no school
E veryone ate all their candy in one day
D ark chocolate is very sweet

Ryan Fisher, Grade 4
Avondale School, AB

Andrea

Andrea

Happy, quiet, busy, and a dancer
Daughter of John and Melissa
Lover of hip hop
Who feels happy and mad
Who needs trees and food
Who gives friendship and hugs
Who fears snakes and tarantulas
Who likes to wear capris and t-shirts
Who would like to see New York and England
Resident of B.C.

Daly

Andrea Daly, Grade 4
Bayview Elementary School, BC

Christmas

C is for Christ
H is for hot chocolate you drink in the cold
R is for Rudolph the red nose reindeer
I is for igloo which you make with the snow
S is for Santa Claus
T is for the tree you put up for Christmas
M is for merry Christmas
A is for animals who migrate in the winter
S is for the snowmen we make with the snow

Parwan Grewal, Grade 4
Micro Education and Consulting School, BC

Kaleb

I am so excited!
    Yes I am!
His name is Kaleb
Don't you understand?
He is very sweet.
He doesn't make a peep
He is my new puppy of three weeks!
I can't bring him home yet.
He is still too young
But that doesn't stop him from having his fun!

Felicia DiPierdomenico, Grade 6
St Anne French Immersion School, ON

Remembrance

Some men of the English went to fight the Germans.
They may not come back
but they did not care,
as long as their families were free.
The noble men moved up,
as the selfish men stand back.
Worried of bloodshed across the field.
Days, months, years went by,
for all those men who died
we stand in remembrance of them.

Maddison Morris, Grade 5
St Noel Chabanel Catholic Elementary School, ON

Growing, Growing, Gone

Eyes open to the smiling sun,
This creature's life has begun,
Paws like tiny cotton balls,
Which touch the surrounding walls,
Tail like a slithering snake,
Oh, what a wonderful jewel they make.

Fur a sandy beach,
Fuzzy as a peach,
Nose pink cotton candy,
Never before have I seen a cat so dandy.

The happy mother cleans her young,
Gingerly with her tongue,
Struggling the creature begins to moan,
"I'm too big for that see how much I've grown."

Staring sadly the mother sighs,
The wild cat runs and the mother cries.

Growing up happens so fast,
Although we want the good times to last.

Eden Slabe, Grade 6
St Catherine Elementary School, AB

Autumn Leaves

L eaves are light as a feather,
E asy to break into pieces.
A utumn leaves start to fall.
V iewing the different varieties and the beauty.
E stimating the exact amount of leaves.
S plendid season, colour, spirit.

Michelle Vu, Grade 6
Holy Cross School, ON

My Rabbit

My rabbit has a habit to never eat carrots until
    the afternoon under the birds' tune.
He races through spaces under the midnight tune
until he finds a place to sleep under the twilight moon.

Justin Harkness, Grade 6
Credit Meadows Elementary School, ON

She Is Me
She lives for what she dies for,
She dies for what she lives for,
She dreams of what she awakens to,
She awakens to what she dreams of,

She is me.
Danielle LaCouvee, Grade 5
Joseph A Gibson Public School, ON

Christmas Fairies
At Christmas time the fairies dance.
they eat the treats
and drink some dew
for presents they give out flower hats
and flower bibs as well
the cups and plates are made of leaves
the clothes are made of gossamer
for a tree they use a branch
for decorations they use stars
a fairy Christmas lights up the sky
but my house shines like north star
Hanna Schmidt, Grade 6
North Saanich Middle School, BC

I'm Sorry
I'm sorry when you were alone,
I feel sorry right down to my bones.

I'm sorry for the disrespect,
and for the times that I would neglect.

I'm sorry for the times I was mean —
I was just a teen.

Friends will come and friends will go,
you're my friend, I'll always know.
Abby Kwawukumey, Grade 5
Forest Hill Public School, ON

Fire and Ice
Fire
Hot, orange
Burning, smoking, blazing
Logs, matches, freezer, ice cream
Freezing, cracking, snowing
Cold, blue
Ice
Justin Baker, Grade 4
Ecole les Cypres, AB

Climbing
A man is climbing, his name is Brock
He is making his way up the rocks
He has on shoes, but no socks.
Kirk Demond, Grade 5
New Germany Elementary School, NS

Thanksgiving
T hanks for the good family
H elping for dinner
A utumn leaves
N o left overs
K eeping thanks from your family
S tuffing is good
G iving thanks
I ce cream for dessert
V arieties of food
I ndian corn
N obody is left out
G ravy
Karly Keall, Grade 5
Muskoka Falls Public School, ON

Thanksgiving
T hankful for all my family I have
H appy times
A pple pie
N ice leaves on the trees
K indness to everyone
S tuffing in the turkey
G reat time to take pictures
I s in October
V isits with family
I t's a holiday
N ice memories
G reat turkey to eat
Brian Moore, Grade 5
Muskoka Falls Public School, ON

Winter
Winter is fun,
We can run,
We can play,
Yes, you may,
We can slide,
We can hide,
I love snow,
Yes, it's so.
Sandra Neufeld, Grade 4
Riverdale School, MB

Remember
R emember people who died
E verlasting
M emories
E ncourage the soldiers
M others lost their sons and husbands
B rothers are wounded
E veryone is sad but our
R espect for those men lasts forever
Casey Mahoney, Grade 4
Linsford Park School, AB

Fall Is Here
Leaves are twirling down from trees
Fall is in the air

Carving pumpkins is so fun
and Halloween is ready to scare

Trick or treating is so great
I can't wait for that night

Flying ghosts in the sky ready to
give you a fright
Brandon Chimko, Grade 4
Avondale School, AB

Thanksgiving
T urkey
H appy
A corns
N o school
K ind
S tuffing
G iving
I love my family
V ase for flowers
I nvite grandparents
N ice weather
G o to Quebec
Curtis Horvath, Grade 5
Muskoka Falls Public School, ON

I Am (Imperfection)
I am the girl
With the messy hair,
I am the girl
With the sad stare.

I am the girl with
The ugly face,
I am the girl
Who stinks.

I am the girl
With the small smile,
I am the girl
Who stared off into space for a while.

I am the girl
With the dirty clothes,
I am the girl with
The perfect grades,
I am the girl with
All these mistakes.

I am: Imperfection
Vivian Hui, Grade 6
William G Davis Public School, ON

Another Day of Autumn

As the chocolate brown, mango, orange, and cherry red
leaves fall to the pine green grass
three by three twirling and swirling.
Kids start wearing scarves and mitts.

They go outside and rake a big huge pile of leaves
so they can have so much fun
jumping into the leaves.

The pile of leaves is full of lovely colours:
cinnamon brown, pumpkin orange, poppy red, and
golden yellow fill the pile children fly into,
then they do it again, again and again!

The wild leaves fly up and down quickly, softly and lightly.
Then the kids go in and enjoy a steaming colourful
mug of hot cocoa, as it settles in their tummies
They happily watch the fall TV shows.

Now it's bedtime.
They hop into their warm cozy beds,
they dream and think about tomorrow
and how it's going to be another awesome day of autumn!

Tori Chenier, Grade 4
Avondale School, AB

Autumn/Fall

Leaves fall
Different colors
Raking up piles
Jumping in them
Pumpkins scarecrows
The weather's getting cold
Coats gloves and hats we wear
So we don't get sick
But watch out after autumn
It snows and…
It's winter!

Kennedy Finamore, Grade 5
St Noel Chabanel Catholic Elementary School, ON

Martin Luther King Jr.

He made freedom come true
He did it all for me and you
He made people not think about the color of skin

Now you're free to be whoever you please
So today think about what he did
For the people of color

If it wasn't for him
You wouldn't be treated like a human being

Martin Luther King did this to fight for what's right!!

Mohamed Yahye, Grade 6
Dr F D Sinclair Elementary School, BC

The Eagle

The eagle soars in the blue blue sky.
My favorite bird goes up up so high.
It gives me a feeling like no one before
It is such a beautiful bird.
When babies are flying they try they try.
So let them go high go high.
When they come back they soar in the sky.
The eagles fly they fly they fly.

Gabrielle Gamblin, Grade 4
Chiganois Elementary School, NS

The Man Who Died

This battle is nothing but a game
These soldiers don't get any fame
Their mothers shed a tear
While their sons fight in fear
All they do is sit and sigh
They really do want to cry
Bullets fly over head
They cry because their best friend is dead
All the soldiers see is red
He shoots trying to get a kill
Who knew he had an iron will
His friend has told a horrible lie
Someone gives him a shove
In the sky flies a dove
His mother is left to cry
As if he only lived to die
She didn't even get a proper good-bye

Shawn Nagra, Grade 5
Dr F D Sinclair Elementary School, BC

The Blue Jay

He makes a sound so loud and so clear,
Showing everyone in the area that danger is near.

His feathers so colourful, all black, white and blue,
The policeman of the forest, for me and you.

While he loves to eat seeds, perched in a tree,
The chattering chipmunk calls out, "Hey, leave some for me!"

As winter begins and the snow starts to fall,
The blue jay cries out, "Go south y'all!"

Abbey Jordan, Grade 6
Hampton Middle School, NB

Autumn

Leaves are falling to the ground
Making piles with no sound
Having fun all year round
When leaves fall to the ground.

Colin Morris, Grade 5
St Noel Chabanel Catholic Elementary School, ON

Difference

I may seem different,
I may seem strange,
But when we really look inside,
We are all a little odd or deranged.
We all have flaws,
Things of imperfection,
but that's the way it was meant to be,
because of God's direction.
Imagine it,
If all people were the same,
How boring and bland life would be,
Like one repeating game.
So you may stare and point,
and laugh at me,
but more our differences than similarities,
is the key.

Devyn Shields, Grade 6
Steele Street Public School, ON

Would You Die for Your Country?

On the 11th month of the 11th day
We think of those who passed away
They risked their lives when they went to war
Now we don't see them anymore

They left their wives and families
And now they're only memories
They left on airplanes trains and boats
Now we have freedom and we can vote

Imagine you were going to fight
For your freedom and your rights
Would you be prepared to die
Would you meet the rally cry

The poppy is a sign you wear
To show that you will always care
For everyone who risked their lives
And now in Flanders fields they lie

Anna Prust, Grade 5
Forest Hill Public School, ON

Autumn

Swish!!!

I pass all of the pretty chestnut brown leaves
as I run through the field.
If I rake all the leaves in this enormous field,
I could make a house!
There are so many leaves!

Autumn is the greatest!
I'm serious it is!

Kaelyn McCarty, Grade 4
Avondale School, AB

Young Poets
Grades K-1-2-3

Note: The Top Ten poems were finalized through an online voting system. Creative Communication's judges first picked out the top poems. These poems were then posted online. The final step involved thousands of students and teachers who registered as online judges and voted for the Top Ten poems. We hope you enjoy these selections.

Top Poem Grades K-1-2-3

Monsters Everywhere

Scary, scary, fright
A very dark night.
A ghost is in my bathtub,
A monster's in my closet,
A zombie's in my drawer…then
I go to sleep,
Snoring all night long.

Levi Bosch, Kindergarten
John Knox Christian School, ON

Top Poem Grades K-1-2-3

At the End of the River

At the end
of the river,
all the frogs
croak and hop
on lily pads
and people
go fish
and catch lots of fish,
at the end
of the river.

Rebecca Leary, Grade 2
Falmouth District School, NS

Top Poem Grades K-1-2-3

Wishes

Give me a smile that will last a lifetime.
Give me purity and beauty.
Give me a big garden of flowers so I can smell them every day.
Give me peace and freedom.

Alexis Leibenzeder, Grade 3
Port Kells Elementary School, BC

Top Poem Grades K-1-2-3

Rainbows

Rainbows are pretty,
I see them all the time
But they seem to disappear,
When I count to nine.

Jenelle Manitowabi, Grade 2
Sioux Mountain School, ON

Top Poem Grades K-1-2-3

Halloween Treats

Halloween, spooky being
Got a cheerful fright
Ghosts are flittering one by one
Haunting us tonight

Trick or treat, running feet
Knocking at the door
I have lots of candy
But I know I want some more…
Please.

Angelina Moro, Grade 1
St. Maria Goretti Catholic School, ON

Top Poem Grades K-1-2-3

Jesus' Birth

Jesus was born on a cold, wintry night.
The star appears to three wise men shining so bright.
He was born in a manger while outside it was cold, dark and forlorn.
That was the little nook where Jesus Christ was born.
Many people came to see him and celebrate his birth in Bethlehem where they rejoiced and sang a song.
The drummer boy played his drums and had not a beat wrong.
All the people were pleased at the new king.
Angels began to sing.
King Herod was mad.
That made God very sad.
He left Joseph a message in his dreams and he ran off and away.
The people then said they had a glorious day.
While they were remembering the wonderful new king they didn't know what could of happened to
  Jesus Christ.
God's only son of the lord who gave himself and sacrificed him for our sins.
He was a wonderful man with courage and strength and Joseph would say
"My son is the only one with miracles. Yes that is him."
We are here to give him thanks and praise with glory.
For him we are sad and after we do something bad we say sorry.
For the old Bible says, that Jesus was born on Christmas Day!

Josephine Rybchuk, Grade 3
St Peter School, SK

Top Poem Grades K-1-2-3

The Sad Poppies

Poppies blow where the field flows
With the rows then it snows
When it is time to go
Wives cry and husbands die.
It is time to cry and say goodbye.

Kaylee Sergerie, Grade 3
Sioux Mountain School, ON

Top Poem Grades K-1-2-3

Glorious Winter

The snow had just fallen, the winds at a blow, children were playing, with eyes at a glow.
The snow-fort they treasured was big and was bright. And surely just surely, it would light up the night.
They built it, they built it, they built it up high. And when it is finished I won't heave a sigh.
The snow has been falling, onto the ground. And when it has melted it will be a small mound.
Oh winter! Oh winter! It comes after fall…and then came a blizzard! We'll all have a ball.
It shows an impression, the snow's a possession. Oh winter is joyous, it's joyous to all…
The fort. Oh the fort! One day it will shine! But to others the bricks will look like some twine.
Those are the enemies of this precious season. But sometimes I sense they don't have a reason.
St. Nick. Yes St. Nick! He comes on a sleigh. But strangely his mammals don't say a neigh.
He'll come in December, when all is dark. Nothing is heard, (Not even a bark!)
The winds at a chill, a house on a hill. Except for the sleigh, all is still.

Jane Smallman, Grade 2
Sydenham Public School, ON

Top Poem Grades K-1-2-3

Leaves

L oading things in the wind. Whoosh! Whoosh!
E verything is orange and crunchy. Scrunch! Scrunch!
A nimals are sleeping in their caves zzzzzz…
V ery rainy and tinkly on roofs. Chick! Chick!
E veryone is cold Brr! Brr!
S cience experiments with leaves that go zap, zap, zap!

Matthew Steinlauf, Grade 3
Ecole Akiva, QC

Top Poem Grades K-1-2-3

Christmas

On Christmas Eve
When I'm asleep
I hear footsteps
In the hallway.
I open my eyes.
I see a flash of red and white!
I know St. Nick is here.

Alyssa Wells, Grade 2
Falmouth District School, NS

Hallowe'en
Rattling skeleton
Haunted house
Spooky zombie
Wicked witch
Hissing black cat
Floating ghost
BOO!
Ryan Stacey, Grade 2
Bayview Elementary School, BC

Fuzzy Wuzzy
My teddy bear is so soft.
A Webkinz is also soft.
But walls aren't soft at all.
Books are also not soft either.
Olivia Frank, Grade 2
Falmouth District School, NS

Ophelia
Ophelia
Clever and thoughtful
Drowning in a river
Hamlet breaks her heart
Sadness
Sophie Hillcoat, Grade 3
Ecole Akiva, QC

Night
Night
Is very, very dark.
Night.
You can hear the wolves howling.
Night.
You can hear the bats squeaking.
Night!
Jacob Caldwell, Grade 2
Falmouth District School, NS

Juliet Is Beautiful
Juliet
Wonderful and beautiful
Loving Romeo with her whole heart
Sad because she could not be with
Romeo
Love
Samantha Jacobson, Grade 3
Ecole Akiva, QC

Hallowe'en
Floating ghost
Hissing black cat
Wicked witch
Spooky zombie
BOO!
Chelsea Wyse, Grade 1
Bayview Elementary School, BC

Oh Gertrude!
Gertrude
Sly and bright
Drinking wine
Makes Hamlet mad
Mother
Chloe Ginsberg, Grade 3
Ecole Akiva, QC

Halloween
H alloween is scary. Hoooo!
A hhhhhh!
L ots of candy. Plop!
L et's get dressed up!
O h, Halloween is spooky.
W owowo! Frightening.
E mily, there is someone scary. Ah Ah!
E mily, time to go. Yahoo!
N ow that's creepy. Ahh!
Emily Eiley, Grade 2
Ecole Akiva, QC

Great Day for Ice Skating
Frozen pond,
Frosty snow,
Clear, blue sky,
Great day for ice skating.
Devon Blackmore, Grade 2
Merritt Central Elementary School, BC

Juliet
Juliet
Beautiful and loving
Pretending to die
Dies for real
Poor her!
Nicole Amir, Grade 3
Ecole Akiva, QC

Leaves
Red leaves
Orange leaves
Brown leaves
Green leaves
Yellow leaves
Dropping
Chelsie Seward-Peall, Grade 2
Bayview Elementary School, BC

Hallowe'en
Wicked zombie
Haunted skeleton
Floating bat
Swooping witch
BOO!
Antonio Mitchell, Grade 1
Bayview Elementary School, BC

Orange
O h so colorful.
R un and collect those leaves.
A nother colorful project.
N o project could look better.
G o to school and show your project.
E verything can't be orange.
Adam Wolfe, Grade 3
Ecole Akiva, QC

Pigs at the Farm
P igs are on the farm.
L et's go to the farm.
O h no! The wheel popped! Pop!
P igs are sleeping in the autumn.
Noah Kader, Grade 2
Ecole Akiva, QC

Orange
O ctober
R ain falls…SPLASH!
A pple trees
N ight
G ames
E njoy Halloween!
Aaron Gurman, Grade 2
Ecole Akiva, QC

Hockey
I love hockey.
Fun
Cool
Crazy!
I love
Shooting the puck
At the net.
I love hockey.
Andrew Manning, Grade 2
Falmouth District School, NS

The Apple
Green or red apples
Crunch crunch crunch
Are sweet
Crunch crunch crunch
Apples are juicy
Crunch crunch crunch
Kiley Kitts, Grade 3
School of Hope, AB

Rain
R ain in the forest.
A ll the leaves fall.
I like jumping in leaves. Yay!
N ow it's fall.
Adam Cohen, Grade 2
Ecole Akiva, QC

Christmas

C is for candy canes striped red and green
H is for holly hung by the kitchen
R is for Rudolph flying in the sky
I is for igloo in the North Pole
S is for singing "Winter Fantasy"
T is for telling secrets on Christmas Eve
M is for Mrs. Claus so funny and bright
A is for apple cider so yummy and sweet
S is for Saint Nicholas on Christmas night.

Corey Cole, Grade 3
Watson Road Elementary School, BC

Rain

R ain in the puddles splish, splash!
A t the park in the fall.
I n the house drinking hot chocolate, slurp slurp.
N o sun anymore.

Jonah Levy, Grade 2
Ecole Akiva, QC

My Dog Cleo

My dog Cleo is a lot of fun.
You can play fetch with her
But she won't give the ball back.
So WOOF!!
If you see a yellow white brown dog
Coming at you,
That is Cleo!
WOOF! WOOF! WOOF!

Olivia Lowthers, Grade 2
Falmouth District School, NS

Christmas Times

C is for carols sung at the church
H is for holly hung on the white roof
R is for reindeer flying in the air
I is for icicles cold and hard
S is for Santa saying "Ho, Ho, Ho"
T is for toys for the good girls and boys
M is for mom making hot chocolate
A is for Abby playing with presents
S is for stockings hung on the fireplace

Abby Cullen, Grade 3
Watson Road Elementary School, BC

Colorful

C old in the night. Whoosh!
O pposite from summer.
L ollipops for Halloween.
O range is the main color.
R eally fun. Whee!
F all is really exciting. Wow!
U mbrellas, you might need. Splish Splash!
L eaves are very colorful.

Aiyana Kaplan, Grade 3
Ecole Akiva, QC

Hamlet

Hamlet
Brave and deceitful
Sword fighting and shouting
Tries to tell his uncle that he knew he was a killer
Tragedy

David Kalichman, Grade 3
Ecole Akiva, QC

The Magic of Christmas

C is for carolers singing "Carol of the Bells"
H is for "Ho, ho, ho" called by Santa Claus
R is for roasting marshmallows by the fire
I is for icicles frozen to the frosted roof
S is for sleigh bells ringing in the sky
T is for tinsel wrapped around the tree
M is for Mrs. Claus making yummy cookies
A is for angel standing at the top of my tree
S is for Santa giving presents to girls and boys.

Isabel Estephan, Grade 3
Watson Road Elementary School, BC

Christmas Days

C is for candy canes hung on the green tree
H is for holly sitting on your door
R is for reindeer pulling Santa's sleigh
I is for icicles hanging in the bright light
S is for singing carols in the night
T is for Tuesday when Santa comes tonight
M is for merry kids every single night
A is for apple cider that sizzles in your mouth
S is for sounds of children with laughter

Kelsey Raja, Grade 3
Watson Road Elementary School, BC

Christmas

C is for candy canes at the North Pole
H is for holly at our home
R is for Rudolph helping Santa get around
I is for icing on our gingerbread house
S is for Santa singing "Ho, Ho, Ho"
T is for trees at our house
M is for mandarin oranges that are tasty and sweet
A is for apple cider that is good and hot
S is for snowball cookies that I eat

Kristen Mehus, Grade 3
Watson Road Elementary School, BC

Hockey

H ockey is fun. SNAP!
O h yeah! The Canadiens scored. DING!
C andy at the arena.
K aylee loves hockey.
E liana does not play hockey. Oh, no!
Y ou would love it too.

Dani Schwartz, Grade 2
Ecole Akiva, QC

Hallowe'en

Hissing black cat
Wicked witch
Floating ghost
Swooping bat
Rattling skeleton
Wicked black cat
BOO!
Aliana Baxter, Grade 2
Bayview Elementary School, BC

Ice Cream

Hi!
I am ice cream.
Oh! Oh no!
It is Mr. Spoon.
He is going to chop me up
Into little pieces!
Now he has me!
Oh no!
A person!
AHHH!
I am going
going
gone.
Elise Lynch, Grade 2
Falmouth District School, NS

Cats

Cats meow.
Meow
Meow
Meow.

Cats purr.
Purr
Purr
Purr.

Cats hiss.
Hiss
Hiss
Hiss.

Cats
Can be fuzzy.
Sarah Sturge, Grade 2
Falmouth District School, NS

Leaves

Maple leaves
Big leaves
Red leaves
Orange leaves
Yellow leaves
Taylor Forsythe, Grade 1
Bayview Elementary School, BC

Bubble Bath

I like to do my math in my bubble bath
Because I can subtract the bubbles in my bubble bath,
One, pop two, pop
I better stop or else all the bubbles will be popped.
Sydney MacDonald, Grade 3
Sioux Mountain School, ON

The Cold Christmas

C is for celebrating all through the holiday season
H is for hot chocolate cooling slowly on the table
R is for reindeer trotting softly on the roof
I is for icing on the holiday cakes
S is for stockings filled with surprises
T is for trees covered with powdery white snow
M is for mandarin oranges being sold in the stores
A is for Advent calendars filled with chocolate and treats
S is for Santa Claus saying "Ho, Ho, Ho" into the cold winter night.
Nicholas Wolter, Grade 3
Watson Road Elementary School, BC

The Shiny Christmas

C is for crunching the snow and making snowballs
H is for hot chocolate melting on your lips
R is for Rudolph dancing and prancing
I is for ice hanging from your house
S is for stockings hung by the bright fire
T is for toys for little girls and boys
M is for mistletoe up up very high
A is for Advent calendar that has chocolate inside
S is for shortbread cookies sitting on the plate, waiting to be eaten.
Hailee Kepes, Grade 3
Watson Road Elementary School, BC

Jolly Christmas

C is for crunchy candy put on the sweet gingerbread houses
H is for holly hung by the fire
R is for ringing bells attached to Santa's reindeer
I is for icy cars getting their engines warmed up so they can go shopping
S is for sounds made by fireworks popping in the sky
T is for tinsel wrapped around the dark green tree
M is for mistletoe hanging right above the chandelier
A is for appetites that grow after singing beautiful carols
S is for songs sung by blue eyed sparrows.
Jessica Stepaniuk, Grade 3
Watson Road Elementary School, BC

Halloween

H alloween is my favorite holiday.
A pples when you eat them, they go crunch crunch crunch.
L ooking at the stars is fun at night and you can hear owls. Whoo Whoo!
L earning in the autumn is so fun!
O h, it's almost Halloween. Yay!
W atch squirrels eat, munch munch munch.
E ating in the fall with snow and syrup is tasty. Yum!
E ach house on Halloween has so much candy.
N o one on Halloween in my family ever gets sick.
Noah Chazonoff, Grade 2
Ecole Akiva, QC

A Snowy Christmas Day

C is for candle burning in the night
H is for hot chocolate when you drink in the winter
R is for Rudolph ready to carry a present
I is for ice hanging on the porch
S is for Santa Claus flying in the bright night
T is for toys that everyone will play with
M is for Mrs. Claus helping Santa Claus
A is for Andrew playing in the snow
S is for snowy day at Christmas time

Andrew Yang, Grade 3
Watson Road Elementary School, BC

A Snowy Day

C is for cookies that are so yummy in my tummy
H is for holly you hang it in the hall
R is for Rudolph when he lights up his nose
I is for icicles hanging from the icy cold roof
S is for snowy winds in the night
T is for tree in the living room
M is for mmm, Santa eating the cookies
A is for adventures that Santa has on Christmas Eve
S is for snow that falls twinkling down

Emily Gotte, Grade 3
Watson Road Elementary School, BC

My Kittens

My kittens are cute.
Liquorice is black and she is the smallest,
Oreo is my favourite but
I think Stripey will be the tallest.
They like to scratch and play with balls,
it drives mom crazy when they climb the walls.

Cassidy Parks, Grade 3
St Carthagh Catholic School, ON

Candy

C olorful candy is good to eat. Mmmm!
A nd my favorite candy is Juicy Fruit.
N aturally we are not allowed to eat gum in school. Uhh!
D elicious candy is chewy and you can make bubbles.
Y ou should win a prize.

Shoshana Nuez, Grade 3
Ecole Akiva, QC

Christmas Joy

C is for carols sung by the tree
H is for holly no one will eat
R is for reindeer guiding the sleigh
I is for icing on the brown gingerbread man
S is for Santa saying "Ho, Ho, Ho"
T is for tinsel hung from the tree
M is for mandarin oranges Santa puts in your stocking
A is for Advent calendar that children eat
S is for stocking hung on the decorated mantle

Zachary Whitehead, Grade 3
Watson Road Elementary School, BC

My Teddy Bear

My teddy bear
is so special.
He is my favourite.
I love him.
He has patches on him.
He sleeps with me every night.

Hunter Sanford, Grade 2
Falmouth District School, NS

Leaves

Scrunching yellow leaves
Big crunching red leaves
Small Birch leaves
Back flipping orange leaves
Tumbling green leaves
Swishing Maple leaves
Dropping brown leaves
Little red tumbling leaves

Amiyah Berard, Grade 2
Bayview Elementary School, BC

Taylor Dickenson

Taylor

Bike rider, funny, lazy sometimes, tall
Son of Lindy and Joe
Lover of watching monster trucks and doing tricks on his bike
Who feels happy and excited
Who needs air and rest
Who gives time and space
Who fears runaway monster trucks and sharks
Who likes to wear blue jeans and a white t-shirt
Who would like to see Alberta and China
Resident of Harewood

Dickenson

Taylor Dickenson, Grade 3
Bayview Elementary School, BC

Fall

Fall is colourful.
Fall is pretty.
Fall is crunchy.
Fall is beautiful.
Fall is the best season!

Matteo Mazzone, Grade 2
St Clare Catholic Elementary School, ON

Fall

B lue rain dropping down.
L ooking up at the sky, it is raining.
A ll the rain falling on the sidewalk. Whoo!
C old outside.
K ids running. Crick Crack outside!

Naomi Malka, Grade 2
Ecole Akiva, QC

Hallowe'en

Rattling skeleton
Wicked witch
Swooping bat
Haunted house
Hissing black cat
Floating ghost
BOO!

Rose Anderson, Grade 2
Bayview Elementary School, BC

Game Boy

Game boy, game boy,
I like game boy. I play it to the left,
I play it to the right.
Game boy, game boy
Such a delight!

Samuel Manitowabi, Grade 3
Sioux Mountain School, ON

Halloween

On Halloween night
Monsters come out
And scare you!
And you will scream!
And they will jump out
And say
BOO!!

Danielle Lynch, Grade 2
Falmouth District School, NS

Leaves

Red leaves
Falling leaves
Maple leaves
Green leaves
Yellow leaves

Ashiel Marshall, Grade 1
Bayview Elementary School, BC

Animals

Animals, animals
I love animals!
Bears
Dogs
Bunnies
Cats
Owls
Fish
Mice.
Some animals live in the north.
Some animals live in the south.
Some animals live in the east.
Some animals live in the west.
I love animals.

Alicia Woodworth, Grade 2
Falmouth District School, NS

Hallowe'en

Wicked witch
Haunted house
Rattling ghost
Hissing bat
Floating skeleton
Swooping black cat
BOO!

Kaitlyn McMahon-White, Grade 2
Bayview Elementary School, BC

Gretel

Gretel
Hungry and poor
Went to a candy house
Saved her brother
Kind

Lauren Rotholz, Grade 2
Ecole Akiva, QC

Whee

Sledding down hills
Over bumps we go
And we all yell
Whee!

Savannah Stewart, Grade 3
Merritt Central Elementary School, BC

Sweet Juliet

Juliet
Sad and sweet
Ready to die
She lost her love
Tragedy

Rebecca Falutz, Grade 3
Ecole Akiva, QC

Hallowe'en

Spooky zombie
Wicked witch
Hissing black cat
Swooping bat
Haunted house
Floating ghost
BOO!
BOO!

Gideon Klimek, Grade 2
Bayview Elementary School, BC

Ophelia's Life

Ophelia
Sweet and helpful
Dies by drowning
She loved Hamlet.
Life!

Aiyana Kaplan, Grade 3
Ecole Akiva, QC

Hallowe'en

Spooky zombie
Floating ghost
Swooping cat
Haunted house
BOO! BOO! BOO!

Ben Smith, Grade 1
Bayview Elementary School, BC

Orange

O n a beautiful day it is sunny.
R ain makes the sound PLOP!!
A nice beautiful rainbow.
N ever go swimming.
G o play in the leaves.
E njoy!

Gabriella Castiel, Grade 2
Ecole Akiva, QC

Potatoes

Potatoes are red,
Potatoes are white.
Potatoes are brown,
And they are round.

We see them in curry,
We see them in chips.
We see them in sandwiches,
And many a dish.

We find them at stores,
Where they come from farms.
They grow underground,
Some places around.

Arsh Raza, Grade 2
Tumpane Public School, ON

Hallowe'en

Hissing black cat
Wicked witch
Swooping ghost
Rattling skeleton
Spooky bat
Haunted zombie
BOO!

Maddison Crichton, Grade 2
Bayview Elementary School, BC

Hallowe'en

Rattling zombie
Spooky skeleton
Ghosts and bats
Witch's house
RIP
BOO!

Dawson Wassell, Grade 1
Bayview Elementary School, BC

Snowy Christmas

C is for choir singing "Rudolph the Red Nosed Reindeer"
H is for hoping you won't get coal
R is for reindeer pulling Santa's sleigh
I is for ice shining throughout the day
S is for Saint Nicholas going down the chimney
T is for toys fun for girls and boys
M is for mandarin oranges packed in a box
A is for Advent calendars with treats inside
S is for stockings you hang on your mantle.

Spencer Braam, Grade 3
Watson Road Elementary School, BC

Chilly

C runchy! Crunchy! I jumped on the leaves.
H er jacket is so light. Brr brr.
I n the fall there are a lot of leaves. Crunch! Crunch!
L ove fall.
L eaves are here and leaves are there.
Y ou know that I love fall.

Hannah Polachek, Grade 3
Ecole Akiva, QC

Hallowe'en

Rattling skeleton
Floating ghost
Swooping bat
Haunted house
Wicked witch
Big goblin
BOO!

Ainsley Allan, Grade 2
Bayview Elementary School, BC

Leaves

L eaves fall in the autumn.
E verybody loves jumping in leaves. Crunch!
A ll leaves are colorful.
V ines sometimes have leaves on them.
E mblem! It's the maple leaf.
S ome leaves are green.

Samantha Cherry, Grade 2
Ecole Akiva, QC

Christmas

C is for coloured lights glowing brightly on the roof
H is for holidays giving time to play in the silver snow
R is for reindeer flying in all conditions even if it's 50 below
I is for icy winds chilling you and your bones
S is for silky soft snow giving the hard ground a thick blanket
T is for tinsel hung on the beautiful green tree
M is for moms making yummy gingerbread houses
A is for angel shining brightly on the top of the tree
S is for Secret Santa giving presents to friends

Cole Gaudreau, Grade 3
Watson Road Elementary School, BC

Justis MacKay-Topley

Justis

Fast, smart, funny, shy
Son of Marney and Jeff
Lover of lacrosse and my family
Who feels happy and energetic
Who needs family and fun
Who gives respect and love
Who fears pit-pulls and strangers
Who likes to wear shorts and under armor shirts
Who would like to see the Ice Palace in Quebec
Resident of Nanaimo

MacKay-Topley

Justis MacKay-Topley, Grade 3
Bayview Elementary School, BC

Family

Without a family there would be no love,
Without a family there would be no fun,
But I am lucky to have a family,
That loves me with all of their heart.

When I am feeling down,
My family makes me feel better,
They hug me and kiss me,
To bring a smile back to my face.

When my family does things for me,
It makes me feel very happy,
But it makes me feel even better,
When I do something for them!

Families were made for each other,
They were made to love one another,
And to help one another,
I know that my family is always going to be there!

Claire Del Fatti, Grade 3
St Clare Catholic Elementary School, ON

Index